PROTOCOLS OF *Liberty*

PROTOCOLS OF *Liberty*

COMMUNICATION

INNOVATION AND THE

AMERICAN REVOLUTION

WILLIAM B. WARNER

THE UNIVERSITY OF CHICAGO PRESS

Chicago and London

WILLIAM B. WARNER is professor of English at the University of
California, Santa Barbara. He is the author of three books, most recently
*Chance and the Text of Experience: Freud, Nietzsche, and Shakespeare's
Hamlet*, and coeditor of *This Is Enlightenment*, published by the
University of Chicago Press.

The University of Chicago Press, Chicago 60637
The University of Chicago Press, Ltd., London
© 2013 by The University of Chicago
All rights reserved. Published 2013.
Printed in the United States of America

22 21 20 19 18 17 16 15 14 13   1 2 3 4 5

ISBN-13: 978-0-226-06137-5 (cloth)
ISBN-13: 978-0-226-06140-5 (e-book)
DOI: 10.7208/chicago/9780226061405.001.0001

Library of Congress Cataloging-in-Publication Data
Warner, William Beatty.
    Protocols of liberty: communication innovation and the American
    Revolution / William B. Warner.
        pages; cm
    Includes bibliographical references and index.
    ISBN 978-0-226-06137-5 (cloth: alkaline paper) —
    ISBN 978-0-226-06140-5 (e-book) 1. United States—History—
    Revolution, 1775–1783—Committees of correspondence.
    2. Communication in politics—United States—History—18th
    century. I. Title.
    E216.W29 2013
    973.3—dc23   2013011347

♾ This paper meets the requirements of ANSI/NISO Z39.48-1992
(Permanence of Paper).

For my children:

Robert, Andrew, Nathaniel,

and Emma

CONTENTS

ACKNOWLEDGMENTS

Everyone who gathers knowledge and ideas to write a book discovers that as authors, each of us is embedded in a sustaining network of personal and institutional affiliation. It is a pleasure to thank those who have helped me think about networking and the American Revolution. My deepest debt is to my longtime collaborator and director of the Re: Enlightenment Project, Clifford Siskin. Special thanks go to those who read the whole manuscript and gave me invaluable advice during its long gestation: my wife, Elizabeth Mac-Arthur, a wise and perspicacious scholar of eighteenth-century France; Ronald Paulson, the generous teacher who first guided me into eighteenth-century studies; and my brother, Jonathan Warner, who is a distinguished biologist and all-around intellectual. I also benefited from readings of parts of the manuscript by three gifted historians: Robert Gross, my colleague Ann Plane, and my old friend and running buddy, William Graebner. In the later stages of writing, Summer Star, an advanced graduate student at the University of California, Santa Barbara (UCSB), gave me invaluable critical and editorial advice.

Early in my work on this project, I received an indispensable grant from UCSB's interdisciplinary Center for Information Technology and Society and its visionary founder, Bruce Bimber. This study grew along with the conversations sustained by conferences in the United States and Europe. I especially want to thank the Scandinavian Eighteenth-Century Novel group, for conversations led by Knut Ove Eliassen, Anne Fastrup, and Helge Jordheim; the Bloomington Enlightenment Seminar, especially Sarah Knott, Konstantin Dierks, Jonathan Elmer, Mary Favret, and the seminar's founder, Dror Wahrman. In seminars and lectures, I have benefited from the critical exchanges initiated by Elisa Tamarkin, Janet Sorensen, and Mark Goble, all at the University of California, Berkeley; by Deidre Lynch and Paul Downes at the University of Toronto and its Munk Center of Global Affairs; by the Eighteenth-Century Group at the University of California, Los Angeles, led by Felicity Nussbaum; by the Danish Society of Eighteenth-Century Studies; and by the McNeil Center, where Toni Bowers was a most generous interlocutor. Finally, I have been lucky to be surrounded by a remarkable group of my colleagues at UCSB, especially Richard Helgerson, Alan Liu, Rita Raley, Mark Rose, Patricia Fumerton, James Kearney, Elizabeth Heckendorn Cook, Matthew Stewart, and Yunte Huang. Each has, in different ways, been an inspiration for me.

Throughout this project I have benefited from the assistance of a series of indispensable archives: the American Antiquarian Society, the Huntington

Library, the New York Public Library, the Massachusetts Historical Society, the Small Special Collections of the University of Virginia, the Library Company of Philadelphia, and the Historical Society of Pennsylvania. Finally, I've received support from the Davidson Library at UCSB, where I received years of personal assistance from Barbara Lansdon. At all these archives, I've learned that during an epoch when archives are being migrated to digital databases, it is all the more important to have gifted guides to explore this vast, complex, new multimedia archive. At the end of the writing process, I greatly benefited, in taming a once-unruly project, from the critical readings coordinated by the innovative editor at University of Chicago Press, Alan Thomas, and the capable acquisitions, copyediting, design, production, and marketing personnel at the Press.

Finally, I wish to acknowledge three publishers for allowing me to rehearse early versions of ideas in the pages of their publications before making their way into this book: Johns Hopkins University Press, for portions of chapter 3 that were developed in "Communicating Liberty: The Newspapers of the British Empire as a Matrix for the American Revolution," *ELH* 72 (2005): 339–61; the University of Pennsylvania Press, where portions of the argument of chapter 1 were first developed in "The Invention of a Public Machine for Revolutionary Sentiment: The Boston Committee of Correspondence," *Eighteenth Century: Theory and Interpretation,* Summer/Fall 50: 2–3 (2009): 145–64; and the University of Chicago Press, for some elements of the argument of chapters 1 and 2, which were first broached in "Transmitting Liberty: The Boston Committee of Correspondence's Revolutionary Experiments in Enlightenment Mediation," in *This Is Enlightenment*, edited by Clifford Siskin and William B. Warner (2010), 102–19.

. . . .

*A*lmost from the moment they could imagine themselves as citizens of an independent nation, Americans have turned to the American Revolution to understand the essential character of their politics. From Lincoln at Gettysburg to the Tea Party of the Great Recession, claims about the meaning of the American Revolution motivate a return to the origin, where Americans have sought to identify America's defining values and ideas: liberty, democracy, religious faith, the public virtue of the founders, popular sovereignty, imperial expansion, racial violence, or multicultural difference. This way of knowing the Revolution obscures the distinctive collaborative politics that Americans developed during the American Revolution, a politics of change that Americans have practiced periodically ever since. Crucial to that politics were innovations in communication that American Whigs developed in the dozen years after the Peace of Paris (1763) and which made their revolution a model that many other nations would emulate. In *Protocols of Liberty*, I study the American Revolution as an event in the history of communication.

Momentous historical events often issue from a nexus of violence and communication. While American independence from Britain ultimately depended upon the spilling of blood on the battlefields of Bunker Hill, Saratoga, and Yorktown, the successful challenge to the legitimacy of British rule in America was the culmination of an earlier communications war waged by American Whigs between the Stamp Act agitation of 1764–1765 and the Coercive Acts of 1774. In response to the first of the Coercive Acts—the Boston Port Bill—Boston Whigs secured a tidal wave of political and material support from throughout the colonies of British America. By the end of 1774, the American secretary at Whitehall, Lord Dartmouth, had received numerous reports from colonial governors of North America, like this report from the lieutenant governor of South Carolina, William Bull:

> I beg your lordship's permission to observe, and I do it with great concern,
> that this spirit of opposition to taxation and its consequences is so violent

and so universal throughout America that I am apprehensive it will not be soon or easily appeased. The general voice speaks discontent . . . determined to stop all exports to and imports from Great Britain and even to silence the courts of law . . . foreseeing but regardless of the ruin that must attend themselves in that case, content to change a comfortable, for a parsimonious life. (July 31, 1774; *Documents* 1975, 154)

Official private letters to Lord Dartmouth confirmed a catastrophic unraveling of British authority in America: colonial legislatures were meeting without the permission, or the presiding presence, of the governor; royal courts were being prevented from convening; and local militia were openly preparing for war. Remarkably similar acts of resistance to British authority, justified by very similar words, were happening hundreds of miles apart at virtually the same time. What may have looked to British ministry like a well-concerted conspiracy were in fact decentralized and self-organizing acts of resistance.

What led to this remarkable dissolution of British power? How did American Whigs fashion this victory over British legitimacy *before* the war that began on April 19, 1775, at Lexington and Concord? How did they prevail in what John Adams would later call "the real revolution," the revolution that occurred "in the minds and hearts of the people?" (Adams 1818, 465). Finally, and more pointedly, how did the American Whigs gather the power to challenge and then replace British authority? Between 1772 and 1774, the ratio of political power shifted in favor of the American Whigs. I say "Whigs" to designate those who rebelled against Britain, so as to avoid the more familiar but tendentious name "Patriot." After all, the Tories of America who remained loyal to King George considered themselves more patriotic than those who rebelled against the British Empire. To understand the shift in power from Tories to Whigs, this book will trace three related communication innovations: the invention of a new political agency, the committees of correspondence; the development of a new genre for political expression, the popular declaration; and the emergence of networks for collective political action, first within Massachusetts and then across all the colonies. The institution of the Continental Congress, as the hub of this network, enabled American Whigs to gather the power to do what successful revolutionaries must do: act together.

It can be difficult to apprehend what is new in a revolution, because revolutionaries almost always emphasize the restorative, conserving, recuperative character of the change they promote. That, after all, is what the *re* in the word *revolution* denotes. Thus American Whigs repeatedly insisted that all their actions were designed to protect a precious legacy that British imperial policy had put at risk: English liberty as it had been codified into law and practice by the Glorious Revolution of 1688. The historian Keith Baker (1990, 2), describing François Furet's contribution to the study of revolution, puts the challenge of apprehending the distinctness of the French Revolution in this way: "Furet insisted on the importance of grasping its character conceptually, as political event and cultural creation. As a series of acts that transformed the situation making them possible, as the creation and experiential elaboration of an entirely new mode of political action, the Revolution had a logic and dynamic of its own, not derivable from the necessity of social conditions or the ineluctability of social processes." The American Revolution, like the French Revolution, initiated a sequence of events that appeared to both contemporary observers and later historians to be unprecedented and surprising. In this study I argue that nothing was more pivotal to American Whig success than what they learned from the dynamic of political crisis: the new practices of association, communication, and generic invention, which, when linked together, produced "an entirely new mode of political action." Because the communication innovations of the Revolution emerged from within the rush of events, I begin this introduction with the political crisis that opened in Boston on March 6, 1770, the day after what Whigs referred to as the Boston Massacre.

AN ANATOMY OF THE AMERICAN CRISIS IN BOSTON ON MARCH 6, 1770

The "American crisis" is the term historians have used to designate that epoch when a contest for authority had opened between royal government and American Whigs. "Crisis" is useful because it is a politically neutral term for describing the Whig challenges to government that so alarmed royal officials. For Whigs, the crisis had been brought on by new assertions of the royal prerogative that American Whigs considered inconsistent with liberty. Derived from the Greek word *krisis*, "decision," the word *crisis* indexes a period of political emergency, suspenseful struggle, fluid events, and impending decision. There was one day, March 6, 1770, the day *after* the Boston Massacre, when the American crisis was expressed as a very literal decision: troops could not, but must, be removed from Boston. What would happen? Here politics assumed its baldest form as a struggle of words and deeds. By the end of the day, no one doubted that the Whigs had won.

For the Tories of Boston as well as for the royal officials in both Boston and London, the events of that day—which featured emergency meetings of both the Massachusetts Council and the Boston Town Meeting—precipitated a catastrophic breakdown of the royal government in Boston. Eighteen months before, the king in Privy Council, acting with the explicit approval of Parliament, had dispatched regiments of British regulars to invest the town, enforce the Townshend Acts, and prevent the sort of riotous behavior visited on royal officials in the Liberty Riot on June 10, 1768. But on the day after the so-called Boston Massacre, the Boston Town Meeting succeeded, through threats that appeared nothing less than seditious, in compelling the lieutenant governor to order the complete and immediate removal of His Majesty's troops from Boston.

While the administration in Whitehall used the events of March 6, 1770, to develop plans for stronger royal government, Boston Whigs saw the same events as justifying a vigilant but restrained defense of their rights and liberties. We can capture the Whig presentation of that day by reading the *Boston Gazette* of March 12, 1770. The paper devoted a full page and a half, bordered in black, to a narrative of the "massacre" and its aftermath. The *Boston Gazette* presents the events of the sixth of March as a tightly plotted drama, one that begins in tragedy but ends in redemption. As we see from the documents embedded in the account, Whig success depended upon an adroit management of public communication.

There are six distinct moments in the account of the day.

1. *"A most shocking scene":* The narrative of the sixth of March begins by placing the bleeding body of Boston at the center of its narrative: "Tuesday morning presented a most shocking scene, the blood of our fellow citizens running like water through King-Street and the merchants Exchange.... Our blood might also be track'd up to the head of Long Lane, and through divers other streets and passages." This blood, the account insists, is *"our"* blood," that of the collective body of the people who have gathered in town meeting. While the blood of the martyrs of the "massacre" at first shocks, this blood also seems to allude to the mysterious power of the blood of Christian sacrifice to sanctify the actions of the town.[1]

2. *The town meeting takes the initiative (11 a.m.):* Rather than answering blood with blood, the town meeting chose a committee of fifteen members to deliver the town's carefully framed three-sentence message. The "vote" of the

---

1. In *The Bloody Massacre*, Paul Revere's famous print showing British regulars firing upon the respectable citizens of Boston, the color red assumes an emblematic character: each print was hand-colored so that the blood flowing out of the respectable citizens represented in the print matches the color of the red coats of His Majesty's troops who fire upon them (Zobel 1970, 211).

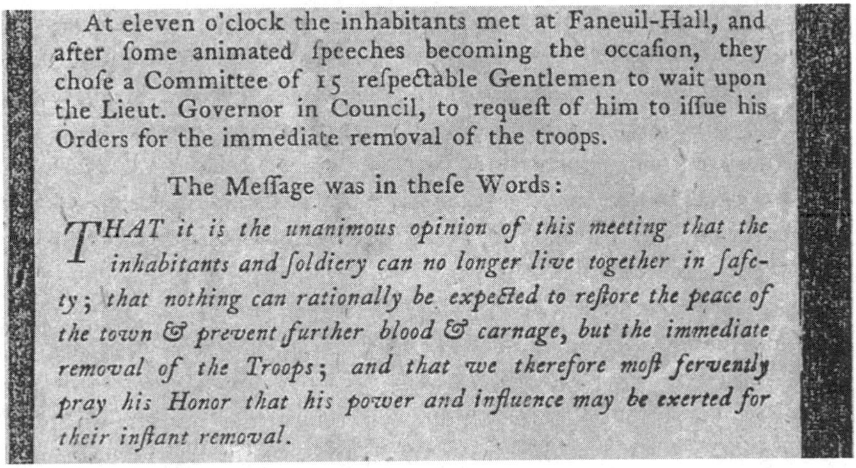

> At eleven o'clock the inhabitants met at Faneuil-Hall, and after some animated speeches becoming the occasion, they chose a Committee of 15 respectable Gentlemen to wait upon the Lieut. Governor in Council, to request of him to issue his Orders for the immediate removal of the troops.
>
> The Message was in these Words:
>
> *THAT it is the unanimous opinion of this meeting that the inhabitants and soldiery can no longer live together in safety; that nothing can rationally be expected to restore the peace of the town & prevent further blood & carnage, but the immediate removal of the Troops; and that we therefore most fervently pray his Honor that his power and influence may be exerted for their instant removal.*

FIGURE 0.1. The March 6 "vote" of the Boston Town Meeting as presented by the *Boston Gazette* (March 12, 1770). The thick black border is a mourning tribute to the "martyrs" of March 5. Photograph courtesy of Special Collections, University of California, Santa Barbara.

---

town is set off within the account and given added importance by its presentation in italics (figure 0.1): "*THAT it is the unanimous opinion of this meeting that the inhabitants and soldiery can no longer live together in safety; that nothing can rationally be expected to restore the peace of the town & prevent further blood & carnage, but the immediate removal of the Troops; and that we therefore most fervently pray his Honor that his power and influence may be exerted for their instant removal.*"

Note that the legitimacy of this "vote" emerges from the fastidiously observed procedures of the town meeting: the framing of a resolution; a vote; a selection of the committee to carry this message, which is respectfully addressed to "his Honor." What gave the town meeting's response power is its claim to express the "unanimous opinion" of the meeting, thereby authorizing the use of the first-person plural "we."

3. *His Honor's reply*: Speaking in the first person, Lieutenant Governor Hutchinson offered the longest communication in the record. He spoke euphemistically of the "unhappy differences" between the inhabitants and troops, and defended his "exertions" to uphold the law. He further insists, against the town's vote, that his power over the troops is limited. "*I AM extremely sorry for the unhappy differences between the inhabitants and troops, I have exerted myself upon that occasion that a due inquiry be made, and that the law may have its*

course. . . . [Since the regiments] *have their orders from the General in New York. It is not in my power to countermand those orders.*" However, because some council members "*have desired that the two regiments may be removed to the Castle,*" the lieutenant governor's message ends with a compromise. Because of its "particular" differences with the town, the Twenty-Ninth Regiment would be removed to Castle William (on an island several miles east in Boston Harbor), and the main guard would be removed from its headquarters opposite the main door of the Town House.

4. *The response of the town (3 p.m. meeting):* The town meeting rejected the lieutenant governor's offer and acted with decision: "it was then moved and voted that" seven members of the meeting "be a committee to wait on the Lieutenant-Governor, and inform him that it is the unanimous opinion of this meeting" that his reply to the town's vote of this morning "is by no means satisfactory; and that nothing less will satisfy, than a total and immediate removal of all the Troops." These words seek to put the town meeting in the position of an aggrieved party who must be satisfied. The partial removal of troops was rejected, negotiation was foreclosed, and the demand of this morning's vote—"a total and immediate removal of all the Troops"—was reiterated. Here, courage takes the form of concise obstinacy.

5. *The Council deliberates and finds a solution:* The Council is represented as speaking with three different voices: the lieutenant governor requests the Council's advice on the town's message; the Council is "unanimously of opinion . . . that the Troops should be immediately removed out of the Town of Boston"; and finally, breaking the impasse, Lieutenant Colonel Dalrymple "gave his word of honor that he would begin his preparations" for the "removal of both regiments to the Castle." The Council had acceded to the demands of the town, and victory of the town meeting was complete. The long, agonizing, and vexed deliberations of the Council, meeting in morning and afternoon sessions, are skipped over with these few words, and the lieutenant governor is given no credit for relenting.

6. *The town meeting savors its victory and takes charge of the security of the town:* The inhabitants expressed "high satisfaction," and "for the security of the Town in the Night" the committee of seven assumed responsibility for setting up a "strong Military Watch." After nearly eighteen months of military occupation, the town meeting had won a promise for the removal of British regulars, and once again could take full responsibility for its own security.

While the *Gazette*'s account of the sixth of March does not conceal the fact that it expresses the Whig perspective of the town meeting, it also strives to establish the objective validity of its account. It does this by weaving its account out of documents that are already part of the public record: the "vote" of the morning town meeting, the reply of the lieutenant governor, the rejoinder of the town meeting, and the final decision of the Council. In fact, almost all the words of the *Boston Gazette*'s account are lifted straight out of the minute book of the Boston Town Meeting, but the record has been abridged so as to create an illusion of an up-tempo flow of acts. This interweaving of documents, by foregrounding actual votes and messages produced by the meetings of the town and the Council, and eschewing the tendentious rhetoric that was widely used by both Whigs and Tories, sought to overcome what was obvious to all in Boston: that, in fact, every aspect of the events of March 5 and 6 were open to dispute. Since these documents were produced by two governing bodies, the town meeting and the Council, that operated according to the law, the whole narrative had a "cooling effect" by appealing implicitly to the rigorous legality of the actions of the day. In response to the irregularity of the riot of March 5, or the specter of civil war that opened on March 6, the *Boston Gazette* account foregrounded communications that were informed by the correct forms of procedure and law.

Yet this media account hid as much as it represented. In order to get the risky brinksmanship of March 6 to follow a streamlined dialectic, back and forth between town, lieutenant governor, and Council, so that the action of the day assumed some of the formal clarity of political drama, the history of the day had to be simplified. The account of the *Boston Gazette* censors out what the three royal officials at the meeting of the Council—Lieutenant Governor Hutchinson, Lieutenant Colonel Dalrymple, and Secretary Andrew Oliver— reported in considerable detail to their superiors in Whitehall and New York. First, the lieutenant governor had given a stern warning to the town's morning committee of fifteen that a resort to force would constitute treason. Second, to the lieutenant governor's compromise offer to remove one regiment, Samuel Adams had offered a sharp rejoinder: "Mr. Adams, one of the committee, told Colonel Dalrymple that if he could remove the 29th Regiment he could also remove the 14th, and it was at his peril if he did not" (Andrew Oliver, *Documents* 1975, 2:53); and, finally, Councilor Royall Tyler insisted "that the people would come in from the neighboring towns, and that there would be ten thousand men to effect the removal of the troops, and that would probably be destroyed by the people, should it be called rebellion, should it incur the loss of our charter, or be the consequences what it would" (Andrew Oliver, *Documents* 1975, 2:53–54). What proved decisive to the deliberations and led all the council, including his close ally and brother-in-law Andrew Oliver, to abandon Lieutenant Governor Hutchinson was the conviction that militia from the surrounding towns were "in motion" to remove the royal troops from Boston by force.

In order to clear the town meeting of the seditious tendency of such a threat, the *Boston Gazette* narrative foregrounds other features of the town meeting's performance: its restraint even when sorely provoked; its observation of customary procedures (voting, appointing committees, and patiently awaiting results); the speed and decisiveness of its deliberations; the simplicity of its demand; and, most importantly, its achieved unity. When the lieutenant governor tempted the town with a compromise measure (of removing one regiment instead of both regiments from the town), the wise, deliberative ethos of the town meeting prevailed. With directness and firmness, the town meeting renewed the demand for "a total and immediate removal" of the troops from the town. The *Boston Gazette* narrative represents the events of March 6 as a triumph of responsible, because disciplined, popular sovereignty. By this account, the passing of the crisis is due neither to royal officials, who prudently relent, nor to the Whig threat of civil insurrection. Instead, successful sovereignty emerges from the collected will of the people, assembled in town meeting, united in purpose, and acting according to correct procedure. The concision of this narrative suggests the magical efficacy of the town meeting's disciplined exercise of self-government, which allowed it to govern the action of others. By the *way* it acted, by its moral resolve, its powerful unity, and by the lively "spirit of liberty" it demonstrated, the town meeting emerged, in the account of the *Boston Gazette*, as the hero of the sixth of March.

As much as ideas or places, events can become mediators of historical change. *How* events mediate history is crucially informed by what actors remember and "learn" from decisive events, like the face-off between Whigs and royal officials on the sixth of March. The diametrically opposed "truths" learned by Whigs and Tories from the events of the sixth of March seeded the future with new political crises. For royal officials, the events of the day intensified their determined efforts to reform "misgovernment" in Massachusetts. In the early summer of 1770, the breakdown of royal authority on the sixth of March became an object of forensic analysis. The Privy Council held emergency meetings and ordered a comprehensive review of royal government in Massachusetts. After extensive research and interviews with eyewitnesses, the secretary of the Board of Trade, John Pownall, wrote a long memo, upon the "disorders, confusion and misgovernment" in Boston over the previous five years, that fit the events of the sixth of March into a succession of increasingly serious challenges to royal government (June 21, 1770; *Documents* 1772, 2:110–28). This important synthetic document offers one of the first versions of the "succession of crises" narrative of the American crisis that would play so important a part in the later historiography of the American Revolution. The memo, which was reviewed and approved by the Board of Trade and the Privy Council, concluded by proposing fundamental changes to the Massachusetts charter (P. Thomas 1987, 195). These included the royal appointment of the Council (rather than its election by the House of Representatives), the requirement that the provincial governor give prior approval of non-routine town meetings, and the appointment rather than election of county sheriffs. Officials were confident that these reforms would restore "vigor" and authority to royal government in Massachusetts. In fact, after the destruction of the tea in Boston Harbor, these reforms were written into law in the Massachusetts Government Act (1774) and became one of the triggers for the American Revolution.

Whigs learned something very different from the events of the sixth of March. By happily resolving a transient crisis, that day provided a tactical model for the future defense of liberty. The lessons of March 6 were woven into the monumental histories that Boston Whigs retold in the annual massacre orations held by the town of Boston between 1771 and 1783. However, in *On Revolution*, Hannah Arendt (1963) offers a more fundamental reason why Whigs took special pleasure in remembering the "public business" of March 6: it gave Whigs access to a new, more active concept of freedom. Arendt argues that the crucial legacy of the American Revolution does not consist in the rights and liberties that American revolutionaries explicitly fought to protect: for example, to take liberties pertinent on March 6, the negatively constructed *freedom from* the posting of troops in the town at times of peace, or the *freedom from* parliamentary taxation without consent. Instead, Arendt argues that the political crisis that led to revolution "threw them into public business" where they practiced a new *freedom to* speak and act. By this interpretation, all the words and deeds of the Boston meeting on the sixth of March and in the many meetings in the weeks that followed—including votes and resolutions, the appointment of committees, the writing of pamphlets, and the institution of the annual oration to commemorate the "massacre" and the success in winning removal of the troops—were not only undertaken to protect rights and liberties that preexisted the crisis. Freedom also, and most crucially, emerged with and in the acts that defended rights and liberties.

In other words, the town of Boston's successful actions on the sixth of March offers an early instance of the happiest harvest of the Revolution: the sort of self-government where freedom will be a concomitant of the exercise of sovereignty. To quote Arendt (1963, 33–34):

Whatever the merits of the opening claim of the American Revolution—no taxation without representation—it certainly could not appeal by virtue of its charms. It was altogether different with the speech-making and decision-taking, the oratory and the business, the thinking and the persuading, and the actual doing which proved necessary to drive this claim to its logical conclusion: independent government and the foundation of a new body politic. It was through these experiences that those who, in the words of John Adams, had been "called without expectation and compelled without previous inclination," discovered that "it is action, not rest, that constitutes our pleasure."

Arendt so values John Adams's insight into the centrality of the "pleasure" of "action" to the revolutionary business of the town meeting and the legislative assembly that she makes it a recurrently quoted leitmotif in *On Revolution*. In this passage and later essays like "What Is Freedom?" (1961), Arendt associates freedom with action: "Men are free—as distinguished from their possession of the gift for freedom—as long as they act, neither before nor after; for to be free and to act are the same" (Arendt 2000, 445–46). Arendt further argues that freedom is only fully realized when it is part of a collective action that unfolds in a public space, in pursuit of a shared principle. While I do not claim that the participants in the Boston Town Meeting shared Arendt's particular philosophical understanding of freedom, her linkage of freedom to collective, principled, public action helps to explain the "high satisfaction" the freeholders and inhabitants of Boston felt on the night of the sixth of March. If they felt joy as they left the day-long meeting and went home that night, or shared in the duty of stationing the Boston militia around the streets of the town as a night watch, their exhilaration must have come in part because the acts of the day had secured Boston from the exasperating constraints of "military power and control." But perhaps the special pleasure of this moment came from another factor: the town had won this victory not through recourse to force, but through a principled assertion of the higher authority of the law.

THE PROJECT OF SYSTEMATIC IMPERIAL REFORM

The success of Boston Whigs in winning the removal of royal troops fortified royal officials in their belief that the British Empire required fundamental reform. As early as 1763 the British administration in Whitehall exhibited what might be called one of the paradoxes of power. Britons everywhere felt the exhilaration of their heady victory in expelling the French and Spanish from virtually all of North America east of the Mississippi. But unlike most of the public, officials on the Board of the Trade and members of the Privy Council also carried the memory of the failure of many previous administrations to exercise the royal prerogative in Britain's American colonies. Out of this combination of new powers and responsibilities, on one hand, and a detailed understanding of the failures of previous administrations, on the other, emerged a steely determination to pursue imperial reform. This administrative mind-set, which includes an odd mixture of resolve and exasperation, may be read in the words that British officials wrote to each other in their private, semi-official correspondence. Here, for example, is General Thomas Gage, the commander of British forces in America, writing in April 1772 from his headquarters in New York to his superior in the War Office, Viscount Barrington. Note that it was the authority of Gage's command that had been abridged by the events of the sixth of March. Now, over two years later, Gage worries that the prevalence of "democracy"—that is, various forms of popular sovereignty as practiced in the American colonies—constitutes a fatal menace to a coherent British Empire. "Democracy is too prevalent in America, and claims the greatest attention to prevent its increase, and fatal effects. It is necessary too that Great Britain should not only assert, but also support that supremacy which she claims over the members of the Empire, or she will soon be supreme only in words, and we shall become a vast empire, composed of many parts, disjointed and independent of each other, without any head" (April 13, 1772; Gage 1933, 2:603; also P. Thomas 1987, 217).

Gage's specter of a headless empire serves as an odd complement to the "many-headed hydra" often used by Tories to represent the unruly masses. An empire without a head, made up of "disjointed and independent" members, requires a union secured from above, namely, through its head, the "supreme" authority of the king in Parliament. Gage's explicit distinction between words and deeds hints at the use of force necessary to support British supremacy in America. But for Gage, a new policy of firmness did not involve imposing tyranny. As Eliga Gould and Peter Onuf (2005, 3) have argued, for British administration "the best way to secure British liberty was by *enhancing* the government's power throughout the empire." For General Gage and the ministry shaping imperial policy, British sovereignty was not inconsistent with British liberty, but the condition for the possibility of it.

After the Peace of Paris in 1763, the British administration developed a systematic program for curtailing the power of the colonial assemblies and extending effective government to the American colonies. That program of reform had many aspects, each executed by a different branch of government:

TABLE 0.1. REFORMS AND RESISTANCE IN BRITISH AMERICA

Type	Example	American resistance
Military	Standing army	Boston Massacre
Legal	Proclamation line; Declaratory Act	Ignoring line; challenge Parliament
Economic	American Board of Customs Commissioners	Liberty riot
Postal	Fixed rates; packet ships	None
Administrative	Secretary of state of America	None
Judicial	Admiralty Court in Nova Scotia	The burning of HMS *Gaspée*
Financial	Direct payment of governors and judges	Boston Committee of Correspondence
"Self-funding through revenue acts"	Stamp Act (1765); Townshend Acts (1767); Tea Act (1773)	Stamp Act riots; embargo on British goods; the destruction of tea

it was *military* (in the stationing of a standing army for defense of the frontier, and in cities like New York and Boston); *legal* (through an act of Parliament, the Proclamation Line of 1763 suspended the westward movement of settlement); *economic* (enforcing the Navigation Acts with new vigor and placing an American Board of Customs Commissioners in Boston [1767]); *postal* (subsidizing monthly packet ships); *administrative* (the creation of the position of secretary of state for the American colonies in 1768 by separating the American colonies from the portfolio of the secretary of state for the Southern District); *judicial* (with the introduction of the admiralty court in Nova Scotia to try customs violators); and *financial* (owing to a secret plan to transfer the payment of governors and judges and other judicial officials from the colonial assemblies to direct payment out of Crown customs revenues in 1770; see table 0.1). The lynchpin of all these administrative reforms was a series of revenue bills passed by Parliament and designed to make all these reforms "self-funding" instead of a drain upon the British treasury: the Stamp Act (1765), the Townshend Acts (1767), and the Tea Act (1773). For officials in Whitehall, these reforms appeared as long-needed measures to renew and improve the empire, by restoring its original principles of government. For the American colonists, however, these measures expressed all the latent violence of the term *reform* in its sense of "form again," and "to be corrected." As John Brewer notes, "[E]very administration creates friction in its attempt to impose order and structure on the entropic enterprise of collaborative human endeavor" (1989, xvi). This reform of administration intensified resistance. With the exception of postal improvements and the administrative change that created the post of the American secretary, every single one of these imperial reforms was actively resisted in the American colonies. Although Parliament retreated on the Stamp Act and rescinded all but one of the Townshend duties, British administration was undeterred. Elaborate pamphlet wars in the mid-1760s, and eloquent sympathy for the colonies in Parliament (led by Isaac Barré, Lord Camden, Lord Chatham [William Pitt], Edmund Burke, and Thomas Pownall) only led administrators to find other less direct means to assert the parliamentary sovereignty, which even these strongest British supporters of American rights believed must undergird imperial rule.

THE CONSTITUENTS OF THE AUTONOMY AND POWER OF BOSTON

Given the determination of British officials to establish the sovereignty of the king in Parliament throughout their American colonies, how did the town of Boston gather the power to challenge British posting of troops on March 6? Historians of Boston and the Revolution have noted some of the constituents of Boston's political cohesion: its wealth from trade; the nature of its dominant religion, Congregationalism; and its robust development of the New England town meeting. However, nothing contributed more to Boston's readiness to take the political initiative in the years leading up to the American Revolution, than the complaisant belief, shared by both Whig and Tory leaders, in the colony's preeminence among the colonies of British America. For most of the first century of British settlement in America, Boston was the largest town in British North America, its most versatile place of trade, and the most important port outside of the West Indies. A ship crossing the Atlantic in a westerly direction from Falmouth, England, to North America would be sailing against prevailing winds and currents. After that six- or seven-week journey, Boston was the first full-service port reached, providing a deep harbor, ship repair, provisions, a merchant's market, and an ample variety of houses of worship and entertainment. Boston developed special importance in supporting the Atlantic trade through shipbuilding, a canny development of the rum trade, and by supporting the fishing fleets of the North Atlantic (Windsor

1881, 2:447). Boston's crucial advantage was its proximity to the richest fishing grounds in the North Atlantic: in the outer banks of Newfoundland, Nova Scotia, and Maine were located the spawning grounds of the cod fishery, and rich sources of whale oil and seal skins, all of which became the object of intense rivalry between the fishing fleets of France and England. Boston's success in the Atlantic trade made it the center of what the geographer D. W. Meinig has dubbed "greater New England," which reached across "six political units, several economic areas, and some cultural variations. . . . Boston was the principal focus of this entire realm, the commercial and cultural capital, as well as the political capital of the most populous and influential colony. It was the chief intelligence center, the point of gathering and dissemination of information between the region and the world" (Meinig 1986, 100–101). While Boston's own idea of its primacy and centrality among the colonies of British America may have been part heroic fiction, it contributed to Boston's willingness to take the lead in forging the Whig initiatives of the American crisis.

The confining physical topography of Boston helped to explain the intensity of its prerevolutionary politics. Memoirs written after the Revolution by Thomas Hutchinson, Andrew Oliver, Mercy Otis Warren, and John Adams, whether Tory laments of Boston's ungovernability or Whig admiration of its vigilance, testify to the palpable proximity of political opponents and the hothouse volatility of its politics. Surrounded by water, linked to the mainland by a narrow isthmus called the Neck, prerevolutionary Boston was described by Thomas Pownall (1949, 86) as shaped "somewhat like a Cross the triangular space however between the stem & branches especially the South end filled up with buildings, the head at the North End rounded." Those who know the modern city of Boston must use their imagination to reverse the "improvements" made by nineteenth-century engineers, who leveled Boston's hills to fill in its bays, and turned a colonial peninsula, which was linked to the world by water, into a modern city linked to the world by road and rail as well. If one uses maps and views to envision the eighteenth-century town of Boston, one finds approximately sixteen thousand inhabitants living on a peninsula of land that is only two miles long, and one and a quarter miles wide. The geography and commercial uses of the peninsula further contracted the spaces for public life. The rather steep hills on the western edge of the peninsula and the ubiquity of commercial wharfs on the eastern and northern edges meant that most of Boston's residences, taverns, clubs, markets, newspapers, and meetinghouses were concentrated on a relatively small grid of streets. Whether inhabitants of Boston were going to work or shop, to church or town meeting, they had to travel a narrow network of roads that developed along a central axis that ran 250 yards up the middle of the peninsula from the Liberty Tree (a large elm near the intersection of Essex Street and Orange Street) to Old North Church. Nearly all the important public buildings and private residences of Boston could be found within two short blocks of that axis, which was defined by these streets: Orange, Newbury, Marlborough, Cornhill, Union, Middle, and North. Proximity encouraged rapid communication. The Boston Whig leaders who lived farthest apart—Paul Revere on the North End, Samuel Adams on Purchase Street, and John Hancock opposite the Common—lived only a fifteen-minute walk from each other. John Adams, the Whig printers Benjamin Edes and John Gill, and Joseph Warren lived between one and two minutes' walking distance from each other (on or near Queen Street and Brattle Street). When Governor Thomas Hutchinson was at his official residence at Province House or Andrew Oliver was summoned from his house on Oliver Street, both men could walk to the Town House in two or three minutes. All these men, whether Whig or Tory, could reach the various meetinghouses—Faneuil Hall, the Town House, and Old South Church—in under ten minutes by foot.

If wealth helped to secure Boston's independence and its topography gave it an intimate scale, Boston's political power depended upon its energetic self-government through the town meeting. Early observers of the Massachusetts town meeting attributed its strength to its egalitarian ethos and its participatory structure. The Reverend William Gordon, who migrated from England to Massachusetts in 1770 and in 1772 became Congregational minister for Roxbury, was struck by the formal equality enjoyed by members of the town meeting: "Each individual has an equal liberty of delivering his opinion, and is not liable to be silenced or brow beaten by a richer or greater townsman than himself. Every freeman or freeholder . . . gives his vote or not, and for or against as he pleases; and each vote weighs equally; whether that of the highest or lowest inhabitant" (Sly 1967, 96). Coming from an English society where deference in speech and government was automatically extended to those of higher rank and learning, Gordon's account, from his 1789 *The History of Rise, Progress, and Establishment, of the Independence of the United States of America*, emphasizes the novelty of the Massachusetts town meeting where each member enjoyed equality in speaking and voting.[2]

---

2. The Congregational system of worship, like all churches in the reform tradition, authorized autonomous challenges to instituted authority. But alone among Calvinist sects, the Congregational Church gave members a direct role in the most important part of church government: the recruitment, hiring, and (occasional) firing of ministers.

Writing over sixty years after the Reverend Gordon, Alexis de Tocqueville (2000, 63) notes that "[t]he New England township unites two advantages that, everywhere they are found, keenly excite men's interest; that is to say: independence and power." He admires the way the town attracts the interest and energy of town members so as to make itself a center: "It is in the township, at the center of the ordinary relations of life, that desire for esteem, the need of real interests, the taste for power and attention, come to be concentrated" (64). For Tocqueville, this political alchemy is made possible by the way freeholders gather in the town meeting to nominate and elect each other to a large number of town offices, with each office exercising a narrow function. Most towns had nearly fifty offices, Boston over two hundred. Tocqueville was fascinated with the sheer number of these town offices, and by the "art" demonstrated by this system of governance, "if I can express myself so, to *scatter* power in order to interest more people in public things" (64). In Tocqueville's highly favorable assessment, New England town self-government reconciled power with order, participation with administration, government with liberty.

The effective power of the Boston Whigs throughout the American crisis depended upon their ability to act with unanimity. This unanimity was grounded in a concept of liberty that was corporate and not individual, Congregational rather than classically liberal. By January 1770, Boston's strenuous efforts to sustain the non-importation agreements against a tide of cheating demonstrated how difficult it was to reconcile the constraints of a collective boycott with liberty. In one essay, the leader of the Boston Whigs, Samuel Adams, interweaves the voices of tavern, street, and town meeting to make his case for a disciplined boycott of English goods. Writing as Determinius, he quotes the complaints of the merchants with these words: "[A]nd now their cry is, 'Where is that Liberty so much boasted of and contended for?' We hear them very gravely asking, 'Have we not a right to carry on our own trade and sell our own goods if we please?' 'who shall hinder us?' "

To counter this proto-liberal language of individual rights, Adams asks rhetorically if an inhabitant of Boston then has the right to set fire to his own house and watch the whole city burn. The essay reaches its rhetorical climax in a stern reproach to those who refuse to recognize the social obligation that grounds their liberty. "Where did you learn that in a state or society you had a right to do as you please? And that it was an infringement of that right to restrain you? This is a refinement which I dare say, the true sons of liberty despise. Be pleased to be informed that you are bound to conduct yourselves as the Society with which you are joined, are pleased to have you conduct, or if you please, you may leave it" (January 8, 1770; S. Adams 1904, 2:5).

Alluding to the indiscriminate voluntarism of the phrase "right to do as you please," Samuel Adams, in the final sentence of this passage, plays on the several meanings of the words *please* and *pleased*. He begins with a polite expostulation: "Be pleased to be informed." While the word *pleased* references the voluntary consent this passage solicits, the appeal is cast in the imperative mood more appropriate to a binding order of a court. What comes in the middle of this sentence is an austere statement of a legal contract that subtends the life in this society, as if to say, "you, citizen, are bound to conduct yourself" in the way the Society is "pleased to have you conduct" yourself. Here the volition that the word *pleased* references shifts from the addressee (the obdurate merchant who would violate the anti-importation covenants) to "the Society." The addressee is left with an obligation, given emphasis by the stark words "you are bound." By using the word *bound*, Determinius argues the existence of a social covenant between members that is as binding and reciprocal as the religious covenant between God and his people. This may explain the harsh conclusion of the sentence—if the addressee cannot accept this obligation, he is informed of his unsavory alternative with a sarcastic politeness: "if you please, you may leave it." This passage summons to the republican cause the authority to shape the community of "saints" that characterized the earliest days of Puritan settlement of New England. Adams seems to be standing at a figurative meeting-house door and expostulating with the wayward merchant, as to the terms of his membership in a "Society" that would be free.

THE CENTRALITY OF COMMUNICATIONS: DEFINING PROTOCOL AND NETWORK

The events of March 6 demonstrate the symbiosis of communication and revolution. Over the course of this book, I argue that innovations in communication allowed American Whigs to gather the power to undertake a revolution. The title of this book, *Protocols of Liberty*, might be heard as an oxymoron, by which protocols are the rules and liberty the release from them. But within the revolutionary movement, liberty and protocols were mutually dependent and flourished together. Protocols are enabling constraints: they enable by constraining. How this is so is explained in part by the history, etymology, and diverse extensions of the term *protocol* over the hundreds of years of its usage. Protocols smooth the progress of some principal communication, which is located nearby. Thus in its earliest use, *protocol* is "the first leaf of a volume, a fly-leaf glued to the case and containing an account of the manuscript, – *Proto-* first + *Kolla* glue" (*Oxford Dictionary of English Etymology* 1966). As such it will ease the use of the document, by defining what is in it, or the larger communication context of which it is a part, or the preliminary agreements that frame the document's circulation. The word came to be used, especially in the diplomatic practice of the French, to designate the mutually agreed-upon legal stipulations that were placed before the text, or body, of the document, so that document could acquire the authority of a law. From this use in diplomacy and law, *protocol* was extended to refer to the "method or procedure for carrying out an experiment, investigation, or course of medical treatment" (*OED*). In this usage from science and medicine, protocols help to assure the formal regularity, reliability, and duplicability of experimental results. *Protocol* is also given an explicitly social reference as "the official rules of etiquette to be observed by the head of state and other dignitaries in ceremonies and relations with the representatives of other states" (*OED*). According to diplomatic protocol, seats at a state dinner are assigned to reflect guests' rank and importance. From this usage *protocol* comes to refer, more generally, to "the accepted or established code of behavior in any group, organization, or situation" (*OED*). Since the emergence in the 1970s of that network of networks called the Internet, "protocols" have become fundamental to the operation of computerized networks, as a "standardized set of rules governing the exchange of data between given devices, or transmission of data via a given communications channel." It seems that the more complex a communication system becomes, the more it needs protocols. Thus every computer on the Internet must observe TCP/IP, where *TCP* = "transmission control protocol" and *IP* = "the Internet protocol." In *Protocol: How Control Exists after Decentralization*, Alex Galloway suggests the way protocols assume a regulatory function within computer networks: "Protocol is a technique for achieving voluntary regulation within a contingent environment" (2004, 7).[3]

The protocols developed by the Boston Committee of Correspondence and voluntarily observed by the other towns of Massachusetts repeatedly used

3. After describing the use of protocols in diplomacy and highway driving (e.g., by staying on the right, unless in the United Kingdom), Galloway offers this thesis: "Viewed as a whole, protocol is a distributed management system that allows control to exist within a heterogeneous material milieu" (2004, 7). While I agree with Galloway's finding that voluntary as well as strict or embedded technical protocols influence the form and content of Internet communication, his use of the loaded term "control" has a perverse effect upon his analysis. While Galloway successfully debunks the libertarian interpretation of the Web, his book often implies that there could be systems of communication entirely free from control and that any system of control is suspect (147).

rules that shaped and constrained, in order to enable, communication. These protocols acquired their binding power by being general, rather than specific to a place or person, mutually observed by the parties to the communication, and so fully internalized that they became virtually invisible. Their repeated use increased their familiarity and authority. Of course, protocols for how we communicate inevitably influence what we communicate. "Protocols," it might be said in echo of Marshall McLuhan, "are the message." Thus, as we have seen in the discussion of March 6, the communication practices of the Boston Whigs embedded certain protocols like corporate action, open public access, and virtuous initiative, which I will discuss below.

By enabling trusted communication, shared and voluntary protocols permit a network to emerge and, once it has emerged, to cohere and do things. American Whigs solved the problem of forging political unity among heterogeneous colonies by networking. A network confounds both our commonsense notion that unity and strength depend upon proximity, and Newton's law of gravitation, that as the distance between discrete bodies increases, their ties must proportionally weaken. Instead, the networking activity of the American Whigs exploited a paradoxical potential of a network: the greater the distance between nodes, the greater the diversity it could accommodate, and the greater its power. A brief look at the long history of the word *network* will explain the usefulness of this term to an analysis of revolutionary communication. The *OED* defines it as "a work, especially manufactured work, in which threads, wires, etc., are crossed or interlaced in the fashion of a net; frequently applied to light fabric made of threads intersecting in this way"; and "an arrangement or structure with intersecting lines and interstices resembling those of a net." Its closest natural analogy is the spider's web. Over the long development of the word from the sixteenth century to the present, the structure and concept of the network was extended to transportation (e.g., turnpikes, canals, the post) and communication (e.g., telegraphy, telephony, the Internet), where its connecting threads were no longer ropes or threads, but the roads, rails, wires, and cables. All these uses of the word *network* have certain common features. Networks are fashioned out of slender threads that can extend to relatively remote nodes. Because they are woven of simple elements, networks have a minimal degree of structure, which can accommodate heterogeneous elements, however, and be woven into the many different patterns that serve their purposes. Modern communication networks are used in several basic ways: (1) to distribute or broadcast something, usually from one source to many receivers (water, electricity, print, radio, and television); (2) for two-way communication (as in postal, telephonic, and computer networks);

and (3) to facilitate acting together (as a commercial firm, a government, or any other political agency). While all three kinds of networks figure in this study, the third purpose for networking is most relevant to revolutionary communication.

How networks function depends upon their topology, which in turn depends upon a mix of physical factors (e.g., the architecture of channels of communication) and protocols (the enabling constraints that determine level of access, who can initiate communication, who reports to whom, and all the nuanced relations of any organizational structure). From the point of view of users, the postal system is a classic example of a distributed topology, represented in figure o.2 as a mesh, where no node on the network is given privilege over another. By contrast, the administrative network of the British Empire offers a classic instance of the hierarchical version of a star topology, where all communication from the colonial periphery (from the twenty-six governors, from military officers, from the admiralty courts, etc.) passed through the centers of administration in Whitehall. In a star topology the "hub" exercises control over the content and generic form, the privacy or publicity of the communication. The administration in Whitehall understood the importance of guarding the integrity of networks vital for communication and control, and, when it moved toward independence, the Continental Congress did the same.

The liberty that the protocols and networks make possible is not about throwing off shackles or being free to do whatever one wants. Instead, during the approach to the American Revolution, the cause of liberty bound its adherents into groups, obliged them to consult with others before they acted, and carried an ethical imperative to shape individual actions so they supported the public virtue of the cause. These imperatives became crucial to the development of a revolutionary movement, and in the actions that this discipline made possible, liberty assumed tangible form. The goal of the Revolution, a polity that would fairly reflect the consent of the governed, was embedded in the protocols and the networking with which the Revolution was conducted. This simple idea had profound implications. It meant that the way revolution was done was at the heart of what could follow from it.

WHAT IS DISTINCTIVE ABOUT THIS BOOK

By putting the ways and means, the practices, and the genres of communication at the center of this account of the American Revolution, I hope to offer an alternative to three familiar accounts of the Revolution: founder's narratives, people's histories, and intellectual history. I will briefly state the appeal

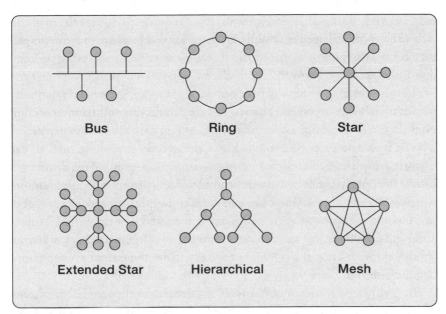

Bus   Ring   Star

Extended Star   Hierarchical   Mesh

FIGURE 0.2. Network topology. One way to represent the flow of information through networks is with their physical and logical topology. The rigidly hierarchical network of the British administration might be presented as a star, where Whitehall is situated at the hub in a raised (hierarchically privileged) center, and each administrative unit is a node on the periphery. The more egalitarian networks that emerged in the American colonies from 1772 to 1774 are best represented as a mesh, where each node can communicate on equal terms with all nodes. To organize the Continental Congress, however, the Whigs of British America had recourse to the extended star, where local town and county committees are the nodes at the periphery, the next level in represents the assemblies and conventions that select delegates, and the node at the center is the presumptive hub, Congress itself. The presumptive equality of the colonies keeps this network flat.

and limitations of each. Seeing the Revolution through the words and deeds of the founders gives us inspiring and sometimes useful exemplars. However, such a history distorts the Revolution by making the founders the *authors* of events. History's expansive horizons morph into the comfortable confines of biography. How can one describe the crucial mediating role of certain leaders without ceding them copyright to a history that is too large and multifaceted to be explained by them? To redress the bias of founder narratives, some historians set out to demonstrate how "the people made the Revolution." These historians advance the irrefutable thesis that it required a wide spectrum of the people to gather the power to pull off a revolution. How can one take advantage of this useful broadening of the Revolution, without accepting the tendentious opposition between "the elite" and "the people," and the replacement of a few founders with equally few "ordinary people"—shoemakers, farmers, soldiers—who are supposed to represent "the people," but somehow never do? Neither founders' histories nor people's histories have adequately explained what it is that sets a critical multitude of the people in motion. Intellectual historians explain revolution by offering a systematic account of the distinctive ideas of people living over two centuries ago. But a history through ideology is troubled by two questions. How can we acknowledge the mediating effects of ideas without supposing that they afflict men and women with delusions and rigid ideologies, now and then sweeping through history the way a virus spreads through a population? More crucially, how do men and women translate their ideas into action?[4]

To grapple with these questions, it is essential to demote "liberty" and "freedom" from the determining role they are often given in accounts of the Revolution. Thus, in spite of their differences, narratives through the founders, the people, and ideas give "liberty" a leading role, as the truth that the leaders grasp, as the right that the people claim, or as the idea that animates all. In these accounts, the Revolution can appear as spontaneous and neces-

---

4. These three approaches have interpreted the events of March 5–6, 1770, in quite distinct ways. The founders' narratives focus on the political manipulations of Samuel Adams, who through the apparatus of the Boston Whig Party he formed and led, enjoyed full control of the town meeting (Hosmer 1885, 295; Harlow 1923, 116; J. Miller 1936, 39). Bancroft attributes the Boston Whig victory on March 6 to the moral, liberty-loving character of Samuel Adams: "His vigorous and manly will resembled in its tenacity well-tempered steel, which may ply a little but will not break" (1866, 5:194). On March 6, when Samuel Adams demanded the removal from Boston of both regiments, a moment captured in Copley's famous 1772 portrait, Bancroft opines: "The vigorous will of Samuel Adams now burst forth in its majesty" (6:343). By contrast, people's histories emphasize the popular agency of the multi-ethnic urban mob, or "motley crew," of sailors and dockworkers who were scattered around the British Atlantic and occasionally rose up, as they did on the evening of March 5, to challenge instituted authority (Linebaugh and Rediker 2000, 213, 232–35). Finally, intellectual historians have emphasized a long-standing English radical tradition that argued that the existence of a standing army in times of peace was incompatible with true liberty. While each of these accounts has some cogency, each narrows our understanding of what happened on March 6.

sary as Delacroix's famous allegorical 1830 painting *Liberty Leading the People* over the barricades. There are two fundamental problems with this approach. First, by placing the British abridgment of fundamental American "liberties" at the origin of revolution and by making liberty the end or telos of revolution, historians give "liberty" the role of an all-purpose explanation and absolute value that simplifies the actual actions that enabled revolution. Instead of a laboriously constructed assemblage, the unity of diverse actors appears as a spontaneous response to a moral imperative, popular declarations are reduced to timeless truths or Whig propaganda, and the communication system of British American—the newspaper linked to the post—is understood as a passive information conduit instead of an active mediator of the crisis. The organizational achievements of American Whigs fade into clever instrumentalities. Second, and somewhat ironically, the privilege given to freedom as the origin and end of the Revolution obscures that event by staying too close to the highly motivated political rationales offered by the Whigs writing in the heat of crisis. Thus, in a 1779 pamphlet, *Observations on the American Revolution*, the Continental Congress begins by stating the political axiom that subtends and justifies revolution: "The great principle is and ever will remain in force, THAT MEN ARE BY NATURE FREE" (Congress 1779, 1; capitals in the original).[5] In the most widely read British pamphlet written about the American crisis, the dissenting minister Dr. Richard Price anchored his Whig defense of the American resistance to Britain by arguing that the idea for which Whigs fight—"liberty"—is, if properly understood, "a blessing truly sacred and invaluable . . . the foundation of all honour, and the chief privilege and glory of our natures" (Price 1776, section I).[6] While construing liberty as an unconditional value helped Congress summon Whigs to the sacrifices of war, an insistence upon the absolute value and power of liberty can become a

5. From my search of databases, this 1779 pamphlet is apparently the first time the struggle was named in print as "the American Revolution," a nomenclature that of course courts an analogy with the Glorious Revolution of 1688.

6. George Bancroft's Whig history of the Revolution engages in the most extravagant inflation of freedom by making it the engine of historical progress. The sentences where Bancroft begins his account of the Revolution show the pivotal role given freedom as an idea that gives history its preordained direction: "The hour of revolution was at hand, promising freedom to conscience and dominion to intelligence. . . . From the intelligence that had been slowly ripening in the mind of cultivated humanity, sprung the American Revolution, which was designed to organize social union through the establishment of personal freedom, and thus emancipate the nations from all authority not flowing from themselves" (1866, 4:12).

black hole into which the particular actions of the Revolution disappear. Instead of beginning with liberty, this study of the Revolution begins with the actions of American Whigs. My account of the Revolution does not ignore leaders, the people, or ideas, but it resituates each by subordinating them to the most decisive Whig communication innovations: the standing committee of correspondence, the genre of the popular declaration, and, finally, the dispersed and decentralized network of American Whigs. In my account of these developments, I have built upon the work of generations of scholars who have studied the post, the committees of correspondence, and the rich media practices of speech, manuscript writing, and print so central to the revolutionary movement in America. While I depend upon these varied veins of scholarship, I offer a fundamental revision of them.

Recent scholarship, perhaps in response to the emergence of the Internet, has begun to explore the full implications of early American postal communication and the networking that it enabled (John 1995; Loughran 2007; Chandler and Cortada 2000; Cohen 2010). In many ways the emergence of the postal system entailed changes as consequential for the eighteenth century as the arrival of the Internet was in our own time. In the eighteenth-century Anglophone world, epistolary correspondence enjoyed unprecedented prestige and popularity (Dierks 2009). It attracted many pedagogical initiatives and became ubiquitous enough to produce powerful linkages across the British Atlantic, developing what one scholar has called "the postal age" (Henkin 2006). The papers of those American Whigs who responded most actively and creatively to the American crisis—Samuel Adams, Richard Henry Lee, Benjamin Franklin, Charles Thomson, George Washington, and John Adams—reveal how trusted private correspondence opened a space for a cooperative development of political resistance to Great Britain. Finally, classic as well as recent studies have demonstrated how merchants—by managing cross-Atlantic trade with agents, letter books, and correspondence—offered an influential early model for exploiting the synergistic effects of networking (Doerflinger 1986; Hancock 1995).

This study of the standing committee of correspondence clarifies its role as the agency that began the Revolution. When George Bancroft was gathering primary materials for his early, magisterial history of the Revolution, he purchased from the heir of Samuel Adams the thirteen bound volumes of the town of Boston's committee of correspondence. This "find" helped to justify giving the Boston committee a prominent place in his history of the Revolution (Bancroft 1866). In the second half of the twentieth century, several important studies of the committees of correspondence were published. Most valuable for me has been Richard D. Brown's pioneering study of the Boston committee (1970), which was followed by studies of committee activity during the political crisis of 1774 (Ammerman 1974), in Philadelphia (Ryerson 1978), and in Virginia (Ragsdale 1996). These studies have given later scholars an indispensable grasp of how the committees functioned and how they shaped revolutionary mobilization. My study seeks to go a step further by explaining why the committees succeeded so spectacularly. I do this, first, by clarifying how the committee served as an engine of local consensus building; second, by arguing that Boston's fortuitous double invention of the standing committee of correspondence and the popular declaration became a decisive model for other Whigs; third, by tracing the steps by which Boston's communication initiatives scale up to become first provincial and then intercolonial; and finally, by describing the protocols that served as the adhesive that enabled a Whig network to emerge, cohere, and act together. I hope what has resulted is a fresh, synthetic view of revolutionary networking.

This book seeks to overcome the partiality of single-channel approaches to a media study of the Revolution. Scholars of the American Revolution have demonstrated how various formats and genres of print served as vehicles of Whig political resistance: the newspaper (Schlesinger 1958; Botein 1975, 1980; Brown 2000a), the pamphlet (Bailyn 1967), the legal document (Ferguson 1994), and public print media per se (M. Warner 1990; Loughran 2007). Thus, for example, Schlesinger and Warner offer two ways to explain how print shapes culture. While Schlesinger turns the press into an instrument for propaganda in the hands of the newspaper printer, who understands himself as "the maker of opinion" (Schlesinger 1958, 61), Warner subsumes the newspaper into a systemic analysis of the (republican) effects of print.[7] These two scholars can stand in for a much larger group of historians and literary critics who produced a dominant theme: that America's distinctive national achievement came from the various ways the nation created itself through writing.

Against these diverse professors of the power of writing, another group of scholars have insisted on the priority of speech, elocution, and orality to a revolution they ask us to understand as a performance (Fliegelman 1993; Looby 1996; Gustafson 2000). These histories of the oral performances of the Revolution explore the larger field where revolutionary sentiments unfold,

7. In spite of the theoretical possibility Michael Warner (1990, 40–41) entertains, that cultures without print might effect these same kinds of communication, Warner ends by arguing that "this universalizing mediation of publicity" so characteristic of republicanism "would continue to find its exemplary case in printed discourse."

where assembled groups and the body of speakers contribute to the performance of meaning. While print scholars emphasize print's fixity, authority, spatial reach, and public anonymity, these speech scholars emphasize the fluidity, authenticity, and local intensities of embodied speech. Their argument for privileging speech results in part from an understanding of the pragmatic imperatives of revolution. It required, they argue, rhetorical skill and the charismatic voices of revolutionary leaders like James Otis, Patrick Henry, and Samuel Adams. However, when scholars are haunted by the charm of the lost voices of the eighteenth century, they can become engaged in a highly speculative or even futile effort to reconstitute the moment of the self-presence of the voice to itself, and of a speaker to listeners, at the moment of successful revolutionary performance.

While print, speech, and manuscript studies have enhanced our understanding of the conceptual logic and rhetorical resources of the writing and speeches of the American founding era, they do so by obscuring the place of each medium in the more complex ecology of communication. While it is conceptually possible to disentangle one media object from the larger aggregation of media, this analytical procedure seems to run counter to the way media actually worked in the seventeenth and eighteenth centuries, where a particular medium acquired its salience within a multimedia buzz of communication.[8]

If one looks at the events of March 6, 1770, as I discussed earlier in this introduction, each media form was embedded in a hybrid media matrix that included speech, manuscript writing, print, pictorial representations, and systems for circulating media, like the newspaper and the post. On March 6, 1770, the most influential media making at the height of the crisis was the "vote" of the Boston Town Meeting. It began as a record in the town's minute book, then morphed into a single sheet that transmitted the political sentiment of the town meeting to the Council. It provoked the lieutenant governor's written reply and the town meeting's brief afternoon rejoinder, reiter-

---

8. Everywhere one looks in the seventeenth and eighteenth centuries, one finds media achieving efficacy by depending upon one another. In studying the ballad, Adam Fox (2000, 5) has demonstrated the complex co-implication of oral, scribal, and print culture for Renaissance England. Robert Ferguson (1994, 433) notes that the political pamphlet, the most ambitious political genre of the American crisis, relies upon the rhythms of speech: "Adrift in a culture still between oral and print modes of communication, the pamphlet often comes closer than even the printed sermon to the rhythms and personal pressure of speech."

ating the sentiment of the "vote." However, the "vote" could not incite and inflect these responses without attaching itself to various non-media: the "body" of the committee of fifteen that carried it up the gentle slope to the Council meeting, the thinking-speaking-gesticulating bodies of speakers who spoke for (and against) the "vote," the particular buildings (the Town House, Faneuil Hall, Old South Church) that became the forum where the "vote" was heard, and the streets of Boston that linked these places and humans. Thus, the distinct power of this modest single-sentence "vote" of the town meeting, which first "speaks" the demand of the town meeting but ends "speaking" through the lieutenant governor's order to remove the troops, arose from the way it merged, virus-like, with the actions and events of the groups, places, and bodies, through which it circulated. The "vote's" condensed power to "speak," and thereby become an "actor" within a political crisis, depended upon a complex network of places, groups, bodies, and genres, as well as other systems of communication like the post and the newspaper. *All* these terms become mediators of the American crisis. This approach understands the American Revolution as part of a capacious, inclusive, and hybrid history, the history of mediation.[9]

A BRIEF OVERVIEW OF THE BOOK

At the center of *Protocols of Liberty* is an account of how, in the midst of a chronic political crisis, American Whigs seized the initiative through a set of interrelated innovations in communication. This begins with the institution by the Boston Town Meeting, on November 2, 1772, of its own standing committee of correspondence. The committee was given the assignment of writing a statement of rights and "infringements" to the other towns of Massachusetts. Their pamphlet overwrote the petition, which was by custom addressed upward with humility to a person or institution of authority, with the public declaration, which was addressed outward to the people of Massachusetts. This simple change in the direction of address carried revolutionary potential (chapter 1). Sent to the other town meetings of the province, the Boston

9. For a full discussion of the rationale for a history of mediation, as alternative to other kinds of history, like the history of ideas, see the introduction of *This Is Enlightenment* (Siskin and Warner 2010). There we define Enlightenment as "an event in the history of mediation," and specify the four cardinal mediations that serve as the conditions of the possibility of Enlightenment.

declaration invited and secured declarations from most of the towns of Massachusetts. The public exchange of the town declarations was a new technique for discovering and focusing public opinion, for expanding political participation, and for mobilizing the Whigs of Massachusetts for collective action. The emergence of a public network of Massachusetts Whigs, based in the town meetings, changed the ratio of political power in the province. This became evident in 1773 when the governor's calculated attempt to reassert his authority weakened him, culminating in his failure to prevent the destruction of tea in Boston Harbor (chapter 2).

While the startling novelty of revolutionary events often occupies the foreground of historical narrative, it is essential to understand the background communication systems that do so much to shape how those events unfold and are transmitted. In prerevolutionary America, Whigs received an enormous "assist" from the open media communication system of the British Atlantic. Throughout the eighteenth century, royal officials in Whitehall had improved the postal system so that it could efficiently support communication (whether by private official letter or public broadside) between the metropolitan center and the colonial periphery. By providing franking privileges (i.e., free delivery) among the newspapers of the American colonies, the post also greatly expanded the reach of the newspapers. But because the post was a public system, through which the letter writer could address anyone, at periodic intervals, with dispatch and privacy, it was available to both challenge and support the empire. Because the newspapers of British America were run for profit by a dispersed group of talented craftsmen, the newspapers linked by post became a communication system that no one controlled. Newspapers could carry articles that celebrated the king's birthday or condemned his policies. When trials for seditious libel failed on both sides of the Atlantic, the newspapers proved to be censorship-resistant. The American crisis confronted British officials in Whitehall with this irony: improvements to the royal post, which they had undertaken to increase the efficiency of imperial administration, were now being used to subvert British authority in America. In 1774–1775, crisis engulfed the postal system: the postmaster general for America, Benjamin Franklin, was fired; the American secretary, Lord Dartmouth, initiated secret invasion of the mails; the royal post in American was dissolved; and a new postal system, under control of the Continental Congress, was instituted (chapter 3).

The second half of this book demonstrates the vigorous productivity of the communication innovations of the Boston Whigs. Between November 1772 and the end of 1774, shared public declarations, which observed a common set of protocols, introduced a communication dynamic that scaled up to reach all thirteen colonies. Parliament's passage of the Boston Port Bill and the other Coercive Acts was the "shock of electricity" that strengthened and expanded this intercolonial network of Whig committees. With Boston "suffering in the common cause of America," Virginia led the distributed network of town and assembly committees in planning the meeting of the First Continental Congress (chapter 4). The meeting of the First Continental Congress in Philadelphia resulted in consequential corporate actions, like the formation of the signed Association, authorizing the formation of committees in every town and county to enforce the economic embargo against Britain. By exercising effective authority over Whigs throughout the colonies, Congress emerged as the de facto hub of the American Whig network (chapter 5). The culminating act of the American Whig network was the writing, ratification, and broadcast of the Declaration of Independence. The Declaration of 1776 was cast in the form of a verbal panorama within which American Whigs throughout the colonies could experience two decisive acts—insulting the king and separating from Britain—as their own actions, but also as necessary events within the expanse of human history (chapter 6). Precisely how such an improbable set of actions happened is the focus of this study.

This brief overview of the narrative arc of this book suggests what is problematic about the use of the American Revolution to advance libertarian or neoliberal political goals. Those who fought the American Revolution did not value liberty at the expense of power, for only by producing a new concentration of shared power could liberty be secured. The rights and liberties in the name of which Whigs fought were not grounded in personal property but emerged from collective political practice of revolutionary resistance. Finally, American Whigs did not demonize government, but used their own carefully nurtured forms of self-government (of town, country, and colony) to create networks that could evolve into new forms of government. The distributed network of American Whigs eventually evolved into a confederation (1781) and then into a federal republic (1789).

While the communication innovations of the American Revolution, as detailed in this study, contributed to nation building, they also became a potent model for resistance to government. Several of the first ten amendments to the Constitution are shaped to assure that the future citizens of the United States would enjoy the right to communicate as the Whigs who made the Revolution did. The distinctive communication innovations of the Revolution—the committee and the declaration and the network—were available to oppose custom, law, and state. The conclusion to this book briefly considers some of the ways others have availed themselves of this revolutionary legacy, in movements for the abolition of slavery, for women's suffrage, for southern secession, and many other American political movements ever since. In deploying the communication innovations of the Revolution, each of these movements found that success depended upon the voluntary use of protocols that could extend once again the collective, public discipline of liberty.

THE INVENTION OF THE BOSTON COMMITTEE OF CORRESPONDENCE AND THE POPULAR DECLARATION

. . . .

For the course of five, six or seven years the town of Boston has invariably been the ringleader and promoter of all the disorders, the discontents, and disturbances. . . . They, Sir, at the latter end of 1772 . . . began to hold town meetings to consider the rights, and of their grievances. They established correspondence with the country towns in the province, in order to revive and rekindle that flame which appeared to them at that time near extinguished. From thence there has been nothing but disorder and confusion, almost all originating, all at last prevailing without opposition in the town of Boston.

— Lord North, speech to Parliament introducing the Boston Port Bill, March 14, 1774

All Accounts of the discontent so general in our colonies, having of late years been industriously smothered, and concealed here; . . . That the true state of affairs there may be known, and the true causes of that discontent well understood, the following piece (not the production of a private writer, but the unanimous act of a large American city) lately printed in New-England, is republished here.

— Benjamin Franklin, preface to *The Votes and Proceedings of the Town of Boston*, February 1773

[T]he votes and resolutions of the town of Boston . . . is a set of ready drawn head[ing]s of a declaration for any one colony in American, or any one distant county in the kingdom, which shall choose to revolt from the British empire, and say that they will not be governed by the King and Parliament at Westminster.

— Solicitor-General Wedderburn, in Privy Council, January 29, 1774

Historians who narrate the American Revolution are wary of saying precisely when it began. Rather than framing our inquiry as a quest for origins, which produces a vertiginous multiplication of remote causes, we can guide our inquiry with a question that allows us to pinpoint critical developments: *How* did the colonies move, during the crucial interval of 1770–1774, from what some called "the quiet time" (of 1771–1772) that followed the repeal of most of the Townshend duties to the emergency meeting of the First Continental Congress? How, in short, did the slowly simmering American crisis turn into revolution? These questions invite us to attend to the methods, mechanics, and media of revolution. In this chapter, I argue that the decisive development came on November 2, 1772, the day that the Boston Town Meeting instituted the twenty-one-member Boston Committee of Correspondence. Although the committee's first task was an apparently modest one—to write a pamphlet stating the rights and grievances of Massachusetts for circulation to the towns of the province—the activities of this autonomous standing committee of correspondence changed the dynamics of the American crisis. Its initial influence was direct. By developing a sustained two-way correspondence with towns throughout Massachusetts, and by extending this correspondence to important centers of political resistance throughout the colonies (Virginia, Philadelphia, Charleston, New York), the committee emerged as an influential counterweight to royal authorities in both America and Britain. In the subsequent two years, the committee replied affirmatively to the Virginia Committee of Correspondence's invitation for an intercolonial communication, publicized "the Hutchinson-letters affair," coordinated Boston's resistance to the Tea Act, and, after the arrival of the Boston Port Bill, developed regular communication with the committees of other colonies so as to manage relief for the city of Boston and plan for the meeting of the First Continental Congress.

The formation of the first, non-legislative committee of correspondence, by becoming a model for others, also had powerful indirect effects on the crisis. An anonymous cataloger of the Bancroft Collection placed the following note upon the first of thirteen volumes of the committee's minute books: "It was through the correspondence of this committee that disaffection spread throughout the English colonies, precipitating the AMERICAN REVOLUTION" (Boston 1772–1775, reel 1). This note suggests that revolution came through media contagion: the "correspondence" of the committee produces a contact that is said to "spread" "disaffection" throughout the English colonies, "precipitating the American Revolution." But the metaphor of spreading disaffection begs the question of how the Boston committee's writing could induce such a far-reaching change, of how this mode of communication communicated revolution.

One answer to this question comes from the correspondence of John Adams. Writing to his second cousin Samuel Adams from Paris in 1780, John Adams describes the committee of correspondence as an invention or discovery that enables widespread political mobilization: "Your Committee of Correspondence is making greater progress in the World and doing greater things in the political World than the Electrical Rod ever did in the Physical. England and Ireland have adopted it, but, mean Plagiaries as they are, they do not acknowledge who was the Inventor of it" (February 23, 1780; J. Adams 1989, 8:353).[1] A few weeks later, in a letter to Thomas Digges in England, John Adams gives more explicit credit to Samuel Adams as the inventor of the committee of correspondence: "The Committee of Correspondence is purely an American Invention. It is an Invention of Mr. Sam. Adams, who first conceived the Thought, and made the first Motion in a Boston Town Meeting, and was himself chosen the first Chairman of a Committee of Correspondence, that ever existed among men" (March 14, 1780; J. Adams 1989, 9:44).

By characterizing the standing committee of correspondence as an "invention," John Adams confers upon the committee form the central traits of a scientific invention: appearing at a discrete moment in time, it is new; but, after its invention, it is open to imitation by others. By emphasizing the person "who *first* conceived the thought and made the *first* motion in a Boston Town Meeting," John Adams figuratively awards his second cousin patent rights. But, by fusing the invention to a human with motives, John Adams negates what is happy, lucky, or fortuitous about the "discovery" of the committee form.[2]

1. In this letter, John Adams is referring to the English movement for radical parliamentary reform that made use of county committees to launch a national "Association" to discredit a corrupt and unrepresentative Parliament (see Black 1963, chapter 2). For the use of committees of correspondence on the American model, see pages 34–42. See also Goodwin 1979, 58–61.

2. Garry Wills notes that *invention* in its earliest meaning is a "discovery" or finding, rather than a fabrication out of the ingenuity of the mind. John Adams's description of his second cousin's role is inaccurate. It was not Samuel Adams but James Otis Jr. who was appointed as chair of the committee (though Samuel soon assumed the role as chair), and John Adams does not seem to have understood the collaborative emergence of the Boston committee I will describe below. More importantly, John Adams's treatment of his second cousin's reputation indulges in an early version of "founders discourse," where wise, far-seeing "founders" shape the history of the Revolution.

As with other inventions—in art, technology, or social organization—the influence of the Boston Committee of Correspondence derived less from its direct efforts, though these were significant, than it did from the indirect, and only gradually apparent, effects of its invention. The Boston Committee of Correspondence modeled the standing committee of correspondence as an agency for collective political action, and, as I will argue below, it spread through the communication protocols vital to the functioning of these committees. The wide imitation of the committee of correspondence by Whigs on both sides of the Atlantic suggests that the potency of this invention flowed from the ease with which others cloned it. It is this dangerous reproducibility of the committee, its power to spawn numberless local committees, that horrified the Tory polemicist Daniel Leonard. Writing as Massachusettensis in January 1775, a few months after the triumph of the committee movement with the First Continental Congress's adoption of the Association,[3] Leonard excoriates the dangerously generative power of the committee of correspondence: "[A] new and, till lately unheard of, mode of opposition had been devised, said to be the invention of the fertile brain of one of our party agents, called a committee of correspondence. This is the foulest, subtlest and most venomous serpent ever issued from the eggs of sedition" (*Boston News-Letter*, January 2, 1775; Leonard 1972, 34).[4]

Out of an impasse in the Whig confrontation with royal authority, the Boston Town Meeting instituted its committee of correspondence as a risky new experiment in Whig communications. In this chapter and the next, I argue that the committee's gradually expanding representative function, of speaking first for the town of Boston and later for the citizens of Massachusetts, derived not so much from its political ideas, which were conventional by design, as from the five communication protocols it observed: correct legal procedure, corporate action, public access, and a general and systematic address to the people that shows virtuous initiative. In this chapter, I describe the particular

3. As an "action of combining together for a common purpose" (*OED*), an association, in eighteenth-century practice, was formed by a group of people who gathered and publicly pledged to one another that they would behave in such a way as to support a specific common goal. So, for example, associations were important instruments in promoting the boycott of British goods in America, and the Virginia Association of August 1774 formalized a trade boycott against Britain that was then adopted and implemented in their own Association by the Continental Congress in October 1774.

4. Leonard's suspicion that "party agents" lay behind the foul birth of the committee of correspondence follows Hutchinson's erroneous suspicion that Benjamin Franklin hatched the Boston Whig plan to establish a committee of correspondence.

political emergency out of which the committee emerged, the canny strategy it developed to authorize itself as a new branch of government, and how it developed the committee's corporately authored pamphlet, *The Votes and Proceedings of the Town of Boston*, as the first popular declaration. The success of the Boston declaration and the development of a network of committees of correspondence in Massachusetts helped to break the repetitive political cycle that had persisted since the Stamp Act crisis, whereby British imperial "reforms," enacted by administration or Parliament, forced American Whigs to scramble and improvise to protect their rights and liberties from imperial encroachment. Because the crises that followed the formation of the committee resemble those that inspired its formation, it is easy to miss what had changed. After November 1772, the Boston Committee of Correspondence had achieved institutional continuity as a "standing" committee: always there and ever ready to act.

THE WHIGS OF BOSTON FACE A MOST DANGEROUS TIME

In the response to the stinging defeat on March 6, 1770, royal officials in Whitehall and Boston worked to reclaim the political initiative. Although the North ministry did not pursue the changes to the Massachusetts charter that had been recommended by the Privy Council in July 1770, Whitehall took a series of steps to strengthen the royal prerogative in Boston. It ordered the lieutenant governor to take possession of Castle William, the provincial fort in Boston Harbor to which British troops had retired in the week after the Boston Massacre; it shifted the American headquarters of the Royal Navy from Halifax, Nova Scotia, to Boston, where a substantial number of the navy's floating fortresses would offer Whigs a useful daily reminder of Britain's military might (Bailyn 1974, 175); it appointed Lieutenant Governor Thomas Hutchinson to be governor of Massachusetts and Secretary Andrew Oliver to serve as lieutenant governor (Hutchinson 1971, 1:80–81). This change enabled Hutchinson to avail himself of his power of appointment and expanded the power of the "government party" in Massachusetts (Bailyn 1974, 177–78). Finally, on December 7, 1770, Whitehall secretly implemented a step that would strengthen the hand of the governor by paying him directly out of customs revenues, a practice that was already followed in many other colonies (P. Thomas 1987, 212). This freed the governor from the dependency that arose from his receiving his salary from the annual appropriation of the Massachusetts House of Representatives. After the success of this change, Whitehall prepared in the spring of 1772 to pay the five judges of the Massachusetts

Superior Court, as well as the attorney general and the solicitor general, out of customs revenues.

Why were these administrative initiatives so alarming to American Whigs? Writing as Candidus in the *Boston Gazette* of September 23, 1771, Samuel Adams explains. If the ministry could raise a revenue through customs duties and use that revenue to pay the salaries of royal officials like the governor, and if the governor could, operating according to instructions of the ministry, delay calling the House of Representatives into session, veto laws of which he did not approve, and prorogue that body whenever it challenged the governor's authority, then the body representing the people of the colony, whether of Massachusetts or New York (and here Adams quotes "the Pennsylvania farmer," John Dickinson), "whose deliberations heretofore, had an influence on every matter relating to the liberty and happiness of themselves and their constituents, and whose authority in domestic affairs at least, might well be compared to that of Roman senators, will find their determinations to be of no more consequence than that of constables" (S. Adams 1904, 2:223–30). In short, American Whigs confronted the possibility that structural changes in imperial administration would push their popular assemblies, their main venue for influencing policy and law, into abject subservience. This would bring on, in Adams's words in a letter to Arthur Lee, "a State of perfect Despotism" (September 27, 1771; S. Adams 1904, 2:233).

At the same time that the royal officials were taking steps to strengthen their power to govern, the Whigs of Boston were losing their cohesion and active sense of purpose. With Parliament's repeal of all the Townshend duties except the tax on tea, Boston merchants had followed New York and Philadelphia in ending boycotts (P. Thomas 1987, 205). While the Whigs in the town meeting and the House kept up their resistance to several administrative measures—the appropriation of Castle William, the convening of the General Court in Cambridge, and the Crown's direct payment of the governor—they did not prevail in any of these struggles. At the same time, the Whig leadership of the province suffered an unsettling loss of cohesion. James Otis Jr. was becoming erratic in his behavior and inconsistent in his support for Whig initiatives; a new coolness appeared in the relationship between Samuel Adams and John Hancock, and this was reflected in Hancock's reluctance to follow Adams on measures before the House as well as his acceptance of a commission from Governor Hutchinson to be the colonel of the Boston cadets (Irvin 2002, 95). Hutchinson hoped that his compromise with Hancock and Cushing on returning the General Court to Boston from Cambridge would finally succeed in "wholly detaching him from" the Whig faction (Hutchinson to

John Pownall [private]; *Documents* 1972, 5:125). Finally, John Adams distanced himself from Boston Whig politics. Sensitive to the criticism that he had received from some fellow Whigs for successfully defending Captain Thomas Preston in the massacre trials, and feeling an increased general disgust with politics, on April 10, 1771, John Adams moved his primary residence from Boston to Braintree, where he stayed until the fall of 1772 (June 6, 1770; J. Adams 1961, 2:6, 63, 68).[5]

In 1771 Governor Hutchinson began to sound a new note of optimism about the vigor of royal government. In a long private letter to the American secretary Lord Hillsborough, Hutchinson wrote hopefully of a "change in the temper of the people" and of the "cure" brought by the active assertion of royal authority. At the same time, however, he counseled against any immediate change in the Massachusetts charter, which he feared would probably be "ineffectual" and only "increase the disorders" of the people (January 22, 1771; *Documents* 1973, 3:32–31). By June 1, 1771, Hillsborough evinced "hopes" that the "respectable inhabitants" and the Council will "preserve the tranquility that has been so happily restored to that town [i.e., Boston]" (*Documents* 1973, 3:103). By 1772 royal officials like Lord Hillsborough were smugly confident that their policy of "firmness" had restored the colonies of British America to a "quiet" in colonial affairs, such that affairs were finally resuming their "normal" course.

By 1772 the publication in Great Britain of news about the political crisis in British America reached a minimum, as measured by reference to "American Affairs" or "American Troubles" in the *Gentleman's Magazine* (see fig. 3.2). After many years in which vituperative challenges to the royal prerogative had kept the political pot boiling, both sides believed—Whigs with anxiety and royal officials with a sense of cautious relief—that the appearance of calm worked to legitimize the government party while it weakened what the governor referred to as "the party of liberty." In response, the Whigs of Boston conducted extensive private and public discussions about what should be done to challenge a royal policy that they saw as steadily encroaching upon their rights and liberties.[6] Often this discussion sounded disheartening notes. By

5. For a description of the disunity of the Boston Whigs, interpreted from different angles, see Bailyn 1974, 204–5; also S. Adams 1865, 1:389–411; Irvin 2002, 94–95.

6. Because the Whig leader, Samuel Adams, is sometimes represented as a party boss, puppet master, and "pioneer in propaganda" (J. Miller 1936), it is useful to note the essentially collaborative nature of Whig deliberations. At the center of this conversation was Samuel Adams, but it included two of his correspondents, Arthur Lee

1771 Boston Whigs privately worried that the people of Massachusetts had fallen into a political sleep. To counter this sentiment, Samuel Adams challenged James Warren's interpretation of the people's "silence" as acquiescence in Hutchinson's rule: "If the people are at present hushd into Silence, is it not a sort of sullen Silence, which is far from indicating your Conclusion, that the glorious Spirit of liberty is vanquished and left without hope but in miracles" (March 25, 1771; J. Warren 1917, 9). In addition, Adams reminded Warren that "[i]t is no dishonor to be a minority in the cause of liberty and virtue."

Adams did not, however, underestimate the urgency of the political moment. In the letter to Arthur Lee, which opens their important correspondence, Adams describes the tactical advantages then enjoyed by British administration:

> Perhaps there never was a time when the political Affairs of America were in a more dangerous State; Such is the Indolence of Men in general, or their Inattention to the real Importance of things, that a steady & animated perseverance in the rugged path of Virtue at the hazard of trifles is hardly to be expected. The Generality are necessarily engaged in Application to private Business for the Support of their own families and when at a lucky season the publick are awakened to a Sense of Danger, & a manly resentment is enkindled, it is difficult, for so many separate Communities as there are in all the Colonies, to agree in one consistent plan of Opposition while those who are the appointed Instruments of Oppression, have all the Means

---

in London and James Warren, a representative from Plymouth. Five other Whigs also played a part in this discussion: the Speaker of the House, Thomas Cushing Jr.; and Dr. Thomas Young, a member of the Albany Sons of Liberty, who, after the Sons of Liberty congress in Annapolis in 1766, had relocated to Boston; as well as Dr. Joseph Warren, Dr. Benjamin Church, and Josiah Quincy. The polemical essays published by these men and their later roles with the Boston committee and the town meeting suggest their active participation in these deliberations. Throughout these deliberations upon the most effective way to challenge the systematic expansion of ministerial authority in Massachusetts, Samuel Adams was less a grand architect than a leader of the conversation. Although Dr. Thomas Young was distrusted by some of the Boston Whigs as an agitator with deist tendencies, his correspondence with a member of the Sons in Albany suggest that he was involved in the early planning for a Boston committee of correspondence (Brown 1970, 47–48, 64). There is additional evidence that Samuel Adams also consulted with James Warren upon his visit to Plymouth in 1772, for Mercy Otis Warren erroneously gave her husband, James Warren, credit for conceiving the idea of the committees of correspondence and transmitting that idea to Samuel Adams (M. Warren 1989, 1:62).

put into their hands, of applying to the passions of Men & availing themselves of the Necessities of some, the Vanity of others & the timidity of all. (April 19, 1771; S. Adams 1904, 2:164)

After sounding an alarm, Adams attributes the administration's strength to American weakness: the population "in general" is inattentive, lazy, busy with private business, and therefore not ready to walk the "rugged path of virtue." Adams notes the operational advantage of the oppressors: they have the means, that is, the money and power, to manipulate the "passions of men" by "applying" to their necessities, their vanity, and their timidity. But in the midst of this familiar lament of the modern political activist, Adams describes the structural problem for those who recognize the danger and want to respond: given the way communities are scattered across all the colonies, "it is difficult . . . to agree in one consistent plan of opposition." This is the problem to which the Boston Committee of Correspondence would be a solution.

For Adams, the past offered lessons with which Boston Whigs might address the present crisis. In three essays published under the name Candidus in September 1771, Adams offered the readers of the *Boston Gazette* a survey of the American colonists' successful resistance to the Townshend Acts, focusing especially on the happy effects of Massachusetts's initiative in writing a circular letter to the assemblies of all the other colonies. From this history Adams extracts a general lesson about the way communication can promote unity: "I have often thought that in this time of common distress, it would be the wisdom of the colonists, more frequently to correspond with, and to be more attentive to the particular circumstances of each other" (September 16, 1771, S. Adams 1904, 2:220). Only by instituting regular and frequent communication, and only by attending sympathetically to the "particular circumstances" of each colony, can the colonists learn that *the cause of one is the cause of all* and thereby counteract the ministerial policy "to divide and thus to destroy" (221–22).

One model for producing unity is described by Arthur Lee. Arthur Lee, a member of the already-prominent Lees of Virginia and younger brother of Richard Henry Lee, served as secretary for the Society for the Support of the Bill of Rights, the organization of radical Whigs that was founded in February 1769 to support John Wilkes in his struggle against Parliament. In response to Lee's description of the workings of this voluntary political association, Adams suggested that the Whigs of British America might be united by forming distributed and independent societies, which, by communicating regularly with each other, could create a powerful transatlantic alliance of Whigs. Although the Boston Whigs never attempted to act on this particular idea, the experimental posture Adams assumes here may explain how, a year later, in the autumn of 1772, Adams and his collaborators found a way to lead Massachusetts into the arduous task of forging a union through remote communication by letter. Like the "societies" Adams envisioned, the committees of correspondence would have an ongoing existence. But success depended not upon a transatlantic or intercolonial correspondence, but upon grounding the committees in the Massachusetts town meetings.

NEWS FROM WHITEHALL TRIGGERS A NEW CRISIS: OUT OF INFORMAL MEETINGS, A NEW INSTITUTION

The Boston committee was forged out of a particular political crisis. On September 28, 1772, the *Boston Gazette* confirmed that British administration had decided to pay judges and other judicial officers out of customs revenues, instead of allowing them to depend upon annual appropriations by the Massachusetts House of Representatives. For the Whigs of Boston, this development meant that events had veered toward a genuine crisis. But was this really a crisis, that is, a time where events are implicated in a decision that will bring changes that could be irreversible? Unlike the Boston Massacre, the inhabitants of Massachusetts would not necessarily see the direct payment of judges by the Crown as a political emergency to which all must respond. For Tories, this administrative change was a reasonable way to secure the independence of judges from influence by a Whig-dominated House. The dispute quickly led to relatively abstruse questions of the best way to secure judicial independence. But for Whigs, this ominous change induced a political crisis that was all the more dangerous precisely because, to an unwary eye, it might appear that nothing of consequence had changed.

Samuel Adams, writing in the *Boston Gazette* of October 5, 1772, under the pseudonym Valerius Poplicola, developed four related points to argue both the existence of a crisis and the proper way for each citizen to respond to it. First, previous modes of communication had failed: petitions to the king had proven useless because, though they reached the "royal ear," they had not "touch'd the royal heart" (S. Adams 1904, 2:334). Second, the fact that this was a dangerous ministerial innovation is described in a tone that is grand, sad, and hyperbolic: "To what a State of infamy, wretchedness and misery shall we be reduc'd if our judges shall be prevail'd upon to be thus degraded to *Hirelings*, and the *Body of the People* shall suffer their free constitution to be overturn'd and ruin'd." Third, Adams poses a fraught question: "Is it not High Time for the People of this Country explicitly to declare, whether they will be freemen or slaves?" Finally, Adams argues that the only recourse in this time of crisis is for men to come together and communicate:

> We are at this moment upon a precipice. The next step may be fatal to us. Let us then act like wise Men; calmly look around us and consider what is best to be done. Let us converse together upon this most interesting Subject and open our minds freely to each other. Let it be the topic of conversation in every social club. Let every Town assemble, Let Associations & Combinations be everywhere set up to consult and recover our just Rights
> "*The Country claims our* active *Aid.*
> That let us roam; & where we find a Spark
> Of public Virtue, blow it into Flame."
> VALERIUS POPLICOLA
> (S. Adams 1904, 2:334–37)

The language of this essay develops the rationale for the new enterprise of the committee of correspondence. The essay is not directed at king or governor, but instead turns away from them to address fellow subjects. We shall see that this is a crucial trait of the new genre of the popular declaration. In its hyperbolic statement of the threat to liberty posed by this policy, Poplicola uses language that does not just describe a crisis, but also seeks to induce one. This Whig rhetoric of crisis appalled the Tories and drew their contempt.

Perhaps counterintuitively, Poplicola's essay modulates its tone by counseling readers to calm their passions by slowing down and coming together. Only as voluntary "associations & combinations" of private citizens will they have the strength and confidence to conduct "calm," "wise," inclusive, and "open-minded" "conversation" about this political crisis. Here the language deliberately avoids the fatalism that might grip a people confronted with a political crisis over which they have little direct control. Poplicola invites his readers to something they *can* do: gather in groups, "open our minds freely to each other," and "converse together upon this most interesting subject." With this exhortation, Adams summons Bostonians to a politics that is local and neighborly. Democratic deliberation at the granular scale of "every social club" is the precondition for gathering popular consent for more ambitious political measures. A new politics can emerge one conversation at a time. The final image—of "roaming" to "find" a transformative "spark" of "public virtue"—neatly condenses the disposition required to advance the cause. Citizens must be deliberate, but also open to fortuitous discovery.

But how could this diffuse conversation be more than mere talk? How could this politically fraught conversation be both sharply focused *and* participatory, both coherent *and* extensive? The Boston Committee of Correspondence was the formal and institutional solution to these imperatives. However, even after news of the direct Crown payment of judges had arrived, those Whigs who favored a town meeting to discuss and counter this threatening development encountered skepticism and resistance from other powerful Whigs. Only on October 14, 1772, after the failure of two petitions for a Boston town meeting, did a third petition, which garnered 106 signatures out of the 692 freeholders eligible to sign, finally convince the selectmen of Boston, the seven men who alone had the power to call a meeting, to issue a warrant for a town meeting. The formation of a committee of correspondence gave pause to Cushing, Hancock, and others. In a letter to the Massachusetts agent in London, Benjamin Franklin, Dr. Samuel Cooper reported pragmatic reasons for this opposition: "[T]his measure was oppos'd by a Number of the most respectable Friends to Liberty in the town, among which were three out of four of the Representatives of Boston, from an apprehension that many Towns, for various Reasons might not chuse to adopt it, and in that Case, the Attempt might greatly prejudice the Interest it was designed to promote" (March 15, 1773; Franklin 1974, 20:112). But there was another more substantial reason for their hesitation. While none questioned the legal right of the House of Representatives to petition the king for redress of grievances, the formation of a standing committee of correspondence to address similar grievances would place that committee in a constitutional no-man's-land: it would be meeting outside of the authority of the General Court, and therefore also outside the authority of the royal governor. It would be meeting while the town meeting was not in session, and apart from the selectmen. In short, as Gordon Wood (1969, 315) notes, Whigs were aware that with this kind of improvised meeting, they might well be "moving into revolutionary ground."

THE WHIGS' RUSE: USING THE THEATER OF POLITICAL IMPASSE
TO JUSTIFY INSTITUTING THE COMMITTEE OF CORRESPONDENCE

The town meeting that first met on Wednesday, October 28, 1772, and was continued each day but Sunday until Monday, November 2, 1772, brought the latent struggle between the Whigs of Boston and the royal governor into a public arena where the political agon acquired the suspense and visibility that we associate with theater or a sporting event. Because political contests in general are composed of the public words and deeds of antagonists, victory will often depend upon the quality of the performance. Since these antagonists had met many times before and knew each other well, their encounter would have a certain generic familiarity. Each adopted a distinct strategy. The Boston Whigs worked to draw the governor out by drawing him in. They would start with a request for information about this "alarming" news of the direct Crown payment of judges, then they would petition the governor that the General Court be allowed to convene and discuss this matter. When these failed, they would proceed with their experiment with a new form of communication, the Boston Committee of Correspondence.

Why, one might ask, request information that the Whigs not only already had, but that they already suspected the governor would refuse to share? The aim was to press the governor, within the public forum of the Boston Town Meeting, to make public the policy they knew he had been ordered to implement, but which the governor was withholding from public knowledge. Winning the governor's public avowal of this policy was less important to the Whig strategy than developing a sharp contrast between their reasonable addresses to the governor and the high and haughty style of his refusals. In other words, because they knew the unyielding posture that the governor was likely to assume, they could script him into a scenario where those qualities would contribute to reconcile even "cautious minds" among the Whigs to the "Unanimity" essential to political action (Samuel Adams to Elbridge Gerry, November 5, 1772; S. Adams 1904, 2:346).

If the Whigs' work was to bring the "alarming" new policy into clearer view, the Tory strategy was to defer the public discussion of this new policy until after it had been fully implemented. To do so, the governor adopted the magisterial tone of one who is calmly confident in his possession of the powers of the royal prerogative. The Tories of Boston boycotted the town meeting entirely, and to the town's initial request for information, the governor insisted that his office made it inappropriate to share "any Part" of his official and private "correspondence as Governor of the Province." Similarly, when the town meeting petitioned the governor to allow the General Court to convene (at the time to which it was then prorogued—December 2, 1772) in order to discuss this new policy, Hutchinson turned away the petition on the legal grounds that to accede to the town meeting's request would be a constitutional violation, because he would then, "in effect, yield to [them] the exercise of that part of the Prerogative, and should be unable to justify [his] Conduct to the King." By sidestepping any discussion of the new policy, the governor avoided an expansive inquiry into the fundamental principles implied by ministry's resort to a direct Crown payment of the judges. The day after the town meeting adjourned, Governor Hutchinson replied with a potent negative to the town's petition that he convene the General Court. Instead, he further prorogued the General Court from December 2, 1772, to January 6, 1773.

When, at 3:00 p.m. on November 2, 1772, the town received and read its second negative from the governor, the whole exchange, which had been going on for six days, might have appeared an exercise in futility. The town had addressed a "message" to the governor requesting information, and the governor had replied no; a petition to the governor to convene the General Court had received another no. But what was thereby staged in the highly public forum of the town meeting was a blockage in the circulation of public information, and it was at this juncture that the Whigs of the Boston Town Meeting introduced their surprise. Throughout all these deliberations, the Whigs had kept the central motive of this meeting—the scheme to institute a Boston Committee of Correspondence—carefully out of view. Only after the governor's second negative had produced a deadlock in communication could the establishing of a committee of correspondence appear to be the town's last and only recourse for continued resistance to Whitehall's intolerable new policy. And here we confront an important paradox with regard to the town meeting's exchanges with the governor. While the town sought to expose the governor as simply "impossible," these exchanges paradoxically made the governor an indispensable relay on the way to new forms of communication. The town first had to request information of the governor in order to turn away from him as a reliable source of information; they first had to petition the governor in order to move beyond petitioning. In sum, engaging the governor with these addresses opened the space for a new kind of address to the towns of Massachusetts.

How did the town meeting justify its pivot, in the crucial last part of the meeting of November 2, 1772, from an engagement with the king's designated representative in Massachusetts to something so very different as the institution of a standing committee of correspondence for communication with the towns of Massachusetts? After reading the governor's refusal to convene the General Court, the town meeting passed a unanimous vote rejecting the governor's reply, and then moved immediately to do two things: it passed a *resolution*, upholding the ancient right to petition, and passed a *motion*, establishing a committee of correspondence.

And thereupon RESOLVED as the Opinion of the Inhabitants of this Town, That they have, ever had, and ought to have a right to Petition the King or his Representative for the Redress of such Grievances as they feel, or for preventing of such as they have Reason to apprehend, and to Communicate their Sentiments to other Towns.

It was then

MOVED, That a Committee of Correspondence be appointed to consist of Twenty-one Persons, to state the Rights of the Colonists, and of this Province in particular, as Men, as Christians, and as Subjects; to communicate and publish the same to several Towns, in this Province, and to the World, as the Sense of this Town, with the Infringements and Violations thereof that have been, or from Time to Time may be made.—Also, requesting of each Town a free Communication of their Sentiments on this Subject.— And the Question being accordingly put—it passed in the Affirmative, *Nem. Con.*

A Committee of Twenty-one Persons was then appointed for the Purposes aforesaid, of which the Hon. James Otis, Esq; is Chairman; and they were desired to Report to the Town as soon as may be.

Attest.

WILLIAM COOPER, Town-Clerk.

The town justified its appointment of the committee of correspondence by building on the most ancient right to political speech—the right to petition. But notice that the town extends the right to petition the king for "such grievances as they *feel*" (in the present) to those they "have reason to apprehend" (in the future). Next they connect the right to petition with the right "to communicate their sentiments to other towns." Finally, in the motion proper, they associate the right "to communicate and publish" "to several towns" with a request "of each town a free communication of their sentiments."

Royal officials were appalled at these proceedings of the Boston Town Meeting. By gathering together the later private and public responses from Governor Hutchinson, the American secretary Lord Dartmouth, Solicitor-General Alexander Wedderburn, and Lord North, I can offer this redaction of the Tory condemnation of the town of Boston's initiative.

Neither the town's careful observation of legal procedure nor its unanimous votes (made possible by the Tory boycott of the meeting) justify illegal motions and these irregular proceedings. The resolution (affirming the right to petition) has no logical or legal relation to the motion that it introduces. Through what rhetorical alchemy has the town of Boston translated the ancient right of petition—that none would deny, and that the House of Representatives was at this very time pursuing through official channels—into a capacious set of communication rights and practices: the right to communicate their sentiments to other towns, and the authority to request a "free communication of their sentiments" back? There is no law or custom that would justify establishing a standing committee of correspondence to take up matters of imperial policy within the colony of Massachusetts. Since the committee has no designated termination date, is this to be permanent new branch of town government?

Such a Tory critique allows us to see that the motions of this meeting, including the appointment of a committee of correspondence to communicate with the towns of Massachusetts, rested upon little more than the "opinion" of the town. In other words, the motions of this town meeting, and the twenty-one-member committee it instituted, were self-authorized. The town's actions rested upon nothing more substantial than the town's collected and independent initiative.

Since the town of Boston was venturing an exercise that had no constitutional support, success would depend upon opening its proceedings to the public so that the "people" could serve as ultimate judges of the legitimacy of the proceedings. Here is where the newspaper tied to the post became an indispensable constituent of the Whig practice of politics. As Whigs who assembled in Faneuil Hall communicated with the governor at Province House, they would have no occasion to meet. Each understood, however, that all they said, did, and wrote would be reprinted in the newspapers, and this understanding had a powerful influence upon all that they *did* say, do, and write. This publicity helps explain the postures assumed by each of the protagonists—why the Whigs were so alarmist and histrionic, the governor so haughty and absolute. Both the town meeting and governor wrote and spoke as though their two-way communications were for each other alone, but each also knew, after years of political struggle in Boston, that every word that the town sent the governor and that he sent back to them would be published in the Boston newspapers in the next few days, reprinted throughout many of the colonies in the coming weeks, and would finally cross the Atlantic to be read by British Whigs and Tories. In fact, in order for the two "actors" to appear in one coherent exchange, political theater needed the media supplement of the newspaper broadcast.

The *Boston Gazette*'s presentation gives the exchange between town meeting and governor the continuity and dialectical precision of stage drama.[7]

7. I use the metaphor of the theater advisedly. While in conventional theater actors pretend that no one is watching from beyond the lights, in political theater everything that is said and done is assumed to be for those who watch and listen. Thus in this political theater, that agon is unframed, or provisionally framed, since all are invited to join in (Enders, 2009, 126). In fact that was the motive of this Whig performance: to spread the theater beyond its first "act," the exchange between the town meeting

Crucial to the "you are there" illusion of becoming an eyewitness to history is something we have noticed before about the British American newspaper: its polemical restraint. The *Boston Gazette*'s narrative account of the three sessions of the town meeting is spare and simple, constituting little more than brief connectives that allow the reader to situate the documents. Thus, before reporting the town meeting's first message to the governor (on October 28), the *Gazette* reports that there was "the coolest and most candid Debate and Deliberation," but does not give the content of that debate. Instead, it presents the flow of documents in the order in which they were produced. On the common space of the page of the newspaper, the exchange takes on the intensity of a debate and the suspenseful character of live theater, where spectator-readers wonder "how it will end." While for Tories, a display of political differences was inconsistent with sound government, for Whigs, conducting political business under the gaze of the public was consistent with their political values. Who could be a more appropriate witness of political development than the people in whose name that business was conducted?

HOW THE BOSTON COMMITTEE CAME TO ACT AS ONE

Whig unity was an arduous achievement, and American Whigs only achieved the unity to act together one committee at a time. By looking at the workings of the Boston committee during its first weeks of operation, we can isolate what was distinctive about this committee and how it came to stand at the beginning of a powerful new politics of change. The Boston Town Meeting routinely appointed committees as agents for the town meeting, but ultimate authority rested with the town meeting. A committee's task was limited in scope. Thus, on November 2, 1772, the new committee was charged with the task of drafting a general address to the people of Massachusetts, which was to do three things: "state the rights of the colonists, and of this province in particular, as men, as Christians, and as subjects"; state as "the sense of this town" "the infringements and violations thereof"; and request "of each town a free communication of their sentiments on this subject." Once this document was completed, the committee was "desired to report to the town as soon as may be." Because this was a complex and potentially fraught task, the town meeting appointed a large body of twenty-one members so that the committee could be various and authoritative enough to represent the prevailing sentiment of

---

and the governor, and gradually to welcome all the towns of Massachusetts onto this political "stage."

the town. Otherwise, the committee could not be an effective agent for the town, and when it returned to the town meeting, its document might be rejected.

Forming a unified committee began with the selection of those nominated to serve. The twenty-one committee members were a cohesive group: seven graduated from Harvard, eight were members of the North End Club, and many had worked together over the years to enforce the boycott against the Townshend duties and the Stamp Act (Brown 1970, 59–60). Secrecy was another way in which the Boston committee helped to secure its own unity. Because leaks of committee discussion could easily abort initiatives before they had time to mature, it was considered essential to hold each committee member accountable for guarding the secrecy of committee deliberations. Thus, on the first day of the committee's meeting, November 3, 1772, the honor of each of the committee members was engaged to assure secrecy: "Upon a motion made and seconded, it was voted unanimously, that each member of the committee be desired to declare to the chairman, that he does hold himself bound in honor, not to divulge or make known any part of the conversation of this committee at their meetings to any person whatsoever, excepting what the committee shall judge proper to lay before the Town or to make known in their capacity as a committee" (November 3, 1772; Boston 1772–1775). The form of this pledge of secrecy—a formal oral declaration to the chairman, evidently witnessed by the whole committee—engaged the full eighteenth-century gentleman's code of honor, by which one's word is one's deed. The recording procedures of the clerk of the committee, William Cooper, also guarded the secrecy of the committee. Within the committee's minute book, Clerk Cooper recorded the formal motions of the committee, but he never recorded the content of discussion or the opinions of individual members. Secret knowledge bound the committee members into one body, and each member's honoring of their pledge of secrecy helped to assure the safety and integrity of the whole.[8]

Several aspects of the Boston committee's operation helped it speak with one voice. Since a quorum was required for any business to be conducted, a small subset of the committee could *not* act for the whole. The authority of the chair, first James Otis Jr. but very soon Samuel Adams, resembled the moderator of the town meeting rather than the committee chair of today: his main job

8. Ironically, one of the committee's most prominent members, Dr. Benjamin Church, eventually spied for the British, though it is not known if he was doing so as early as 1772 (American National Biography Online).

was to advance the discussion and business of the meeting. The agenda of the committee seems to have been developed collectively. The chair was not authorized to act alone on behalf of the committee, except when charged by the committee to do so. Upon those rare occasions when the chair of the committee was absent, the meetings still went forward. Of almost equal importance was the clerk, William Cooper, who kept the minute book, recorded and archived the correspondence from and to the committee, signed letters from the committee, and attested to the authenticity of broadsides in the name of the whole committee. The clerk's public role prevented the chair from emerging as the de facto public "face" of the committee, or from allowing the committee to appear as little more than the "mouthpiece" of the chair. That Cooper also served as clerk of the town meeting helped to assure an ongoing institutional link between the two bodies.

This elaborate system for collective action is evident in the committee's first major task, the drafting of the pamphlet to be sent to the towns. On the first day of its existence, the committee of twenty-one appointed three subcommittees with three members each, which at first met separately to draft the three parts of the pamphlet, and then met together (six times) to join the parts into one so it could be forwarded for review by the town meeting. At the end of the successful completion of this first task, the Boston committee was composed of the minds and bodies of twenty-one members who had engaged in corporate acts of deliberation, writing, and reading. For the purposes of its communications, twenty-one Boston Whigs embedded themselves in the committee and channeled their diverse sentiments through the speech and writing of the committee. By subordinating individuals' views and voices to the communications of the committee, the committee could aspire to the power that their representative function promised: to speak for all of the freeholders and inhabitants of the town. Once they were "in" the committee, members inevitably found that the committee of correspondence, like any other rule-bound and media-specific form of communication, constrained communication. A reading of the minute book of the committee suggests that, like many modern committees, the committee of correspondence depended upon accepting the presumptive equality of its members by giving each a (formally) equal voice and vote in its business. Because even a single dissonant voice could paralyze its work, the committee habituated its members to showing deference to the opinions of others. In this way, committees became a machine for achieving consensus. After habitual use, these modes of operation were internalized. The committee's forms of communication ceased to appear arbitrary or consciously utilized, and the members blended into a committee. To grasp the strangeness of this phenomenon, it is useful to consider these habituated Whig committee members the way the Tories and the British did, as a dangerous new political entity, "committeemen."[9] The disciplined corporate language of the committee allowed it to realize its remarkable potential: although a small group, it represented many others; though secret, it devised public measures; though local, its language could reach across an empire.

Neither the warrant for the town meeting that founded the committee (on November 2) nor the town meeting (on November 20) that voted unanimously to approve the work of the committee described the Boston Committee of Correspondence as a *standing* committee of the town. That is, it was not explicitly given the crucial authority to schedule and authorize its own meetings and send off communications on behalf of the town, or to continue in existence for years without periodic reauthorization. However, in some sense continuous existence was implied by its very name and charge: to *be* a committee of correspondence implied that its tasks were by its very nature open-ended. In addition, there were early signs of the committee's expected longevity. From the first meeting, Clerk William Cooper developed a capacious and well-organized archival system for the committee: a chronological log to hold the minutes of each meeting as well as an alphabetical log to hold the correspondence with the various towns. The committee quickly settled upon its preferred meeting place and time: one of the selectmen's two chambers on the third floor of Faneuil Hall on Tuesday evening (at first 5:00–7:30 p.m.; after March 1773, 6:00–9:30 p.m.). Although not founded as a standing committee, the Boston committee's own success—in writing and then distributing the pamphlet for the town, and in corresponding with the other towns—allowed it to emerge as a committee that gradually assumed executive functions more proper to government.

THE BOSTON DECLARATION

It is easy to underestimate the Boston committee's pamphlet, *The Votes and Proceedings of the Town of Boston*. It has none of the authoritative learning or easy elegance of John Dickinson's *Letters from a Pennsylvania Farmer* (1767–1768). It does not marshal the solid legal arguments of the Stamp Act pam-

9. While he was imprisoned in New York, Ethan Allen described one of his fellow prisoners as a "committee man"; in suffering imprisonment in New York with this man, William Miller of West Chester County, Allen found that "the word rebel or committee man was deemed by the enemy a sufficient atonement for any inhumanity that they could invent and inflict" (Allen 1779, 100).

phlets of 1765–1766, nor of John Adams's newspaper debates with Captain William Brattle or Daniel Leonard. It lacks both the lucid structure and literary elevation of Jefferson's *A Summary View of the Rights of British America* (1774), and the sting of the fusillade-like sound bites that Paine would develop in *Common Sense* (1776). Among the influential political literature of the American Revolution, the *Votes and Proceedings* appears as a drab, and perhaps even ugly, duckling.

The problem begins with its anodyne title. Rather than foregrounding its inflammatory topic (the British "invasion" of the rights of the American colonists) or the boldness of its action (calling for a correspondence among the towns of Massachusetts), the title page protests too much through its use of expressive typography—the town is "assembled" "ACCORDING TO LAW"; its proceedings are "*Published by Order of the Town*"—and by including an "attested copy" of the vote of the town meeting forming the committee that writes the document (see fig. 1.1). On first reading, the *Votes and Proceedings* may also appear as a confusing miscellany of Boston Whig writings cobbled together from the minutes of two town meetings, the town's communications with the governor, a political pamphlet, and a letter to the towns of Massachusetts. Finally, the *Votes and Proceedings* suffers from its mixed authorship: it was written by a committee, a circumstance that weakened its consistency of argument, tone, point of view, and literary quality.

In spite of these liabilities, however, the text produced by the Boston Committee of Correspondence and endorsed by the town meeting turned out to have a potency of life in it that surprised its first readers and has baffled later historians. The *Votes and Proceedings* might be said, in Milton's famous defense of books, "to preserve as in a vial the purest efficacy and extraction of that living intellect" of the Boston Whigs, as it had developed over the course of seven years' resistance to British rule. Viewed in relation to the arc of events that led to the outbreak of war on April 19, 1775, the *Votes and Proceedings* might also be said to have scattered words that, like the fabulous dragon's teeth Milton references in *Areopagitica*, "sprang up armed men." How could this prerevolutionary writing have had such potent effects? When Benjamin Franklin republished the Boston pamphlet in London in the spring of 1773, his preface recognized that the novelty of the *Votes and Proceedings* arose from its corporate authorship and performative agency. In his preface, Franklin notes that this "piece" was not "the production of a private writer, but the unanimous *act* of a large American city" (Franklin 1976, 84–85; emphasis mine). In this chapter and the next, I explore how words can *do* what they describe, and reshape the political context within which they are inserted. Like the performatives

THE

VOTES and PROCEEDINGS

OF THE

FREEHOLDERS and other INHABITANTS

OF THE

Town of BOSTON,

In Town Meeting affembled,

ACCORDING TO LAW.

[*Publifhed by Order of the Town.*]

To which is prefixed, as Introductory,

An attefted Copy of a Vote of the Town
at a preceeding Meeting.

——————————

BOSTON:
PRINTED BY EDES AND GILL, IN QUEEN-STREET,
AND T. AND J. FLEET, IN CORNHILL.

"I do" or "I declare war," the Boston committee's words turn political discourse into political action.[10] Most obviously, this text "acted" because the motion to accept the report of the Boston committee received a unanimously favorable

10. Franklin's preface to the pamphlet was written in February 1773, but not published in London until June 1773. Franklin's characterization of the *Votes and Proceedings* as a "declaration" proves insightful and prescient. I follow Franklin and John Phillip Reid, who justifies this terminology in *The Briefs of the American Revolution* because of the way the document anticipated the Declaration of Independence of 1776 in grounding its statements of rights and grievances in a doctrine of natural rights (*Briefs* 1981, 2–3).

vote within the town meeting; this rendered the *Votes and Proceedings* the official "vote" of the town of Boston. This performance was public because it was the product of a committee, which submerged the opinion of private writers into corporate authorship that was also highly public: all twenty-one members of the committee were listed in the text as well as in the newspaper notices that describe the town meetings leading up to its formal adoption.

For Tory observers, the boldness of its statement of opinion gave the *Votes and Proceedings* a different kind of agency: the edgy notoriety of an "act" that authorities might find actionable insofar as it should be judged seditious. When Alexander Wedderburn surveyed the damaging effects of "votes and resolutions of the town of Boston" upon the loyalty of the colonists of Massachusetts, he characterized it as "a *declaration* for any colony in America . . . which shall choose to revolt from the British Empire" (Franklin 1974–2012, 21:62; emphasis mine). The *Votes and Proceedings* was apparently the first instance of the most distinctive genre of modern political writing, the popular declaration. To track this important generic innovation, I begin by making sense of the hybrid structure of the *Votes and Proceedings*, showing how it established its authority through its incorporation and redirection of two traditional constituents of the petition, the statement of rights and the list of infringements and grievances, by replacing the deferential address to authority with an egalitarian address to fellow citizens. Second, I account for the remarkable influence of the *Votes and Proceedings* by considering the three ways it circulated: as a Whig political pamphlet grounded in a neo-Roman theory of liberty, as the script for oral readings performed in towns throughout Massachusetts, and, finally, as a letter that elicited replies from 140 Massachusetts towns, which then took the Boston declaration as a model for their own.

The complex, carefully contrived structure of the *Votes and Proceedings* advances two different goals. In order to establish the authority of the town meeting, the *Votes and Proceedings* is given an elaborate frame: parts 1, 2, 4, and 5 are taken directly from the minute book of the town meeting. These sections carry the evidential force and documentary realism I have noted in the discussion of the eighteenth-century newspaper's reprinting of public documents. These documents strive for neither polemical clarity nor dispassionate commentary; instead, they share the exact words with which the town meeting established a committee of correspondence (part 1), took up the report of the committee on November 20, 1772 (part 2), moved to accept the amended copy of the report of the committee on November 20, 1772, and arranged for its publication and distribution (part 4). Finally, to demonstrate the town's attempt to resolve the crisis within the traditionally prescribed system of political communication, the town places four texts in the appendix (part 5) that document the town's political impasse with the governor. All this framing material securely attaches the writing at the center of the *Votes and Proceedings*, what I am calling "the embedded pamphlet" (part 3), to the matrix of its emergence: in the town meeting, in its exchange with the governor, and within the political crisis proclaimed by the Boston Whigs in response to the news of the direct Crown payment of the judges of the Superior Court.

If the document's frame is procedural and businesslike, the document itself—the text written by the committee, amended and accepted by the town meeting, as an address to the other towns of Massachusetts—is full of the fiery rhetoric of crisis. This embedded pamphlet shifts from the calm certitude of a statement of rights, to the indignation of the list of infringements of those rights, to the rousing letter of correspondence to the other towns of Massachusetts. The letter of correspondence to the other towns has a contradictory double logic. On one hand, the letter serves as the conceptual and rhetorical climax of the embedded pamphlet, with its formal statement of rights and list of infringements. On the other hand, it serves as a cover letter and readers' guide, by narrating the town meeting's conflict with the governor. The letter's urgent personal tone and style of address seek to establish the trust and solidarity that will encourage other towns to write back.

The impetus for the formation of the Boston Committee of Correspondence and the composition of the Boston declaration arose in part from the gradual decay of the only legitimate method for registering complaint within the monarchy: the petition of right for redress of grievances. While the colonies had used petitions to address Parliament during the Stamp Act crisis, and had petitioned Parliament to repeal the Townshend duties, the lack of success of these petitions meant that the king became the increasingly favored addressee of colonial petitions. In the same years that the town meeting and the Boston Committee of Correspondence were developing the popular declaration, the Massachusetts House had recourse to petition the king to challenge new policies of Whitehall: to oppose the direct payment of governors (July 14, 1772), to oppose the direct payment of the judges of the Superior Court (March 6, 1773), and to advocate the removal of Governor Hutchinson and Lieutenant Governor Peter Oliver (June 23, 1773).

The ancient right of petition was rooted deep within the constitution of the monarchical form of government. The act of petitioning presupposes and reiterates the covenant by which a monarch extends his "protection" to subjects, who in their turn vow "allegiance" to their monarch (Bushman 1985, 51–53). It is this reciprocal bond that opens up a special mode of protected political speech, by which subjects may submit their grievances to the monarch in the form of a petition. A good king will show that he *is* good by a readiness to receive the petitions of his loyal subjects; a loyal subject will show his or her loyalty by the way each petitions the king or queen. Because the petition builds upon the instituted hierarchies of eighteenth-century monarchy, its forms of address may seem fawning to modern ears. However, a perusal of the colonial-era journals of the House of Representatives of Massachusetts or the House of Burgesses of Virginia reveals that the petition was an utterly routine channel of government. It was the pervasive method by which subjects brought their needs and projects before their elected assemblies. When a town wanted to expand its land holdings, or settlers on the frontier had suffered grievous losses in Indian wars, or when a wounded veteran needed a stipend to survive, each of these parties would frame a petition to their assembly.

British Americans of the eighteenth century understood the right of petition as one of the fundaments of English liberty. The Bill of Rights of 1689 stated "that it is the right of the subjects to petition the king, and all commitments and prosecutions for such petitioning are illegal." Indeed, this right was understood to go back to Magna Carta. To have legal grounds for a petition, a subject must have a grievance, which, as Garry Wills has noted, is more than a simple gripe, but, in the words of John Adams, is "a violation of an essential British right" (Wills 1979, 59). Because it arises from the abrogation of some fundamental right of the subject, the grievance threatens "to dissolve the constitution" (Blackstone 1769, 1:244). Therefore Blackstone, in his *Commentaries on English Law*, lists the right to petition as one of the "rights" of the subject (1:143). Because petition involves a mutually acknowledged asymmetry of power, it was understood to be particularly crucial that the petitioner be protected from punishment for petitioning, for such a punishment would constitute the highest tyranny (Zaret 2000, 88). Like the freedom of speech later enshrined in the First Amendment to the US Constitution, the ancient right of petition serves as what might be called a guardian right, for without the right to petition, how could a subject defend any other right?[11]

11. Zaret (2000, 87) notes that during the English Revolution, Royalist insurgents who opposed the new power of Parliament affirmed their right to present "just desires of the oppressed in a petitionary way (the undoubted right of the subject) and the very life of their liberty itself." In my general synthetic account of the petition of right, I have drawn upon the scholarly accounts of David Zaret, Richard L. Bushman, and Pauline Maier. Zaret's account is particularly cogent for describing the repurposing of the petition of right for political resistance; Bushman (1985) describes the normative

To mitigate the potentially disruptive impact of the petition and soften the asperity of its complaint, it was essential that a felicitous petition observe certain forms and protocols: the petitioner reaffirms the covenant between ruler and ruled by asking for protection and vowing allegiance, petitioners lower themselves in humility before the petitioned as they would in prayer; the petition displays the dependency of petitioners, and their adherence to the law; and finally, the tone and manner of the petition must be, in terms developed by David Zaret, *deferential* ("an apolitical flow of information" [92] that is particular, local and the fruit of direct experience), *juridical* (adheres to the existing legal constraints and does not appeal to popular will), and *spontaneous* (does not evidence premeditation and political organization), and, finally, the petition must also observe the *proper procedures* (by submitting the petition through appropriate mediators).[12]

THE *VOTES AND PROCEEDINGS* CONSIDERED AS A PAMPHLET THAT SIMULATES A PETITION

The first readers of the *Votes and Proceedings* must have been puzzled as to *what* it was. The title suggests that it documents the votes and proceedings of the Boston Town Meeting, and, strictly speaking, this is the case. But this title offers a deceptively neutral-sounding wrapper for what I have labeled the "embedded pamphlet." The pamphlet itself offers a sustained polemic against the policies of the administration of George III. In its topic and stance, it resembles countless Whig pamphlets written and published in British America since the Stamp Act crisis of 1765. Indeed, soon after its publication, the *Votes and Proceedings* was apparently given the informal name of "the Boston pamphlet" (Raphael 2002, 33). Scholars have admired the eighteenth-century pamphlet's supple variety of form, length, and topic, and its efficacy in bringing a coherently developed argument before the public with "a rare combination

---

system as it operated in the colony of Massachusetts; and Maier (1972, 206–7) offers a briefer account of the breakdown of the petition.

12. The conventions of the petition were often honored in the breach. In his study of the practice of petitioning during the English Revolution, David Zaret shows that during the Civil War, petitions to the Parliament and the king often pushed the limits of, or simply violated, every one of the prescriptions for a proper petition. During the lead-up to the American Revolution, a number of petitions observed the forms but contravened the spirit of the protocols for petitioning. See one especially shocking mock petition to the king composed by Isaiah Thomas and published in the *Massachusetts Spy* on September 10, 1772 (*Documents* 1973, 5:190).

of spontaneity and solidity, of dash and detail, of casualness and care" (Bailyn 1965, 5). The pamphlet's low cost and small size (when compared to a book) made it easy for the Boston committee to distribute. The *Votes and Proceedings* is also like many other prerevolutionary pamphlets in the way it oscillates between two characteristic rhetorical stances: on one hand, an "earnest insistence on presentation," which assumes that readers will recognize and assent to the truth of a well-framed argument, and, on the other hand, "a spirit of invective and outraged condemnation," directed at those many readers who might resist its truth (Ferguson 1994, 433–34).

Although the themes of the *Votes and Proceedings* were familiar, the form chosen for this pamphlet must have given its early readers a sense of uncanny familiarity. The first two parts of the polemic are cast into the conventional verbal formulas of a traditional petition: first the statement of rights, and then the enumeration of the "infringements and violations" of those rights. The incorporation of the two cardinal elements of the petition enabled the town to claim the protection customarily extended to the petition. But there is something highly provocative about the usage of these familiar formulas in the *Votes and Proceedings*. As I have noted in the discussion of the petition form, what opens the protected space for a political complaint by the petitioner is the address to authority, which must be placed *before* the statement of rights and grievances. By its omission of the humble address to authority, the town of Boston has moved its communication outside of the protection that the English constitution provided for the petition to authority. This explains why royal officials found the *Votes and Proceedings* to be of "unwarrantable" and "dangerous tendency" (Governor Thomas Hutchinson to the General Court, February 16, 1773), "very extraordinary" (Lord Dartmouth to Hutchinson, March 3, 1773; *Documents* 1973, 6:95), and a generic model for those "who choose to revolt from the British Empire" (Alexander Wedderburn, January 29, 1774; Franklin 1978, 21:63).

While royal officials recognized that there was something dangerously seditious about this pseudo-petition, they failed to grasp the larger ambition of the framers of the *Votes and Proceedings*. Its statement of rights is so comprehensive and systemic that it recalls other foundational English constitutional instruments that used legal means to challenge and circumscribe royal authority, like the Declaration of Rights (1689) and Magna Carta (1215). The *Votes and Proceedings*' list of "infringements and violations" had grown so long that it criticized every aspect of British rule in the colonies: the collection of customs duties, the stationing of troops, rule by issuing of instructions by the king in Privy Council, the expansion of the royal courts and admiralty courts, the direct payment of royal officials, the regulation of trade, and even the rumored proposal for an American episcopate. The Boston committee's subtle shift in terminology—from "grievances" to "infringements and violations"—is telling. While in the eighteenth century "grievance" is a legal term for a violated right, it still carries the older sense of an inflicted "grievance," derived from the old French *grever*, "to harm," and thus an "infliction of a wrong" or "injury" by another (*OED*). By using "infringements and violations" instead of "grievances," the *Votes and Proceedings* uses a more remote, less personal, and more neutrally legalistic way to describe what British rule has done to American rights. In this way, the writers increased the distance between the freeholders of Massachusetts and their harmful government.

DEPLOYING THE NEO-ROMAN THEORY OF LIBERTY

Skeptical readers of the *Votes and Proceedings* were not just put off by its misuse of the petition or its comprehensive critique of British rule. They were also dismayed that it propounded a concept of liberty that Tory readers considered flawed and impractical, the very one that had proved so dangerous to government in the English Revolution (1642–1649). At the very center of the *Votes and Proceedings* was the thesis that the Crown's plan to pay the judges of the Superior Court directly, when considered as the last in a long train of British infringements and violations of American rights, would, "if accomplished, complete our slavery" (Boston 1972, 20). To royal officials the claim appeared subversive of any legitimate authority or constitutional government. Because of its difference from later nineteenth- and twentieth-century understandings of political liberty, this concept of liberty has appeared extreme and hyperbolic to later historians, at times more an "ideology" that succeeded through "propaganda," than a judgment based upon facts as American Whigs assessed them. But here intellectual historians can help us recover the internal logic of the concept of liberty invoked by the Whigs of Boston.

In *Liberty before Liberalism*, Quentin Skinner has described the essential constituents of what he calls "the neo-Roman theory of liberty," a cluster of ideas developed out of early modern European interpretations of Roman history, law, and political theory—ideas that proved subversive of authority before, during, and long after the English Revolution. In its essentials, it is the same idea of liberty that was used by the Whigs of British America to frame and motivate their political struggle. *Neo-Roman theory*, a term preferred by Skinner to *republicanism*, literalizes the metaphor of the body politic with the observation that both individual human bodies and the state can be healthy or sick, and both can lose their liberty. This deep coupling of the state and citizen means that a state's loss of freedom renders personal liberty impossible and transmutes the citizen into a slave. Ideally, government should enable each individual citizen to exercise an equal right of participation, though it is understood that this entails complex acts of representation. The civic liberty and expansive participation of the citizens in the government of a free state helped explain the "glory and greatness" of the Roman republic and the early Greek republics. The *virtu* and valor of citizens strengthens the republic rather than arousing the jealousy of kings and tyrants. Virtue, power, and greatness can then flow from the liberty of a free state of free citizens (Skinner 1998, 61–65). However, if a change comes about so that the people are ruled by laws and bodies that they do not control, citizens become slaves. By "slave" neo-Roman thinkers rely on the definition from Roman law: slaves, like children, are those who are not *sui juris*, that is, not "within their own jurisdiction or right," but *in potestate*, "in the power of someone else" (41). A state can lose its freedom through conquest, but it is endangered in the colonial condition as well (50).

In an argument that is particularly pertinent to Boston Whigs in 1772, neo-Roman theorists maintain that state or people can lose their liberty if they are exposed to the prerogative power of rulers acting outside the law, *even if these powers are not exercised.* "If you hold your freedom and felicity as a subject 'at the will of another' (Francis Osborne) you are already living in a condition of servitude" (Skinner 1998, 71). So, for example, when at the beginning of the English Revolution Charles I claimed control of the militia, the neo-Roman theorists insisted that his potential power to use the force of a standing army in time of peace—a power that would make his word law—abrogated the liberty of all (73). Only in the absence of such a threat can the state and its people enjoy what the British constitution should secure, "the empire of laws and not of men" (75).[13] Other ideas follow from this expansive, legalistic definition of liberty. Neo-Roman theorists refuse to confine liberty to the minimalist idea of "negative liberty," first defined by Hobbes but later developed by liberal thought: that freedom merely consists in an absence of constraints upon

---

13. In his protracted debate with Daniel Leonard (Massachusettensis), published under the name Novanglus, John Adams argues that British government should be understood as a republic. "If Aristotle, Livy, and Harrington knew what a republic was, the British constitution is much more like a republic than an empire. They define a republic to be *a government of laws, and not of men*. If this definition is just, the British constitution is nothing more nor less than a republic, in which the king is first magistrate" (J. Adams 1979, 2:314).

speech, movement, or contract. Liberty can only sustain itself through activity: "it is only possible to escape from personal servitude if you live as an active citizen under a representative form of government" (77). Most crucially, neo-Roman theorists of liberty like John Milton argued that a free people must always have the right and power to remove their ruler (75–76).

This account of the neo-Roman theory of liberty is a useful corrective to the way Bernard Bailyn describes the interplay between idea and action in *The Ideological Origins of the American Revolution*. For Bailyn, the theory of liberty that Skinner describes is a highly coherent "ideology," which, by specifying the meaning of liberty and slavery, virtue and corruption, legal sovereignty and usurping power, became the framework through which American Whigs conceptualized their political relationship with Britain. This American Whig ideology, a homegrown variety of Britain's own opposition "country party" ideology of the early eighteenth century, is in place before any particular event occurs, but it predisposes American Whigs to believe that the ministry in Whitehall was conspiring to *enslave* them. In Bailyn's words, this "belief" served as an "accelerator" to "opposition"; the "denial" of conspiracy "only confirmed" Whig suspicion of the "conspirators"; then, "overwhelming evidence" of conspiracy "in the end propelled them into Revolution" (Bailyn 1967, 95). Bailyn's analysis therefore has the effect of discrediting the American Whig political anxiety that he describes with so much precision. Bailyn argues that the American Whigs' belief in conspiracy was sincere, historically consequential, but, ultimately, a delusion (144).

My study of the Whigs of Boston suggests an alternative to Bailyn's analysis. While Bailyn's scholarship offers a psychological insight into American Whig anxiety, it does not qualify what has been richly documented by the so-called imperial historians like Lawrence Henry Gipson or later scholarship by Peter D. G. Thomas: the determined institutional effort by Whitehall to reform and strengthen imperial administration (see introduction). Boston Whigs were quite clear-eyed about these plans to make the empire governable. While for Thomas Hutchinson, these reforms would merely bring the English constitution back into balance, for American Whigs, Whitehall's official reforms *were* a "deliberate conspiracy to destroy the balance of the constitution and eliminate their freedom" (Bailyn 1967, 144). In his "Note on Conspiracy," Bailyn sets aside the Whig worry that there was a ministerial "design" to enslave the American colonies. But neo-Roman theory makes design beside the point. It is the bare fact that the Crown has stationed a standing army in Boston in a time of peace so that the word of the magistrate could now have the force of law, or that the Crown, through the direct payment of judges, could now exercise control of the Massachusetts Superior Court, that has already translated the colonists of Massachusetts into a condition of "slavery." It was these particular policies that had precipitated a political crisis. The ruler's possession of the *potential* power to enslave enslaves.

American Whigs valued power and liberty as positive benefits that were mutually constitutive. By contrast, Bailyn describes the Whig theory of power as essentially negative: "the dominion of some men over others, the human control of human life: ultimately force, compulsion ... aggressiveness: its endlessly propulsive tendency to expand itself beyond legitimate boundaries" (1967, 56). Opposite to power is the "sphere" of "liberty and right," which must be defended as "delicate, passive, and sensitive" (58). In the third part of the *Votes and Proceedings*, "the letter of correspondence to the other towns," we shall see how the Boston Whigs stage the pathos of endangered liberty in terms that resonate with Bailyn's. But by characterizing the American Whig ideology as organized by a Manichaean opposition between, on one hand, the encroaching power of the state (and its corrupt politicians) and, on the other, the passive liberty of individual subjects, Bailyn confers upon American Whig liberty an essentially liberal cast as a negative freedom *from* the illegitimate effects of power, rather than the freedom *to* gather and use power. By contrast, in the *Votes and Proceedings*, "liberty" is represented both as fragile *and* as what can move its defenders toward action; "power" is represented as dangerously insinuating *but also*, in the modern positive sense, empowering.

The double potentials of both power and liberty help to explain the double movement of the *Votes and Proceedings*. In a defense of liberty against power, the town of Boston first used its statement of rights and list of infringements to stage the spectacle of endangered liberty. But this labor of representation has drawn upon the latent reserves of liberty found within the freeholders and other inhabitants of the town of Boston: to call a town meeting, to form a committee of correspondence, to write and publish the *Votes and Proceedings*. In this way, depicting liberty as passive becomes an action. Rousing others to defend liberty gathers power, and using their freedom to communicate with one another increases their collective power. In all these ways the town meeting of November 20, 1772, sought to gather the sort of power over the direction of events that it had earlier achieved on March 6, 1770. Robert Ferguson (1994, 366) has described the sort of writing that gathers power by uniting a diverse group of readers and auditors: "As the creators of a consensual literature for a diverse and divided citizenry, the leaders of the Revolution write to reconcile and, thereby, to control. They seek to encompass difference within a consciously communal perspective." This reconciliation of differences serves the document's second distinctive feature: it was fashioned as a script to be read in the town meetings across Massachusetts.

THE *VOTES AND PROCEEDINGS* CONSIDERED AS THE SCRIPT FOR ORAL PERFORMANCE IN TOWN MEETING

Central to the gambit of the *Votes and Proceedings* is the transmission of the political message of the Boston Town Meeting to town meetings throughout Massachusetts. Such a communication would bypass the General Court, which the governor refused to convene, and penetrate to the local foundations of political power in Massachusetts. Only if the *Votes and Proceedings* were made the business of each town meeting and read aloud by the diverse elected moderators before the assembled meeting, would it achieve an institutional centrality that no other pamphlet, however elegant or persuasive, had ever achieved (Brown 1970, 46–48). Many of the formal features of the *Votes and Proceedings* made it appropriate for reading in the town meetings.

Length: The text to be read is short enough—thirty-six small pages rendered in large font—to be read in about forty-two minutes (without the appendix). This means that, even with the customary second reading, the whole presentation of the *Votes and Proceedings* would come in around ninety minutes, well under the usual two hours of sermons in New England religious services during this period.

Repetition: The central themes of the *Votes and Proceedings* are repeated frequently throughout, so even the most casual listener will grasp its argument.

Accessibility: The *Votes and Proceedings* has none of the allusiveness, Latin quotation, or irony found in gentlemanly political discourse. Instead, as vernacular political theory, it is written in a direct, plain, and "honest" style that optimizes it for aural apprehension by the freeholders of middling knowledge and intellectual acuity. The authors build their argument by using familiar formulas like "life, liberty and property," the concept of natural rights, the necessity of maintaining the equilibrium of powers in the English constitution. This restatement of general Whig principles can then serve as a general statement of the Massachusetts mind.

Orality: By describing its own reading within the Boston Town Meeting of November 20, on the very first page of the *Votes and Proceedings*, the document foregrounds its user-friendly orality and offers a textual prompt to other towns.

In all these ways, the writers of the *Votes and Proceedings* sought, by both what they said and how they said it, to be accessible and intelligible to the overwhelming majority of Massachusetts Whigs. This inviting lucidity was crucial because the *Votes and Proceedings* would succeed only if the selectmen, who alone possessed the power, actually called town meetings. In fact, in the three months following the publication of the *Votes and Proceedings*, scores of Massachusetts towns held meetings to consider it, and, by April 1773, 119 towns had drafted formal written responses to the Boston Committee of Correspondence.

The *Votes and Proceedings* came to life in the town meetings in three ways: as the formal business of the town meetings of Massachusetts; as a printed script to be read aloud; and as a translation into politics of the religious jeremiad.

The Votes and Proceedings *becomes the business of each town meeting:* For reasons of law and history, the *Votes and Proceedings* was delivered to Massachusetts towns that had remarkable autonomy and power. In accordance with the rules and procedures, the selectmen had the power to convene a town meeting. Once properly convened, the meeting could deliberate upon questions, pass resolutions, and take actions. So when they received a printed pamphlet-letter from the town of Boston, most towns took up in their turn the fundamental questions of rights and the list of grievances as they had been broached in Boston. The solicitor general of Great Britain, Alexander Wedderburn, found it an "extravagant absurdity" that the town of Petersham, whose resolutions he mockingly quoted, would dare to deliberate upon imperial policy and the English constitution. The Petersham town meeting evidently did not agree (Franklin 1978, 21:62–64).

Media shift from print to speech: As a pamphlet, the *Votes and Proceedings* carried the virtues of print: fixity, authority, portability, and the power to "act at a distance." But when a moderator of a Massachusetts town meeting took that printed document into his hands and read it aloud, the *Votes and Proceedings* acceded to some of the media traits of the spoken word. Brought to life by the breath and distinct tonalities of the moderator's voice, the words of the *Votes and Proceedings* became part of a live performance, where, embodied by the moderator, they were broadcast to the assembled town meeting, the members of which were united by their common experience of a performance heard in the same place and time. When the moderator reached those passages in the *Votes and Proceedings* that modulate into the "purple prose of liberty," the moderator could speak with a charismatic sense of urgency, which might rouse the united body of the town meeting to action.

A political call that is aligned with a religious one: Although the reading of the *Votes and Proceedings* was undertaken within the confines of a secular institution, the meetinghouse where the town assembled was almost invariably also the town's Congregational church. Thus the moderator spoke from the same raised lectern where the town's minister gave his sermon and scriptural lessons every Sunday. This physical location helped to enhance a homology that is carefully developed by the mode of appeal and the argument of the *Votes and Proceedings*. The appeal of the *Votes and Proceedings* repeats the basic gestures of the jeremiad: by targeting modern sources of sin and threats to the commonweal; by calling attention to the contrast between founding virtue and contemporary backsliding; and, finally, by making a call for renewal (Elliott 1994, 260–63). However, the *Votes and Proceedings* translated the religious argument of the jeremiad into secular terms. The religious jeremiad argued this way: God has made a (religious) covenant with Christian believers, but when they break that covenant (through sin and backsliding), they must be recalled to the word of God's law. The political jeremiad makes an analogous argument, but instead of internalizing the judgment, the censure is instead directed to another. The king and Parliament have made a political covenant with the people of Massachusetts, but now that those authorities have broken their covenant (by violating colonialists' rights and by their own corruption), they must be recalled to the word of the English constitution. In spite of its dire warnings, however, the *Votes and Proceedings* has the distinctive trait that Sacvan Bercovitch (1978, 6–7) discerns in the American jeremiad as its "unshakeable optimism" and "unswerving faith in the errand in the wilderness."

The Votes and Proceedings *Considered as "a Letter of Correspondence to the Other Towns" of Massachusetts*

The most innovative and operationally significant section of the *Votes and Proceedings* was "the letter of correspondence to the other towns." It constitutes the last sixth of the thirty-six-page embedded pamphlet and is placed directly after the enumeration of the British infringements and violations of American rights. It is worth noting the oddity of this ordering. Since this letter, as we have noted, serves as a kind of cover letter and reader's guide for the whole document, explaining the occasion of the formation of a committee to write the *Votes and Proceedings*, why was it not placed first? The letter *could* not be placed first because it was extraordinary, a document outside of the customary modes of political communication. To justify the writing of this extraordinary letter, the statement of rights and list of infringements and violations had to be placed first, so the political crisis triggered by the direct payment of judges can be described by the Boston committee as requiring the last recourse of this letter. But who is to receive and redress these complaints?

The letter of correspondence solves this problem of address and at the same time develops a new genre of communication, one where entirely new statements can be made. The first two parts of the *Votes and Proceedings*, the statement of rights and the infringements and violations of those rights, had been cast in a familiar idiom: addressed to no one and everyone ("the world"), its formulations strove to be general, objective, and legally correct. By contrast, the very first sentence of the letter assumes a new tone and character.

> Gentlemen,
> We, the Freeholders and other Inhabitants of *Boston*, in Town-Meeting duly assembled, according to Law, apprehending there is abundant Reason to be alarmed that the Plan of *Despotism*, which the Enemies of our invaluable Rights have concerted, is rapidly hastening to a completion, can no longer conceal our impatience under a constant, unremitted, uniform Aim to enslave us, or confide in an Administration which threatens us with certain and inevitable destruction.

The first sentence cues the reader to the four new coordinates of this writing. The letter begins by specifying the writer with the first-person plural pronoun "we," who are identified as "the freeholders and other inhabitants of *Boston*, in town-meeting duly assembled, according to law." This awkward formula, which describes *who* writes at the same time that it claims the *right to write*, indirectly acknowledges the unlicensed character of this communication. As a letter, it is dignified but informal, personal yet concerned with public matters (Dierks 2009). Here the candor of the letter aims to win the confidence of its readers. Second, the letter (and the whole *Votes and Proceedings*) is *addressed* to the "Gentlemen" of the "other towns" of the province of Massachusetts. The use of the term *Gentlemen* is not merely respectful. It also suggests that the letter is written to win the disinterested concern with, and reflective attention to, public matters that was a hallmark of eighteenth-century gentlemen. Third, the first sentence begins the main polemical work of the letter: it explains why "we" can no longer "confide in . . . administration" and have therefore embarked on this extraordinary address to the other towns of the province. Pivotal to justifying this letter is ministry's new scheme to pay judges directly, which offers "abundant reason to be alarmed that the plan of *despotism*, which the enemies of our invaluable rights have concerted, is rapidly hastening to a completion." Finally, as the title of this final section of the *Votes and Proceedings* makes clear, the writers hope that, because of the alarming crisis, this will in fact become a "*letter of correspondence*," that is, one that will initiate an ongoing reciprocal communication among the towns of the province.

The letter of correspondence to the other towns makes explicit what had been implicit for most of the *Votes and Proceedings*. The change of the direction of address, from the king in Parliament to the people of the province, from vertical to horizontal, from up to out, from one to many, carries a revolutionary potential. The *Votes and Proceedings* declares or clarifies its provocative redirection of the complaint of the petition from an instituted authority to the people. The petition to authority is morphing into a popular declaration. It is a "popular declaration" because, by the way it is written and is intended to function, it confers unprecedented authority upon the opinion of the people. The Boston committee's bold redirection of its complaint from those who possess the legal authority to receive it to the other towns of Massachusetts solved a discursive problem that would also be faced by two later documents, the Declaration of Independence of 1776 and the Constitution of 1787. The conundrum might be put this way: the writers of the document found that they did not as yet have the authority to write as they wished. So they drew that authority from the people they addressed. They wrote *as if* they had the authority to speak for their addressees. This communication act is founded on a hypothetical proposition: "*If we communicate our sense of the political crisis to you, and if you respond by affirming our sense of a common crisis, then, after the fact, our letter of correspondence will have been legitimate.*" This throws the tense of the communication into the future anterior: if you respond to this letter in the right way, we *will have had* the authority to make this bold address to you.

The letter of correspondence folded the statement of rights and grievances into a new form of public declaration. First, the letter offers a careful self-justification for the Boston Committee of Correspondence embarking upon this new form of communication. By announcing a moment of extraordinary crisis, by posing imponderable questions of the towns, and by offering a narrative of the town meeting's futile attempt to seek redress on the question of judicial salaries through exchanges with the governor, the crucial innovation—the formation of the committee and the address to the towns—appears as a natural, rational, and even mild recourse. While the letter "declares" the reasons for this innovation, it also intensifies the crisis by asking each town to "lay" the *Votes and Proceedings* "before your town," and by asking each town to frame its own reply to the issues raised by the *Votes and Proceedings*. "A free Communication of your Sentiments, to this Town, of our common Danger, is earnestly solicited and will be gratefully received" (33). Every word in the phrase "a free communication of your sentiments" indexes a constituent of this experiment in communication: these communications are to be *free*, because they are not constrained by the protocols of the traditional petition, or by mediation through the town's elected delegate to the provincial assembly. Following eighteenth-century usage, "sentiments" here implies a mix of idea and feeling.[14] The sentiments are important because they are *yours*.

The Boston committee's request for "a free communication of your sentiments" gets its full rhetorical force by the way it is mingled with the spectacle of liberty in distress. The dialectical movement of the passage, which follows this request for communication, is designed to take the reader and auditor through an emotional roller coaster. I have numbered the three sentences.

> A free Communication of your Sentiments, to this Town, of our common Danger, is earnestly solicited and will be gratefully received.
>
> [1] If you concur with us in Opinion, that our Rights are properly stated, and that the several Acts of Parliament, and Measures of Administration, pointed out by us, are subversive of these Rights, you will doubtless think it of the utmost Importance that we stand firm as one Man, to recover and support them; and to take such Measures, by directing our Representatives, or otherwise, as your Wisdom and Fortitude shall dictate, to rescue from impending Ruin our happy and glorious Constitution.
>
> [2] But if it should be the general Voice of this Province, that the Rights, as we have stated them, do not belong to us; or, that the several Measures of Administration in the British Court, are no Violations of these Rights; or, that if they are thus violated or infringed, they are not worth contending for, or resolutely maintaining;—should this be the general Voice of the Province, we must be resigned to our wretched Fate; but shall forever lament the Extinction of that generous Ardor for Civil and Religious Liberty, which in the Face of every Danger, and even Death itself, induced our Fathers, to forsake the Bosom of their Native Country, and begin a Settlement on bare Creation.
>
> [3] But we trust this cannot be the Case: We are sure your Wisdom, your Regard for yourselves and the rising Generation, cannot suffer you to doze, or set supinely indifferent, on the brink of Destruction, while the Iron Hand of Oppression is daily tearing the choicest Fruit from the fair Tree of Liberty, planted by our worthy Predecessors, at the Expense of their Treasure, and abundantly water'd with their Blood. (Boston 1772, 33–34)

This passage was printed as an excerpt in the *Boston Gazette* (November 23, 1772) and reprinted in many of the newspapers throughout the colonies in

14. The usage of the term *sentiment* in the *Votes and Proceedings* joins rather than opposes emotion and ideas. This is consistent with Lord Kames's 1762 definition of *sentiment*: "Every thought prompted by passion is termed a sentiment" (*OED*).

the following weeks.[15] It tenders the central claim of the *Votes and Proceedings*, which might be condensed this way: if "a free communication of your sentiments" allows us to achieve public consensus, then together we can become a powerful new agency for opposing British administration. To support this claim for the transformative effect of a publicly shared consensus, this elaborate rhetorical period goes through three movements, each corresponding to one sentence: the initial proposition, its reversal, and then a reversal of that reversal.

1. Proposition: "If you concur with us in opinion" (about rights, administration, and the rest), then you will "doubtless" think it of the "utmost importance" that "we stand firm as one man."
2. Reversal: "But if [you do not concur] . . . , we must be resigned to our wretched fate" (i.e., enslavement to British power).
3. Reversal reversed: "But we trust this cannot be the case: We are sure . . . [you will agree to defend] the fair tree of liberty."

At first glance the passage may offer a fairly simple proposition for the towns it addresses. Join us in "standing firm as one man," and together we will defend the "fair tree of liberty" from the "iron hand of oppression." However, if one reads the passage within the specific context of the Boston Whigs' address to the towns, where consensus must be consistent with the freedom of all the towns, if one attends to the rhetorical machinery that propels the passage forward, and if one takes account of the communications network the Boston committee was trying to build, the passage appears more complex. To begin with, even the "we" that speaks for the Boston Whigs is open to question. Since the "we" of the pamphlet is generated by the writing that also presupposes it, a certain wishful fictionality clings to this "we." This passage of the *Votes and Proceedings* postulates, in a proleptic fashion, the moment *after* the *Votes and Proceedings* are read/heard by the towns, and *after* the towns have responded to Boston, confirming their shared recognition of "our common danger." The passage's vacillation, between a securing of and the loss of a collective "we" (that would include both Boston and the other towns), may reflect

15. Here are some of the publication dates for reprinting this passage following the *Boston Gazette* publication on November 23, 1772: *New Hampshire Gazette*, November 27, 1772; *New London Gazette*, November 27, 1772; *Providence Gazette*, November 28, 1772; *Pennsylvania Gazette*, December 2, 1772; *Virginia Gazette* (Purdie and Dixon), December 17, 1772. This list suggests the speed and efficiency of this distribution network.

the suspense the Boston Whigs felt as to how or whether the other towns of Massachusetts would respond to their communication.

What are we to make of this passage's three-part movement from "standing firm as one man" to the disunion of a failed consensus to a postulated gathering under the "fair tree of liberty?" "To stand firm" in defense of liberty was broadly associated by British and American Whigs with Cato's brave defense of Rome's republican liberties against Caesar's ultimately successful imperial ambitions.[16] However, the Boston Whigs had no interest in serving as Cato-like solitary martyrs to lost liberty. Instead, through this act of communication, they proposed to the other towns that they collectively "stand firm as one man." These words use the trope of personification to make plausible that the diverse 260 towns might, by sharing ideas and feelings, become "one man." While such a union may be usefully threatening to their political adversaries, it would also compromise the autonomy of each town. So this personification is also embedded in a simile: the towns are not to become one man, but to "stand firm *as* one man." Only through a loose, incomplete, or provisional union could the freeholders and inhabitants of the many towns of Massachusetts engage in the "free communication" to which this passage calls them. However, a failure to achieve a concurrence of opinion, and the partial union that would entail, would leave their liberty vulnerable to the "measures of administration." So in the second movement of this period, the cowardly retreat of the sons who fail to live up to the heroic deeds of "our fathers" is expressed through their vacillating opinions (opinions that, it is worth noting, are at variance with the central arguments of the Boston committee): "if . . . the rights . . . do not belong to us; or . . . [there have been] no violations of these rights; or . . . they are not worth contending for." But, the reminder of a common debt to "*our* fathers," who bravely faced "danger" and "death itself" in beginning a "settlement on bare creation," prepares for the countermovement, which brings the rhetorical period to a culmination in one loaded, pathetic image. What is finally at stake in this struggle is "the fair tree of liberty, planted by our worthy predecessors, at the expense of their treasure, and abundantly water'd with their blood."

The threat to Liberty, here figured as a tree, is rendered as a rape, a theft, and a ravishment, by the "iron hand of oppression" which is "daily tearing the choicest fruit from the fair tree." This "hand of oppression" figures the British ministry as "iron," in its extension of a machinelike imperial system. Here

16. For the various ways Cato inspires imitation, within many different British, American, and French political contexts, see Ellison 1999 and Dillon 2004.

natural liberty is put at risk by imperial machinations. "The tree of liberty" (instead of that firm "one man") becomes the figure favored to secure a consensus on the threat to American liberty. This horticultural image displaces the human developmental narrative of the family romance so frequently used to frame prerevolutionary relations between the "parent state" and her colonies. The passage does not critique what might be called the Tory family romance, grounded in Filmer's *Patriarcha* and found in the *New England Primer*, the writings of Peter Oliver, and of many others, which figures the "parent state" as a father or mother, who deserves the filial love, permanent subordination, and ongoing obligation of grateful colonies. But neither does the passage offer the Lockean alternative by which a colony develops through education and experience from a dependent child to an independent adult, where the imperial relation could one day become a legal and contractual one among equals (Fliegelman 1982). The idea of "the fair tree of liberty" acknowledges debts to earlier generations: this New England tree may still carry some of the original virtues of Anglo-Saxon liberty that England has now forsaken; this fair tree of liberty was "planted by our worthy predecessors" at the "expense of their treasure" and "watered with their blood. " But the image introduces an alternative idea about the progress of liberty. Because liberty does not advance through families and their bloodlines, the only way for it to survive is to transplant it from an old to a new world.

The shift from British familial metaphor to a horticultural metaphor helps to develop the idea that only in America can there be a new growth of freedom. The fruitful "plantation" of European colonies translates European humans, animals, and horticulture, so that they both enrich and benefit from the new world into which they are planted. Because New England liberty needed to be defended from encroaching enemies, especially French Catholics and Native Americans, it not only required treasure (money, labor, and love), but it also had to be "watered" with blood. This mythos of New England settlement is elaborated in the sermons and political writing of the period. It is given an amplified formulation in Samuel Adams's private letters and anonymous public writings between the years 1765 and 1769.[17] Adams's argument for the special

17. Samuel Adams's concept of the rights of the colonists within the empire was part of a larger consensus that had emerged over the previous century and included, to quote a valuable new book by Craig Yirush (2011, 77), an empire "based on the equal rights of all of the king's subjects; the grounding of those rights outside the realm in the efforts and risk taking of the settlers themselves; the confirmation of these rights in charters and other royal grounds . . . and the transformation of what the settlers saw as a 'wilderness' into flourishing civil societies."

flourishing of liberty in New England develops along these lines: because they carried the ancient rights and liberties of Englishmen with them, because the earliest New England settlers were not sent or sponsored by the British state, because they received no direct or indirect subsidy from others (and this was very different from both the failed and successful Virginia settlements), because they had no grand proprietor-investors behind them (the way Pennsylvania and Maryland did), because they emigrated to preserve their religious freedom from encroachment, because of the bitter privation upon their arrival (arriving in December, they survived only by eating clams from the sea), for all these overdetermined and rather differently grounded reasons, it is claimed that *the first English settlers of New England knew freedom as their original and natural condition* (S. Adams 1904, 1:7–297). But in an odd extension of the argument, the Boston Committee of Correspondence also argued something new: that only by embracing their American freedom could they possess the ancient English liberty abandoned by the British.[18]

This mythos of the organic growth of liberty in New England is condensed in the passage's climactic invocation of the "fair tree of liberty." This figurative tree offers an oblique reference to one very literal tree (fig. 1.2). If the British associated the survival of the Stuart monarch with the mighty Royal Oak that saved Charles II from capture at the battle of Worcester in 1651, the Whigs of Boston honored their liberty under one particular huge and ancient elm. It was planted in 1646 soon after the founding of Boston (1630), near the intersection of Essex and Orange Streets. Located in the front yard of Deacon Jacob Elliott, it was made available by its Whig owner to the Whigs for public use as a protected site for oppositional political speech. Paradoxically, its status as private property helped to protect it from the legal manipulation of public agencies (like the governor or His Majesty's army) to which it might have been vulnerable if it were located on Boston Common. This elm became the focal point of Boston's agitation against the Stamp Act on August 14, 1765, when Andrew Oliver, one of the officials assigned to sell stamps, was hung in effigy from one of its branches. In the seven years that followed, the "Liberty Tree" (as it was formally named on a plaque erected on September 11, 1765) became the place where the Boston Whigs assembled in public meetings, devised a

18. This points to the idea of the westward progress of civilization; Isaac Barré dubs the American Whigs "the Sons of Liberty"; Burke admires them because they can "snuff the approach of tyranny on every tainted breeze." For the paradox that early Americans prided themselves for cleaving to English liberty with more purity than the British, see Tennenhouse 2007 and Tamarkin 2007.

FIGURE 1.2. The Liberty Tree at the corner of Essex and Orange Streets. The caption reads: "The world should never forget the spot where once stood Liberty Tree, so famous in your annals—*La Fayette in Boston*." From Snow (1825, 266). Courtesy of Houghton Library, Harvard University.

mock court, punished Tories accused of collaborating with British ministry, and started their marches (Schlesinger 1952; Fischer 2005, 27).

In gathering under the tree of liberty, each member of the community assented to the discipline of speaking with and through the larger gathering. In this moment, and through the same discursive acts of speech and writing with which he assented to disciplined participation in a collective political body (like the town meeting or a committee of correspondence), each subject recognized himself as free at the same time. The *Votes and Proceedings*, the New England town meeting, and the Congregational Church all, in various ways, sought to subsume individual liberty into communal freedom. In this reconciliation, they contrast with modern liberal and neoliberal concepts of freedom. David Hackett Fischer, in *Liberty and Freedom*, offers a way to grasp the productive tension between these two senses of freedom through an analysis of the etymology of the terms *liberty* and *freedom*, words that in the eighteenth century and our own time are usually treated as synonyms. While *liberty* is derived from the Latin word that "meant unbounded, unrestricted, and released from restraint," and becomes associated with the rights of individuals, towns, and colonies, the English words *free* and *freedom* are derived from the Indo-

European words *dear* or *beloved*, and have the same root as *friend*. A "free" man meant, in Fischer's formulation, "someone who was joined to a tribe of free people by ties of kinship and rights of belonging" (2005, 5). Only if we grasp that liberty brings autonomy through rights, and freedom involves one in a binding attachment to and responsibility for the community, can we understand how liberty and freedom came to be interpreted as what motivated the settlement of New England: how they bound the early colonists into a single community, and (during the approach to revolution) how they justified disciplined collective action in its defense. This expansive concept of a liberty that is both individual and communal helps to explain why the specter of liberty's loss induces such intense anxiety.[19]

If we link this figural tree (in the *Votes and Proceedings*) and the literal elm (in Boston), a cluster of related ideas are subsumed under "the fair tree of liberty." The fact that the Liberty Tree was tough and ancient suggests the antiquity of English rights; its vast size connotes the greatness of liberty; and its longevity suggests that liberty may (or *should*) survive from the dim past into the distant future. Yet, because the tree is alive, it is vulnerable to disease, fire, and cutting, just as liberty itself is vulnerable to sudden destruction or gradual decay. The thought of the loss of this ancient and precious living endowment—once it is destroyed, it is lost forever—produced the sentimental solicitude, anxiety, and dread that suffuse this climactic passage from the *Votes and Proceedings*.

In 1772, the recent uses of the "Liberty Tree" by Boston Whigs gave it particular salience for forming committees of correspondence throughout Massachusetts. Because Boston's Liberty Tree was a place of voluntary assembly, political speech, and symbolic protest, the tree also became a metonym for the voluntary association of the Boston Whigs throughout the last eight years of protest (1765–1772). The defense of the freedom to protest and to be heard is thereby condensed into the protective embrace of the figural tree of liberty. The figure of the "fair tree of liberty," as presented at the climax of the *Votes and Proceedings*, not only naturalized the human desire for liberty; it also invited all the towns of Massachusetts to assume a place beneath the(ir) "fair tree of liberty." In this way the towns of Massachusetts could achieve a new unity by joining their "brethren" in a freely communicated consensus, under

19. For the fundamental dependence of the public sphere upon the private citizen, see Habermas 1991. Elizabeth Dillon (2004, 32–34) shows how the identity of the subject in the political public sphere—through a process of "subjectification" that she borrows from Lacan—leads to subjects' free assent to its "determination" by the social.

Boston's Liberty Tree. By associating their own communication technologies for uniting (through speech, writing, town meetings, and committees) with the organic-natural-arboreal "tree of liberty," and opposing it to the oppressive iron machines of British power, the Boston committee concealed what was machinelike, repetitive, protocol-controlled about their own technology.

By the way the *Votes and Proceedings* incorporated and overwrote the petition to authority and made the freeholders and inhabitants of the town meetings of Massachusetts the ultimate tribunal of their political cause, the Boston Committee of Correspondence invented the modern popular declaration. But the committee's motive was political mobilization rather than generic innovation. Writing, publishing, and disseminating a message was a covert way for those who composed the declaration to offer themselves as leaders of a "movement." By speaking in a collective first-person plural "we," the committee first represented themselves and then those for whom they spoke: the Boston Town Meeting. At the same time, the committee clearly aspired to have its sentiments accepted as representative for those whom they addressed. As Robert Ferguson (1994, 367) writes with regard to the Second Continental Congress, to proclaim a self-evident "truth" will also "introduce and impose an explicit political group, the new holders of truth in North American, the 'we' of the document." Acceptance of the truth implied acceptance of this group of political leaders. But success depended not upon language or genre alone; it depended on whether and how the other towns would respond. It depended on whether they would take the *Votes and Proceedings* as an actual "letter of correspondence," by writing back to the Boston committee. How that happened will be the focus of the next chapter.

2

THE PROTOCOLS OF THE DECLARATIONS AND THE ECLIPSE OF ROYAL POWER IN MASSACHUSETTS IN 1773

. . . .

In opening their correspondence, the Boston committee and the committees of the town learned that what can be done often depends upon how it is done. Thus Boston's request to the other towns for a "free communication of your sentiments" had to achieve a delicate balance between two distinct imperatives. The "correspondence" opened by Boston would be sufficiently unconstrained that each town could share their true opinions. But, at the same time, Boston wished to draw other towns into alignment, or "correspondence" (in a second sense of that word), with its particular view that Massachusetts faced a common political emergency. To honor the formal legal equality of all the towns, the *Votes and Proceedings* of Boston claimed only to speak for itself, and with an air of neutral inquiry, noted that the affair of the judges "being of public Concernment, the Town of Boston thought it necessary to consult with their Brethren throughout the Province . . . [so] the collected wisdom of the whole People, as far as possible, be obtained" (Boston 1772, 32). These words make the pamphlet sound like a modest request for comment. But by the comprehensive scope of its statement of rights and list of infringements, by the keen edge of its polemic against the British ministry, by the rousing passion of its sentiments, the committee's address invited each town to take the Boston declaration as a model for its own. Leading by example is still leading. However, only if each town's communication was formally unconstrained, and thus "free," would their responses contribute to the political power that the Whigs of Boston sought to gather.

If the *Votes and Proceedings* was to succeed, it had to travel a complex communication path. It was available by December 1, 1772, and by December 14 the *Boston Gazette* reported that the *Votes and Proceedings* had been delivered to the selectmen of four-fifths of the 260 towns and districts of Massachusetts. Because Boston's initiative could achieve its purpose only though a robust response from the other towns, the weeks following the publication of the *Votes and Proceedings* were most likely a time of suspense for the Boston Whigs. By contrast, Governor Thomas Hutchinson was confident that the busy farmers of the towns of Massachusetts had better things to do than gather in town meetings. In a private, unofficial letter, Hutchinson wrote mockingly to John Pownall, the secretary of the Board of Trade, that, having left behind "their old spirit of mobbing," "the only dependence left [for the Boston Whigs] is to keep up a correspondence through the province by committees of the several towns, which is such a foolish scheme that they must necessarily make themselves ridiculous" (November 10, 1772; *Documents*, 1772, 5:218). Hutchinson's initial confidence and the Boston Whigs' uncertainty might be explained by the intricate and time-consuming procedures that each town would be obliged to observe in order to call a meeting and respond to the *Votes and Proceedings*. But by the third week of December, news of a number of town meetings was being circulated by the newspapers and reported in private correspondence. The Boston Whigs became exultant, and the governor "was greatly alarmed" (Hutchinson 1936, 3:265–66). Each side knew that every town that met, read the *Votes and Proceedings*, and then responded affirmatively to the Boston committee, increased the political influence of the town of Boston and its committee. In fact, both in number and character, the responses of the towns exceeded the fondest hopes of the Boston Whigs. By the middle of January 1773, 56 towns had held a town meeting and framed their response to the Boston Committee of Correspondence. These towns had responded *before* receiving news of the governor's provocative opening address to the General Court on January 6, 1773. By April 1773, 119 towns had responded to the Boston committee, and by the end of September 1773 the responses of at least 144 towns and districts had been received. Figure 2.1 documents the initially rapid, but then steady, response of the towns to the *Votes and Proceedings*.[1]

The Whigs and Tories who witnessed the spread of the committees of cor-

---

1. The numbers I have used come from my study of the logs of the Boston committee and correspond with the numbers developed by Richard D. Brown. I have documented the date of response of most replies to Boston from the log of the Boston Committee of Correspondence, where the date of the receipt of a response from a town is reported on the date of each (usually Tuesday) weekly meeting. Several factors are responsible for the significant lag time between when the various town selectmen first received the *Votes and Proceedings* and when the town's written response was recorded in the minute book of the Boston committee. These include the delay in calling a first town meeting, the time it took to write a committee response and then convene a second town meeting, and, finally, the distance each response had to travel back to Boston. Richard Brown, who checked Boston's records against the town records of ninety-three towns, argues that these numbers are conservative because the Boston log is incomplete.

The Response of the Towns of Massachusetts to the *Votes and Proceedings*

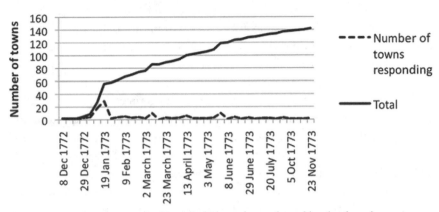

FIGURE 2.1. Response to the *Votes and Proceedings*, plotted by the date that town responses were received at a meeting of the Boston Committee of Correspondence and inserted into their minute book by the town clerk, William Cooper. Eventually 144 of the 260 towns and districts of the province replied to Boston.

respondence in 1772–1774, and the many historians who have written about them ever since have competed to find the best language to express their transformative influence. The ardent Whig and early historian of the Revolution, Mercy Otis Warren, uses language that suggests the emergence of a new system of communication: it was through the committees of correspondence, she wrote, that "an intercourse was established, by which a similarity of opinion, a connection of interest, and a union of action appeared, that set opposition at defiance, and defeated the machinations of their enemies through all the colonies" (1989, 1:62). But for Tories like Daniel Leonard, the committees of correspondence were not a beneficial instrument but a viciously corrupting one: "the foulest, subtlest and most venomous serpent, that ever issued from the eggs of sedition" (Massachusettensis, letter 3, January 2, 1775; Leonard 1972, 34). For Leonard, Chief Justice Peter Oliver, and Governor Thomas Hutchinson, the committees spread sedition rather than unity, a poisonous discontent with government, and even the fire of rebellion. It is thus appropriate that Governor Hutchinson uses Blackstone's precise terminology for sedition in describing Boston's "innovations" to be "of dangerous nature and tendency." In his study of the Boston committee, Richard D. Brown (1970, 92) describes

The Protocols of the Declarations ⇥ 77

the Boston committee as having a "catalytic role" in encouraging "the most elaborate general expression of provincial opinion that Massachusetts had ever witnessed."

While each of these accounts grasps an essential feature of the committees of correspondence, all mischaracterize the communication dynamic the committees set going. How did the committees engender the "union of actions" that Mercy Otis Warren's history foregrounds? The surprising generative power that so appalled Leonard? The enhanced influence of the Boston Whigs that the propaganda historians emphasize? Or the unprecedented "general expression of provincial opinion" that Brown documents? All these accounts center attention upon the words and ideas that the Boston committee transmitted through a one-to-many broadcast: from itself to the towns of Massachusetts. Whether those words have the redemptive moral virtue celebrated by Whig commentators like Warren, or the seditious "bad tendency" excoriated by the Tories, or the "catalytic" effects described by Brown, in each case, communication is understood as a top-down, one-to-many broadcast: a single vector that stamps each town with a message "made in Boston." Whether radical Whig ideas were imposed by Boston upon the towns or were already latent in the towns, they were brought into public view by Boston's broadcast and the towns' enthusiastic reception of it. In both cases, communication is connective and functional rather than productive.

What these accounts of the committees of correspondence miss, and this chapter takes up, is the manner in which two-way communication between Boston and the towns produced something quite new, a distributed network of political actors. With the emergence of a network of the towns in the winter of 1772–1773, the communication among the towns of Massachusetts became constitutive and primary: the network enabled the towns to assume new roles and postures, and to enter into new political relations. For both Boston and the towns who responded to it, communication could not be reduced to its modern sense—as simply "imparting information or knowledge"—as if the agents of communication remain unchanged as information moves from point A to point B. Communications within the network of the towns had effects that were psychic, somatic, and social. Rather than connecting what was preexistent, communication changed those brought into communication, yielding, as Mercy Otis Warren suggests, a new "connection of interest" and "unity of action." To Tory observers like Leonard, the transformation of the political climate wrought by the committees was dismaying in its suddenness. The network of the towns activated an earlier sense of what it means "to communicate": "To give to another as a partaker; to give a share; to share in, partake, use in common." In the earliest entries in the *OED*, the ritual of Christian communion is the chief example of the incorporating and binding potential of communication. The etymology of *to communicate* further suggests the way communication actively associates or links humans to one another: from Latin, *communicat*: "to make common to many, share, impart, divide"; derived from *communis*, a compound of *com* (together) + *munis* (bound, under obligation; *OED*). Within this network of the towns, the shared writing and speech of the Massachusetts towns bound them into a new relationship with one another. These words became, in Milton's phrase, vigorously productive.

THE RESPONSES OF THE TOWNS
TO THE *VOTES AND PROCEEDINGS*

A robust network of the Massachusetts towns would never have emerged in 1773 if the town selectmen who received the *Votes and Proceedings* in December 1772 had done nothing; or responded to the Boston committee with their own letter of approval or disapproval; or instructed the town's elected representative to the General Court to respond on behalf of the town. Instead, each town that responded did something much more ambitious and time consuming: they mobilized the resources of the town meeting to organize themselves into a body coherent enough to make their own general political statement as a reply to their fellow subjects in Boston. To achieve consensus and legitimacy for this effort required following an arduous set of procedures:

1. First, after receipt of the *Votes and Proceedings*, the selectmen of each town issued a warrant for an official town meeting. In at least one town, a petition from town members preceded the selectmen's issuing of a warrant.

2. After an oral reading of the *Votes and Proceedings* within the meeting, and preliminary discussion, the meeting elected a committee to frame a response to the town of Boston. As I have noted in the previous chapter, the procedural language for doing this was embedded in the *Votes and Proceedings*. In selecting this important committee, the town meeting had to choose members out of its own body who had the intellectual acuity to grasp and respond to the ideas of the Boston committee, as well as possessing a sympathetic understanding of their neighbors such that they could draft a document that would represent

the opinions of the town. The committee was sometimes a temporary reporting committee or, as in fifty-eight responding towns, a new "standing" committee of correspondence (Brown 1970, 122).

3. A second town meeting was convened to consider the committee's draft response. After hearing, considering, and amending the report of the committee, the town meeting voted (almost always unanimously) to accept the town's resolves and/or letter of instructions.

4. Finally, the town's committee of correspondence (or the selectmen) transmitted its response to the Boston Committee of Correspondence.

The form of that response is significant. Rather than simply adopting the *Votes and Proceedings*, as one town did, almost all the responding towns issued an elaborate formal statement on the political crisis that the Boston committee had described. Although the statement might take the form of "resolves" or "instructions" to their representative, these statements were a political declaration: they included a statement of rights, a list of grievances, and an address to the Boston committee, which had a general public character. At the center of these declarations there was a strong kernel of ideological consensus: first, each town asserted, either explicitly or implicitly, that it had the right to express its opinion on any matter that touched basic liberties; second, most towns declared that Parliament's expansive claims to sovereignty in America were unfounded and must be rejected; third, almost every responding town asserted that the ministry's plan to pay judges out of Crown revenues would "complete the system of despotism" (Plymouth Resolves, *Boston Gazette*, December 14, 1772). Throughout the declarations of the towns there breathes a neo-Roman theory of liberty: if government ever wins the legal or operational authority to subvert our liberties, even if they have not yet exercised that authority, we are *already* slaves.

Writing their own declaration was the way that each town articulated its independent political sentiment at the same time that it linked their own town to Boston and the other towns of the province. By responding, each town registered its own responsibility to the political crisis; by translating the issues at the center of the crisis into their own words, they localized the crisis, transmitting it back outward, but in slightly different terms. Upon this discursive occasion, too, too much intellectual novelty might block the connection each town was seeking to secure. The writing and sharing of these declarations participated in a symbolic exchange, whereby those who gave and received these declarations were saying "by what you say to me and I say to you, I see that you're one of us, and I hope you will agree that we are one of you." Like a potlatch or Christmas, the expenditure of effort on all sides appears extravagant, but like these gift economics, the larger purpose of an exchange of declaration is the formation of one trusted system for political communication.[2] A crucial by-product of this exchange has been noted by virtually every commentator since the eighteenth century: it greatly broadened active political participation.

While responding towns shared a common political doctrine, the tone and style of each declaration affirmed the distinct character of each town. We can capture these differences of tone and character by looking at brief excerpts from the responses of four towns. In 1772, as its declaration reveals, the town of Cambridge, originally Newtowne, considered itself the intellectual equal of the larger town of Boston. The Cambridge declaration took up the idea of the blood and treasure sacrificed by our "ancestors," as argued in the Boston declaration, but embedded it within a long formal period, which summarized the history of settlement from the first settlers to the present day.

> We Freeholds and other Inhabitants of Cambridge . . . Do therefore with true patriotic spirit, declare, that we are and ever have been, ready to risk our lives and fortunes in defense of this Majesty King GEORGE the Third, . . . So, on the other hand, are as much concerned to maintain and secure our invaluable rights and liberties . . . [which] were purchased at no less price than the precious blood and treasure of our worthy ancestors, the first settlers of this province, who for the sake of those rights left their native land, their dearest friends and relations, goodly houses, pleasant gardens and fruitful fields, and in the face of every danger, settled a wild and howling wilderness, where they were surrounded with an innumerable multitude of cruel and barbarous enemies; . . . yet aided by the smiles of indulgent heaven, by their heroic fortitude . . . they subdued their enemies before them. (*Boston Gazette*, December 21, 1772)

The effect produced is one of elevated indignation, earnest pathos, and learned authority. If Cambridge was trying to best Boston in the oratorical power of its performance, the town of Pembroke wrote a declaration of no-nonsense legal economy. Written in ten carefully ordered, comparatively short resolves, Pembroke approached the crisis with an emotionally restrained but highly logical exposition: "*Resolved*, That it is particularly necessary, in the present alarming crisis of our affairs, to give our opinion, and cause it to be

---

2. I am here indebted to an unpublished talk given by Christoph Raetzsch, of the Technical University of Berlin, entitled "Symbolic Exchange Revisited." "The Legacy of Baudrillard," conference at University of California, Santa Barbara, 2008.

known, that not a few men only, of factious spirits, as has been falsely represented, but the whole body of the people complain and are uneasy. *Resolved*, That acts of the British parliament made for, and executed within the limits of this province, are in our opinion against law and the most essential principles of our constitution" (*Boston Gazette*, January 11, 1773). Pembroke's rhetorical discipline gives added weight to its final warning: that if British ministry persisted in its "measures" and enforced them "by fleets and armies," it must lead to "the total dissolution of the union between the mother country and the colonies."

If Pembroke was restrained, Petersham was extravagant. Located on the western edge of Worcester County, Petersham answered Boston's call by offering to share their homes should Boston need them or, if they find that they were both chased off by British military might, to seek refuge with "the aboriginal natives of this country" which would offer "more humanity & brotherly love" than our "mother country." Urgent, sincere, and prone to unrestrained hyperbole, Petersham declared that the direct payment of judges would "complete a system of bondage equal to any ever before fabricated by the combined efforts of the ingenuity, malice, fraud, and wickedness of man." At the end of its declaration, Petersham's rustic frontier spirit modulates into the millenarian faith of a revival meeting: they would rely "no longer on an arm of flesh, but on the arms of that all-powerful GOD, who is able to unite the numerous inhabitants of this extensive territory, as a band of brothers in one common cause" (*Boston Gazette*, January 18, 1773).

In fashioning its declaration, the town of Gorham—in Cumberland County, Maine, then still part of Massachusetts—found a vivid way to justify confronting those "who are attempting to enslave us, and who desire to wallow in Luxury upon our Earnings." Gorham may have been far from the metropolis it addressed, but it had firsthand experience that it cockily invoked. Picking up the same thread of the *Votes and Proceedings* that Cambridge had extended, Gorham drew upon its recent history of Indian warfare to give the "blood and treasure" topos a startlingly literal turn: "We have those amongst us, whose Blood streaming from their own Wounds watered the Soil from which we earn our Bread! Our Ears have heard the infernal Yells of the native Savage Murderers—Our Eyes have seen our young Children weltering in their Gore, in our own Houses, and our dearest Friends carried into the Captivity by Men more savage than the Savage Beasts themselves!" (*Boston Gazette*, February 15, 1773). In this specimen of frontier gothic, "blood," "gore," and a plethora of exclamation marks helped to translate the courage required for facing the merciless Indians into the resolve to join Boston in facing down the British.

While the declarations of the towns of Massachusetts performed their political autonomy, many towns also acknowledged Boston's leadership by expressing their gratitude to the metropolis. Roxbury's expression of thanks is one of the most elegant: "That the sincere and hearty thanks of this town be given to the inhabitants of the town of Boston for the great readiness and care discovered by them to do all that in them lies to preserve the rights, liberties and privileges of the people inviolate when threatened with destruction." While most of the towns gave their thanks more briefly, they followed the same formula: the town thanks Boston for the virtues it has displayed in communicating to us. By turns, towns expressed their gratitude for Boston's "vigilance and care" (Cambridge), "vigilance and activity" (Charlestown), "moving so seasonably and wisely" (Ipswich), "vigilance and patriotic zeal" (Gorham), "seasonable and prudent care" (Salisbury), and so on.

Compliments to Boston, found in nearly all of the towns' declarations, helped to consolidate the link between Boston and the other towns in several different ways. First, they explicitly affirmed that Boston was right to initiate communication and that the citizens of this town were pleased to be included in this communication. Second, the expression of gratitude offered a tribute to Boston's special virtue or valor in the cause. More subtly, it preempted the feelings of jealousy of Boston's leadership that might be harbored by large, important towns like Cambridge, Concord, and Salem. Finally, these thanks made it clear that the towns welcomed further communication, something that Pembroke made explicit in its letter to the Boston committee: "We are ready and willing to hold a correspondence with you and the other town committees of correspondence within this province, when, and so often as it shall be thought necessary" (*Boston Gazette*, January 11, 1773). But, it is worth noting, there are also clear limits to the deference shown Boston. Opening such a channel of communication did not forfeit the formal legal equality of the towns, and no town pledged to follow Boston wherever it might go.

THE PROTOCOLS OF THE DECLARATIONS

No doubt the towns' public testaments had revealed a convergence of opinion on the questions of colonial rights and liberties and the limits of parliamentary sovereignty. But although this kernel of shared opinions was necessary, it was not sufficient. After all, a consensus against parliamentary taxation of the colonies had existed as early as the agitation seven years earlier during the Stamp Act protests. Nor did the increased citizen involvement in provincial politics in itself assure the formation of a network of towns.

What created a network was the towns' observation, within their diverse declarations, of a common set of protocols. These protocols were first embedded by the Boston committee in the *Votes and Proceedings*, and then observed by each of the town declarations. Protocols enabled and constrained the declarations of the towns by accepting certain ground rules for communication. Protocols, as intricate guardians of communication, cannot be reduced to either the form (like a letter) or the content (an idea), but, as we shall see, they influence both. The protocols of the Massachusetts declarations embedded certain common values like public spiritedness. But, more crucially, by enabling trusted communication, these shared and voluntary protocols permitted a network to emerge and, once it had emerged, to cohere and do things.

Here are the five protocols observed by the declarations of the towns of Massachusetts. In order to ground their declaration in precedent, law, and the "constitution," each town took up issues, conducted its meeting, and achieved consensus by following correct *legal procedure*. Because only unanimity would enable each town to speak its declaration with one voice, the town meetings and the committee deliberations were managed so as to observe the *corporate action protocol*. In order to project the effects of each declaration outward, the resolves and instructions were published so that they could become generally known. The circulation of warrants before the town meeting and the wide newspaper distribution of the declarations observed *the public access protocol*. Because the declarations offered a systematic account of the rights and grievances of all the citizens of Massachusetts, but eschewed the old petition to authority, they became a *systematic and general address to the people*. Finally, if these declarations were to avoid being words spoken by rote, they had to be written in such a way that they were imbued with the virtue and valor, and the freedom-loving independence, of those who spoke them. This could only happen if each corporate speaker observed the *virtuous initiative protocol*.

The Legal Procedure Protocol

The declarations of the towns of Massachusetts were developed in the face of royal officials who believed that they were "unwarrantable" and of "dangerous nature and tendency" (Hutchinson, Speech to General Court, February 16, 1773; *Briefs* 1981, 84). However, precisely because the declarations of the towns had a dubious legitimacy, and might, as the governor's words suggest, be seditious, each town was careful to follow correct legal procedures in framing its declarations. We have seen how the town of Boston followed ancient tradition in framing its petition to the governor (to convene the General Court), such that, when the governor rejected the petition, this refusal provided a rationale for transmitting their *Votes and Proceedings* to their "fellow citizens" in the other towns. The very title *The Votes and Proceedings of the Town of Boston* reminds its reader that Boston had followed correct procedure. Its title page further insists that the town meeting was "assembled, ACCORDING TO LAW." From the first warrants and motions of the Boston Town Meeting, to the carefully kept minute book of the Boston Committee of Correspondence, to the placement of the signature of the town clerk, William Cooper, upon each "attested" copy of the *Votes and Proceedings*, the town called attention to its exact observance of law and precedent.

Virtually every responding town demonstrated the same careful observance of legal procedure. So, for example, Ipswich reported near the end of its accepted resolves: "The foregoing report being read, and after mature deliberation the same was put to vote, paragraph by paragraph, and passed in the affirmative, *nem. con.*" The legal proceduralism observed in measures of dubious legality should not be viewed as cynical window-dressing. It was rooted in each town's attachment to the constitutional foundation of its own political body. The vast majority of towns were originally chartered by the General Court, which was in its turn established by the royal charters (first in 1629 for the Massachusetts Bay Colony, and then in 1691 for the Province of Massachusetts Bay). Careful attention to received procedures, evident in both the town meeting and in the meeting of town committees, reaffirmed a town's tie to the unwritten English constitution, the ultimate legal foundation of the political order. Even so, this passion for "the ancient constitution" transmitted contradictory political impulses. Because it aimed to preserve a valued tradition, it could present its project as a conservative one; but because it wished to return to the original root of things, it might also justify a radical critique of current political policies. From the English Revolution to the American Revolution to the Reform Bill agitation of the nineteenth century, upholding the true spirit of the "ancient" English constitution became the leading rationale for opposition to the existing political order.

The Corporate Action Protocol

Corporate action emerges when the members of one political body—a town meeting or a committee of correspondence—develop a consensus that is successfully expressed in a laboriously fashioned legal instrument: the resolves, instructions, and votes that make up a declaration. In order to "speak" for the town, the declaration required the formal unanimity of the town meeting. The final vote ratifying the declarations was almost invariably passed unanimously, "*Non contradictem*," with no one in the negative. To observe the corporate action protocol must have required patient deliberation and a pains-taking revision of the precise wording necessary to achieve consensus. For each responding town, the central challenge was how to manage things so that the long-standing differences of town life—of rank, of interest, and of personal-ity—were overcome for the sake of a single common declaration. Some towns were unable to reach consensus. In the case of Barnstable, on Cape Cod, the division between two prominent townsmen, James Otis Jr. and Representa-tive Edward Bacon, and their respective supporters, prevented the town from offering full support to Boston (Brown 1970, 135–36). In Marblehead, Elbridge Gerry initiated a successful effort to develop resolves for transmis-sion to the Boston committee (*Boston Gazette*, December 14, 1772), but soon after, twenty-nine inhabitants of the town publicly protested the Marblehead resolves, as well as its formation of a "committee of grievances" (*News-Letter*, December 31, 1772; Brown 1970, 112–13).

The unanimity achieved by the vast majority of towns depended upon in-corporating the equal voices of the freeholders and inhabitants who partici-pated in the meetings. While leaders inevitably emerged who, by reason of the trust others had in them, successfully expressed the concerns and ideas of the town meeting, nonetheless, because each member had a vote in the final adop-tion of a common declaration, the surest pathway to a sustainable unity was to respect the formal equality of the members of the meeting. In this regard, the town meeting and its committees did not resemble the public sphere as conceived by Habermas, where a liberal plurality of competing discourses, in-terests, and opinion is sustained rather than overcome. In acting together and forging themselves into a temporary or provisional unity, the Massachusetts Whigs were not liberal but republican (Arendt 1963, 73–79; Wood 1993). The achieved unity of a common declaration gathered and directed the political power of the town, so that it could be transmitted outside the town. Then each town could become a node within a larger heterogeneous unity, the network of Massachusetts towns.

The Public Access Protocol

From the warrant issued for the town meeting of November 2, 1772, the aim of the Boston declaration was to "communicate and publish [the rights and in-fringements] to the several towns in this Province, and to the World" (Boston 1772, iii). The double address of the declaration, "to the several towns" and "to the World," points to the two kinds of communication undertaken by the *Votes and Proceedings*. It was both the beginning of the one-to-one networking of Boston and other individual towns and a one-to-many broadcast, from Boston to anyone in the "world" who read their communications in the newspaper or in the *Votes and Proceedings*. From the beginning, the Boston committee conducted its communications before the public. By making the formation of the Boston Committee of Correspondence so visible to readers of the newspaper, by replacing the official private petition with a published declaration, by publishing its pamphlet-letter to the towns (in print rather than manuscript form, which nonetheless mimes the personal address of the letter), and by reprinting the declarations of selected towns as they were received, the Boston committee observed the public access protocol for communication. In addition, once the declaration of Plymouth was reprinted on December 7, 1772, the responding towns of Massachusetts would know that their own declaration might be published as well. In all these instances, the aim of publication was to place the actions of the towns before the tribunal of public opinion. In implementing political acts in clear view of the public, the towns of Massachusetts built upon the open, public, and distributed character of the newspaper and the postal system. Making things public was both a general value (of open and transparent dealing) as well as a calculated strategy (for mobilizing the sentiment of the people).

By making the new associations of the towns so publicly visible, the Whigs of Massachusetts secured themselves against the accusation that they were engaged in secret plotting against the government. While each town's declaration localized the political crisis, their publication also allowed each town to step boldly onto the stage of history so as to retransmit the crisis in its own words. The effect produced was one of a serendipitous harmonic convergence. Because the names of the town committee members were invariably reprinted with the resolves of the town, each member came into public view as worthy of praise or blame.[3]

3. As they appeared in the Boston newspapers, the declarations of the towns began to resemble a contest to develop the most spirited expression of an ardent attachment to liberty. Such a contest for fame is suggested by a notice, labeled "To the PUBLIC," which was published in the *Massachusetts Spy* on January 21, 1773. By way of recognizing the towns that had responded, it proposed that "all of the proceedings of the towns in Massachusetts province, for the preservation of the rights of America, be collected and published in a volume; that posterity may know what their ancestors have done in the cause of FREEDOM." This would allow each town of Massachusetts to "be recorded in this catalogue of FAME, and handed down to future ages." Although this project was never undertaken, the public spectacle of the diverse responses of the Massachusetts towns stimulated interest outside of the province. On January 25, 1773, the *Boston Gazette* published an item that suggests the far-flung glory that towns were achieving:

The Protocol of a Systematic and General Address to the People

One doesn't have to think the way the Tories of Massachusetts did to acknowledge the audacity of the Boston declaration. The ambition of the *Votes and Proceedings* is evident from both its systematic character and its general address. The pamphlet presents a systematic account of rights: first through a description of the "natural rights" of the colonists of the province "as men"; then an account of their "rights as Christians"; and, finally, an account of their "rights as subjects." By foregrounding the interrelation of three distinct parts of the whole subject, and by moving from the most general (as "men") to the most particular (as "subjects"), the *Votes and Proceedings* imitates the generic traits of countless Enlightenment systems, like that found in Locke's *Second Treatise on Government*, which is cited in the first section of the *Votes and Proceedings* (Boston 1772, 5).[4] This three-part discussion of rights prepares for the Crown's "infringements and violations" of those rights. In length and scope—there are eleven infringements named—this list is given a comprehensive character. The systematic design of the Boston pamphlet, however much it may fall short of its philosophical predecessors, helped to ground its authority. Although it was written out of the particular political experience of the Boston Whigs, the *Votes and Proceedings* was fashioned into a general address to the people of Massachusetts. In making systematic arguments about rights and grievances that touched *all* the king's subjects of Massachusetts, in striving to reach *all* the towns in the province, in fashioning a popular declaration for (all) "the world" to hear, the content and rhetoric of the Boston committee's pamphlet observed the protocol of a general address to the people. Here the drafters of the Boston declaration, and the many committees who imitated Boston by writing their own declarations so they were also systematic and general, cast their ideas in the mode of Enlightenment universality: they sought to say what would be true for *all* the people.

The *Votes and Proceedings* and the declarations of the other towns applied an inclusive political strategy to written political discourse that the town meeting applied in other times of political emergency. On the day after the Boston

---

"EXTRACT OF A LETTER FROM PHILADELPHIA, DATED DECEMBER 28, 1772: 'WE HAVE NOTHING NEW OF AN INTERESTING NATURE STIRRING AMONG US; BUT YOUR TOWN MEETINGS, RESOLVES, &C. BEGIN TO EXCITE THE ATTENTION OF THE PEOPLE IN THESE PARTS'" (capitals in the original).

4. For a more comprehensive discussion of the centrality of the genre of system to the Enlightenment in Britain, see Siskin 2010.

Massacre and in the days before the threatened landing of East India tea, the Boston Town Meeting sponsored what they called meetings of "the body of the people." These meetings included tax-paying freeholders, but could also include women, apprentices, servants, and other non-tax-paying male inhabitants as well as nonresidents.[5] In addition, the annual orations and funerals that followed the Boston Massacre included a still larger public body, by including families with children. This inclusiveness was no doubt a way to expand political power: the more who are gathered, the more power one demonstrates and has. A systematic and general address to (all) "the people" became a way to include, in principle, the largest possible audience for one's address. Of course, Enlightenment political practice never lived up to its theoretical universalism. However, the Enlightenment's failure to include women, servants, blacks, and Native Americans in its general address opened up a tension between what is said and done that later actors (from the slaves who petitioned the Massachusetts General Court in 1773 to Mary Wollstonecraft in 1792) would use to challenge and change the rules for participation. Notwithstanding its theoretical and practical deficiencies, the general address to the people was a success in the way it incited a correspondent response from Whigs in the towns throughout Massachusetts.

The Virtuous Initiative Protocol

In order to link the towns of Massachusetts into one network, the declarations of each town had to act together, according to correct legal procedure, through a general address to the people that was both systematic and public. But each town also had to demonstrate the independent initiative and public virtue that Boston had shown. So, for example, I have noted that the "letter of correspondence with the other towns" was cast as a rather loaded moral test. The letter insisted that each of the towns of Massachusetts, and every inhabitant of those towns, had to choose between "standing firm as one man to recover and support" our rights, or alternatively, to sit "supinely indifferent," "while the iron hand of oppression is daily tearing the choicest fruit from the fair tree of liberty" (Boston 1772, 33–34). In other words, the town of Boston asked each town this pointed question: Do you have a "share of public virtue remaining" (Boston 1772, 34) such that you can join us in responding to this political crisis? Just as the collective worship of a Congregational church

5. For the participation of women in the Boston meetings of "the body of the people" held during the tea agitation, see Forbes 1942, 187; and Raphael 2001, 22.

rests upon the belief and conscience of each of its members, and its collective prayers upon the faith of each believer, so the cardinal unit of each town's declaration is the virtue of each individual who becomes joined in a declaration. Here *virtue* means more than the familiar modern definition as acting according to "recognized moral laws or standards of right conduct" (*OED*, 2). The eighteenth-century Whig makes public virtue the touchstone for legitimate political action by drawing upon an earlier sense of *virtue* as "a power or operative influence inherent in" a supernatural or human being (*OED*, 1a). In other words, in eighteenth-century Anglo-American political culture, virtue was both the energy source and the moral guide of action. Three days after the formation of the Boston committee on November 2, 1772, Samuel Adams invoked this sense of virtue in a letter written to Elbridge Gerry, one of the two representatives from Marblehead. Adams urges Gerry to seize the political initiative by forming a committee of correspondence in Marblehead, so "that Boston is not wholly deserted." To explain the quality that is needed to act, Adams draws upon the Latin sense of *virtu* ("manliness, valour, worth, etc., from *vir*, man" [*OED*]), and quotes "a letter I received not long ago from a friend of mine of some note in London, wherein he says, 'your whole dependence under God is upon your own Virtue, (*Valor*)'" (November 5, 1772; the friend is Arthur Lee; S. Adams 1904, 2:347). Here, and throughout the eighteenth century, in celebrations of moral exemplars from Cato and Richardson's *Pamela* to George Washington, virtue was understood as an inner strength and courage that enables one to stand alone, to speak boldly when others are silent, and when tested, to act with "spirit," that is, with energy, attention, and readiness.

The imperative for each town to show its public virtue offers another reason why declarations of the towns, though written in response to the Boston declaration, had to be more than an expression of sympathy and support for the metropolis. Public virtue could not come from Boston alone. It was therefore morally essential that each of the towns of Massachusetts formulate, publish, and declare its own declaration. Each town had to start anew, by declaring its sense of the political crisis in its own words. In this way, each town meeting, and each individual of the town meeting, would confirm that they were possessed of the virtue, the spirit, and the courage to be worthy members of "the cause" of liberty. While each town's declaration was a response, it was also a beginning. That each town and individual demonstrated virtuous initiative, even while they acted together, helps to explain the character of the network that emerged through the use of these protocols. The diverse declarations of the towns of Massachusetts generated a network that was voluntary, bottom-up, and distributed in its topology. The moral and political power of the towns stayed distributed throughout the network, rather than flowing toward one place, such as Boston. This explains why individual towns could later undertake measures that showed greater boldness than Boston, as, for example, in late August 1774, when the farmers, craftsmen, and others from the middling ranks in Worcester County assembled thousands of men to prevent the meeting of the royal court at the county seat in Worcester (Raphael 2002, 59–89). The virtuous initiative protocol means that the declaration of each town became a new instance of what Hannah Arendt has described as the "miraculous" human power to begin.[6]

For the Whigs of Massachusetts, the declarations could bind them in an exalted and redemptive common cause only if they "breathed" a spirit of public virtue. But for this binding process to work, the readers of these declarations had to accept the sincerity of the claims to virtue made in each declaration. Because virtue is an inner quality, it could only be evidenced by how each town wrote and "utter[ed]" its virtue. In the public and private exchanges between Boston and the other towns, public virtue functioned as an outward sign of inner merit, as a fraternal handshake to fellow Whigs, as a shared code, as a wink of humanity. As the crisis intensified, private correspondents used appeals to their public virtue as a way to expand trusted communication. Thus, Richard Henry Lee's first letter to Samuel Adams, written on February 4, 1773, in response to alarming news about the legal powers granted the Gaspée commission, explicitly linked an appeal to their shared virtue to the opening of a new channel of trusted communication: "to be firmly attached to the cause of liberty on virtuous principles, is a powerful cause of union, and renders proper, the most easy communication of sentiment" (Lee 1911, 1:82).

The same factor that made a show of public virtue indispensable to the Whig cause—as virtue is hidden in each human breast—opens it to skeptical questioning. For Tory readers, the publicity of these declarations called into question the virtue they would transmit. Tories construed the grim seriousness of the Whig claim to public virtue as nothing more than a way to varnish sedition with morality, to incite the mob with political enthusiasm, and to disguise a far-flung political combination, in fact engineered by a few Boston

6. For a general theoretical discussion of the "miracle" of forgiving and beginning, see Arendt 1998, 230–47. For the miraculous power to begin as central to human freedom, see Hannah Arendt's 1961 essay "What Is Freedom?" There she emphasizes that for the Greeks and Romans, political freedom entailed virtuoso performance (Arendt 2000, 447).

radicals, with the fiction of each town's political independence. Furthermore, Tories argued that if the Boston Whigs actually believed that their seditious opposition to royal authority constituted a form of public virtue, they were as "deluded" as those in the towns that they misled.[7]

THE BOSTON COMMITTEE OF CORRESPONDENCE CLOSES THE CIRCUIT OF COMMUNICATION AND A NETWORK EMERGES

The careful observation of the protocols of the declarations made the constituents of a network publicly visible. However, it would still require the multifaceted communication work of the Boston committee to weave a network that would be coherent enough to act together. To this end, the Boston committee coordinated two distinct kinds of communication: one-to-many public broadcasting and one-to-one and one-to-few networking, that is, private correspondence between itself and the various committees of the responding towns. Each had its particular traits. Broadcasting, whether in a speech or publication, reached many minds with one message; it was vertical and implicitly hierarchical (because it raised the makers over the receivers of meaning). At its most powerful, a broadcast could become an "event" in the public life of the community, as the publication of the *Votes and Proceedings* did. Networking, by contrast, whether it unfolds in conversation or letters of correspondence, has the diffuse plurality of discrete communications. In its topology it is horizontal, and because all those who use the network are media makers, it is comparatively egalitarian. At its most influential, networking can forge the diverse agents on the network into a unity coherent enough to act together.[8]

7. See Peter Oliver's *Origin and Progress of the American Rebellion*, where he fulminates against Samuel Adams's "psalm singing Myrmidons" (1961, 74). The word "deluded" began to sound through Tory assessments of the American crisis in this period. Spoken by Tories with an air of condescension, the assumption that Whigs were "deluded" suggested that (1) Whigs, Quixote-like, held madly misguided theories, (2) that most had been misled by a few conspirators, but also, more generously, (3) that these subjects could be reclaimed from their delusion by strong argument, or if this failed, by stronger measures.

8. Elsewhere I have sought to develop a systematic topology, across the long history of media, of the traits of broadcasting and networking (W. Warner 2007). The rise of the Internet was linked with a reductive and tendentious opposition between the oppressive regime of big media broadcasting (in film, radio, television), enforced by strict copyright, and the supposedly liberation potential of networking, where, in one for-

Thus, in the winter of 1772–1773, when the twenty-one members of the Boston Committee of Correspondence gathered each Tuesday at 5:30 p.m. in one of the selectmen's two chambers on the third floor of Faneuil Hall, the Boston committee engaged in both broadcasting and networking. After a reading of the communications of each town that were received that week, the committee selected a few to send to the newspapers for publication. By April the five newspapers of Boston had published the declarations of over forty towns, about a third of those who responded. In this way, even some very obscure towns—like Petersham and Gorham—received their fifteen minutes of fame. By flooding the Boston newspapers, the Boston committee allowed the response of each town to add to a building consensus: supplemental iteration of similar but distinct declarations helped to build the authority for the way Whigs framed the political crisis (Lakoff 2002, 2004). In addition, this public display of these first responses may have motivated slower towns to convene their own town meetings and respond to the *Votes and Proceedings*.[9]

While newspaper publication displayed the solidarity with Boston of diverse towns, private correspondence was used to nurture a more personal and ongoing relationship between towns and what those towns referred to as "the metropolis." Thus, as early as December 1, 1772, the Boston committee appointed a subcommittee of three to compose a first draft of a reply to the town of Plymouth, which was then referred back to the whole committee before being sent to that town. By late December, a committee of five emerged to draft responses to the various other towns. Each draft was returned to the whole Boston committee for reading and revision, which then sent it to the town in question as a response of the whole committee, under the signature of the clerk, William Cooper. The replies were consistent with the deference shown

mulation, "information wants to be free." But, in fact, each mode of communication is highly variable, not tethered to any particular medium (like paper, electronic signal, or wireless), and is in fact often co-implicated with one another. The effectiveness of the Whig committees of correspondence emerged from their ability to switch with agility between networking and broadcasting.

9. The rate of publication varied considerably over the period between December 1772 and summer of 1773. At first the letters were a novelty, and they were published in more than one paper. This was particularly true of the first responders: Plymouth, Marblehead, Roxbury, and Cambridge. But over the course of the winter, the *Boston Evening News*, the *Boston Post-Boy*, and the Tory *News-Letter* lagged the two staunchly Whig papers, the *Boston Gazette* and the *Massachusetts Spy*. The *News-Letter* stopped publication of the declarations in January (Brown 1970, 91).

to each town in the *Votes and Proceedings*: they were carefully targeted to the individual town (rather than being boilerplate); they encouraged, praised, and sometimes even flattered a town; they occasionally communicated important news; and they implicitly embraced the idea of the equality of the towns (Brown 1970, 125–31). One-to-one correspondence deepened, broadened, and enhanced the staying power of the network of the Massachusetts towns. Network communication brought the Boston committee into private but official communication with a large number of town committee members who had never served on the General Court. By the third month of 1773, the Boston committee had built a list of corresponding committees with which it could communicate by letter or printed broadside. When political crisis brought correspondence from and with Rhode Island, New Hampshire, Virginia, and Philadelphia, the Boston committee seamlessly extended its network to committees throughout the colonies.

The success of the *Votes and Proceedings* encouraged the Boston Committee of Correspondence to use the broadside to develop a new channel of communication with the towns of Massachusetts. When Governor Hutchinson, in his speeches to the General Court, accused the Boston committee of being illegal, dangerous, and unwarranted, the town meeting appointed a committee to vindicate its committee. The result was a broadside that was transmitted directly to the towns of Massachusetts by the Boston committee. The broadside defended the formation of the Boston committee and the declarations of the other towns by appealing first to the Boston Town Meeting's careful observation of legal procedure as outlined in the Massachusetts charter, then to "the great and perpetual law of self preservation," and finally to the ancient right to petition. It rejected the governor's claim that the committee had "invited every other Town & District in the Province to adopt the same Principles," by insisting that "every Town which has thought it expedient to correspond with this [town] on the Occasion have acted their own Judgment [*sic*] & expressed their own principles" (S. Adams 1904, 3:3–12).

There were several distinct advantages to communication by broadside over publication in the newspapers. Newspapers were published once a week, mixed political information with a mélange of other news and advertising, and were under the editorial control of their printer, who might choose to give the communication less prominence than the Boston committee desired. By contrast, the broadsides of the Boston committee were composed, printed, and distributed under the direct control of the Boston committee. Each could be timed to the moment of political exigency, rather than waiting for a newspaper day. Finally, by transmitting information from one political body directly to another, these broadsides began to take on some of the character of communication among the nodes of a quasi-administrative network. The Boston Committee of Correspondence used broadside broadcasts to the 260 towns and districts of Massachusetts at least eleven more times between 1773 and 1775.[10]

The broadsides that were produced and distributed by the Boston Committee of Correspondence between 1772 and 1775 track the whole arc of the imperial crisis in Massachusetts, from the defense of the formation of the Boston Committee of Correspondence against the governor's challenge to the committee's legitimacy (March 30, 1773) to the text of the Boston Port Bill (May 12, 1774), from the king's speech in Parliament of December 12, 1774, condemning "the most daring spirit of resistance . . . in Massachusetts Bay" (January 20, 1775), to the committee's promotion of measures to block the passage of supplies to General Gage's army on the eve of the Battles of Lexington and Concord (February 25, 1775). These broadsides all observed the protocols of the declarations as described above: they followed correct legal procedure, acted as a corporate body, encouraged public access through a general address to the people, and throughout demonstrated their commitment to the ideal of public virtue. But each of these broadcasts also does something more: it translates the intensifying political crisis into a shared communication. This periodic broadcasting by the Boston committee allowed even the remotest towns of Massachusetts to feel that they were in direct contact with "ground zero" of the political struggle in Boston. Many towns wrote back to offer their support. Most importantly, the stream of writing (and some speech) that the Boston committee exchanged with the other towns helped to make the "we" of the *Votes and Proceedings*—one that was hopeful, tentative, and rhetorical—actual. The "we" that filled the broadsides began to denote the diverse inhabitants of the towns who had joined Boston in its political initiative. Thus, after the arrival of East India tea in Boston Harbor, five neighboring town committees joined the Boston committee in composing these words, which were circulated to all other towns by broadside: "We are in duty bound to use our most strenuous endeavours to ward off the impending evil, and we are sure that upon a fair and cool inquiry in to the nature and tendency of this ministerial plan you will think this tea now coming to us, more to be dreaded

10. A few of the controversial broadsides were sent only to towns that had already responded to the Boston committee.

than plague or pestilence" (Broadside in Consequence of a Conference, November 23, 1773, Early American Imprint no. 12693). This "we" denominates the Boston committee and the committees of the other towns as a loose network of subjects who were beginning to learn how to speak and act together. After the battle of Lexington and Concord, that "we" would take the form of a large army that gathered around Boston and accepted Washington's leadership.

HOW A "WONDERFUL" "CONCURRENCE OF CAUSES" CHANGED THE RATIO OF POWER IN MASSACHUSETTS

The emergence of the network of the towns with the Boston committee at its center created a new context for politics in Massachusetts. Over the first six months of 1773, the Whigs experienced a palpable increase in their power while there was a concomitant decrease in the authority of royal government. But *how* did this happen? Changes in political power are difficult to discern and seldom visible. When John Adams moved himself and his family back to Boston from Braintree in late November 1772, the political climate seemed very menacing for the Whig cause. In a letter to the famous Whig historian Catharine Macaulay, which he copied into his diary at the end of the year, John Adams declared that the "system of a mean, and merciless administration, is gaining ground upon our patriots every day." Lamenting the fall of "the flower of our genius, the ornaments of the province," Jonathan Mayhew, Oxbridge Thatcher, and James Otis Jr., Adams observed that "the body of the people seem to be worn out, by struggling." Faced, like Hercules, with the choice between virtue and vice, Adams was convinced that, given "what a Mass of Corruption human Nature has been in general, since the Fall of Adam, we may easily judge what the Consequence will be" (December 31, 1772; J. Adams 1961, 2:75). But only two months and one week later, Adams's reading of the political weather had changed dramatically. Instead of attributing Whig weakness to fatigue and moral failings, Adams discerned a "wonderful" pattern in the working of Providence: "I have never known a Period, in which the Seeds of great Events have been so plentifully sown as this Winter. A Providence is visible, in that Concurrence of Causes, which produced the Debates and Controversies of this Winter. The Court of Inquisition at Rhode Island (i.e. the Gaspée commission), the Judges Salaries, the Massachusetts Bay Town meetings, General Brattles Folly, all conspired in a remarkable, a wonderfull Manner" (March 4, 1773; J. Adams 1961, 2:78). What had changed Adams from anxiety to jubilation, from black prognostications to hopeful confidence, was a palpable change in Whig fortunes in Massachusetts. This shift was discernible in "the debates and controversies" triggered by the *Votes and Proceedings* and the declarations of the towns, in replies of the House to the governor's speech to the General Court, and in the much less important episode (included with a certain personal vanity) of John Adams's own debate in print with General Brattle.

This shift in the ratio of power was shaped by two interconnected trends, both unfolding over the course of 1773: the gradual emergence of a new agency, the network of the towns with the Boston Committee of Correspondence as its hub, and the politically fraught communication events of the first six months of 1773. These include (1) the governor's three speeches to the General Court (in January–March), (2) the publication of Hutchinson's old private letters to ministry (in June), and (3) the dispute triggered by the arrival of the East India Company tea (in November–December). The governor's attempt, in his opening address to the General Court on January 6, 1773, to shut down this unprecedented exchange among the towns had the paradoxical effect of accelerating the networking of the towns. The official private letters of the governor and lieutenant governor, which, written before the Boston Massacre, advised their superiors on ways to strengthen Crown government in Massachusetts. Their publication greatly diminished the effective authority of Governor Thomas Hutchinson. Governor Hutchinson's failure to prevent the destruction of the tea destroyed that authority.

These events produced a cascade of effects that weakened British government in Massachusetts. In describing these episodes, I explore how each is linked to the Boston Committee of Correspondence and the network that emerged around it, and I trace the flowing together, or, to use John Adams's suggestive phrase, the "concurrence of causes," of these communication episodes. As noted earlier, political power—whether it is expressed as authority, sovereignty, or legitimacy—often appears abstract, dynamic, and uncertain. However, it becomes quite visible at those moments when agents discover whether they have the leverage *to make others do what they want them to do*. By the last months of 1773, a new test of relative power assumed the tangible shape of the 114 chests of tea that arrived in Boston Harbor on the ship *Dartmouth* on November 28, 1773. The *Dartmouth*'s arrival precipitated a struggle as to whether the tea would be landed, as the governor, British ministry, and the law required, or the tea would not be landed, as the Whigs insisted.

Event 1: The Governor's Speech and the Reply of the House

I have laid before you, Gentlemen, what appeared to me to be the true Constitution of the Province, and recommend an Adherence to it because I believed it would restore us to and continue us in that happy State in which we flourished so long a Course of Years.

— Governor Thomas Hutchinson, speech ending the session of the General
   Court, March 6, 1773

In politics the exercise of power often takes the form of performance. On January 6, 1773, Governor Thomas Hutchinson used the persuasive power of his words and ideas, his body and his gesture, to deliver a speech convening the General Court. In the months and years that followed, this speech and the debate with the Massachusetts Council and House of Representatives that it explicitly invited came to be understood by both Whig opponents and British administration as a strategic blunder. So how did it come to be that Governor Hutchinson penned and delivered a speech that stated "the true constitution" of the British Empire and Massachusetts's place in it? Since, in the previous three years, Hutchinson had made no general speech to the representatives and councilors, both Whigs and Tories were surprised by this action (Hutchinson 1936, 3:267). Royal officials were also surprised by the governor's gambit. At least since the Boston Massacre, Whitehall had developed a policy to strengthen government in Massachusetts that consisted of some strategic retreat (removing troops from Boston, repealing most of the Townshend Acts), administrative "firmness," covert measures (like the direct payment of governor and judges), and a trust in the salutary effects of a sustained dispute-free interval of normality and "quiet." One of the ways Governor Hutchinson and other colonial governors advanced this policy was by proroguing, or suspending, the meetings of the elected assemblies, so as to remove the institutional setting within which political opponents might air their grievances. It was consistent with this policy that the governor took no public notice of the *Votes and Proceedings* upon its publication. After all, petitions and pamphlets could not disturb the positional authority that Thomas Hutchinson still enjoyed as governor and as chief representative of royal authority in the province.

The responses of the towns changed the political climate in Massachusetts, changed the calculations of the governor, and stirred him out of his deliberate silence. As more and more towns responded, and none but a dissident minority from the town of Marblehead spoke in public opposition to the Boston declaration, the governor worried that ever more towns were publicly committing themselves to ideas that declared their independence of the sovereignty of the British Parliament. On the day after his speech, in a candid private letter to John Pownall, the secretary of the Board of Trade, the governor worried that he would be "charged with bringing on a fresh dispute," but explains his decision this way: "I was loath to bring this point before the Assembly but when I saw that by neglect the several towns without understanding what they were doing would have *bound* themselves by their resolves and their Representatives would have thought themselves *bound* to do nothing in the General Court contrary to the resolves of their towns, I found myself under the *necessity* of stating the case between the kingdom and the colonies" (January 7, 1773; *Documents* 1974, 6:45; emphasis mine). While he speaks with a legal scholar's condescension about the people's limited "understanding" of their own declarations, Hutchinson also registers an administrator's alarm about the implications for royal government. By following the Boston declaration with their own, towns were binding themselves and their representatives so that the General Court, when the governor finally convened it, would automatically follow the political course laid out by the Boston committee in the *Votes and Proceedings*. Then, through a "dangerous plot" Hutchinson reports to Lord Dartmouth that he has discovered, the seditious notions that had spread from Boston to many of the towns and translated into instructions to each representative would bind the House of Representatives to reiterate these notions, which would then be conducted through a "circular letter" to "all the Assemblies on the continent" (Thomas Hutchinson to earl of Dartmouth, January 7, 1773; *Documents* 1974, 6:44; see also Hutchinson 1936, 264–65). In other words, the towns' declarations were a threat to which Governor Hutchinson could not *not* respond.

In convening the General Court, Hutchinson sought to channel the errant ideas about the limits upon parliamentary sovereignty, now circulating among the dispersed towns of the province, into a constitutional forum where instituted hierarchies were expressed in the procedures of the General Court, a place where he enjoyed considerable control over proceedings. By convening the General Court on brief notice, the governor hoped to prevent any more towns from giving their representatives binding instructions, as the towns of Roxbury, Cambridge, and Charleston had recently done. Because the governor knew that his speech would be reproduced by all the newspapers of Massachusetts and New England, he hoped that a systematic statement of the constitution of the British Empire would discourage any more towns from meeting in response to the Boston declaration. In at least one regard, Governor Hutchinson's gambit achieved its end. Over the next two months,

FIGURE 2.2. The Representatives' Hall (1882 restoration). The Speaker of the House sat at a large table with the clerk on the right-hand (south) side of the room. The four Boston members sat front and center on the first bench. To hear the governor's opening address to the General Court on January 6, 1773, the members would go through the door and across the hallway to the Council Chamber, visible on the other side of the staircase (Massachusetts 1980, 138–39).

from January 6 to March 6, 1773, Hutchinson succeeded in managing the time, place, and manner of a political exchange so that they had all the institutional decorum, correct procedure, and dialectical precision appropriate to constitutional issues of great moment. The governor's speech to the General Court received written replies from the Council and the House, which, in turn, were answered by a second speech of the governor, which, in its turn, attracted written replies by the Council and the House, which were, in their turn, answered by a third speech from the governor on March 6. The governor made his third speech the "last word" in this two-month-long debate by proroguing the General Court at the end of his speech.

The protocols of the General Court gave an initial advantage to the governor by enabling him to control the rhythm and form of communication. On the morning of Wednesday, January 6, 1773, the governor was notified by a

FIGURE 2.3. The Council Chamber (1882 restoration). The fragmentary record suggests that the governor sat at the head of a long, narrow, rectangular table, which extended into the center of the room, with his back to the large window between the two fireplaces. The governor would preside over twenty-eight councilors, who sat in armchairs, wearing high wigs and scarlet robes. For an address to the House, members would sit on benches (Boston 1889, 208–24).

committee of five members of the House of Representatives that a quorum of the representatives out of the total 139 elected that year were now gathered in their chamber at the Town House.

Then "A Message from his Excellency the Governor by the Secretary" was carried to the House chamber (see fig. 2.2): "Mr. SPEAKER, His Excellency the Governor is now in the Chair, and directs the Attendance of this House in the Council Chamber" (Massachusetts 1980, 137). The character of debate that unfolded after the House was summoned to the Council Chamber is illuminated by the spaces within which the Governor's communications unfolded (see fig. 2.3).

The governor's "chair" was in the Council Chamber, set between two large royal portraits, in front of the large windowed doors, and it offered architectural support to the governor at the moment he asserted the royal prerogative.

After the representatives had proceeded to the Council Chamber and heard the governor's speech, "the Speaker having obtained a copy," the representatives returned to their own chamber. Over the two months of the debate, only *he* was permitted to speak. Only he enjoyed the advantage of casting his ideas into the immediacy of speech where his tone of voice and bodily gesture could inflect the meaning in a live oral performance. However, most of those who followed this debate read it in printed form, first in the newspaper or later as a pamphlet, where all seven installments of the debate were gathered. Once the debate was reduced to print, the media asymmetry of the "live" debate, whereby the governor spoke and the Council and House wrote, was effaced. For readers throughout the empire, the debate had the irresistible rhythms of an agon. Although it was framed in abstruse legal and constitutional arguments, it cast the dispute between the parent country and the colonies into a formal debate where each reader could decide for himself or herself which side had "won." While the governor controlled the initial venue of the exchange, he could not control either the arguments of his opponents or how that debate might be scored by the many readers that it attracted in Massachusetts, in other colonies, and in London.[11]

In a sense Thomas Hutchinson's whole career had prepared him for the moment when he delivered his speech to the House and Council. At the age of sixty-one, Governor Hutchinson had served for over three decades with distinction in the Boston Town Meeting, as representative for Boston, as Speaker of the House, as councilor, as chief justice of the Superior Court, as lieutenant governor, and for nearly two years as governor. He had published the most authoritative scholarly history of Massachusetts Bay, in the early history of which his family had played a prominent founding role. One of his ancestors was Anne Hutchinson. The Hutchinsons had flourished for generations as merchants and had formed powerful alliances with his wife Margaret's family, the Sanfords of Rhode Island. In the only account of his personal appearance, by his rival James Otis Jr., Thomas Hutchinson was described as "a tall, slender, fair-complexioned, fair spoken, very good gentleman." Self-confident in his rank, his wealth, and his intellectual ability, proud to be the first American-born governor of Massachusetts, Thomas Hutchinson opened the session at the very height of his personal vigor and political power. The language of his speech exudes a confidence that his legal analysis is irrefutable on the grounds

11. Hutchinson's speech was reprinted in the London daily, the *Public Advertiser*, on March 4, 1773; Arthur Lee replied to it on March 4 and 8. Answers to the governor by Council and House were published in April.

of history, logic, and law. By the end of the speech, he apparently believed that his exposition had been so compelling as to bring enlightenment to most of those who heard him. The next day he wrote to John Pownall, "At [the end of] the delivery of the speech the members seemed to be amazed, three-quarters of them having taken for granted that all that had been done by Parliament was arbitrary and unconstitutional without having ever been informed what is their constitution. I flatter myself that it will be of service" (Hutchinson to John Pownall, secretary of the Board of Trade, January 7, 1773; *Documents* 1974, 6:45). In the days after his speech, Hutchinson seems to have fallen prey to the thespian fantasy that he had delivered a performance so compelling that it had turned the political tide in Massachusetts. Thus, over the next two months, he defended his communications initiative by incorrectly claiming that the speech had arrested the town meetings and town declarations around the province.

In his three speeches to the General Court, Hutchinson offered two fundamental reasons to reject the *Votes and Proceedings* and the meetings it provoked. First, the arguments of the Boston Town Meeting threatened to undermine the proper relationship of each subject to "our" king.

> I will not particularize these Resolves or Votes and shall only observe to you, in general, that some of them deny the supreme Authority of Parliament, and so are repugnant to the Principles of the Constitution, and that others speak of this supreme Authority, of which the King is a constituent Part and to every Act of which his Assent is necessary, in such terms as have a direct Tendency to alienate the Affections of the People from their Sovereign who has ever been most tender of their Rights, and whose Person, Crown and Dignity we are under every possible Obligation to defend and support. (*Briefs* 1981, 17)

These words embed a reproach within an argument. Hutchinson argues that a challenge to the supreme authority of Parliament fails logically because the king is a "constituent part" of Parliament. But they have the further effect of alienating "the affections of the people from their sovereign." This constitutional argument exposes the latent cruelty of Boston's *Votes and Proceedings*: the king has ever been "tender" of the people's "rights," and "we" are therefore "under every possible obligation to defend and support" the "person, crown and dignity" of the king. By reminding his auditors of the highly personal obligation of each subject to show loyalty to their sovereign, Hutchinson was inviting the members of the House to join him in the "we" who uphold the authority of the king against those in Boston and the other towns who had called it into question. By the second speech to the General Court, the governor went on the offensive with much more direct and sweeping attacks on Boston and the other towns who supported it. Of these developments Hutchinson writes, they "appeared to me to be so unwarrantable and of such a dangerous nature and tendency, that I thought myself bound to call upon you in my speech at opening the session, to join with me in discountenancing and bearing a proper testimony against such irregularities and innovations" (second speech to House and Council [the governor's rejoinder to the Council and House's reply to the governor's first speech], February 16, 1773; reported in *Boston Gazette*, February 22, 1773). By making this charge so explicit, the governor increased the stakes and the intensity of the political confrontation.

At the center of the governor's legal refutation of the declarations of the towns were two uncompromising arguments. First, against the idea that the British colonists left parliamentary sovereignty behind them in England when they crossed the Atlantic, and were instead granted a local assembly to *be* their parliament in America, Hutchinson recounted the many implicit and explicit ways in which British Parliament had continued to exercise legal sovereignty over Massachusetts. Second, and still more provocatively, against the Whig claim that, through its charter's "compact" with the Crown, the colonists carried all the ancient rights and liberties of Englishmen across the Atlantic, Hutchinson argued that though the "gift" of the royal charter had conferred certain rights and liberties, other rights once enjoyed in England, like the ability to vote for members of Parliament, must necessarily be abridged by the very fact of removal from the mother country.

This debate came to a conceptual and rhetorical climax in one exchange. In his first speech, Hutchinson declared that "I know of no Line that can be drawn between the supreme Authority of Parliament and the total Independence of the Colonies: It is impossible there should be two independent Legislatures in one and the same State, for although there may be but one Head, the King, yet the Legislative Bodies will make two Governments as distinct as the Kingdoms of England and Scotland before the Union" (*Briefs* 1981, 20). Here, Hutchinson is elaborating one of the truisms of eighteenth-century political theory, that since there can be no *imperium in imperio*, or as the *Votes and Proceedings* translated it, no "government within a government," true sovereignty must be indivisible. Since the American Whig notion of "one head" with two "legislative bodies" is a monstrosity, the colonies had either to accept the "supreme authority of Parliament" or to claim "total independence." In reply, the House fashioned a canny rejoinder. First, the members seem to have accepted the constraints of Hutchinson's choice.

If there be no such Line, the Consequence is, either that the Colonies are the Vassals of the Parliament, or, that they are totally Independent. As it cannot be supposed to have been the Intention of the Parties in the Compact, that we should be reduced to a State of Vassallage, the Conclusion is, that it was their Sense, that we were thus Independent ... [and] may it please your Excellency; and if they interfere not with each other, what hinders but that being united in one Head and common Sovereign, [the colony and the mother country] may live happily in that Connection, and mutually support and protect each other? (71–72)

Building on Hutchinson's loaded choice between accepting parliamentary supremacy and "total independence," the House replies that within the governor's own logic, they could avoid being vassals only if they were in fact "independent." Using his historical example, they could coexist the way England and Scotland had before the Union (1707), with two political bodies, "united in one head and common sovereign."

But, rather than leaving things there, the House went one important step further. The House members picked up the crayon to draw lines that the governor's constitutional analysis had declared impossible to draw. Conceding the difficulty of this constitutional project, the House proceeded to imagine a new body that might garner the power to draw new lines in the constitution. "If your Excellency expects to have the Line of Distinction between the Supreme Authority of Parliament, and the total Independence of the Colonies drawn by us, we would say it would be an arduous Undertaking; and of very great importance to all the other Colonies: and therefore, could we conceive of such a Line, we should be unwilling to propose it, without their Consent in Congress" (72). While the House continued, with a certain coy modesty, to refrain from the "arduous undertaking" of drawing the line between parliamentary supremacy and independence, to draw it would require the power that could only come from mutual "consent"; and that could only be achieved through a general "congress" of the colonies.

One purpose of Hutchinson's opening speech to the General Court was to draw out the radical implications of the theories being advanced by the Massachusetts Whigs. He succeeded in doing so. By using words like "total independence," he drew a line that he was daring his opponents to cross. When they proceeded to cross that line, or to "conceive" of ways in which lines could be entirely redrawn, by calling a general congress of the colonies, the debate then carried Whigs and Tories closer to another kind of line—the line of battle. Whig readers widely admired the House's clever way of turning Hutchinson's words and concepts against him (Arthur Lee to Samuel Adams, June 11, 1773; Lee 1829, 1:229). However, when administrators in Whitehall read the responses of the Council and House in the *Public Advertiser*, they saw the debate in a very different light than Hutchinson intended. A wise administrator should know the difference between what *could* be said, based on the law and logic of a case, and what *should* be left unsaid, based upon prudent forethought about the effects of saying it. When royal officials in Whitehall read the replies of the Council and the House, they were appalled to find a de facto declaration of independence. In a conversation on March 5, 1773, Lord Dartmouth expressed his distress to Benjamin Franklin in terms that foregrounded the way the House's very public performance would now oblige Parliament to act: "It is impossible that Parliament can suffer such a Declaration of the General Assembly (asserting its Independency) to pass unnoticed" (Franklin to Cushing, May 6, 1773, referencing a discussion of May 5; Franklin 1976, 20:200–201). Upon his arrival in London in early July 1774, Hutchinson questioned Lord North on the severity of Parliament's modification of the Massachusetts Charter in the Massachusetts Government Act (1774), and why it had been passed without granting the colony the chance to defend its behavior. Lord North replied that "the behavior of the Council and House," "upon the Declaration of Independence" in their debate with the governor, already fully justified Parliament's reform of Massachusetts government (Hutchinson 1971, 1:181).

There is a double irony in Hutchinson's brave attempt to stem the tide against royal authority in Massachusetts. The first irony: by convening the General Court and taking up the issue of parliamentary supremacy, Hutchinson had done precisely what the leaders of the Boston Town Meeting had sought to achieve through the petition that they had carried to Province House on October 31, 1772: engage in a public airing of the constitutional underpinnings of royal policies like the direct payment of judges. A second irony: as we have noted, in letters on January 7, 1773, Hutchinson told of a "dangerous plan" to spread the false political doctrine of the colonies' independence of parliamentary authority from Boston to the other towns, to the House of Representatives, and finally to all the other colonial assemblies. To forestall such a "plan," the governor convened the General Court and gave his speech. Ironically, the two-months-long debate helped to bring about the result he hoped to avert. The Council and House publicly declared their broad agreement upon all fundamental political principles with the Boston committee and the other towns. When the Speaker of the House received a letter from the Speaker of the Virginia House of Burgesses announcing the formation of their committee of correspondence, and proposing regular communication, the House readily agreed.

This episode suggests the political perils of *clarifying* relations of power. On January 6, 1773, Hutchinson began his attack on the Boston committee by accusing it of making a covert thought all too public: "[T]he authority of the Parliament . . . has been, by many, denied. What was, at first, whispered with Caution, was soon after openly asserted in Print . . . and [after] having assumed the Name of legal Town Meetings . . . [it was] passed as Resolves, . . . placed upon their Town Records, . . . and printed & published in Pamphlets and News-papers" (*Briefs* 1981, 17). To counter the pernicious effects of this publicity, Hutchinson's speech imitated the analytical clarity, the candor, and the publicity of these declarations. In other words, he aimed to correct a seditious clarity and openness by stating, openly and clearly, the constituents of the "true constitution." To the public glare of false thinking, he would bring the light of reason.[12] But Governor Hutchinson's superiors in Whitehall quickly came to the conclusion that Hutchinson had forfeited the advantage to administration of preserving some ambiguity about the nature of parliamentary authority. Dartmouth acknowledged to Hutchinson that the latter's arguments may have been "justified in the intention," but "how far it was or was not expedient to enter so fully in your speech into an exposition of your own opinion in respect to the principles of the constitution in the colony I am not able to judge" (March 3, 1773; *Documents* 1974, 95). Hutchinson correctly understood this tepid support as a rebuke. Lord Dartmouth's alarm led him to initiate a private back-channel correspondence with the House Speaker, Thomas Cushing Jr., hoping that he could convince the Massachusetts House to rescind its part in the debate with Governor Hutchinson. But, as Benjamin Franklin wryly commented to Lord Dartmouth, the House "cannot withdraw their Answers till [Governor Hutchinson] first withdraws his Speech; which methinks would

12. After Thomas Hutchinson moved into exile in England in the summer of 1774, he found that his debate with the Council and House was widely known and widely admired by the British political elite. Thus, on July 29, 1774, at Pope's Grotto at Twickenham, now owned by Mr. Welbore Ellis, Hutchinson offers this account of the conversation: "They all agreed that the whole indivisible supream authority [of Parliament] never could be parted with. 'Mr. Hutchinson' says Lord Beauchamp, 'the controversy with your Assembly has set that point in so clear, so convincing a light, that it never will be denied again. We used to have it in all debates thrown in our way, but not one word was said against it in either House of Parliament during the whole business of the Colonies last session'" (Hutchinson 1971, 1:198).

be an awkward Operation" (Franklin 1976, 20:201). Like the partners in a failing relationship, each side feels the burden of words that have been mercilessly explicit, are too well remembered, and are irretrievable.

Event 2: Franklin's Leaks; or, The Hutchinson Letters Affair

Over the course of the American crisis, two streams of correspondence linked Massachusetts and the centers of imperial power in Whitehall and Westminster. The first, the administrative correspondence, consisted in the periodic, official two-way correspondence between the American secretary in Whitehall and the governors (and other royal officials of British America), which were copied into large folio logs and constituted part of the official record. In addition, there was also a second robust private correspondence upon public matters between royal officials in America and their friends, patrons, or would-be patrons in Britain. It is from this second, private, unofficial correspondence upon official matters that the packet of eighteen letters at the center of the Hutchinson letters scandal came. They were selected from a larger body of letters written to Sir Thomas Whately, member of Parliament, coauthor of the Stamp Act, secretary to the former prime minister, George Grenville, and, at the time the letters were sent to him (1767–1769), a de facto leader of the opposition in Parliament.[13] Alongside these two streams of correspondence among royal officials there was another official transatlantic communication link, the correspondence between colonial legislatures and their agents. In 1772–1773, the most important correspondence linking the Massachusetts Whigs to London was the official communication between two highly trusted and influential Whigs: Benjamin Franklin, the agent for the House of Representatives, and Thomas Cushing Jr., Speaker of the House. The Hutchinson letters affair happened when royal and Whig communication channels crossed: the content of unofficial royal communications from America to Britain was sent back to America within the Franklin-Cushing Whig communications channel, and then publicized.

This packet of eighteen letters became incendiary when touched by hands and read by eyes for which they were not intended, thereby shifting them out of private reading spaces and into public ones (see fig. 2.4). From their original home in the collected correspondence of Sir Thomas Whately, "a Gentleman

13. The correspondence of royal officials, sometimes even private letters, was sometimes used in redacted form by the ministry in Whitehall and the Board of Trade to write memos justifying changes in policy, for example, in the wake of the Boston Massacre or the Tea Party.

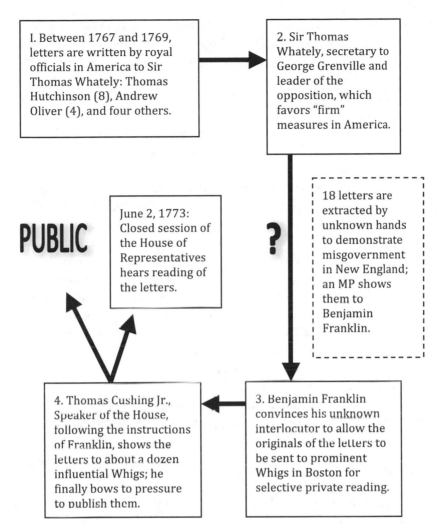

I. Between 1767 and 1769, letters are written by royal officials in America to Sir Thomas Whately: Thomas Hutchinson (8), Andrew Oliver (4), and four others.

2. Sir Thomas Whately, secretary to George Grenville and leader of the opposition, which favors "firm" measures in America.

PUBLIC

June 2, 1773: Closed session of the House of Representatives hears reading of the letters.

?

18 letters are extracted by unknown hands to demonstrate misgovernment in New England; an MP shows them to Benjamin Franklin.

4. Thomas Cushing Jr., Speaker of the House, following the instructions of Franklin, shows the letters to about a dozen influential Whigs; he finally bows to pressure to publish them.

3. Benjamin Franklin convinces his unknown interlocutor to allow the originals of the letters to be sent to prominent Whigs in Boston for selective private reading.

FIGURE 2.4. The circulation of "Copies of Letters Sent to Great Britain by His Excellency Thomas Hutchinson, the Hon. Andrew Oliver . . ."

of Character and Distinction" selected letters that demonstrated the state of misgovernment in New England, and the need for "firm" measures. The packet of letters circulated among officials in Whitehall and Westminster, until it came into the hands of a member of Parliament, who had strong Whig sympathies and was in conversation with Benjamin Franklin on the sources of the antagonism between the mother country and her American colonies. That member of Parliament may have been Thomas Pownall Jr., the former governor of Massachusetts, and the stalwart defender of the colonies in his speeches in Parliament (Franklin 1974, 20:419, "Tract"). Within this conversation, the letters were used by their purveyor to convince Franklin of the active role of American royal officials in promulgating harsh measures, like the deployment of British troops in Boston. At the urging of Franklin, the holder of the letters permitted Franklin to send the packet of originals to the Speaker of the House, Thomas Cushing, so that, through a strictly limited disclosure of these private letters, Whig leaders in Boston would shift their resentments from the British ministry in Whitehall to the Tory leadership in Massachusetts.

By sending this packet of letters to Massachusetts, Benjamin Franklin hoped to engineer a salutary shift in attitude. Instead he ended up demonstrating the unpredictable effects of publicizing sensitive political information through three features of this dubious act of transmission. First, Franklin understood his delivery of the letter packet as fully consistent with his balanced and moderate Whig pro-empire, pro-American position. Franklin insisted that in sending the private letters to Massachusetts, he sought to restore rather than undermine the loyalty of the Massachusetts Whigs to imperial administration in Whitehall. Second, against his explicit instructions, Massachusetts Whigs made the letters public, and against his expectations, they produced an uncontrolled fury against both the governor and his superiors in Whitehall. Finally, after he publicly acknowledged his central role in the affair, the deputy postmaster general of the North American colonies was exposed as a violator of the secrecy of the mails.[14] After the public humiliation adminis-

14. Even after the letters were published, they continued to enmesh Franklin in a variety of unpleasant consequences. After their publication in London, William Whately, the brother of the dead Sir Thomas Whately, publicly accused Commissioner John Temple of stealing them, and Temple defended himself in the newspapers. Only after William Whately had been injured in an interrupted duel, and the parties were threatening to fight again, did Franklin go public to announce, "I alone am the person who obtained and transmitted to Boston the letters in question." In this public notice, published on Christmas day 1773 in the *London Chronicle*, Franklin vindicated himself by insisting upon the public rather than private character of these letters: "They were not of the nature of *'private letters between friends'*: They were written by public officers to persons in public station, on public affairs, and intended to procure public measures" (Franklin 1974, 20:515). Franklin defended his release of information the way most leaks of classified government documents have been justified ever since: if public measures are being conducted in secret to the public's disadvantage, the exposure of secret communications may, by destroying public trust in public officials, serve the public interest.

tered by Solicitor General Alexander Wedderburn at an open meeting of the Privy Council, Franklin was summarily fired.

The letter packet that Franklin sent to Speaker Cushing was a politically fraught time capsule with the power to give the public a disconcerting new view of the mind of their governor. The context into which Benjamin Franklin sent the letter packet made a controlled private reading by a carefully selected group of Whig leaders implausible. Events had brought Massachusetts politics to a boil, and the arrival of the letters only increased the temperature. Once the letters were published and read, they served to *unmask* the two most important royal officials in the province, Thomas Hutchinson and Andrew Oliver. That is the metaphor that the Reverend Samuel Cooper used to describe the effect of the publication of the letters: "They have had great Effect: they make deep Impressions wherever they are known. They strip the Mask from the Authors who under the Profession of Friendship to their Country have been endeavoring to build up themselves and their Families upon it's Ruins" (Samuel Cooper to Benjamin Franklin, June 14, 1773; Franklin 1974, 20:234). Suddenly one of their own, Thomas Hutchinson, appeared actively complicit with the years of British oppression. No part of any of the eighteen letters caused more dispute, and proved more damaging to Thomas Hutchinson, than one ambiguous sentence that touched upon the core value of Anglo-American political culture, liberty. "I never think of the measures necessary for the peace and good order of the colonies without pain. *There must be an abridgment of what are called English liberties.* . . . I doubt whether it is possible to project a system of government in which a colony 3000 miles distant from the parent state shall enjoy all the liberty of the parent state" (January 20, 1769, Boston 1773, 16; emphasis mine). For Tories, these sentences were entirely consistent with the speech of January 6, 1773, and they evidenced the governor's commendable candor about the geographical imperative that required, if the colonies were to be governable by Britain, some abridgment of "English liberties." Tories emphasized Hutchinson's practical though reluctant conclusion that distance required such an abridgment. Whigs shifted their attention from Hutchinson's self-proclaimed "pain" to his advocacy of an imperial policy that would entail an "abridgment" of the "English liberties" of his fellow countrymen.

In the wake of the publication of the letters, it must have been difficult for Thomas Hutchinson to make eye contact with some of his lifelong acquaintances as he passed them on Cornwall or King Street. Governor Hutchinson's letters to Whitehall in the weeks after the publication of his old letters confirm a catastrophic decline in his influence. In his first letter to Lord Dartmouth, Hutchinson vigorously rejects the effort by Whigs to use the letters "to inflame the minds of the people and to cause them to believe the letters to be highly criminal." At the same time, he concedes that it would have been difficult to prorogue the House while it was working against him, because "if I had put an end to the session the construction would have been that I was conscious of my guilt." Hutchinson asks for a leave of absence from his post for nine or twelve months, so he can come over to England, either to protect his "reputation and character," should that be necessary, or to take care of his "private affairs" (Hutchinson to Lord Dartmouth, June 26, 1773; *Documents* 1974, 6:165). But in his letter to Lord Dartmouth of July 2, 1773, the General Court had been prorogued, a petition for his removal had passed, and Hutchinson sounds chastened and defensive. He enters into the details of the charges against him—of reviving the dispute about parliamentary supremacy, of secretly promoting reform of the Massachusetts charter—and refutes them. But in a private letter written the next day to the secretary of the Board of the Trade, John Pownall, Hutchinson acknowledges the effectiveness of the effort by House and Council to undermine his position: "It is immaterial to both whether their resolves are true or not: they carry weight with them among the people, . . . every attempt by me to support government will meet with much greater opposition than it ever has done or than it will do from anybody else." Like a cancer patient unable to control the affliction that has overtaken him, Hutchinson is resigned to the loss of his personal authority to govern. Of this long struggle against the "popular party" in Massachusetts, he writes: "I have withstood them as long as I could but I am now left without any support in the province." He only hopes that "whenever it shall be thought proper to supersede [him]" that he receives "some appointment not dishonorary" (Hutchinson to John Pownall, July 3, 1773; *Documents* 1974, 6:180–81).

After the cataclysm of the publication of his correspondence, Thomas Hutchinson proved to be a keen critic and observer of the new power that had risen to overtake him: the committee. In a letter to Lord Dartmouth of July 1, 1773, Hutchinson offers a brief survey of what might be called the "rise of the committee."

We have now subsisting in this province committees of correspondence in most of the towns of the province, committees of the House and Council to correspond with their respective agents to effect the removal of the governor and lieut.-governor and for other purposes, a committee of correspondence of the House to concert, with committees of other Assemblies, measures and to give information etc. The persons who have been most active in promoting the principles of independency are members of one or more of these committees, act without any control, and make themselves of great importance among the people. (July 10, 1773; *Documents* 1974, 6:183)

The activity and apparent staying power of these committees prepares his reader for Hutchinson's remarkable conclusion of the letter, a clear statement of his sense of the shift of power in the province: "There is no interior power within this government from which a proper remedy can be had." In other words, Whitehall must devise outside power to bring to bear upon the province. However, Hutchinson warns that a mere royal declaration will not do.

Event 3: The New Ratio of Power Is Proven in the Disposition of the Tea

Because the relative power of political agents is abstract and immaterial, power is proven in the event. So once the first of the tea ships, the *Dartmouth*, sailed into Boston Harbor late on Saturday, November 27, 1773, a struggle began between royal officials, who were determined to unload the tea consistent with English law, and Whigs, who were equally determined to prevent it. This struggle would issue, as every American schoolchild knows, in the destruction of the tea on the night of December 16, 1773. But how did the Whigs prevail in this contest? What became crucial was the ratio of forces on the ground and what each side could *do* to make the other side comply with its will. Only a rather detailed account of the interplay of forces on the ground will allow us to understand how events led British Whigs to an act that authorities would finally view as a step too far.

Historians have described the chain of circumstances that precipitated this crisis and prepared the ground for this face-off in Boston. On one hand, since Parliament did not anticipate the resistance that the Tea Act would incite, it is sometimes said that Parliament "stumbled" into the tea crisis. On the other hand, in designing the Tea Act, the North administration intentionally affirmed Parliament's right to tax the colonists by keeping a three-penny-per-pound tax on tea. The motive of the legislation was less to tax the colonists than to bail out the East India Company, whose London warehouses were filled with unsold tea and which had recently caused widespread financial distress by threatening to suspend its dividend (Labaree 1979a, 62). Once the special terms of the bill, with its appointment of tea consignees and the increased British control of colonial trade it portended, became known, fierce resistance developed in the four large trading centers to which the tea was making its cross-Atlantic voyage. Resistance in New York (which began at a merchants' meeting at the Coffee House on October 15, 1773) and in Philadelphia (which featured a mass meeting at the State House on October 16, 1773) led to the tea consignees of those towns resigning their commissions in November and December. By December 3, 1773, the same would happen in Charleston, South Carolina. News of New York's and Philadelphia's resistance to the tea reached Boston by early November, and Boston found itself in the unfamiliar position of playing "catch-up" in formulating resistance to British measures offensive to American liberty. On November 5, 1773, the Boston Town Meeting adopted Philadelphia's eight resolves opposing the East India Company tea.

At the moment of the arrival of the first of the tea ships, the *Dartmouth*, on November 27, 1773, Tories and Whigs enjoyed complementary strengths and weaknesses. Because of political reverses, Governor Hutchinson was more determined than ever to enforce the Tea Act in Massachusetts. Although Boston Whigs tried to intimidate them into resigning their commissions, all five of the tea consignees of Boston, who included two of the governor's sons, refused to do so. Instead the consignees petitioned the Council for support. Although the Council refused to take steps to protect the tea consignees from popular intimidation, when the crisis intensified, the tea consignees fled to the safety of Castle William, where they rode out the crisis under protection from Lieutenant Colonel Leslie's regiment. By the beginning of December, Governor Hutchinson was confident that the legal situation meant that time was on his side. Since customs law required that the tea be landed within twenty days after it had gone through customs, the tea would have to be landed by December 17, 1773. The governor ordered Admiral Montagu, the commander of the naval ships in Boston Harbor, to position navy ships to prevent the tea ships from leaving the harbor with their tea. However, there were also weaknesses in the governor's position. Governor Hutchinson had decided that he could not use military means to force the landing of the tea, either by using marines stationed on navy ships or Leslie's regiment on Castle William, because of what he had learned on March 6, 1770 (Hutchinson 1936, 3:313; Labaree 1979a, 147). In addition, by leaving Boston for the calm and relative security of his suburban estate in Milton, Hutchinson escaped physical coercion, but he also lost moment-to-moment contact with the flow of events on the streets of Boston.

The Whigs worked with a different set of weaknesses and strengths. They had no way to force the tea ships to leave Boston Harbor. Through urgent demands directed at shipowners and, after their arrival, ship captains, Boston Whigs were able to convince owners and captains to bring their ships "below" the castle (and its potent batteries) and dock their ships at Griffin's wharf for the unloading of all their cargo, excepting tea. This move gave them physical control of the tea. Owners and captains of the three ships also promised not to unload the tea, unless forced to do so by proper authorities "for their own security" (December 16, 1773; Boston 1883, 10–17). The balance of Tory and Whig power led to the impasse that held from November 29 to December 16: the tea was not landed, but the three tea ships holding the 340 chests of tea—the *Dartmouth* (owner Francis Rotch), the *Eleanor* (owner John Rowe), and the *Beaver* (part-owner Francis Rotch)—were not allowed to return to London. Since the Whigs had the power to prevent the tea from being landed and the Tories had the power to prevent its being shipped back to England, the Whigs developed a witty but brutal alternative: throwing the tea into Boston Harbor.[15] When two to three hundred Whigs went on board the ships disguised as "Mohawks" and threw the contents of 340 large chests of tea into Boston Harbor, they encountered no resistance from the military ships anchored nearby. Naval officers had been given no orders for responding to this contingency, so they didn't. The Whig solution to the impasse surprised local Tories, delighted most of the inhabitants of the towns, and shocked officials in Whitehall (Labaree 1979a, 152). It could only be ventured because the ratio of power in Boston Harbor permitted it.

The Whig resistance to the tea in Boston was more rather than less effective because it was led by distributed but interconnected agencies with overlapping membership: the "sons of liberty" (November 2–4), the town meeting (November 5–8), the selectmen of the town meeting (November 28–29), and the various clubs that seem to have played a key role in organizing the destruction of the tea (December 16). The agency that gave the resistance to the tea coherence, continuity, and geographic reach was the Boston Committee of Correspondence. It sent out two broadsides to the towns, on November 23 (stating the determination of Boston Whigs not to allow the landing of the tea) and on December 1 (containing news of the arrival of the *Dartmouth*, the proceedings of the town meetings of November 5 and 18, and "the meeting of the people" of November 29–30). In response to these communications, the Boston committee received letters from eighty towns about tea, twenty of them towns that had not previously written the Boston committee. The Boston committee also initiated communication with New York, Philadelphia, Portsmouth (NH), and Bristol, Newport, and Providence (RI). But the most consequential initiative was the joint meeting that the Boston committee called and led on the afternoon of Monday, November 22, at Faneuil Hall with the committees of

15. In his February 19, 1774, testimony before the Privy Council about Boston's huge meeting of November 29, Captain James Hall reported "that Dr. Young said the only way to get rid of the tea was to throw it overboard and destroy it" (*Documents* 1975, 8:53).

correspondence of four neighboring towns: Roxbury, Dorchester, Brookline, and Cambridge (Brown 1970, 159). This committee of committees laid the groundwork for taking immediate action once the tea arrived. When news of the arrival of the first tea ship was received on Sunday, November 28, the Boston committee wrote the other four towns so that they could alert a large number of inhabitants for their respective towns to appear on Monday morning of November 29 for a meeting of what was often called "the body of the people." It was this huge meeting of five thousand, with inhabitants of five neighboring towns, which met over two days and developed the framework for a successful resistance to the landing of the tea. When the meeting of November 29–30 dissolved itself, it assigned the Boston committee the task of assuring that the measures applied to guard the *Dartmouth* were extended to the next tea ships that arrived (Boston 1883, 20:14; Carp 2010, 108–40).

Governor Thomas Hutchinson had long deplored the latitude that the Boston Town Meeting had claimed to intervene in questions of imperial administration. So the sudden calling of a general meeting of "the body of the people" in response to the arrival of the *Dartmouth* must have appeared to the governor as a particularly blatant method of extending the authority of the town meeting. A meeting notice, posted around the town and published in the *Boston Gazette* on Monday, November 29, 1773, urged the populace to attend an extraordinary meeting. Just as eighteenth-century ships often had to be quarantined because they carried the much dreaded smallpox, so this notice informed inhabitants of the town that the *Dartmouth* carries an "article"—the "detested," "pernicious" "TEA"—which, by threatening the town's political life, is "that worst of plagues." Note the twofold simplification worked by this summons. Instead of mentioning any of the profusion of agents or abstractions that might have been associated with the East India Company tea—Parliament, the Tea Act, the rights of the colonies, or taxation—the notice confers upon the "machinations of tyranny" the physical facticity of an invading commodity. The notice also insists, with the indexical word *this*, that upon "THIS DAY" a moment of crisis, of uncertainty, an accelerated temporality has arrived. This *this* opens a moment for action: when the bells sound through the town at nine o'clock, all are called to come, meet, and act together to forestall this dreadful visitation.

Crowds gather power and enhance their legitimacy through the numbers that they gather. The word *body* in the phrase "the body of the people" had a precise eighteenth-century sense: the "body" means the "trunk" rather than an extremity, the "main" rather than periphery, the "principal" rather than a secondary part; and thus, most simply, it means the "majority" of the people

(*OED*). By summoning a huge meeting of "the body of the people," the Whigs of Boston delivered an implicit threat to shipowners, captains, and tea consignees: noncooperation with the body of the people would be problematic for those seeking to do business in Boston. In addition, the meeting acted directly by appointing twenty-five men to go on board the *Dartmouth* and serve as a night watch over her cargo. (This group included Paul Revere and the printer of the *Boston Gazette*, Benjamin Edes.)

At his estate in Milton, the governor learned of the meeting, and "seeing the powers of government thus taken out of the hands of the legally established authority," sent the sheriff of Suffolk County to the meeting on November 30 (Hutchinson 1936, 3:309; see fig. 2.5). The governor objected to the meeting on the grounds that (1) while it observed some of the conventions of a legal town meeting (selected a moderator; the Boston town clerk, William Cooper, kept minutes; it sought to "consult, debate, and resolve"; it adjourned and reconvened the meeting); (2) it violated the proper procedures of the town meeting (no advance warning through a legal warrant; it was not limited to voting freeholders of the town; the meeting of the body of the people allowed inhabitants of many nearby towns to participate). For this reason, the governor leveled his strongest charge against the meeting: it was "openly violating, defying and setting at naught the good and wholesome laws of the province, and the constitution of government under which they live." So the governor commissioned Sheriff Greenleaf to go to the meeting and read the governor's proclamation, one that is consistent with the Riot Act of 1715. In its operative clause, the governor proclaims: "I warn, exhort and require you and each of you thus unlawfully assembled forthwith to disperse and to surcease all further unlawful proceedings at your utmost peril." This language echoes the verbal formula of the Riot Act, which "commandeth all persons, being assembled, immediately to disperse"; and the act specifies the "peril" of which the governor warns: that those who "continue together for an hour after such proclamation shall be guilty of a felony," punishable by death.[16]

In his later *History*, Thomas Hutchinson acknowledged that in sending the proclamation "he knew he could say nothing which would check the usurpers" (1936, 309). Why did the governor lack the power to enforce his order to disperse? In a letter written two days later on December 2, 1773, to the American secretary, Lord Dartmouth, Hutchinson described the various attempts to

16. For a discussion of the social ambiguity around the value of riots, which were seen as an expression of both natural exuberance and social breakdown, see Ronald Paulson, *The Art of the Riot*. For a discussion of the Riot Act of 1715, see Paulson 2010, 5.

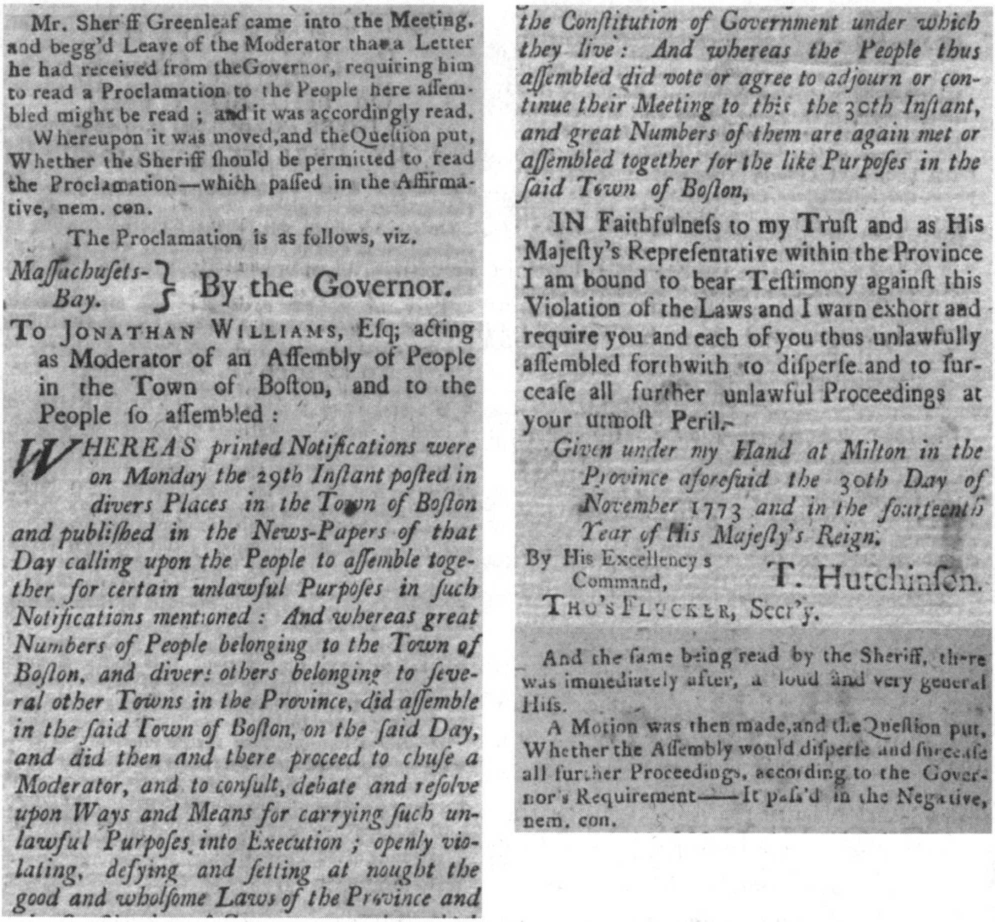

Mr. Sheriff Greenleaf came into the Meeting, and begg'd Leave of the Moderator that a Letter he had received from the Governor, requiring him to read a Proclamation to the People here assembled might be read ; and it was accordingly read.

Whereupon it was moved, and the Question put, Whether the Sheriff should be permitted to read the Proclamation—which passed in the Affirmative, nem. con.

The Proclamation is as follows, viz.

Massachusets-Bay. } By the Governor.

To JONATHAN WILLIAMS, Esq; acting as Moderator of an Assembly of People in the Town of Boston, and to the People so assembled :

WHEREAS printed Notifications were on Monday the 29th Instant posted in divers Places in the Town of Boston and published in the News-Papers of that Day calling upon the People to assemble together for certain unlawful Purposes in such Notifications mentioned : And whereas great Numbers of People belonging to the Town of Boston, and divers others belonging to several other Towns in the Province, did assemble in the said Town of Boston, on the said Day, and did then and there proceed to chuse a Moderator, and to consult, debate and resolve upon Ways and Means for carrying such unlawful Purposes into Execution ; openly violating, defying and setting at nought the good and wholsome Laws of the Province and

the Constitution of Government under which they live : And whereas the People thus assembled did vote or agree to adjourn or continue their Meeting to this the 30th Instant, and great Numbers of them are again met or assembled together for the like Purposes in the said Town of Boston,

IN Faithfulness to my Trust and as His Majesty's Representative within the Province I am bound to bear Testimony against this Violation of the Laws and I warn exhort and require you and each of you thus unlawfully assembled forthwith to disperse and to surcease all further unlawful Proceedings at your utmost Peril.

Given under my Hand at Milton in the Province aforesaid the 30th Day of November 1773 and in the fourteenth Year of His Majesty's Reign.

By His Excellency's
  Command,   T. Hutchinson.
THO'S FLUCKER, Secr'y.

And the same being read by the Sheriff, there was immediately after, a loud and very general Hiss.

A Motion was then made, and the Question put, Whether the Assembly would disperse and surcease all further Proceedings, according to the Governor's Requirement——It pass'd in the Negative, nem. con.

FIGURE 2.5. Riot Act: the governor's proclamation to disperse a meeting to protest the tea is read at Old South Church on November 30, 1773, by Sheriff Greenleaf. It was greeted with a hiss and then put to a vote; "it passed in the negative, *nemine contradicente*" (*Boston Gazette*, December 6, 1773). Photograph courtesy of the American Antiquarian Society.

intimidate the tea consignees and applauded their as yet successful resistance. He also described his response to the illegal meeting:

29th last, on which day I went early to town and met the Council who declined advising to any measure respecting this unlawful assembly in particular, and I had nothing left but in my name only to require them to disperse; and the next morning I sent the sheriff to the assembly with a declaration against their proceedings. I am sensible the proper way would have been for the justices to have required the sheriff to raise the posse and disperse them, but no justice dared to do it and no other posse except the meeting itself would have appeared. As they have printed these proceedings one of the copies shall be enclosed. (*Documents* 1974, 6:249)

This letter no doubt made very interesting reading in Whitehall. It must have seemed astonishing that a legally binding proclamation of His Majesty's royal governor, cast according to the formula of the Riot Act, could be translated by the meeting into a resolution, put before "the body of the people," and unanimously voted down, "*nem. con.*" By the implication of the governor's own account, his invocation of the Riot Act was addressed not so much to the meeting, where he knew it would fail, as to his superiors in Whitehall, where he might at least be seen as trying to sustain the forms of British law. Conversely, the confidence of the meeting of the body of the people was not only grounded in their unanimous opposition to the Tea Act. It also derived from their careful observation of the protocols of the declarations of the towns: legal procedure, corporate action, public access, and virtuous initiative. Seldom in the long political struggle leading to the Revolution had the face-off between royal power and "people power" been staged so baldly. The year that had begun so hopefully for the governor, with his energetic address opening the General Court, had modulated at midyear to painful disclosures, and ended with the people of Boston voting down his last futile effort to assert the royal prerogative.

THE POST AND NEWSPAPER

IN BRITISH AMERICA

A COMMUNICATION SYSTEM IN CRISIS

3

. . . .

In the opening chapters of this study, I described the many different agents that stoked the American crisis: town meetings and committees, "votes" and declarations, bodies, rhetoric and ideas. In this chapter I will consider the media-communication system of the British Empire, seeking to understand how it also functioned as a mediator of the American crisis. Because of the dispersed character of the British Empire, the circulation of information depended upon the royal post and the newspapers that it carried. Letters and newspapers were the medium for communicating, in a copious, timely, and periodic fashion, information that was vital to administration, to trade, and, in the 1770s, to the crisis that became revolution. This chapter considers the post and newspaper together because in eighteenth-century British America they had the coherent character of a system: their many parts (postal offices, deputies, riders, protocols, newspaper printers, presses, subscribers, and the open system of the colonial newspaper) contributed to a whole. As in all systems, these different parts "talked to each other." As we shall see in this chapter, the improving zeal of postal reformers and printers also imbued this communication system with many of the values and projects of Enlightenment, including the global expansion of commerce, religion, and empire; the correspondence of the learned within a "republic of letters"; and a more general diffusion of knowledge.[1] To study this system, this chapter reverses the perspective of chapter 1. Instead of tracing how an event like the formation of the Boston committee was represented through media, I shall describe the formal features of the royal post, the Anglophone newspapers, and the newspaper distributed by post, so we can understand the constraints imposed, as well as the opportunities opened, by that system for those who sought to bolster the coherence of empire and those who challenged it. In the second

1. For a more extended discussion of the integral relationship between Enlightenment and the history of media and mediation, see the introduction to Siskin and Warner 2010, 1–33.

half of this chapter, I will consider how, during the American crisis, a communication system that was first developed to support empire was repurposed to subvert it.

THE FORM AND DEVELOPMENT OF THE
EIGHTEENTH-CENTURY BRITISH POST

While the British public postal system took nearly a century to emerge from the state postal monopolies of the Tudor and Stuart monarchs, the century of continuous improvements to the eighteenth-century post effected as fundamental a mutation in communication practices as the Internet has in our own day. The postal system increased the speed, regularity, and geographic reach of communication. It required the development of new public infrastructure (the post office, the turnpike, transatlantic packet ships for the Royal Mail) and a uniform system of addresses (street names and eventually numbers); it encouraged the development of new genres of writing that were public (the weekly or daily newspaper, the critical journal) or private (familiar letters), new forms of literacy (letter writing, fast reading), new forms of entertainment (the novel), shifts in the rhythms of the day (letter writing before breakfast, solitary writing and reading, sharing responses to published books with correspondents), and, finally, new associations for the purpose of knowledge or politics (scientific corresponding societies, revolutionary committees of correspondence). With the emergence of the public post, the letter, considered as both a material object and a mode of writing, achieved its modern ubiquity. All of this allowed much wider public access to information of all kinds.

But what *is* the post? Here are five of the basic communication traits of the post. First, the post is a public (rather than private) system that is therefore open to all who can read and write, or can have those actions performed on their behalf. Second, it utilizes a uniform set of protocols so as to realize the postal principle, "the idea that people can communicate with one another by letter" (Siegert 1999, 5). Third, the post offers reliable, periodic delivery so that one can imagine sustaining two-way communication for an indefinite period. In this way, the post becomes a new matrix for long-distance human associations. Fourth, the post values dispatch or speed, by which it reduces social distance, but also enlarges the social field of potential actors. Fifth and finally, the post promotes the assumption that postal communication is (or can be) private, a privacy secured by the fold, the seal, or, after the eighteenth century, the envelope. This (presumptive) privacy makes writing a personal letter a privileged site—along with the intimate conversation and the diary—for thinking through and expressing *how one really feels.*[2]

By enlarging the geographic reach of correspondence, the post extends the power of writing. To do its work, the post coordinates a complex, heterogeneous network of humans, objects, and places linked together by a dense group of protocols. By protocols, I here refer to the generally accepted constraints that enable communication: address schemes, schedules, rate structures, administrative procedures, and proscriptions, for example, against the theft or invasion of the mails. To conceptualize how the post comingles materiality and immateriality, imagine the eighteenth-century postboy, riding at relatively high speed on a horse, traveling over a road or turnpike, carrying a pouch of letters and newspapers, each of which observes certain standard conventions of address and genre.

The post extends one of the central features of writing, communication at a distance. While the privacy of the post encourages one-to-one and one-to-few communication, by transmitting newspapers and broadsides, the post also enhances print's special power: to make things public by broadcasting to "all." Finally, considered within the long history of communications, there is a strong affiliation between the post and those later communication technologies that, by communicating by wire or air, cede their material and tactile connection with the sender. The telegraph, the telephone, and the Internet each have their distinct technical potentials and trajectory of institutionalization, but each also builds upon the five general features of the post as a public system, through which anyone may be openly addressed at periodic intervals with dispatch and privacy.

Postal histories describe the gradual, and often halting, institutionalization of the British-American postal service over the course of the "long" eighteenth century. These histories describe a metamorphosis of the post from a monopoly patent, sold by Tudor and Stuart sovereigns, to meet the essential communication needs of the state, into a service conducted to benefit the public. The landmark moments in this change in Britain were the official

2. Obviously this account of the post is normative and ideal. While it is the goal of the postal system to deliver the missive/message from sender to receiver, the functioning of the post in the actual world leads to every kind of communication failure: temporal delay, physical destruction of mail, address failures that land letters in the dead-letter office, mistaken delivery, and calculated interception and reading by someone other than the intended addressee (whether it is a prying friend or a prying state).

opening of the service to the public (1657–1660) and the breakthrough Act of IX Queen Anne (1710; see box 3.1). These made the postal service a branch of government with an explicit postal monopoly for carrying the mail. They instituted a general London post office, a postmaster general, deputy postmasters for the various towns, a surveyor of roads, and, finally, uniform rates throughout England, Scotland, Ireland, and the colonies. The great theme of postal histories is one of improvement, requiring financial investment and ingenious human effort. It took tireless reformers like Ralph Allen and Benjamin Franklin to discover and implement important additional operating principles of the postal system. Ralph Allen circumvented the star topology of the British postal network where the six main post roads radiated from London (Lewins 1864, 58) by developing secondary post roads (and sorting stations) for "cross letters," and thus shortening delivery distances by exploiting the elegant simplicity of the address protocol (name of addressee, building/street and number, town). Benjamin Franklin developed an intricately redundant record-keeping system to keep critical mediators of the post (the deputy postmasters and their riders) honest. All the postal reformers exploited economies of scale, whereby a decrease in the price for postage could increase numbers and general revenues and the improvement of speed and reliability discouraged potential competitors. Finally, the post required reconfiguring spaces and places so as to accommodate circulation and delivery. This was achieved through the improvement of roads designated as post roads, the standardization of street names, and the imposition of numbering to make each place addressable within the postal system. Retrospectively, all these practical improvements helped to realize what one might call the "systematicity" of the system. The steady institutionalization of the postal system over the course of the eighteenth century also involved a gradual shift of postal user, from selective use by members of the economic and social elite to a more frequent and widespread use by both elite and middling ranks of both sexes. In these changes, the postal system both reflects and promotes the changes we associate with modernity: the expansion of economic activity, literacy, political participation, and the achievement through letter writing of greater personal agency for people of middling social ranks.[3]

3. For a comprehensive study of the central place of letter writing in the expansion of the power of those in middling ranks, see Dierks 2009. Dierks surveys the pivotal role of letter writing in middle-class schemes of self-improvement, empire building, commercial expansion, and revolution.

BOX 3.1. THE GRADUAL EMERGENCE OF THE
BRITISH-AMERICAN POSTAL SYSTEM

Pre-1660: Tudor and Stuart monopoly patent provides postal service through postal stations (with fresh horses) for the delivery of state communications between Westminster and outlying towns of England.

1660 reform: The post becomes a legal public service.

1710: Queen Anne Postal Law
   General Post Office established in Whitehall.
   Appointment of a postmaster general (who is now a cabinet
      member) and deputy postmasters in outlying towns.
   Structure: six postal roads radiating from the London Post Office.
   Post office enjoys a monopoly on carrying of letters with legal
      exceptions (for letters accompanying goods in trade; for ship
      captains; for courts of justice; for travelers).
   Standard postal rates set (by weight and distance) for Great Britain,
      Ireland, and the colonies.

1720: Ralph Allen improvements
   Deputy postmaster in Bath: Ralph Allen wins a government patent
      to provide postal service off of the main post roads.
   Development of "cross posts" for sorting and transmitting "bye
      letters" overcomes the "star topology" of the original postal system.

Post-1760 reforms and 1765 Postal Bill
   Regular packet service between Falmouth, England, and New York,
      and then Charleston, South Carolina.
   30 percent decrease in rates for American colonies.

1753–1763: Franklin improvements
   1753: Surveying of roads and defining of new routes (April–
      November).
   1753: Instructions to deputy postmasters with printed spreadsheets
      for disciplined bookkeeping to keep riders and deputy postmaster
      honest.
   1758: Post becomes the de facto distribution system for delivery
      of newspapers; uniform rates are established (i.e., "network
      neutrality").

Box 3.1 continued

1763: Six-month tour to incorporate Canada and southern British America within system; other improvements (e.g., overnight [33-hour] delivery between Philadelphia and New York).

1773–1775: the Continental post replaces the royal post.
   November 1773–June 1774: Hugh Finlay makes "Survey of the Post Offices."
   Spring 1774: William Goddard proposes formation of a "Constitutional" post, to which most royal deputy postmasters move by May 1775.
   July 1775: Congressional committee on the post (first appointed May 29, 1775) reports its proposal and Congress votes to institute the Continental post; Benjamin Franklin is appointed postmaster general.
   December 27, 1775: the central post office of the royal post in New York closes.

THE CENTRAL FEATURES OF THE EIGHTEENTH-CENTURY ANGLOPHONE NEWSPAPER

In the years before the American Revolution, newspapers were not what liberal Whig histories would later try to make them: a forum for the "free" exchange of diverse opinions. Neither were newspapers what both sides in the Revolution, Tories and Whigs, wished they would become: an ideological beacon to guide and inform the people. Although newspapers accounted for 80 percent of the type set in British America, and demonstrated a remarkable facility for absorbing other print and manuscript genres (like the broadside, the oration, the pamphlet, the manuscript letter, and even book chapters), newspapers were also the ugly ducklings of eighteenth-century print media. Newspapers of the eighteenth century were quite variable in both form and content, and they were often held in dubious repute by readers who nonetheless became addicted to them. British newspapers like the *London Gazette* and the *London Chronicle*, as well as the collection of newspaper articles in the *Gentleman's Magazine*, circulated throughout British America, and the main cities and towns of North America had a steadily increasing number of their own newspapers.[4] Paradoxically, what may, from a modern prospective, look like weaknesses in the eighteenth-century newspaper, in fact, enabled it to become a robust and supple matrix for revolutionary communication. To understand this paradox, I will describe four features of the prerevolutionary newspapers.

A Diffuse Collection of Print with Dubious Authority

To the modern eye, colonial newspapers lack many of the elements that give newspapers coherence. There is no general reportorial perspective claiming to tell us "what's happening now," no editorial overvoice to tell us what it means, and no attempt to connect the items published to each other. In *The Public Prints: The Newspaper in Anglo-American Culture, 1665–1740*, Charles E. Clark describes the general rules that determined the layout of the earliest newspapers: the most remote (news from Constantinople and St. Petersburg) is placed before the less remote (London), and the earliest events come before the more recent. In this way, the eighteenth-century newspaper aspired to become a telegraphic, historical record of the time. But these ordering principles in the colonial newspapers were applied in an erratic fashion. Thus an advertisement for candles is placed on the front page of the *Pennsylvania Gazette* alongside "A dissertation on the laws of excise" (March 31, 1773). The same page might juxtapose a reward for an escaped indentured servant and the speech of George III opening Parliament. Letters, articles, ads, and grain prices are assembled in an additive, disconnected fashion and organized with such a weak principle of subordination that their rhetorical effect is paratactic. The reader is left to sift through a cacophony of different voices (often disguised with pseudonyms or veiled by anonymity). For those scanning the single-folio, four-page, three- or four-column newspaper that became standard in the later eighteenth century, coherence of perspective is latent, an effect of

---

4. Several factors made the prerevolutionary decades a time of expansion for newspapers: swift increases in general population between 1750 and 1770 (from one to more than two million, from one-twentieth to one-fifth of the population of the British Empire [Wood 2002, 6]); an "oversupply" of printer's apprentices in the principle cities (e.g., Boston, New York, Philadelphia) produced an outward migration to start newspapers; and the newsworthy quality of the political crisis itself helped to encourage a doubling of the number of newspapers between 1763 and 1776, and then doubling again between 1776 and 1790 (Clark 2000). Schlesinger (1958) reports forty-two newspapers on the eve of Revolution in thirteen colonies.

editorial bricolage and the reader's active discernment. In sum, one might say, eighteenth-century newspapers use the written record not so much to represent the world, but to assemble its written record.

Some of what was published in the eighteenth-century newspaper is of very dubious accuracy. Wanting precise and accurate information about the Crown commission investigating the Gaspée incident, Richard Henry Lee wrote Samuel Adams on February 4, 1773, despairing of ever having "a just account of this affair" "at this distance, and through the uncertain medium of the newspapers" (Lee 1911, 82). The *New York Gazette* reprinted from the *Edinburgh Evening Post* a satiric meditation on the unreliability of newspapers: "the four winds (the initials of which make the word NEWS) are not so capricious, or so liable to change, as our public intelligences" (August 4, 1783). No wonder, this observer concludes, the newspapers must qualify the truth value of their information with these convenient phrases: "we hear; they write; it is said; a correspondent remarks, with a long list of ifs and supposes." Several factors explain these limitations of the eighteenth-century newspapers, especially when compared with the newspapers of the nineteenth and twentieth centuries. As a nascent media institution, the eighteenth-century newspaper was usually published by a talented printer (rather than a formally educated editor) who did not write his own paper. Such a printer would have been too modestly situated to put his opinions before his readers in the authoritative tones attempted by the editors of the future. In an epoch before the professionalization of news gathering, the printer-editor had no correspondent or reporter to file authorized reports under his or her own name. Finally, the liabilities of the eighteenth-century newspaper resulted in part from the network for news exchange into which each paper was inserted. The content of each paper came from a selective reprinting from the tide of newspapers that came through the mails, from interviews with local sea captains and merchants recently arrived in port, and from official documents from the governor or the colonial assembly (Clark 1994, chapter 4). The canny editor sorted and selected articles for printing, guided by his own common sense, ideological inclinations, and ear for local interests. At the end of this cutting and pasting, many items were published anonymously, abridged, with the wording of the original usually transmitted intact, and with or without the date, place, or newspaper of origin. This often left the reader uncertain about the source or authenticity of the text. Because the newspaper lagged behind other print forms like the book in organizing responsible writing under the signature of the author, it has an especially erratic relationship to the modern demand for accountability.

Vitiated by the Problem of Distance

In spite of the various improvements to the postal system over the course of the eighteenth century, matter printed in London could take five to six weeks to travel to North America, and the fastest travel between the cities of coastal British America were as follows: two days (New York–Philadelphia), five to six days (Boston–New York), nine days (Boston–Williamsburg), twenty days (Boston–Charleston, SC).[5] Customary travel times were significantly longer, and publication lagged accordingly. Thus the usual interval for a reprinting in the *Virginia Gazette* (published by Purdie and Dixon) of a news item from the *Boston Gazette* was a month and one day. In short, those reading their newspapers at least seven decades before the advent of electronic communication understood that even the most "current" news had decayed during the substantial interval required to carry the report to the place where it could be read. These eighteenth-century readers were used to living on space-time islands that periodically received reports from other space-time islands, recording conditions that had already changed, sometimes in substantial ways. The effects of this temporal delay can be amusing and ironic. When contradictory news ricocheted around the empire, the response of newspaper printers seemed to be to treat their sources as printed texts to be passed on to their readers, even when these reports had a drastically different tendency. The printer of the *Providence Gazette*, John Carter, must have taken pleasure in juxtaposing a long report from General Burgoyne about his successful conquest of the great American fort at Ticonderoga (on July 11, but not made public in Whitehall until August 25), with an official notice that the Continental Congress had voted to have a gold medal struck to commemorate General Gate's victory over Burgoyne at Saratoga on October 17, 1777.

Independence and "Openness"

When he started the *Boston News-Letter* in 1704, John Campbell aspired to the official status of the *London Gazette* by using the words "published by authority" on his newspaper's masthead. However, Campbell's *News-Letter* was a commercial enterprise rather than a government-sponsored paper of record. Later in the century, several colonial newspapers explicitly asserted their independence with a telling expression: "open to all parties, but influenced by

5. See Fischer 1994, appendix S, 324–25: "Spread of the news of the first shots at Lexington." The commencement of military hostilities, which justified the use of express riders to spread the news at maximum speed, offers a profile of the fastest time of American communication in 1775.

none." (This identical language is used in the prerevolutionary period by Isaiah Thomas's *Massachusetts Spy* [Boston], the *Connecticut Current* [Hartford], and, with a slight variation in language, Rind's *Virginia Gazette* [Williamsburg].) A paper run on an "open" system asserts a brave independence from "influence" and contempt for the narrowness of faction. The printer offers the paper as a public vehicle for communication, "open" to print ads and opinion of a broad spectrum of the town. A newspaper was seen by some as open and public in much the same way that stagecoaches or public houses of the period were. As James Green has pointed out in his account of Franklin's strategy with the *Pennsylvania Gazette*, this strategy was both commercial and political.[6] If a printer was explicitly partisan, opponents would not run ads in the paper or bring other print business to the printer. In the relatively small commercial towns of British America, this loss of business could close down a paper. An open, nonpartisan newspaper also discourages the launching of competing papers. Even in times when papers began to function as explicitly political agents—as when Draper's Tory *News-Letter* of Boston refuted the accounts of the meeting of the town of Boston offered in Edes and Gill's *Boston Gazette*, and Trenchard and Gordon had replaced Addison as models for journalistic writing—both Boston papers published documents and opinion pieces from each side of the Whig and Tory divide. All papers, however explicit and obvious their political commitments, sought to appeal to the whole public.

One News Commons Facilitating Free Exchange

Several factors helped forge the eighteenth-century post and newspapers into a news commons that resembled, in certain ways, the news services set up by Reuters and Associated Press (AP) in the nineteenth century. First, the transportation infrastructure was improving. A reformed postal system made the system of packet ships, stagecoaches, and postal couriers a slow, but increasingly effective, system for transporting newspapers. The practice of the free mailing (or "franking") of copies of American newspapers among all the printers in the colonies continued into this period and greatly facilitated the free borrowing of print items among the papers of the empire. The close ties between master printers and their former apprentices created close networks of affiliation, most notably among those descended from Samuel Green (of Boston) and trained by Benjamin Franklin (Schlesinger 1958, 57). When he

6. Also see Clark 2000, 255–57. For a more ample discussion of the development of the free and "open" press in America, and the stresses it faced during the Revolution, see Botein 1975, 1980.

became deputy postmaster general for the northern half of the American colonies, Benjamin Franklin decided that it was proper to open the mails equally to all newspapers (this policy is discussed below in more detail). Second, there was no functioning system of copyright for materials first printed in a newspaper equivalent to that provided for books published in England. For this reason, colonial and provincial newspapers could draw articles from the *London Gazette*, the official site for publishing news of Crown and government; the *London Chronicle*, the most influential independent news source in the metropolis; and the *Gentleman's Magazine*, itself a compendium of articles culled (in 1774) from fifty-one British papers, as well as literary and scientific writings. By the time of the Revolution, the forty-two newspapers of the North American colonies and eighty to ninety British papers throughout Great Britain had developed into a heterogeneous decentralized news commons that treated the print found in other papers as "shareware" to be adopted and modified according to each paper's needs and interests.[7]

In eighteenth-century British America, the emergent institutions of the post and the newspaper gradually achieved operational integration: the post enhanced the circulation of newspapers, and the newspaper provided the post with its most visible and publicly influential content. By 1774, there were thirty major post offices and thirty-two minor ones through the length of British North America.[8] The post delivered the newspapers and private letters that were aggregated to compose as much as 90 percent of the non-advertising content of each colonial newspaper. So as to associate the newspaper with the latest "news and advices," that is, those that had (just) arrived by post, many newspapers used the word *post*, or *packet*, or more classically *mercury,* in their title.[9] After the printer had set and printed his (or her) paper, the post delivered the newspaper to its many nonlocal subscribers. The dependence of every news-

7. The figure of eighty to ninety British newspapers depends upon the compilation developed by Hannah Barker (1998, 111–12). This includes about fifty provincial newspapers for the year 1780, at least ten papers in Ireland and Scotland, and for London twenty-six papers: nine dailies; eight triweeklies, and at least nine weeklies (Barker 1998, 23). Note that the *London Gazette*, the official paper of record, which is "published by authority," should not be confused with the daily *Gazetteer*.

8. For a somewhat different total of sixty-four post offices, see Dierks 2009, 191. Approximately thirty of those were "major post offices"; see Cappon 1976, 32.

9. For example, the *Boston Evening Post*, the *New York Gazette*, the *Weekly Post-Boy*, the *New York Gazetter* or *Weekly Mercury*, the *Pennsylvania Packet*, the *Newport Mercury*. The invocation of the post seems to have been more frequent with provincial newspapers in both Britain and America.

paper printer upon the post for the receipt of other newspapers and the distribution of their own helps to explain why many early eighteenth-century newspaper printers also served as their town's postmaster. As postmaster, newspaper printers could assure the distribution of their own paper and benefit from the franking privilege—the right to send and receive letters and newspapers free of postage. The vital dependence of newspapers upon the post is apparent from the way newspaper printers would even adjust their day of publication to the arrival of the post, so that they would have time to incorporate the latest news in their paper.[10] If the newspaper depended upon the post, it also sometimes served the post. As deputy postmaster general, Franklin began the practice of advertising in the newspaper the names of those who had letters awaiting them in the local post office (see below).

The post exerted a subtle but important influence upon the form of enunciation in the newspaper. The new content contributed by newspaper printers often consisted of essays by local authors, cast in the genre of a letter. These brief essay-letters, which became particularly important with the onset of the Revolution, might be addressed to the printer or cast as a response to an earlier essay-letter. But this letter was an odd hybrid: while it was written by a private citizen, it was usually signed with a pseudonym (Puritan, Cato, Junius, American Junius, etc.), and its implied addressee was the public of all readers. One might therefore conclude that this general address means that these were not "real" letters. But the letter form, by foregrounding the fact that writing comes from the point of view of a single writer, helped to legitimize the newspaper's accommodation of a capacious variety of opinion. While newspapers implicitly legitimized the critical perspective of the one writer, as if to say, "this private opinion is worthy to be added to the public discourse on this matter," they also qualified the authority of the essay-letter, as coming from just one observer. These essay-letters usually avoid the polite usages of the educated elite (e.g., a Latin exergue, references to Roman history, legal jargon, etc.). The

10. The reliance of each paper upon numberless other papers encouraged papers to time their publication date to the flows of information. William Goddard, in announcing the publication of the *Maryland and Baltimore Journal and Advertiser* on August 20, 1773, explains the day of publication of Wednesday through reference to the newspaper transmission route upon which he must depend and which he would also help sustain: a rider from Philadelphia to Maryland carrying "the Massachusetts, Connecticut, New-York, Pennsylvania and sometimes the British and Irish papers, and be enabled to publish the Journal, with the freshest Advices, deliver it to the customers in Town."

informality and directness of the letter form accommodated the everyday phrases and spontaneous tones of the coffee shop, tavern, or club. In this way the accessible language and lively, social inflection of oral genres—conversation and debate—flowed into the printed newspaper.[11]

BENJAMIN FRANKLIN AS ENLIGHTENMENT COMMUNICATIONS ENGINEER

While the form of the post and newspaper was the work of many hands (and many years), we can explore how values were translated into the post and newspaper, by exploring the communications engineering of eighteenth-century America's most influential printer and postman, Benjamin Franklin. This will enable us to see how the post and newspapers became active embodiments of the values of those who designed and used them. Benjamin Franklin embraced a cardinal premise of Enlightenment communications: that new techniques and technologies of communication, like the post and newspaper, by accelerating and widening the circulation of information, and the diffusion of knowledge, would necessarily produce improvements in society, economy, and politics. In many of the activities of his life, Franklin linked expanded public communication to the discovery of a unity beneficial to all. Sometimes this project took a quite explicit form. When war with France threatened the colonies of British America in 1754, Franklin printed the "Join or Die" snake in the *Pennsylvania Gazette* (May 9, 1754), attended the Albany conference to coordinate colonial defense with Britain's Iroquois allies, and then penned the Albany Plan of Union in the form of a petition to Parliament (Franklin 1987, 378–82). When

11. When Benjamin Franklin published his satiric "Edicts of the King of Prussia" to mock British claims to the right to tax America, he made sure that visual cues to the oral reading of the piece were printed by the *Public Advertiser*. However, when the "Edicts" were reprinted in the *London Chronicle*, these visual cues were stripped away. In a letter to his son, William Franklin, the royal governor of New Jersey, Benjamin lamented their loss: "It is reprinted in the *Chronicle*, where you will see it, but stripped of all the capitalling and italicking, that intimate the allusions and mark the emphasis of written discourses, to bring them as near as possible to those spoken: printing such a piece all in one even small character, seems to me like repeating one of Whitfield's Sermons in the monotony of a school-boy" (October 6, 1773; Franklin 1974, 20:438). Franklin has no doubt that "written discourses" need the supplement of italics and capitalization so readers "get" the allusions and observe the tonal emphasis that will be needed if the "Edicts" are to achieve full realization in a (silent) reading that approximates the vitality and nuance of spoken performance.

the colonies were at war with the united British Empire, Franklin composed the Continental Congress's first draft of "the Articles of Confederation and Perpetual Union" (July 21, 1775; Franklin 1974, 22:122–25). But Franklin's promotion of unity extended beyond speculative plans for political unity. Many of Franklin's business enterprises (his almanac, magazine, and newspaper) as well as the many new projects for public improvement that he describes in *The Autobiography* (for example, the Pennsylvania Academy, the circulating library, fire and militia companies, etc.) were intended to improve Philadelphians by increasing the number and variety of their associations. Such a unity was compatible with the "open plan" with which he conducted his newspaper, the *Pennsylvania Gazette*. But, one might object, does an increase in communication promote unity or difference, consensus or disagreement? Here Franklin's personal reticence, his mild temperament, and the catholicity of his intellectual cosmopolitanism informed his political posture. For Franklin, unity did not entail the ideal oneness of mind and body celebrated by classical republicanism, nor did it strive for pragmatic unity, pursued in the early 1770s by Whig leaders like Samuel Adams, Charles Thompson, and Richard Henry Lee, as necessary if American Whigs were to act together in confronting Britain. Instead, unity needed to be only just "good enough" to hold the empire together. The unity that Franklin valued was open and loosely woven, plural and tolerant, as befits the least religious, most philosophically ironic of the founders.

Unity was more than an all-purpose social ethos for Franklin. With the intensification of the American crisis, unity also became a carefully sustained political position. Franklin understood partisanship and extremism as the sources of disunity, and he consistently set himself against them. Franklin's satires used a genial irony to expose the limitations of every particular ideology. His political writings upon the American crisis sought out a middle ground where Britons might recognize the enormous benefits of American trade, and Americans might embrace the advantages of their position within a great empire. The arduously achieved balance in Franklin's political posture helps to explain how he was able to sustain a steady correspondence, throughout the American crisis, with conservative Tories (like his son, the governor of New Jersey, William Franklin; and the Speaker of the Pennsylvania Assembly, Joseph Galloway) as well as staunch Whigs (like the Bostonians James Bowdoin and the Reverend Samuel Cooper). Franklin's commitment to the politics of unity led him to assume the role of a middleman. By serving as the agent for four colonial assemblies in London—Massachusetts, Pennsylvania, New Jersey, and Georgia—Franklin positioned himself between America and Great Britain, so that he could mediate their differences. This effort to sustain a "good enough unity" lasted so long (into 1774–1775), that it became quite uncomfortable. In the wake of the destruction of the tea, the British solicitor general Alexander Wedderburn came close to accusing Franklin of treason. Even after years of service as American ambassador to France, doubts lingered among some American Whigs, as to whether Franklin was a truly loyal American.

In his role as an influential communications engineer for both the post and the colonial newspaper, Franklin translated values, like unity and openness, into basic operational protocols. To demonstrate Franklin's work as communications engineer, I will focus on three initiatives undertaken by Franklin, his "Instructions to Deputy Postmasters" (1753), his "Apology for Printers" (1732), and his "Further Instructions to Deputy Postmasters" (1758). In each of these texts, Franklin promoted *unity* by applying a *uniform* set of protocols so that the communication system would have *universal* value and usefulness.

Franklin Configures the Post as a System That Will Not Leak Letters, Packages, and Revenue

When Isaac Newton labeled one part of his *Principia Mathematica* "The System of the World," he did so because he understood forces like gravitation to be universal in their operation, in the precise sense that gravitation is "universal" in "[e]xtending over, comprehending, or including the whole of something specified or implied; prevalent over all" (*OED*). In his role as postmaster general for North America, Benjamin Franklin sought to implement a different, less speculative and more pragmatic, but nevertheless universal system. The Queen Anne Postal Act of 1710 was universal in its reach because it made the royal post ultimately responsible for letters circulating through the whole British Empire. Precisely because it recognized carefully specified legal exceptions (letters carried by travelers for friends and family; bills of lading carried by merchant ships; papers served by courts of law; and "ship letters" carried between ports by captains), the Postal Act asserted monopoly control over all the letters within all British possessions. When he was appointed co–postmaster general with William Hunter of Virginia in 1753, Franklin devised a remarkable set of instructions and an accounting system, so that the royal post in America could begin to make good on its claim to universality.

By 1753 Franklin had already served sixteen years as deputy postmaster for Philadelphia and for several years as comptroller for the postmaster general (Franklin 1964, 208). Franklin understood that the royal post, like any system of transmission, was only as strong as its weakest link(s). Because postal rates were very high, because direct supervision of riders and deputies was impossible, and because surveys of far-flung post offices were necessarily infrequent,

Franklin knew that cheating the postal system was not uncommon. Among the twenty-odd major post offices in British North America at that time, delivering mail "off the books" was fairly easy, and deputies and riders could profit handsomely by doing so. Franklin's task was to stop the leakage of letters and revenue from the royal post. Franklin implemented the reforms of 1753 in three distinct ways. First, from April through November 1753, Franklin, in his role as (financial) comptroller of the American post, took a tour of inspection, where he met deputy postmasters, inspected their records, planned new routes, and improved old ones (Butler 1928; Culligan 1968, 11). By December 1753, and after he and Hunter had been appointed "Co–Deputy Postmaster Generals" for North America, Franklin sent out instructions to his deputies, describing their essential duties. At the same time, he sent the deputies a complex set of directions, which explained how deputies should keep their accounts and complete their quarterly reports to the postmaster general in Philadelphia. Included with the directions are filled-out forms as well as blank ones.

Franklin's "Instructions given by His Majesty's Deputy Postmaster Generals for North America to Their Deputy Postmasters" have an oddly equivocal character. Each injunction uses the imperative voice to specify the "best practices" of the postal deputy, but at the same time, each exposes an evident vulnerability of the postal system. Here is a highly selective redaction of one of the printed broadside instructions addressed individually to each of the postal deputies scattered across British America from Savannah, Georgia, to Falmouth, Maine. Newly appointed deputies would also get these printed instructions (Franklin 1974–2012, 5:161). In redacting Franklin's very minute directions, I am blending his language with my sense of the larger purpose that motivated these orders.

You, the Postal Deputy, should . . .

Offer public transparency, by displaying a framed table of postal rates on the wall of your post office and adhering to them exactly.

Prevent leakage from the system, by keeping your post office in a secure, separate and dedicated place, *by* not hiring riders without a certificate from a prior master testifying to their honesty and diligence, *by* examining "strictly" any rider arriving later than they should, and, if he cannot give a "just reason," to notify his master by next post, *by* checking seals of mail bags coming into your office, and *by* not opening sealed bags of "through mail" without due cause (and reporting the fact and reason to us), and finally, *by* not trusting others for the postage of letters, unless you assume full financial liability.

Enhance the speed of the post by not delaying the mail for anyone out of friendship or as a compliment, and delivering letters by penny-post (where possible), by the day after a letter was received. If a letter is not picked up after one month, publish a notice in the newspaper; after two months, mark it as a "dead" letter, and forward it to the General Post Office in Philadelphia.

Sustain the financial health of the postal system, by welcoming advance payment of postal fees, *by* refusing to extend the post-free ("franking") privilege from yourself to others, *by* keeping a record of all money received by you, and *by* filling out postal accounts every quarter upon the day of the solstice, and forwarding "schedule D" to the General Post Office in Philadelphia.

And finally [in an instruction that asserts the postmaster generals' operational control of the system], *accept our authority, by* faithfully discharging your duties and following all the instructions you receive from the Controller and us, and if you commit a misdemeanor, *by* accepting replacement by another and transfer of records to them, according to our order.

Reading this selection of Franklin's instructions changes our sense of the post through a change in scale: we move from the abstract to the specific, from an ideal system to a network of fragile, interdependent parts, the proper operation of which depends upon a host of contingencies. Indeed, historical evidence suggests that, in spite of the oaths that were required of deputies and riders, almost all the imperatives of these instructions were occasionally or periodically violated.

Given the dispersed and decentralized nature of this postal network, how could the postmaster general promote this uniformity, monitor breakdowns in the postal system, and make each of its agents financially accountable? In response to these imperatives, Franklin developed a remarkable accounting system for his deputy postmasters. At the same time that he mailed the instructions, in late 1753, Franklin sent a broadside including directions and printed sample accounts of four "schedules" that each postal deputy was to keep, in large folio volumes, as an essential part of his duties.[12] The ingenious complexity of these schedules resulted in part from the formal difference between the

12. The editors of *The Papers of Benjamin Franklin* have reprinted the directions and schedules that were sent on December 24, 1774, to Thomas Vernon, the new deputy postmaster of Newport, Rhode Island. Without doing an exhaustive search, the editors report finding other postal commissions in the form of the same printed letter for Marblehead (1758), Trenton (1764), Hartford (1767), and Skenesborough, New York (1771) (Franklin 1972, 5:452n6).

modern and the eighteenth-century post. Long before prepayment with postage stamps became normative in the nineteenth century, postage fees were almost always collected at the time of delivery either from the addressee or someone acting for them.

Here is a brief description of the four interconnected schedules that Franklin developed so each postal deputy could correctly track two types of information: the mail collected for delivery through other post offices and the mail received for delivery at his stage (fig. 3.1). The subtle interlocking character of these schedules helped to give the General Post Office crucial information about what was happening throughout the postal system.

Schedule A covers letters received by overland riders or ship for delivery at this stage. This schedule offers an alphabetical list of the names of each letter's addressee, the weight of the mail, and the pounds, shillings, and pennies that are collected from them. By recording the postal fees collected by the postal deputy, schedule A represents the *credit* to the postal system through letters delivered by this office.

Schedule B covers letters sent from this stage. This schedule lists, under date and postal destination, the bundles of letters collected by this office and sent to other post offices for delivery. By summarizing the weight and value of every bundle of letters gathered at this office for other post offices, schedule B represents the *debit* to the post system of letters gathered at this office.

Schedule C covers letters received for delivery (as in schedule A), but now arranged not by individual letter and addressee, but by the origins of postal packets, with added information on weight of unpaid letters, "way letters" (picked up by riders on the road at this "stage"), undercharged and overcharged letters, paid letters, missent letters, and ship letters, whether paid or unpaid. Schedule C represents a refined assessment of the *credit* due to the postal system through the letters delivered by this office.

Schedule D is the quarterly report to the postmaster general to be filled out on each solstice, that is, upon Lady's Day (March 25), Midsummer (June 24), Michaelmas (September 29), and Christmas (December 25). Schedule D gathers and condenses the information of the other schedules under two headings. Part 1 is labeled "Debtor the Post office," and it lists all of the *income generated by this office.* The second part of schedule D is labeled "Credit with the General Post-Office of America," and it lists all of the *credits owed to this office,* including the deputy's own quarterly salary. If the deputy collected more for delivered mail than this credit, the postal deputy would send cash to the postmaster general with schedule D. If not, the deputy would carry a "balance carried to the Credit of the General Post-Office" at the bottom of schedule D.

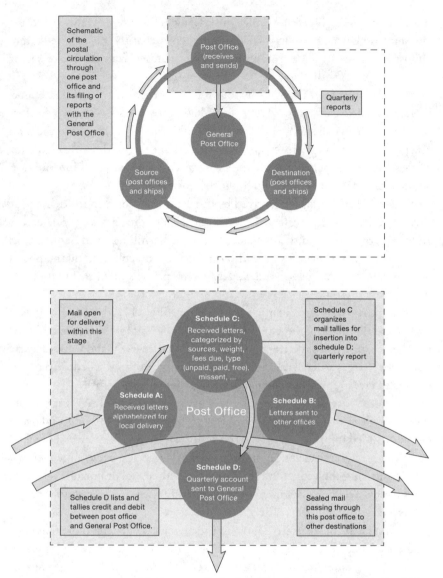

FIGURE 3.1. Schematic of the system of schedules developed by Benjamin Franklin to reform the post office of British America in 1753. The top circle on the upper schema, marked "Post Office," corresponds to the large central circle in the bottom image ("The Post Office").

These four interlocking schedules promoted two related purposes: they prescribed a uniform nomenclature for reporting the flow of mail through each office, and they turned each deputy into an auditor of his own office as well as a contributor to the audit of the whole postal system. With the arrival of quarterly reports at the General Post Office in Philadelphia, the postmaster general and his comptroller would undertake a reconciliation of accounts, calculating the amounts due from and to different post offices, as well as the amount that was to be sent to the General Post Office in Whitehall. This accounting system was also designed to enable the postmaster general to do a forensic analysis of breakdowns in the system. Thus, for example, a comparison of the Williamsburg deputy's schedule B (number and weight of letters sent to Boston) and the Boston deputy's corresponding schedule A and C (letters received from other offices, and their aggregate weight) would allow the postal comptroller, or the postmaster general, to locate letters "lost to the system," whether through negligence, error, or fraud.[13]

Franklin's instructions and directions strive to develop an architecture for the post that would make it a system in the full eighteenth-century sense of that term. To be a system, each part had to be related to every other part so as to compose a whole, with a clear boundary between what is within and outside the system. The imperative voice of the instructions seeks to secure the boundary between the royal post and its fraudulent alternatives. Franklin's accounting system not only anticipated the ghostly flows of background information found in all modern bureaucracies, it also allowed the postal system to acquire the distinctive feature of all systems, the power to "talk to itself."[14]

Skeptics of systems, whether they are speculative (like Newton's) or pragmatic (like Franklin's), have good reason to wonder whether we should construe Franklin's ambitious 1753 redesign of the American post as an elegant,

13. When Franklin was residing in London, accounts and revenue were sent to him so that he could make these calculations. That Franklin could be quite strict with his postal subordinates about reporting requirements is evident from a December 2, 1772, letter that Franklin sent to John Foxcroft, who, during Franklin's long residence in London, was managing the deputy general's central North American office. Foxcroft, rather than sending the schedules, which would allow Franklin to understand the postal revenues in North America, had sent an account, which, in Franklin's words, "lump'd in one Article of £5649 2s. 3½d. without any State of the Accounts of the several Offices to support that Article. It is therefore rejected. And I can make no Settlement till you send it me in the usual form" (Franklin 1975, 19:414).

14. On the nature of the "system," as one of the most important genres for developing Enlightenment knowledge, see Siskin 2010.

but ultimately wishful, construction, or as a normative account of how the post in America actually functioned. There is historical evidence that riders and deputies continued to "game" the system to their advantage.[15] Perhaps the best way to consider Franklin's instructions and directions are as hortatory appeals and financial incentives meant to gradually pressure deputies and riders to move their practice toward the norms of a system that might never to be realized, but could be asymptotically approached. The postal service that resulted was a mix of old usages, publically asserted norms, and their self-serving deformations. Even with this practical qualification, the increased revenues of the North American post suggest the overall success of Franklin's reforms of 1753. While the American post ran a deficit between 1753 and 1757, after that year it earned the Crown a substantial annual profit.[16]

15. After Hugh Finlay was appointed surveyor of the American posts in 1773, he took an extended tour of the North American post in 1773–1774, from Quebec to Charleston, South Carolina (see Finlay 1774). Finlay reported efficient and apparently reputable postal deputies in many towns, especially those in New England. But he also found much that dismayed him: neighbors helping themselves to mail at post offices that were left always "open," riders and stagecoach drivers carrying letters at a discount outside of the postal system, riders who had developed local constituencies that insulated them from the discipline of postal deputies, a kindly deputy who declined to collect fees from the indigent recipients of letters, missing postal horns, and postal records that were incomplete or chronically late. Quite predictably, the efficiency of the post varied by region, with the best postal service in large towns and in New England, and the worst in the more sparsely settled south. The operational lapses of the royal post of 1773–1774 reflect both the intensification of the American crisis and chronic limitations of the colonial post. However, I do not agree with Trish Loughran's (2007) witty and engaging contrast between the sort of "fantasy" of efficient imperial communication, as theorized through Benedict Anderson's concept of "imagined communities," and the broken-down and "chaotic" postal system that she finds through her reading of Finlay. Because Loughran makes normative the sort of national union and speedy communication that develops in the middle of the nineteenth century, in the wake of the institution of the telegraph and railroad, she dismisses the postal and newspaper communication that existed in the American colonies before the Revolution as incapable of overcoming an ingrained localism. But this ignores an obvious fact: the sort of communication and concerted action practiced before the Revolution, which strongly relied upon the post and newspaper, was good enough to enable the Whigs of British American to unite and conduct a war against British imperial power.

16. In his *Autobiography* (1964, 208), Franklin reported that he and William Hunter invested over £900 in the first four years of holding their offices (1753–1757), before the colonial post began to make the profit that would allow the system to pay off this debt and allow each to receive the £300 annual salary. Figures from Culligan are, for

The Printer Benjamin Franklin Argues for a Press That Balances
Liberty and Libel, Openness and Editorial Responsibility

Although Franklin's position as deputy postmaster general made him an ambitious architect of communication, the printing business occasionally confronted him with the more mundane question of what should and what should not be printed. I have noted above that Franklin's newspaper, the *Pennsylvania Gazette*, was run on the "open," nonpartisan system embraced by most colonial printers. But this did not insulate him from problems. When he printed an advertising circular that seemed to show disrespect to the clergy, and the advertisement was "struck up around town as usual," indignant readers canceled their subscriptions to his newspaper and vowed to give Franklin no more business. In the offending ad for a ship offering passage to Barbados, the circular concluded with this note: "N.B. *No Sea Hens nor Black Gowns will be admitted on any Terms.*" To defend himself against his angry readers, Franklin published "An Apology for Printers" (*Pennsylvania Gazette*, June 10, 1731). Franklin insisted that he did not understand the insult that came from linking clergy to "Sea-Hens," for "I never saw the Word *Sea-Hens* before in my Life; nor have I yet ask'd the meaning of it." But Franklin extends his self-defense by describing special features of printing as well as the reader tolerance necessary if printing was to thrive as a public benefit. Since print concerns itself with opinion, everything that is printed tends to "promote some, or oppose others," and from this fact results "the peculiar unhappiness of that business," that a printer cannot make a living without giving "offense to some." Franklin then sketched the pragmatic protocols that both printer and readers must embrace if printing, and especially newspaper printing, was going to support a robust circulation of diverse opinion. First, it was "unfair for the reader "to expect to be pleased by all that is printed." Because of the immense variety of opinion, printers were trained that when men differ, "both sides ought equally to have the advantage of being heard by the public" because, in an echo of Milton's *Areopagitica*, "when truth and error have fair play, the former is always an overmatch of the latter." Because of the detachment from partisanship their profession required, printers "naturally acquire[d] a vast unconcernedness as to the right or wrong opinions contained in what they print." Cultivating a phlegmatic neutrality, they printed "things full of spleen and animosity, with the utmost calmness and indifference." If, by contrast, they were to print only what they themselves believed and approved, "an end would thereby be put to free

---

1753–1757, deficit of £943 16s. 1d.; for 1758–1762, surplus of £1,438 9d.; for 1769, surplus of £1,859; and for 1774, surplus of £3,000. See Culligan 1968, 12–13.

writing"; and, alternatively, if they "determined not to print any thing . . . [but what] would offend no body, there would be very little printed." The low quality of what was printed was due in large part to the low taste of "the People," who, Franklin notes, would quickly buy up "Robin Hood's Songs" while an edition of "David's Psalms (an excellent Version) have lain upon my Hands above twice the Time" (Franklin 1974, 1:197–201).

So far Franklin's "Apology" promotes the two interdependent virtues— reader tolerance and printer neutrality—essential if printers are to open their press to writers of diverse opinion. Franklin has presented printing as though it were as universally inclusive as the post. But then he endorses what we might call the critical vocation of the printer, which, in modern journalistic jargon, makes him a "gatekeeper." In the "Apology," Franklin notes that printers often stifle "bad things" "at their birth," and then, shifting to the first person, Franklin assures his readers that "I my self have constantly refused to print any thing that might countenance Vice, or promote Immorality," or libels "that might do real injury to a person," and this in spite of "the profit it might bring" or the "resentment" expressed by those refused access to his press. In his *Autobiography*, written many years later, Franklin even seems to mock the "liberty of the press" that his "Apology" had implicitly defended. By taking responsibility for the social effects of what he published, Franklin adopts a restrictive rather than liberal stance toward "libeling and personal abuse." Above all the paper must meet his "contract" with his readers to provide what is "useful or entertaining" (Franklin 1964, 165). The latter formulation of course echoes, updates, but also reverses the order of, Horace's familiar characterization of poetry as being that which is *dolce et utile*, "sweet and useful." Taken together, the "Apology" and the *Autobiography* suggest the artful balance necessary in the media policy Franklin practices. While most of the argument of the "Apology" makes the case for the newspaper as a commodious medium for a liberal circulation of opinion, the "Apology" and the *Autobiography* also argue against a mechanical understanding of the newspaper as automatically open to any writer who will pay.

Postmaster General Benjamin Franklin
Officially Extends the Post for Newspapers
In the "Additional Instructions to Deputy Postmasters" in 1758, Postmaster General Benjamin Franklin officially extended the post so that it served as the distribution system for the newspaper; with this order, every newspaper had equal access to that system. Franklin filled in a part of the backstory for this postal order in his *Autobiography*. He described the substantial advan-

tages to Andrew Bradford, the printer of the rival *American Weekly Mercury*, which arose from his also serving as deputy postmaster for Philadelphia: "it was imagined he had better Opportunities of obtaining News, his Paper was thought a better Distributer of Advertisements than mine" (Franklin 1964, 126–27). Bradford used this advantage against Franklin by refusing Franklin the free newspaper distribution by post that Bradford enjoyed as postal deputy. However, like many of the threads of the *Autobiography*, this situation underwent a happy reversal of fortune. In 1737, Colonel Spotswood of Virginia, the postmaster general for North America, discovered some "negligence" and "inexactitude" in Bradford's postal accounts, so he took the commission from Bradford and offered it to Franklin (172). Now it was Franklin's turn to enjoy the economic advantages of being both postal deputy and newspaper printer. Franklin was "satisfied" but did the handsome thing: "My old Competitor's Newspaper declin'd proportionably, and I was satisfy'd without retaliating his Refusal, while Postmaster, to permit my Papers being carried by the Riders" (172). Franklin's account follows a pattern often found in the *Autobiography*. An anecdote is presented with pleasing and mild equanimity, it offers an apparently impartial factual account, but it almost always ends up making Franklin look very good and his rival not very good at all. On closer inspection, Franklin's representation of his own behavior toward Bradford does not stand up. In fact, Franklin *had* retaliated against Bradford, by closing the mail to the *American Weekly Mercury*, for at least several years (Franklin 1964, 172.n3; 1974–2012, 2:235–36). It was only much later, after he had become postmaster general, that Franklin found a way to assure equal access to postal distribution by all newspapers.

The "Additional Instructions" issued by the General Post Office on March 10, 1758 (printed in *Pennsylvania Gazette*, April 20, 1758), follows a pattern familiar in the long history of media. A major shift in policy—making the American post the legally recognized agent for distributing newspapers throughout the colonies—is disguised as a merely practical response to problems. So the postal order begins with an account of the "inconveniences" to both the postal system and the newspaper printer of the present situation. The increased quantity of newspapers had become "burdensome to riders," some of whom were demanding exorbitant fees from readers, out of which the post received no remuneration. Printers did not know who was receiving the newspapers that were requested from afar, and they had no easy way to collect subscriptions from these remote readers, or to know if a subscriber had died or departed or gone bankrupt. In this way the post was clogged with "papers to no purpose." While newspapers had become a problem for the post, Franklin's solution also upheld the long-standing alliance of the post and newspaper, by reaffirming the value of the newspaper. Franklin insisted upon the importance of "not discouraging the Spreading of News-papers, which are on many Occasions useful to Government, and advantageous to Commerce, and to the Public."

Franklin's solution made the post the distribution system for newspapers by incorporating them into the fee structure of the postal system. Delivery of papers to subscribers became contingent upon their paying a per annum delivery fee based on distance; deputies were to pay riders for delivery, and supervise them so that they would not overcharge; deputies (and their riders) would also collect subscription fees and were to be awarded a 20 percent commission for their labors; finally, to further protect the integrity of this newspaper delivery system, deputies were to send new subscription orders to newspaper printers only if the subscriber was, to quote Franklin's order, "in your Opinion responsible, and such as you will be accountable for." These reforms effected a remarkable expansion of the postal system: the post bent toward the distribution and subscription needs of the newspaper, and the newspaper took up a sanctioned place within the postal system. Rather than understanding these changes as a dramatic reversal of earlier practice, Franklin's "additional instructions" should be seen as an incremental but systematic improvement of an earlier, too haphazard, codependence of the newspaper and the post. By making this relationship formal and legal, rather than casual and customary, Franklin expanded the charge of the post and improved the delivery of newspapers, for it became the deputy, rather than a freelance rider, who took responsibility for newspaper distribution. One implication of this policy change was hidden from view, but highly consequential, and it returns us to Franklin's rivalry with Bradford. By making the post the distribution system for newspapers, the new policy implicitly committed the post to doing what Bradford did not do for Franklin, and Franklin did not at first do for Bradford: *treating all newspapers the same way*. By formalizing a uniform set of codes and practices for the distribution of newspapers by post, Franklin's 1758 order offers an early instance of the "common carrier laws" and the concept of "network neutrality" developed in much later years for the telephone and the Internet.

COMMUNICATION, EMPIRE, AND THE AMERICAN CRISIS

Before communication became a vexed problem within the unfolding American crisis, the post and newspaper served as vital and routine supports of empire. As with earlier state-sponsored postal systems, like those developed by the Roman Empire and the Holy Roman Empire, the royal post sustained the one-to-one, one-to-few, and one-to-many communications that were essential for the transmission of the edicts, proclamations, and laws of the king in Parliament, as well as the communications of the American secretary to the governors and other royal officials throughout the colonies. Information also flowed by post from the colonies back toward British administration in Whitehall. In this way, the post sustained the secure two-way networking indispensable to exercising administration at a distance. The initiation in 1754–1755 of a monthly postal packet service between Falmouth, England, and individual American ports (New York, Jamaica, Charleston) was an expensive war measure that was accepted after 1763 as part of the cost of empire. All these steps helped to unify the empire by strengthening the communications within it.

Over the same period, the newspaper, too, emerged as an essential constituent of empire. Founded in 1665, the *London Gazette* announced on its masthead that it was "published by authority," and, functioning as the newspaper of record, published the texts of royal proclamations, the news of public ceremonies, and other salient events in the life of the royal family (births, marriages, birthday balls, movements, etc.). One purpose of this news stream was to inspire the loyalty and affection of His or Her Majesty's subjects. It also publicized the central initiatives of government as well as new appointments, military commissions, ongoing diplomacy, and so on. The *Gazette*, which was published twice a week by the later part of the eighteenth century, also reprinted standard news items of the eighteenth-century newspaper: reports from remote cities like Constantinople, war news, grain prices throughout Britain, shipwrecks, marriages, deaths, and the dreaded bankruptcies that turned being "gazetted," that is, publicly exposed as a bankrupt, into a verb (*OED*). Because the *Gazette*'s important official communications were reprinted by local newspapers throughout Great Britain and the colonies, the *London Gazette* served as the broadcast hub for disseminating the policy directives and viewpoint of administration throughout the empire. This broadcasting function was a crucial complement to the networking performed by official private letters of royal officials on both sides of the Atlantic.[17]

17. Here is a fairly conventional, abstract, and formal account for the difference between networking and broadcasting. As a mode of communication, networking involves one-to-one communication; its topology, or the shape of communication flow, is horizontal, symmetrical (i.e., network users all tend to be doing the same sorts of things), decentralized (the job of making meaning is widely distributed), and thus (at least potentially and comparatively) egalitarian. Access to networks is usually relatively easy and "cheap," content is user-controlled, an extemporaneous informal style

The efficiency and plasticity of this broadcasting system can be demonstrated with George III's "Proclamation for the Suppressing of Rebellion and Sedition" (August 23, 1775). This edict was first published as a broadside, reprinted in the *London Gazette* and then reprinted in most colonial newspapers, for example, the *Penn Ledger* of November 4, 1775, and *Newport Mercury* of November 13, 1775. On November 14, 1775, Governor William Tryon of New York reprinted the king's proclamation embedded within his own broadside. Although the *London Gazette* offered royal government an effective point of entry into a broadcasting system, the king's government did not enjoy a broadcaster's monopoly. Balanced critical commentary on the proclamation would likely appear in the *London Chronicle* and the *Gentleman's Magazine*, while opposition commentary would find a place in the *Public Advertiser*. The colonial newspapers carried commentary and criticism of the king's proclamation, and on December 7, 1775, the *Pennsylvania Evening Post* printed "The Answer of the Congress to the King's Proclamation."

In founding the *London Gazette*, the administration of Charles II showed that it had learned a crucial political lesson of the English Revolution: that printed material had significant influence upon public opinion, and that shifts in opinion could undermine the authority of the sovereign. From the earliest years of printing in Europe, authorities in both church and state understood the opportunities and perils of the new medium: print could transmit the word of God or heresy, the proclamation of the monarch or sedition. For this reason, during the first two centuries of print, states in Europe enforced strict control of printing by restricting the number of printers, by requiring licensing before publication, and by visiting severe and sometimes mortal punishments upon violators. However, after 1688, the newspapers in the British Isles underwent a commercialization, expansion, and liberalization similar to that which

---

flourishes, and there is less regulation than in broadcasting. Broadcasting features one-to-many communication; its topology is invariably represented as vertical, asymmetrical (broadcasters are doing something very different than those receiving the broadcast), centralized, and, thus, implicitly hierarchical. Several traits of broadcasting are implicated in one another: access is difficult and expensive, the broadcaster enjoys control of content, and broadcasters tend to develop fixed generic conventions and correct usage. Historically, broadcasting has brought more regulation than networking. Sometimes this regulation is represented as a technological necessity. The notion that networking is more egalitarian or democratic than broadcasting pivots on two terms of this contrast: because network users are both the receivers and senders of messages, networking puts its users in charge of content formation; and second, access to networks, especially in the United States, has been comparatively easy and cheap (W. Warner 2007).

transformed the post. When, in May 1695, Parliament allowed the old Licensing Act of 1662 to lapse, within that month five new newspapers had started, and by the end of the year, nine more. As papers expanded in number and variety over the course of the eighteenth century, newspapers became responsive to questions of local interest and expanded coverage beyond those kinds of information circulated by the *London Gazette*. They accommodated a broad spectrum of the writing of the age, from the moral essays in the style of the *Spectator* to the political polemics in the style of *Cato's Letters*. The prosperity and independence of these commercial printing enterprises meant that they proved remarkably resistant to state prosecution, even when, after 1770, they published writing that the British administration considered seditious.

As an incoherent collection of items from somewhere else, and as a commons facilitating exchange, run on an "open" system, these newspapers resembled the trading system as envisioned by those Whig theorists who preached the transformative benefits of a free circulation of goods. The eighteenth-century newspaper is an institutional embodiment of the Whig promotion of circulation: the circulation of material goods (by providing information such as tables of commodity prices in different regions, by reporting the arrival and departure of ships, by publishing advertisements); the circulation of public opinion and public knowledge; and of course, the circulation of the newspaper itself. In this way the eighteenth-century newspaper, whatever its explicit politics, advanced the Whig and liberal credo—given expression across the century from Joseph Addison's *Spectator* #69, the visit to the royal Exchange, to Adam Smith's *The Wealth of Nations* (1776)—that increases in circulation would bring spontaneous increases in wealth, power, and liberty. For the Whig apologists of empire, Britain's "blue water policy"—free trade and a strong navy to clear the world's oceans for that trade—was to be contrasted favorably with the restricted and monopolistic trading policies of the French, Dutch, Danes, and Spanish, which developed a host of ways to favor the mother country at the expense of the colonies. For Whigs, the reward of this ever-expanding trade was to be an "empire of liberty," a sovereignty compatible with liberty, because that empire would be woven together by flows of commerce and knowledge that were non-coercive and beneficial to all.[18]

18. Skeptics of this ideology of empire—from the eighteenth century to the present—pointed to the periodic resort to force in forging an empire: in conquering native lands and peoples (from Ireland to New England to Madras), in enforcing the Navigation Acts, and in competing with rival powers in a series of wars with Spain, the Netherlands, and France. See the introduction to Edward Said's *Culture and Imperialism* (1994).

The ideal of an empire founded in the free circulation of goods and information was haunted by this contradiction: there was nothing in this system of circulation that guaranteed the British control of the flows of goods and information in their Atlantic empire. Viewed from a certain angle, this Atlantic system was centered in London and the British government and was controlled from there. Thus, when the king opened Parliament each autumn, the text of his speech was broadcast through the empire by reprinting it in the newspapers of the empire. However, the eighteenth-century newspaper must not be confused with the highly centralized, top-down broadcasting systems developed for radio and television in the twentieth century. While newspapers occasionally cast one message broadly, they did so from within a highly decentralized system of production by artisan printers. The Atlantic trading system and the Atlantic newspaper system were difficult to control for the same reasons: they sponsored flows of goods and information among a diverse group of producers, distributors, and consumers. The authority to make decisions (to buy/not to buy; to print/not to print) was distributed through a system that was essentially multilateral, nonhierarchical, and horizontal in its topology. These flows had no necessary or systemic center. The primacy of England was based in the traditional location of administration (in Whitehall), custom and culture, and the sheer economic scale and dynamism of London. While the king in Parliament controlled the administrative apparatus of empire from the center, there was nothing in the nature of this communication or commercial infrastructure that assured the primacy of this center. The American Revolution demonstrated precisely how the flows of goods and information that underpinned this Atlantic system could be redirected to challenge the traditional centrality of Britain. The newspaper supported by the post proved to be as open to reconfiguration as any other kind of trade.

The American crisis increased the quantity, urgency, and stakes of communication. It engaged the active interest of many writers and readers, who turned to letter writing and newspaper reading to glean the facts, express anxiety, suggest solutions, network, argue a point, or simply share their worries.[19] As the

19. In "Early American Journalism: News and Opinion in the Popular Press," Charles E. Clark documents the increase in newspapers, with their numbers doubling in two time frames: between 1763 and 1775, and between 1775 and 1790. On the eve of independence, there were forty-two newspapers and eighty-two presses in the thirteen colonies (Gross 2002, 245–64). There was a huge upsurge in political printing before the Revolution, with American imprints reaching a peak in 1774–1776; there were one thousand for 1775, though many were half-sheet broadsides (Green 2000).

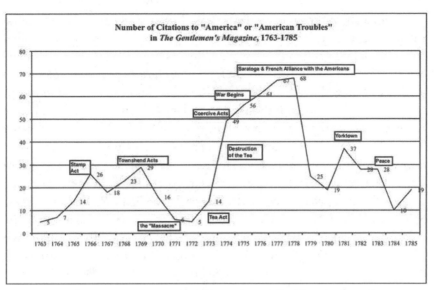

FIGURE 3.2. The American crisis through articles cited in the *Gentleman's Magazine* from 1763 to 1785. This graph represents the "temperature" of the American crisis, as viewed from the metropolitan center of the empire. Reading chronologically from the left, the two small spikes, for the Stamp Act and Townshend Acts, index the vexing disputes about the terms for British taxation of the colonies. Notice that the Boston Massacre was barely noticed by British newspapers. It lies at the beginning of the "quiet time" (1770–1773) between the repeal of most of the Townshend Acts and the destruction of the tea. The climactic crisis began in the spring of 1774 with the Coercive Acts. However, once France and Spain entered the war on the American side, the focus of the British reader shifted from "American troubles" to the starker problem of national survival.

---

political crisis deepened, some readers in Britain complained that coverage of the American troubles had grown so extensive as to be "tedious." The editors of the *Gentleman's Magazine* reported this response and defended their coverage of the "American troubles"—which in 1774 and 1775 comprehended nearly one-fourth of the magazine—by predicting that in the future these current events would prove to be most "interesting" to mankind. One way to track the intensity of the American crisis, as it appeared from London, is to chart the number of articles devoted to "America" or "the American troubles," the terms used in the index of the annual volume of the *Gentleman's Magazine*, against key events in the crisis (fig. 3.2).

Whigs on both sides of the Atlantic found a variety of ways to use the newspaper to support their political struggle. The colonial newspapers printed essays like John Dickinson's influential "Letters from a Pennsylvania Farmer" as well as official documents like the formal resolutions passed by colonial assemblies.[20] Sometimes the newspaper was used as a more urgent and rudimentary medium for communication, such as a large-font notice, "The TEA SHIP being Arrived," in the first column of the first page of the *Pennsylvania Gazette* (December 27, 1773). The notice was used to call every "inhabitant who wishes to preserve the liberty of America" to meet "at the State-Houses, this morning precisely at ten o'clock to consider what is best to be done in this alarming crisis." After the arrival of news of the Boston Port Bill, the *Pennsylvania Packet* of May 30, 1774, created a "you are there" effect by aggregating accounts of the political emergency from geographically dispersed locations: the reading of the Boston Port Bill at the Boston Town Meeting of May 13, 1774; an account of the newfound unity of a New York Whig meeting of May 26, 1774; the arrival in Philadelphia of Paul Revere; and the report that a Philadelphia committee of merchants had decided, in a meeting of May 30, 1774, to suspend business on June 1, 1774, the day the Port Bill went into effect. This flow of news was blended with vigorous Whig opinion pieces—from London, Glasgow, and Philadelphia—to create a panorama that was less reflective and balanced, more urgent and activist, than that achieved by some London media organs, like the *Gentleman's Magazine*. In a June 24, 1776, issue of the *Pennsylvania Packet*, published on the cusp of independence, its printer, John Dunlap, made quite explicit the relationship between a political crisis, the newspaper's detailed and steady communication, and the unanimity of the people he hoped that his paper would inspire: "In times like the present, it is necessary that the chain of political occurrences should be observed and communicated to the people without any material interruption; as no people can be expected to be unanimous in the pursuit of measures, of which they are not alike informed."

While the private official correspondence of royal officials between Whitehall and the American colonies provided the secure networking essential for directing imperial policy, American Whigs, in order to mature their own political measures, developed trustworthy private correspondences. The inten-

20. The twelve letters of John Dickinson, signed "A Farmer," offer a splendid example of the broadcasting potential of newspapers. The series was first published in William Goddard's *Pennsylvania Chronicle*, and then reprinted in nineteen colonial English-language newspapers in 1767 and 1768. There was also extensive, and generally favorable, critical commentary on the series (Kaestle 1968, 323–59).

sification of the political crisis, in the years between 1765 and 1775, prompted the opening of many new correspondences among American Whigs. Here, for example, is the way the leader of the Virginia Whigs, Richard Henry Lee, opened his correspondence with Samuel Adams, someone whom he would have "known" through his presence in the newspaper, but had never met.

> Sir,
>
> From a person quite unknown to you, some apology may be necessary for this letter. The name of my brother, Dr. Arthur Lee, of London, may perhaps, furnish me with this apology. To be firmly attached to the cause of liberty on virtuous principles, is a powerful cause of union, and renders proper, the most easy communication of sentiment, however artfully disunion may be promoted and encouraged by tyrants, and their abettors. (February 4, 1773; Lee 1911, 1:82)

The hesitation with which this letter begins arises from its acknowledged violation of an important protocol of gentlemanly politeness: that one does not write someone to whom one has not been introduced. However, Lee immediately offers two justifications: that Adams is already in correspondence with his brother, Arthur Lee, and that to be "firmly attached to the cause of liberty on virtuous principles" means that they are *already* joined by the same cause. As a warrant for this fact, Lee puts his faith in the Boston Whig leader and makes himself vulnerable to Adams by stating, at the end of this passage and throughout the rest of the letter, sentiments that British authorities would find seditious. At the end of the letter, Lee notes that "the freedom with which this letter is penned" shows that he understands himself to be "writing to a firm and worthy friend of the just rights and liberty of America." Although this letter is justified by a practical purpose (getting more exact information about the Gaspée commission), the heady sense of joy that Lee's language exudes arises from more than its message. It comes from this letter's fraternal, and even erotic, potential to bind two strangers as "communicants" in the cause of liberty. The gradual development of American Whig correspondences into a dense Whig matrix of communications became one of the constituents of the emergence of a revolutionary dynamic in 1774–1775 (Maier 1972, 222–24).

RECONFIGURING THE ROYAL POST AS THE CONTINENTAL POST

The plasticity of both the newspaper and the post in the years before the Revolution suggests that we should not think of them as having the rigidity of "infrastructure" (of pipes, roads, or wires), but instead conceptualize them as pliant and active mediators of the political crisis. Since both sides in the political struggle understood the critical importance of the post and the newspaper, both became contested ground as each side sought to reshape the communication system for their own purposes. Because the royal post was a hierarchical structure, whose postmaster general, deputy postmaster generals, and postal deputies were Crown appointments, royal officials in Whitehall believed it to be resistant to takeover by the colonists (*Gentleman's Magazine*, June 1774, 285). This may have seemed all the more true because Benjamin Franklin was resident in London for most of the twenty years before his dismissal. By July 26, 1775, however, the Continental Congress confirmed the recommendations of a postal committee (which included Franklin, Richard Henry Lee, Samuel Adams, Philip Livingston, and Thomas Willing) by establishing the Continental Post Office in Philadelphia with Benjamin Franklin as its postmaster general (Butler 1928, 161).[21] The remarkably quick, eighteen-month metamorphosis of the royal post into the Continental post can be narrated in two interdependent stages.

Stage 1: Whitehall reclaims control of the post in British America from Benjamin Franklin. The Hutchinson letters scandal leads to the firing of Benjamin Franklin and the appointment of Surveyor Hugh Finlay as his replacement to serve with John Foxcroft. Lord Dartmouth uses his legal power to open letters carried by the royal post to monitor political sentiment as well as Whig machinations.

The ominous implications of this event were spelled out in Franklin's letter of February 15, 1774, to Thomas Cushing, and in the anonymous "A Letter from London" extracted from it for publication in the papers. Franklin represents his dismissal as deputy postmaster general and describes some recent postal orders as evidence of Whitehall's determination to extend much greater "influence" over the American post office (*Boston Gazette*, April 25, 1774; Franklin 1972, 21:83) As noted above, Franklin had followed the formation of committees of correspondence in Boston and other towns in Massachusetts with keen interest. Here, as a former postmaster general, Franklin warns American Whigs of the vulnerability to political manipulation of their com-

---

21. With an order of May 12, 1777, Congress recognized the military importance of the post by ordering that "that all post-masters, post-riders, and persons immediately concerned in conducting the business of the post office, ought to be exempted from all military duties; and that it be recommended to the Legislatures of the different States, to exempt such persons accordingly" (Congress 1777, Evans no. 15669).

munications: "Orders have already been given (*this may be depended on as fact*) to the American Postmasters General . . . not to fill vacancies of value till notice of such vacancies be sent to England. . . . It is plain from hence, that *such influence* is to be a part of the system; and probable, that those vacancies will be for the future be filled by officers from thence [i.e., London]. How safe the correspondence of *committees* along the continent will be, thro' the hands of *such* officers, is now worth consideration" (*Boston Gazette*, April 25, 1774; italics in the original; Franklin 1972, 21:83). These 1774 warnings by Franklin were justified in 1775. Since systematic invasion of the mails could be legally ordered by the secretary of state (as had been done during Jacobite rebellions earlier in the eighteenth century), in 1775 the American secretary, Lord Dartmouth, ordered a team of eight clerks to organize as a team in the New York post office to open, read, copy, and then reseal mail coming from and going to the American colonies on the monthly packet ship from New York to Falmouth, England.[22] One priority was monitoring the communication of American agents like Arthur Lee and Benjamin Franklin. Dartmouth also ordered a random sample of letters to be opened, so as to gauge the opinion of American Whigs and to inquire whether the carrot-and-stick approach pursued by administration was working (Flavell 2001, 403–30). But Dartmouth's manipulation was the last gasp for the royal post. Regular packet service ended on September 28, 1775, and the royal post in New York closed on December 27, 1775. The royal post in British America had dissolved.

Stage 2: William Goddard promotes a "constitutional post" for British America, and in July 1775 Congress institutes the Continental post.

What gradually replaced the royal post in the years of 1774 and 1775 began with the enterprising efforts of the printer William Goddard. Although Goddard had had very uneven success as a newspaper printer in Providence, Philadelphia, and Baltimore, he had a keen sense of the danger of a manipulation of Whig communications by the ministry in London. In the spring of 1774, Goddard traveled throughout New England, seeking support for what he called the "constitutional post." The motive for establishing a "constitutional post," as argued in the minutes of the Boston Committee of Correspondence and their letters to other committees in March and April of 1774, was formulated with

22. In his account of the Whig attacks upon the royal post and the development of the Continental post, Konstantin Dierks (2009, 208) notes that after the closure of the royal post office in New York, a team of eight secret service agents was supervised by Anthony Todd to inspect the royal mail for political and military information.

great urgency in a broadside Goddard printed on April 30, 1774, in Boston, entitled "The Plan for Establishing a New American Post-Office." Goddard's broadside expressed deep suspicion of the now "unconstitutional" royal post as guided by "ministerial" "hands," which now held "all the social, commercial and political intelligence of the continent"; these sinister hands could "by a Ministerial Mandate" stop and open private letters, construing their contents "into treasonable conspiracies," or prevent the circulation of "our News-Papers, those necessary & important alarms in Time of public danger."

It was fitting that Goddard got his strongest support and encouragement from the Boston Committee of Correspondence, and other committees (in Marblehead, Salem, and Portsmouth) to which the Boston committee recommended Goddard's scheme. For although Goddard borrowed some features of the royal post, the proposed "constitutional post" was not hierarchical, and like the committee network he relied upon, the post he envisioned would acquire its coherence from the bottom up, by distributing initiative, power, and responsibility through localities. Resources to start the post in each town would come from the subscriptions of local merchants and governments, and these subscribers would then regulate rates and appoint local deputy postmasters, who would then hire riders and furnish locks and keys for the mails. The postmaster general, elected annually by the votes of provincial committees of correspondence, would receive general accounts and allow deputy postmasters a commission (Goddard 1774; Butler 1928, 157–58; Schlesinger 1958, 190–92). Although the Goddard broadside made the movement to an American post sound revolutionary, for Whig postal deputies, there was little change necessary. By May 1775, thirty deputy postmasters had renounced their connection with the royal post (Butler 1928, 160). In spite of direct lobbying by Goddard in Philadelphia, Congress did not adopt the "constitutional post" as envisioned by Goddard (Dierks 2009, 192–206). In July 1775, Congress instituted a postal service under its own direct control. Congress's appointment of the old royal postmaster general, Benjamin Franklin, to the new position of postmaster general for the Continental post confirmed a change that was hardly any change. Subsequent enhancements of the Continental post, like the instituting of an express service between Congress and military commanders, helped to strengthen the post service for waging war. The ease with which the royal post morphed into a Continental post reflected the broad shift in popular sentiment toward war with Britain (Dierks 2009, 206–14).

As the political crisis intensified, it became increasingly difficult to sustain the open and neutral press, one that could balance the interests of both Whigs and Tories. In Boston, Isaiah Thomas found that his *Massachusetts Spy* had to choose one side or the other, and in New York, James Rivington's effort to print the Tory point of view in the *New York Gazetter* embroiled him in a host of troubles (Schlesinger 1958, 222–27). It was of course part of the common sense of the eighteenth century that liberty of the press could easily shade into license, political censure into seditious libel. Administrative authorities on both sides of the Atlantic tried to police the boundary between responsible newspaper publication and a license that threatened the authority of government. Franklin's gentle mockery of a client, who cried "liberty of the press" to justify printing a libelous notice in Franklin's paper, suggests that the appeal to the freedom of the press could be inconsistent or self-serving (Brown 2000b). However, rather than castigating American Whigs for their failure to realize a modern liberal concept of the freedom of the press as a general right, it is more useful to see American Whigs, along with their English precursors—from John Milton (*Areopagitica*, 1644), and Trenchard and Gordon (*Cato's Letters*, 1720–1721), to contemporary British Whig allies, like John Wilkes or the writer of the Junius letters—as the developers of an emergent concept of freedom of the press (Botein 1975). To do so allows us to see how a central protocol of American communication, one later given constitutional protection by the First Amendment, emerged from the exigencies of prerevolutionary politics.

The issue of the "liberty of the press" repeatedly framed Boston's struggle around how far a newspaper dared to go in criticizing Crown government. On the last day of February 1768, Edes and Gill of the *Boston Gazette* published an essay by "A True Patriot" (Dr. Joseph Warren) that offered a scathing critique of Governor Bernard, without naming him. Bernard took the piece to the governor's council and requested that they take action against the newspaper for its "virulent Libell against me" and its "blasphemous abuse of Kingly Government itself." Although the Council voted to condemn the piece, it declined to recommend that the attorney general indict the paper for publishing it. Thomas Hutchinson, acting in his role as chief justice of the Superior Court, then convened a grand jury, on March 8, and deploring the "True Patriot" and other recent publications of the *Boston Gazette*, which "bordered very near upon High Treason," urged the jury to take action. "Shall our first Magistrate be thus slandered with impunity in an *infamous* Paper? . . . To suffer the licentious Abuse of Government is the most likely Way to destroy its Freedom." After pondering the governor's impressively learned case for a night, the grand jury reconvened and voted not to indict. Bernard and Hutchinson decided against indictment by sole authority of the attorney general, and the Whig writers published articles canvassing their victory in the cause of liberty of the press (Stern 2010, 231–46).

On November 14, 1771, Isaiah Thomas's *Massachusetts Spy* published an attack on Governor Hutchinson, written by one "Mucius Scaevola," attacking the British administration's decision to pay the governor directly, from funds raised by customs, rather than having the governor receive his salary through annual appropriation of the House of Representatives of Massachusetts. The governor's attempt to check the strident critique of the ministry by Mucius Scaevola follows the three-part rhythm of what one might call a "free press incident": an act of expression in print (1) provokes an attempt to curb the expression through sanctions (2). The silenced party then appeals to general constitutional principles to defend their right to freedom of expression (3). In the attack, Mucius Scaevola insisted that "[a] ruler, independent on the people, is a monster in government; and such a one is Mr. Hutchinson; and such would George the third be, if he should be rendered independent on the people of Great-Britain. A Massachusetts Governor, the King by Compact, with this people may *nominate* and *appoint*, but not *pay*: for his support he must stipulate with the people, and until he does, he is no legal Governor; without this, if he undertakes to rule, he is a USURPER" (*Massachusetts Spy*, November 14, 1771). Scaevola continues that the "pretended Governor" should be punished as "a Usurper" and "the Council, according to the charter, should take upon itself the government of this province." It is not surprising that Hutchinson read this as a fundamental challenge to the authority of both himself and the Crown.

The Mucius Scaevola piece is characteristic of Thomas's newspaper for the way it carried challenges to authority beyond the point where authorities would find bearable but short of the point where it would cause broad public offense. The governor convened the Council and won their agreement to have the printer Isaiah Thomas sued for seditious libel. This had several effects. First, it provoked a series of articles in the *Boston Gazette* and the *Massachusetts Spy* invoking and defending freedom of the press against the governor's efforts to limit that freedom. Second, when Isaiah Thomas refused to appear before the Council, they summoned Sheriff Joseph Greenleaf, "generally reputed to be concerned with Isaiah Thomas" in publishing the *Spy*, to appear before them. Finally, when Greenleaf also refused to appear, the Council declared him in contempt and dismissed him as justice of the peace in Plymouth County (Schlesinger 1958, 141). In February 1772, the chief justice of the Superior Court failed to win an indictment against Thomas from a grand jury (Hutchinson to Hillsborough, April 10, 1772; *Documents* 5:64), though the administration considered taking Thomas directly to court "on information." Hutchinson finally declined to do so because the Council strongly advised of the disturbance this might cause among the people. Hutchinson's experience here repeated the difficulties experienced by the British Parliament in suppressing the speech acts of John Wilkes throughout the 1770s, as well as the problems the ministry had, during the summer of 1770, in prosecuting the newspapers that had reprinted the notoriously harsh essays of Junius.[23]

What resulted from this failed prosecution, and others like it in England and New York, was a de facto expansion of press freedoms. Joseph Greenleaf, writing to the readers of the *Boston Gazette* after his dismissal by the Council, showed a keen sense of the dangerous legal precedent that might have resulted from his cooperation with the governor in prosecuting the *Massachusetts Spy*. "The proceeding alarmed me, as I judge it WHOLLY illegal, for I could have no idea of the legality of erecting a court of INQUISITION in this *free country*, and could find no form for such a citation in the province of law books: My duty to my country therefore forbad my paying any obedience to it, especially as it might hereafter be used as a precedent" (*Boston Gazette*, January 13, 1772). But the governor's effort to punish Isaiah Thomas is in fact entirely consistent with English law. After the expiration of the Licensing Act in 1695, freedom of the press meant that printers enjoyed freedom from "prior restraint," that is, restraint prior to publication. But sanctions after publication continued to be part of English law. This key legal distinction was made by Sir William

---

23. For discussion of the litigation pursued by the Crown against John Wilkes and the *Public Advertiser* for publishing Junius, see Rea 1963 and Barker 2000. In London, the government's prosecutions of newspapers led to the formation of an "Association for the Liberty of the Press," which marshaled a remarkable comprehensive defense of freedom of the press (*New York Gazette and the Weekly Mercury* [published by Gaine], January 8, 1776). The failure of prosecutions against newspapers considered libelous led the North ministry to develop an alternative, economic assault upon a hostile press. In a speech to Parliament on April 24, 1776, Lord North promoted a bill doubling the tax on newspaper by launching a broad attack upon the "idle foolish curiosity" that has made newspaper reading so popular, a speech in which he also remarked upon the dangerous effects of the "libelous falsehoods" circulated about "cruel, ambitious, and tyrannical ministers" by "no less than 12,230,000 newspapers" printed each year (*New York Gazette* [Gaine], November 18, 1776).

Blackstone, in two sentences from his *Commentaries on English Common Law* (1769, 4:152): "The liberty of the press is indeed essential to the nature of a free state: but this consists in laying no *previous* restraints upon publications, and not in freedom from censure for criminal matter when published. Every free man has an undoubted right to say what sentiments he pleases before the public: to forbid this, is to destroy the freedom of the press: but if he publishes what is improper, mischievous, or illegal, he must take the consequence of his own temerity." In refusing to obey the governor in pursing legal action after publication, Greenleaf ignored the tradition outlined by Blackstone, and instead appealed to a higher duty and law: "The freedom I now contend for, is, a right of resistance, or rather withholding my obedience, when unlawfully commanded. . . . But if a Justice of the Peace may be dismissed from his office, because he refused to be examined about a common News-Paper," if he may be dismissed because he is "supposed by people in general to be concerned with the printer," or any other person, that the governor has conceived a dislike to, "we are in a pitiable case."[24]

The Greenleaf-Thomas-Hutchinson free-press incident, like the *Boston Gazette*–Bernard-Hutchinson case before it, helped to establish the fact that, by the fall of 1771, there was no practical way for the governor or the Council to censor the local newspapers in Boston.[25] In other words, a year before the founding of the Boston Committee of Correspondence, and two years before the agitation against the Tea Act, these incidents secured the operational latitude needed by the American Whig press. Freedom of the press—and its oral cognate, freedom of speech—emerged as one of the cardinal protocols of revolutionary communication. Freedom of the press did not emerge as a value for the reasons emphasized by liberal thinkers like John Stuart Mill in the nineteenth century: that diverse voices might compete in the "marketplace of ideas." For both Whigs and Tories, a disinterested quest for truth took second place to other concerns. Instead, American Whig republicans valued free-

24. Greenleaf himself may have been the pseudonymous author Mucius Scaevola (Schlesinger 1958), or, as Richard D. Brown (1970, 63) suggests, the essay might have been written by Dr. Joseph Warren. For an account of how the Greenleaf incident prodded Governor Hutchinson to develop his own government-sponsored newspaper, the *Censor*, between November 23, 1771, and May 1772, see Bailyn 1974, 197–99.

25. For a similar struggle around freedom of the press, see the accounts of Alexander McDougall's becoming the "Wilkes of America" when he was charged with seditious libel for the December 1769 pamphlet, *To the Betrayed Inhabitants of the City and Colony of New York* (Maier 1972, 192).

dom of the press and freedom of speech in three distinct, but related, ways: as a pragmatic mode of articulating resistance in a moment of political crisis; as a symptom of freedom as a spiritual possession of the people; and as a way boldly to perform or enact that freedom.

VIEWING "THE MEDIA" AS PART OF THE HISTORY OF MEDIATION INSTEAD OF A TOOL OR AN ENVIRONMENT

That British America enjoyed a robust communication system that was open, public, and free of government control had powerful but ironic effects during the Revolution. The decentralized system for circulating information around the empire had been inspired by liberal Whig principles and developed to support a British trading "empire of liberty." That system was then used by American Whigs to subvert the empire. It is possible to say, for example, that the newspaper circulated by post enabled and sustained the invention of the committee of correspondence, the circulation of the popular declaration, and the emergence of the American Whig network. As we have seen, the robustness and autonomy of the communication system of British America made it difficult for royal officials to block challenges to their authority that they viewed as seditious and inflammatory. So, for example, we can speculate that if Governor Hutchinson had enjoyed the proscriptive control of the newspapers that he actively pursued in 1768 and 1771, and if he had enjoyed direct control of the royal post, the towns of Massachusetts could not have networked themselves together so freely and publicly. This is a way of thinking about the influence of media upon history that is familiar, useful, but also limiting. It may view the newspaper as an "engine of propaganda" (Schlesinger 1958), or both post and newspaper as an element of the media that "works us over completely . . . as environments" (McLuhan 1967, 26). Media and postal institutions begin to appear as fixed a part of the communication "infrastructure" as the roads, pipes, or transportation systems of a modern city. By separating media and history as cause to effect, this leads to the familiar conclusion that media determines history.

If we look more closely at the political ecology of revolutionary Boston, however, it becomes difficult to sustain the familiar modern opposition between "the media" and society, politics, and so on. Thus, as we have noted above, the "votes" and resolutions that were passed by the town meeting and recorded in its minutes often appeared virtually unchanged in the newspapers. An editor of the *Boston Gazette*, Benjamin Edes, participated in the tea meetings and was chosen to be one of those who helped prevent surreptitious unloading of the hated tea. Whig leaders of the town meeting, like James Otis Jr. and Samuel Adams and others, occasionally gathered in the Queen Street offices of the *Boston Gazette* on Sunday evening to complete opinion pieces that would appear on Monday morning. Finally, and perhaps most tellingly, there is an affinity, but not a simple causal relationship, between the general address of the newspapers linked by post and the general scope of the rights claims made by the American Whigs. By taking our cue from these various links between the communication system and the words and deeds of the Revolution, it is possible to place them in a common frame. The traits with which I have characterized that communication system—operational autonomy, openness to the public, freedom of government control, the sponsorship of ideas that are boldly critical, circulation across the expanses of the empire—cannot really be separated from the communication protocols used by the Whigs as they formed themselves into committees and composed popular declarations, which observed correct legal procedure, encouraged public access, acted together, and showed virtuous initiative by venturing a systematic and general address to the people. Both the communication system and the popular declarations were active mediators of the Revolution, both helped network the Whigs of the colonies together, both are informed by a common set of protocols, and both are part of the history of mediation.

4

THE WHIG NETWORK SCALES UP

INFLECTING THE CRISIS FROM

WILLIAMSBURG

. . . .

In May 1774 the news arrived that Parliament had passed the Boston Port Bill, which closed Boston Harbor as a punishment for the town's destruction of the tea. In the weeks that followed, American Whigs worked so that the committee system could scale up to unite most of the colonies of British North America. There are several noteworthy features of this networking. First, it was pursued as a measured response to events, and without those events networking would not have scaled up so quickly. Second, while networking created a new and more powerful agency, the network that emerged deferred defining the full scope of the measures that it would undertake, for example, a full embargo upon trade with Britain. In part, deferring decisions was a way to avoid conflicts; in part, the network of agents simply did not know, without more communication, where consensus lay. Finally, as we shall see in this chapter, the network provided American Whigs a particularly effective way of preparing for, but staying open to, as yet uncertain future developments. In other words, networking is preparatory, cautionary, and provisional: it prepares for a future it cannot yet envision.

A network analysis of the Whig response to the American crisis offers an alternative to an analysis that emphasizes the prior design and secret intentions of revolutionary leaders. As we shall see in the discussion of the Continental Congress, historians have tended to parse Whig leaders into "radicals," "moderates," and "conservatives." So, for example, the "radical" Samuel Adams has sometimes been credited (or blamed) for being the first American Whig leader to fix upon independence as the proper goal of the struggle with Britain. However, a careful reading of his writings, as Pauline Maier's (1976) exhaustive research has shown, demolishes that theory. If one looks into the written record, a very different picture emerges: even among the most ardent Whigs, and even in their private communication, there is a marked reticence about defining the specific goals of political struggle. Whig leaders cleaved to generalities (like the claim to "our full and ancient English rights") for two reasons: first, to avoid discovering differences and opening divisions among themselves, and second, because they knew that the precise remedies of the political crisis could emerge only through the ongoing exchange with the powerful but erratic nation on the other side of the Atlantic. Resolving the American crisis would be an involuntary collaboration.

THE PROBLEM UNITY, THE SOLUTION NETWORKING

Even before the news of the Port Bill arrived in Boston, Massachusetts Whigs responded to the suspense and uncertainty of the moment by relying upon the incipient network of committees that had developed over the previous eighteen months, first in the province and next in the colonies. The success of the committees of correspondence gave the Whigs of Massachusetts a calm sense of resolve and self-confidence. After the close of the House session in March 1774, the committee of correspondence of the Massachusetts House wrote to its agent in London, Benjamin Franklin (March 31, 1774; Franklin 1978, 21:165–66).

> By the vigilance and Activity of Committees of Correspondence among the several Towns in this Province, they have been wonderfully enlightened and animated. They are united in sentiments and their opposition to unconstitutional measures of Government is become Systematical. Colony communicates freely with Colony. There is a common Affection among them, the *communis sensus*, and the whole continent is now become united in Sentiment and in Measures of opposition to tyranny.
>
> Signed, Samuel Adams, John Hancock, William Phillips, Captain William Heath[1]

What gave the Massachusetts committee the confidence that "the whole continent" would join Massachusetts "in measures of opposition to [British] tyranny"? By the sequence embedded in this paragraph, it all started with "the vigilance and activity of committees of correspondence" of Massachusetts. Their communication, by enhancing the energy and intelligence of their poli-

---

1. I have used the Franklin edition transcription, which is consistent with S. Adams (1904, 3:88–89), while including the Latin phrase from William V. Wells's nineteenth-century transcription of a manuscript written by Samuel Adams (S. Adams 1865, 2:46): *communis sensus*. It explains and gives weight to the "common affection among them." Because the manuscript has now worn away in this place, the editors of the *Papers of Benjamin Franklin* have omitted the Latin gloss (Franklin 1978, 21:166n1). The first draft of this letter was evidently written by Samuel Adams, who served as chair of the House committee of correspondence.

tics, had made them "wonderfully enlightened and animated." By working together, the committees of towns had developed an opposition that was "systematical," so the communication of each could become a single part of a more encompassing system. This system of communicating committees had spread, so "colony communicates freely with colony." From this mutual communication there was now a "common affection" among the people, glossed in Latin as "communis sensus." Venturing a hopeful prognostication, the committee suggests that the same *communis sensus* that had united the towns would serve as the bonding agent for a new intercolonial unity.

Massachusetts's prospectus for colonial unity describes the networking that had brought the Whigs of British America into a common sentiment or affection during the previous eighteen months and prescribes more of it: its own efforts to network the towns of Massachusetts as well as the initiative of the Virginia Committee of Correspondence to network together the assemblies of the thirteen colonies of British America. Through its confident posture, the Massachusetts committee elides the extensive work necessary to produce an effective intercolonial unity. Ironically, events in Britain were conspiring to advance that project. The Massachusetts committee's letter is dated March 31, 1774, the very day when the king received the Boston Port Bill from the House of Lords and signed it, thereby giving it the force of law. By closing Boston's harbor and moving royal government out of Boston, the bill would do much more than American Whigs could have done on their own to extend, strengthen, and activate the incipient intercolonial network of American Whigs. Only by configuring themselves into a network could the colonies reconcile diversity with unity.

What a network can do depends in part upon its shape, or topology. The network that was built through the initiatives of the Boston Committee of Correspondence betrayed a telling ambiguity. On one hand, because it relied upon the one-to-one private communication of the distributed postal network—and because it often exploited the traits of the distributed system of the newspapers, which was open, public, and censorship-resistant—the network of the towns had the flatness and equality of a distributed network, where initiative rested with the many nodes, in this case the towns, linked through the network. On the other hand, the network that emerged through the labors of the Boston committee had many traits of a star topology, where nodes are linked through a central hub, rather than to each other. Although the network of the towns was not obliged by law or protocol to pass communications through the network hub in Boston, it always did; and although the towns were free to communicate with each other, instead of through Boston, they apparently never did (Brown 1970, 132–33). So in spite of the Boston committee's insistence upon the formal and legal equality of all the towns of Massachusetts, and in spite of their efforts to support that presumptive equality with sometimes specious flattery, the Boston committee succeeded in winning the leadership position that it overtly disavowed. The declarations by which the towns responded to the Boston declaration set a communication system going that installed the Boston committee as the hub of a network with a star topology, albeit one that was officially flat and nonhierarchical. Boston's status as the hub of the network assured that the Boston Committee of Correspondence emerged as the network's privileged center of calculation. Only the Boston committee could broadcast broadsides throughout the province, call meetings with other towns, and set the agenda for those meetings. This suggests one of the virtues of a star topology: it allowed a small and cohesive group at the hub to initiate and guide collective action.

Because each colony of British America jealously guarded its equality as a separate legal polity and "country," even this relatively egalitarian form of star network could not be used to network the other colonies. The colonies could only be united by a distributed network where each member enjoyed formal equality. In this chapter we shall see that this is what the Virginia House of Burgesses initiated. It was based upon what is called a "mesh topology," where each node is connected with every other node (see fig. 0.2). The rigorous equality of this kind of network makes it very robust: if one node goes out, it does not disable the network. A distributed network has other distinct advantages over the star topology: initiative and invention can come from anywhere on the network; it is especially capable of accommodating complexity and heterogeneity; and it is highly flexible (Kelly 1994; Castells 1996). In 1774 each of the thirteen colonies charted its own pathway to linking into the emerging network. However, there were also drawbacks to a distributed, mesh topology: these networks could be as chaotic as an unmoderated meeting, and, perhaps most critically, broad consensus was essential if the network was to act.

We can translate into networking terminology the problem for members of the Whig network posed by the political emergency that was triggered by news of the Boston Port Bill. "How can we reconfigure and scale up the American Whig network of committees so that it has the robust, broadly participatory and egalitarian character of a distributed network *and* the cohesion and ability to decide and act most characteristic of a network organized by a star topology?" This is the implicit issue with which Whigs across the colonies grappled in May and June of 1774. Their response was to gather in committees and other meetings to authorize a new place for deliberation, a general congress, so that it could serve as a hub that would unite and direct the distributed network of American Whigs. Only then would Whigs enjoy an intercolonial unity that was strong yet open, coherent but loose enough to compete with the decisiveness and coordinated effort that the British ministry and Parliament had demonstrated in passing and implementing the Coercive Acts.

We will begin our investigation of this intercolonial networking initiative in medias res, by tracing the agile response of the Virginia House of Burgesses and their committee of correspondence, during the last week of May 1774, as they reacted to the shocking news of the Boston Port Bill.

WILLIAMSBURG, MAY 24, 1774–JUNE 1, 1774

> *We had been sitting in Assembly near three weeks, when a quick arrival from London brought us the Tyrannic Boston Port Bill, no shock of Electricity could more suddenly and universally move—Astonishment, indignation, and concern seized on all. The shallow Ministerial device was seen thro instantly, and every one declared it the commencement of a most wicked System for destroying the liberty of America, and that it demanded a firm and determined union of all the Colonies to repel the common danger.*
> — Richard Henry Lee to Arthur Lee, June 26, 1774 (Lee 1911, 114)

Richard Henry Lee's account to his younger brother, Arthur, in London offers a remarkable instance of the sudden fold in time that characterizes revolutionary temporality. It begins in ordinary time ("we had been sitting in assembly near three weeks") into which there arrives an unexpected "shock." Because it has the sudden response-inducing effect upon the body of "a shock of electricity," the Port Bill must move everyone, in a fashion that is both physical and emotional.[2] Then comes a moment of collective insight: punishing Boston alone, since it was only one of four American ports that had refused the East India tea in 1773, was a "shallow ministerial device" to divide the colonies. This leads to the ominous Whig interpretation of British motive: it is the beginning of "a most wicked system for destroying the liberty of America." This conclusion justifies the political goal of the Whigs in Williamsburg: "a firm and determined union of all the colonies to repel the common danger." Lee's

---

2. Because of the extensive experiments developed around electricity in the eighteenth century, it was understood to have features that make Lee's simile here, and Jefferson's, cited below, most apt: like the news of the Port Bill, electricity operates quickly; it can surprise its victim and be painful; and it produces an involuntary response in the body.

Tuesday, May 24: **The Virginia House of Burgesses designates June 1, 1774, a day of prayer.** The Burgesses take note of "the hostile invasion of the city of Boston, in our Sister Colony of Massachusetts bay, whose commerce and harbor are to be stopped by an Armed force, deem it highly necessary that the said first day of June be set apart, by the members of this House, as a day of fasting, humiliation, and prayer, devoutly to implore the divine interposition, for averting the heavy calamity which threatens destruction to our civil rights, and the evils of civil war."

Thursday, May 26: **Dissolution of the Burgesses.** Governor Dunmore summons the House to the Council Chamber, and waving the resolution of the House in his hand, declares it to be "conceived in such terms as reflect highly upon his Majesty and the Parliament of Great Britain; which makes it necessary for me to dissolve you; and you are dissolved accordingly."

Friday, May 27: **A rump group of 89 of the 122 Burgesses meets to form an association in the Apollo Room of Raleigh Tavern.** It advises "on the expediency of appointing deputies from the several colonies of British America, to meet in general congress, as such a place annually as shall be thought most convenient."

language evidences several of the proverbial features of revolution, by which events have taken on the novelty, uncertainty, and violence of a storm. In the hectic week that followed the arrival of news of the Boston Port Bill, events in Williamsburg, like events in Boston on March 6, 1770, and on December 16, 1773, acquired the paradoxical double character of a moment of crisis. Because what was happening appeared urgently important and fraught with consequence, and because events demanded a quick response, *time seemed to speed up*; but because all that was happening was unusual, vivid, and intensely felt, *time seemed to slow down*. There was a portentous sense that actions undertaken this day may have effects that would prove irreversible.

The arc of events that unfolded in Williamsburg in the last week in May 1774 is represented in box 4.1. While these events are often narrated to display the vigilance and courage of the leading Whigs of Virginia, I would like

Sunday–Monday, May 29–30: After receiving an **express letter from the Annapolis Committee of Correspondence,** which includes the letters from the committees of Philadelphia and Boston, Chairman Peyton Randolph convenes the 25 Burgesses remaining in the town at his Williamsburg mansion. They write and sign a letter to the other Burgesses, urging them to collect "the sense of their respective counties" and to meet in Williamsburg on August 1, 1774, to consider the advisability of suspending imports from and exports to Great Britain.

Tuesday, May 31: **Virginia Committee of Correspondence** transmits copies of letters from the north to committees to the south (North Carolina, South Carolina, Georgia); in writing to committees to the north, it acknowledges receipt of their letters and wishes "it had been in our power to have done any thing more decisive, at present."

Wednesday, June 1: **Observation of a day of fasting, humiliation, and prayer.**

to underscore another skill they evidence: the agility with which the Virginia Whigs changed course and revised their actions to meet the challenges and opportunities provided by, and their obligations to, the intercolonial network of committees of which they were a part. The Virginia Whigs' first translation of the news of the Boston Port Bill was the successful motion of the House of Burgesses to observe the first of June as a day of "fasting, humiliation and prayer." The motion was a compromise between the more active measures favored by the most ardent Whigs, led by Richard Henry Lee, and those many members who worried that any strong measures—like proposing an immediate boycott upon imports from Britain—would provoke a dissolution of the House by the governor before important business could be completed. Thomas Jefferson, writing forty-seven years later, at the age of seventy-eight, recalled how Richard Henry Lee, Patrick Henry, Francis Lightfoot Lee, Jefferson himself, and three or four others, bypassed the "older members" of the House and met in the Council Chamber, "for the benefit of the library in that room. We were under conviction of the necessity of arousing our people from the lethargy into which they had fallen as to passing events; and thought that the appointment of a day of general fasting & prayer would be most likely to call up & alarm their attention" (Jefferson 1984, 8).

By passing a resolution to appoint a day of "fasting, humiliation, and prayer" for the House, and by printing the resolve as a broadside that could be quickly sent to the towns throughout Virginia, the burgesses settled upon what was the period's most powerful tool for amplifying, broadcasting, and framing the significance of important developments. Such a day of fasting and prayer propelled the community out of the ordinary diurnal round of rising, working, and eating, and into a communal gathering at an extraordinary midweek divine service, where there would be prayers and, in the words of the broadside, "a sermon suitable to the occasion." While it is impossible to know how completely the first of June was observed throughout the colony, Jefferson's autobiography offers an account of what happened after the members of the House returned to their home counties: "We returned home, and in our several counties invited the clergy to meet assemblies of the people on [Wednesday] the 1st of June, to perform the ceremonies of the day, & to address to them discourses suited to the occasion. The people met generally, with anxiety & alarm in their countenances, and the effect of the day thro' the whole colony was like a shock of electricity, arousing every man & placing him erect & solidly on his centre." Jefferson here uses the same electric shock metaphor as Richard Henry Lee, but in addition to the "anxiety and alarm" that Lee's letter describes, the communal observation of the day helps "arouse" "the people" from their political "lethargy," and, perhaps through self-reflection promoted by the day, strengthens "every man" by "placing" him "erect and solidly on his centre." For the small band of Whigs shaping events in Williamsburg in the last week of May 1774, the electric shock of the Port Bill had to be used to activate and mobilize the people.

The burgesses' second translation of the Boston Port Bill came the day after the governor's abrupt dissolution of the House on Thursday, May 26. In a hastily convened meeting of eighty-nine of the burgesses, Speaker Peyton Randolph led a rump meeting five hundred feet west of the House of Burgesses, down Duke of Gloucester Street, in the Apollo Room of the Raleigh Tavern. According to the English constitution, since the House had been dissolved, such a gathering had no more legal standing or political authority than any other group of eighty-nine men meeting in a tavern. In order to overcome this liability, the group emulated some of the legal procedures of the dissolved House: they were led by Speaker Randolph serving as moderator, and they communicated their actions to the other colonies through the committee of correspondence, which had been appointed by the House. Practicing the politics of the weak, the Virginia Association's actual action was very limited, and corresponded in certain ways with what the Boston Town Meeting did after the Massachusetts governor refused to convene the Massachusetts House. As with the publication of the *Votes and Proceedings*, printing "An Association, signed by the 89 Members of the late House of Burgesses" as a broadside allowed eighty-nine members of the "late House" to take its argument against British coercive measures directly to the public. However, in order to secure all those eighty-nine signatures, the resulting signed association was so moderate as to be indecisive. While it reaffirmed the boycott on East India tea, and warned that "the unconstitutional principle of taxing the colonies without their consent" might, in the future, "compel us against our will, to avoid all commercial intercourse with Britain," for now the association showed a judicious deference for their creditors: "A tender regard for the interest of our fellow subjects, the merchants and manufacturers of Great Britain, prevents us from going further at this time." While the association urged the "expediency" of "appointing of deputies, from the several colonies of British America, to meet in general congress" annually, the association did not develop any mechanism for Virginia to select its own deputies. On Saturday, May 28, the eight members of the Virginia Committee of Correspondence met under the chairmanship of Peyton Randolph, and dispatched the freshly printed broadsides of the association under a cover letter that invited each colony to "furnish us with" "your Sentiments" upon the "propriety of appointing Deputies from the several Colonies of British American to meet annually in general Congress" (Virginia House of Burgesses 1905, 138). Besides Randolph and Richard Henry Lee, the committee of correspondence included three more of the seven Virginia delegates to the first Congress. The letters were sent to the committees of all the colonies.

But on the very next day, Sunday, May 29, an express arrived for Peyton Randolph that worked a sea change in Virginia's political posture. The threefold communication that Virginia received from other colonies on the Whig network over the weekend of May 28–29, 1774, provoked it into a new, more active and effective translation of the political crisis. After reading the letters written from the three committees of correspondence of Boston, Philadelphia, and Annapolis, Randolph gathered the twenty-five burgesses still left in the town at his mansion, quite near the governor's palace. After a discussion conducted on Monday, May 30, the Virginia Committee of Correspondence sent out a new communication to all the other burgesses. The letter described the "most piteous and melancholy situation" of the inhabitants of Boston, and the Boston Town Meeting's resolution that "the most effectual assistance which can be given them by their sister colonies will arise from a general association against exports and imports, of every kind, to or from Great Britain."

Most of the twenty-five gentlemen present, after taking "the business under our most serious consideration," now thought "it absolutely necessary . . . to enlarge [their] late Association, and that [they] ought to adopt a scheme of non-importation to a very large extent." But admitting that "being so small a proportion of the late Associates," they could not change the general association, they therefore "invite[d] all members of the late House of Burgesses to a general meeting in this city on the first day of August next." Most crucially, they asked that each burgess take "an opportunity of collecting the sense of their respective counties." As we shall see below, the broadening of the base of county participation greatly enhanced the power of the Virginia Association when it was finally "enlarged" in August 1774.

The course modifications of the Virginia leadership in Williamsburg in the week of May 24–June 1, 1774, suggest the difficulty, as new information flowed in and the influence of the network of committees was felt, of getting Virginia's local response and verbal "translation" of the Boston Port Bill "right." While Virginia's first translation of the crisis responded to news of the Port Bill, and the second to the governor's dissolution of the House, the third translation of the crisis emerged from the synergies of the intercolonial network of committees of correspondence. In the three-part "chain letter" that arrived at Peyton Randolph's house on May 29, 1774, the burgesses could now trace the effort of Boston, Philadelphia, and Annapolis to translate the news of the Port Bill into words and "resolves," which could then be transmitted to the other committees on the network. Before examining how this packet was received in Virginia, it will be useful to characterize this communication dynamic.

Each time a particular node on the network received a letter, other agents from other places were brought into the particular location where committee members convened, deliberated, acted, and wrote; then, their translation of the received communication was pumped back out of the locale into the larger network of committees. Each committee node found its own actions enhanced, but also constrained, in at least three ways: by the patriotic wish and the pragmatic need to work in concert with the other committees on the network, by learning from the ideas and formulations of the other committees, and by its own shifting strategic judgment about what was now possible. Up and down the Atlantic coast, Whig committee members were now learning what it meant to be linked to a network: they had to speak at each moment with a double voice. On one hand, they had to *articulate local priorities, concerns, and ideas* so that the local connection to the larger network was secured. On the other hand, the goal at each node was to find a formulation that could be heard and embraced at the other locales on the network to the point where their words expressed the *collective sense of the whole network*. Both sides of this project of translation necessarily entailed an abstraction and simplification of the dense matrix of local concerns and interests. Within this communication exchange, actors on the network were made to act as well as making others act. All who were linked influenced each other reciprocally. If this system of communication was working well, it became difficult to say who was doing what and where initiative originated.

It is not difficult to surmise the surprise and pleasure that were stimulated by the arrival of the packet from Annapolis at Peyton Randolph's beautiful mansion on the north side of Market Square on May 29, 1774. Out of the packet would have emerged Boston's letter of May 13, 1774, along with multiple copies of the "vote" of the town meeting, intended for each colony who received the letter; the May 21, 1774, letter of the Philadelphia Committee of Correspondence, which was written not to Virginia, but to the Boston Committee of Correspondence, and copied to the colonies southward, thereby augmenting Boston's communications with Philadelphia's response; and, finally, the letter from Annapolis, written by the Annapolis members of the Maryland Committee of Correspondence, and responding to the communications from both Boston and Philadelphia (see box 4.2). For leaders advocating Virginia's commercial resistance to the Port Bill, this multifaceted communication aggregated information from three out of four of the most important commercial centers to the north: British America's third largest port (Boston, 510 miles away); its largest port (Philadelphia, 250 miles away); and the largest port on the Chesapeake (Annapolis, 150 miles away). At each node of the network, a complex situation was put into words that sought to shape the crisis. By taking a concise overview of the translation of the Port Bill fashioned in each of these places, we will be in a position to understand the new translation of the Port Bill developed by Virginia Whigs on May 29–31.

BOSTON, MAY 13, 1774

In its letter, the Boston committee communicated alarm, urgency, and a cry for help. The text of the Boston Port Bill had been brought by the *Harmony* into Boston Harbor on May 10, 1774, the ship that also carried the royal official charged with enforcement, the commander in chief of British forces in America and the newly appointed governor, Thomas Gage. While Gage conferred at Castle William with Governor Hutchinson, whom he was relieving,

Boston, 13 May 1774
GENTLEMEN:
The Town of Boston is now suffering the stroke of vengeance in the common cause. I hope they will sustain the blow with a becoming fortitude; . . . It is expected by their enemies, and feared by some of their friends, that this town singly will not be able to support the cause under so severe a trial; as the very being of every colony, considered as a free people, depends upon the event, a thought so dishonorable to our brethren cannot be entertained, as the town will now be left to struggle alone. . . . I have inclosed a copy of the Town's Vote for each of the colonies southward of your province, which I beg you to forward with all possible dispatch, together with your own sentiments thereon.
    Your humble servant, Samuel Adams

At a meeting of the Freeholders and other Inhabitants of the Town of Boston . . . on Friday, 13 May 1774.
Votes, that it is the opinion of this town that if the other colonies come into a joint resolution, to stop all Importations from Great Britain and Exportations to Great Britain and every part of the West Indies till the act for blocking our harbor be repealed, the same will prove the salvation for North America and her liberties; on the other hand if they continue their exports and imports there is high reason to fear, that fraud, power, and the most odious oppression, will rise triumphant over right, justice, social happiness and freedom.
    Attested: William Cooper, Town Clerk

Philadelphia, 21 May 1774
To collect a sense of this large city is difficult. . . . A respectable number of the inhabitants of this city was, however, assembled last evening in order to consult what was proper to be done . . . the inclosed resolves were passed. By what means . . . a reconciliation, and future harmony with our mother country on constitutional principles may be obtained

is indeed a weighty question; whether by the method you [of Boston] have suggested of non-importation and non-exportation agreement, or by a general congress of deputies from the different colonies, clearly to state what we conceive our rights, and make a claim or petition of them to his Majesty in firm but decent and dutiful terms, . . . are now the great points to be determined; that we have great reason to think, would be more agreeable to the people of this province . . . the former may be reserved as the last resources that should the other fail.

Your humble servants, signed in behalf and by order of the Committee of Correspondence

Annapolis, 25 May 1774
We this morning received a letter from the committee of correspondence of Philadelphia inclosing their resolutions with a copy of a letter and vote of the town of Boston. . . . [W]e shall anxiously expect your resolutions, in the mean time we propose the sense of the people be taken at their meetings on the following heads. [(1) an immediate stop to all exports; (2) the Association by an Oath; (3) no suits for any debts due; (4) this province will break off all trade with violating colonies.] We have the most sanguine hope that Maryland will cheerfully cooperate with your colony to any extent of non-importation and non-exportation.

Signed—Charles Carroll, Thomas Johnson, Samuel Chase, J. Hall, William Paca, Matthias Hammond, Stephen West

the Boston Whigs read the bill with dismay. The Whig leadership convened a meeting of the Boston Committee of Correspondence as well as an informal meeting of the people on May 12; it also "warned" a legal town meeting for May 13.[3] The Boston committee then wrote a letter, including the official "vote" of the town meeting, and sent it posthaste by Paul Revere, southward (from Hartford to New York to Philadelphia). The subscription to the letter, asking each recipient south of Philadelphia "to forward it with all possible dis-

3. The record is ambiguous on whether there was an unofficial meeting of the people on May 12. Letters from Samuel Adams to Elbridge Gerry and to the New Hampshire Committee of Correspondence on May 12, 1774, seemed to suggest this, but the records of the town make it clear that only the meeting of May 13 was official.

patch with their own sentiments," turns the Boston letter into a kind of chain letter (S. Adams 1904, 109). That is, it imposes a double obligation upon each committee receiving the letter: to fashion some sort of response to Boston's explicit plea for support and to forward both the Boston letter and their response to the committees of colonies south of them. In this way, each node on the network became an active relay: a place to pause, deliberate, and write; but also to reply *and* forward a constantly growing web of correspondence.

The Boston committee's brief letter was calculated to incite indignation at the injustice of Britain's response to the destruction of the tea. The inhabitants of Boston were "tried and condemned and [were] to be punished . . . without their having been even accused of any crime committed by them" (S. Adams 1904, 3:107–8). But rather than reject the position of the aggrieved victim, Boston embraced it so that it could become a rallying point for American Whigs. The town of Boston allegorizes itself as Liberty "suffering the stroke of vengeance in the common cause," hopes to have the strength to "support the cause under so severe a trial," where the "being of every colony, considered as a free people, depends upon the event." The pathos of the letter contrasts with the critical alternative outlined by the "vote" of the town: if the other colonies will stop all trade with Great Britain, it will "prove the salvation for North America and her liberties"; but, if they do not, "fraud" and "power" will "rise triumphant" over "social happiness and freedom." The rhetoric of Boston's language was shaped to guide each committee's deliberation into confronting the pointed question upon which everything depended: "do *you* consider Boston to be suffering in the Common Cause, feel and resent the injury, and will you therefore immediately suspend your trade with Britain?" (S. Adams 1904, 110–11).

PHILADELPHIA, MAY 20–21, 1774

While Boston had a committee of correspondence that had been operating continuously since November 1772, and served as an effective agency for active Boston Whigs, Philadelphia's response to the Port Bill unfolded in a political climate and organizational context that were confused and diffuse. While merchant committees had been organized to oppose the Townshend duties, and Whigs in the city had mobilized British America's most effective resistance to the East India tea, there was no standing committee of correspondence in the province or city to receive Boston's communication. So, when Paul Revere rode into town on May 18, 1774, it fell to a few active Whig leaders—Charles

Thomson, Joseph Reed, and Thomas Mifflin—to improvise a response. They persuaded the locally influential John Dickinson to join their effort by attending a hurriedly called meeting of merchants and other important citizens at City Tavern on May 20.[4] The rather chaotic meeting at City Tavern was reported much later by Reed and Thomson to have featured a "pathetic" reading of Boston's letter by Reed; the promotion of vigorous measures, spoken with "more warmth and fire" by Mifflin; and then a moderating motion by John Dickinson to request that the governor convene the Pennsylvania Assembly. The meeting also formed a committee of nineteen, which blended active Whigs with rather more restrained merchants, to respond to Boston as well as the colonies to the south (Ryerson 1978, 41–43; Thomson 1879, 277–78).

The letter that the Philadelphia committee addressed to Boston (and copied for transmission to Annapolis and Williamsburg) translates the contrary currents of the politics of the city into a tentative response to the crisis. The committee is mindful of the limits of its own authority: "to collect a sense of this large city is difficult," and even when this is done, the committee must not "consider themselves as authorized to judge or act for this populous province." Rather than joining the struggle to which the Boston letter summoned the colonies, Philadelphia's letter positions the city as a peacemaker seeking "reconciliation, and future harmony with our mother country." The Philadelphia committee suggests that "if satisfying the East India Company for the damage they have sustained, would put an end to this unhappy controversy," it is confident "that neither you nor we, could continue a moment in doubt what part to act." Setting aside Boston's urgently proposed remedy, a full and immediate embargo on trade with Great Britain, Philadelphia prefers a more moderate measure: "a general congress of deputies from the different colonies," "clearly to state what we conceive our rights, and make a claim or petition of them to his Majesty in firm but decent and dutiful terms." While the equivocating moderation of Philadelphia's response to Boston disgusted some Philadelphia Whigs (like Thomas Mifflin and Charles Thomson), their communication with the network of committees, and their joining at least eight other colonies in the call for a general congress, helped to strengthen the Whig intercolonial network.

4. For an attempt to synthesize the fascinating but sometimes contradictory and self-serving narratives of Joseph Reed and Charles Thomson, see Ryerson 1978, 40–42. For "Joseph Reed's Narrative" and Charles Thomson's corrective, partially disguised account, in a letter to William Henry Drayton, see Thomson 1879, 269–86.

There are several reasons that the communication from the Annapolis Committee of Correspondence would have been particularly important to Virginia. First, in spite of their differences, geography made Maryland and Virginia sister colonies: between them they shared the Chesapeake Bay, with the Potomac River as the boundary between the colonies on the western shore of the Chesapeake. South of that boundary, Virginia was defined by three rivers (the Rappahannock, the York, and the James) and two important towns, Williamsburg and Yorktown. To the north, Maryland featured two towns, the capital of Annapolis and the urban port of Baltimore, as well as the great Susquehanna River. Together the two colonies had economies centered on tobacco, and together they accounted for virtually all of that very lucrative and important trade.[5] But this meant that Maryland shared the same imbalanced economy, with planters highly indebted to Glasgow merchants, and, in 1772–1774, the dismal collapse in the price of tobacco and the ensuing credit crisis (Ragsdale 1996, 168–72). This economic climate made a ban upon exports much more attractive than it would have been in earlier, more prosperous times. But if the economic crisis helped to create a context for vigorous political measures, the Annapolis committee faced organizational challenges. In late May, Maryland's assembly was not in session, and only part of the committee of correspondence was on hand in Annapolis to respond to Boston's cry for help and Philadelphia's response to it. Nonetheless, on May 25, 1774, the Annapolis committee developed a remarkably spirited and robust response for transmission to Virginia (Ammerman 1971, 169–80; 1974, 28–30).

In framing its response, the Annapolis committee had to balance the imperative to respond quickly to the communications that it received from Boston and Philadelphia with an awareness, like that of the Philadelphia committee, of its limited power to act alone. In other words, it had to transmit local ideas and interests, take initial steps to gather more dispersed Maryland

---

5. Although the colony of Maryland was much smaller in population and landmass than Virginia, it provided nearly one-third of the total tobacco trade with Britain from British America (Cappon 1976, 26). Out of the five most important exports to Britain from North America, which totaled on average £2,000,000 between 1768 and 1772, here is the distributed percentage value in pounds sterling of each commodity: tobacco, 44.1 percent; wheat, bread, flour, 26.3 percent; rice, 14.6 percent; fish, 8.9 percent; indigo, 6.1 percent. This suggests the enormous economic value of the tobacco trade for parties on both sides of the Atlantic.

opinions, and transmit and inflect the information it had received from the north. It did this in three different ways. First, by holding an Annapolis town meeting (attended by about eighty) and forming a committee of correspondence, it could translate the sense of the town and its leaders into a possible plan for network-wide action. Second, although the Annapolis committee of correspondence included five people who were also on the officially authorized eleven-member Maryland Committee of Correspondence (John Hall, Thomas Johnson Jr., William Paca, Matthias Hammond, and Samuel Chase), that group fell just short of the six-member quorum that was required by the authorizing motion passed by the Maryland assembly the previous October. It therefore could not pass resolves that "spoke" for Maryland or its legislature. So it acted to become the de facto hub of a network with a star topology: it sent its suggested resolves to Baltimore and five counties, asking them to meet and consider copies of the communication from Philadelphia and Boston. The committee also proposed that each act upon four topic "heads," a list that pointed toward vigorous measures in Maryland: that there be an "immediate stop" to all exports, soon to be followed by a stop to imports; that the "association" to enforce the embargo "be on oath"; that there be a suspension of any local "suit(s) for the recovery of any debt"; and that this colony would break trade with colonies who refused to join the majority in the embargo. But third, rather than wait for a response from these six places, the Maryland committee also functioned as a relay point on the network for north to south transmission, a position that obliged it to act in a timely fashion. Therefore, by the end of a very busy day, it sent an express letter to Peyton Randolph, chairman of the Virginia committee, with their four proposed resolves, as well as the important enclosures from Boston and Philadelphia. Not wishing to appear as though it was directing the great colony of Virginia, nor promising to take Virginia's direction, the Maryland committee ends by expressing "the most sanguine hope that Maryland will cheerfully cooperate with your colony to any extent of non-importation and non-exportation," and that "a cordial and free intercourse will be established" with Virginia, culminating in "withholding our tobacco" from Great Britain.[6]

6. Ammerman exaggerates the influence of the Annapolis letter on Virginia. The documents in *American Archives* show that the Annapolis meeting was too far out in front of public opinion, making it subject to harsh rebukes by petitioners and other meetings, who especially protested the idea of suspending the courts of law in Maryland ("A Publication of the Enclosed Protest, Supported by Considerable Number of the Inhabitants of the City of Annapolis," signed by over 170; Force 1836, 1:23).

When the twenty-five burgesses gathered at Peyton Randolph's house at ten in the morning on Monday, May 30, an oral reading of the three letters from the committees of Boston, Philadelphia, and Annapolis must have taken up much of the early part of the meeting. Although there are no records of the discussion that followed, by reading the letter subsequently composed for absent members of the House of Burgesses, we can surmise something of how these communications changed the direction of Whig political measures in Williamsburg. The letter from the Philadelphia committee, by supporting a "general congress," lent support for the stronger call for a "general congress" to meet "annually," which Virginia had already advanced. The letter and vote from Boston focused more urgent attention upon the measure that the association of eighty-nine had already discussed without full resolution: a ban upon imports and exports from Great Britain. While Philadelphia's temporizing upon that issue might have been discouraging, the enthusiasm of the Annapolis committee for considering an "immediate stop" on exports, followed by a later suspension of imports, helped move sentiment among this group of twenty-five burgesses toward a need for stronger measures. Obviously, a successful embargo upon tobacco required full and enthusiastic participation by tobacco growers and traders in both colonies. With the need for a decision on this momentous question, but a lack of anything resembling a quorum, it became essential to gather the burgesses again for what would come to be called "the Virginia convention." But how was this group of burgesses, who obviously lacked the governor's constitutional authority to convene the House, to convince the ninety-seven absent burgesses who were scattered through the sixty-one counties of this largest of all the American colonies, to come the many miles to Williamsburg for an illegal convention? Here are the words they used: "We flatter ourselves it is unnecessary to multiply words to induce your compliance with this invitation, upon an occasion which is, confessedly, of the most lasting importance to all America. Things seem to be hurrying to an alarming crisis, and demand the speedy, united councils of all those who have a regard for the common cause. We are, gentleman, your most affectionate friends, and obedient humble servants." It may seem odd to "induce" "compliance" with an "invitation." However, the urgent personal appeal, by "your most affectionate friends, and obedient humble servants," is justified by an utterly untypical moment, a time outside of ordinary time, when "things seem to be hurrying to an alarming crisis." It is this unprecedented crisis that demands "speedy, united councils" of all who "have a regard for the common cause." In this moment, the twenty-five burgesses say, *your* sense of responsibility will surely "induce your compliance with this invitation." What has given this group of twenty-five burgesses and the committee that writes for them the authority to demand "compliance" to this "invitation" is their obligation to the network of committees up and down the Atlantic coast: "LAST Sunday Morning several Letters were received from Boston, Philadelphia, and Maryland, on the most interesting and important Subject of American Grievances." In other words, these extraordinary communications in a time of crisis and the call for collective action they reiterate obliges this small group of men to rally Virginia to act.

HOW A LOOSE INCIPIENT INTERCOLONIAL NETWORK OF COMMITTEES WAS DEVELOPED

Virginia's organizational initiatives in late May 1774 turned out to be crucial to convening the general congress of the colonies in Philadelphia. But before considering how the congress was gathered, it is worth asking how towns and cities from Portsmouth, New Hampshire, to Charleston, South Carolina, had managed to develop a coherent and unified response to the Boston Port Bill. How did it come to be that by May 1774, there were already established political agencies—committees of correspondence authorized by towns, counties, and colonial assemblies—to assume responsibility for formulating a local response to the Port Bill and communicating these responses to others? How did each committee know the address and the principals in other colonies? Finally, how is it that they had already developed the ideas and protocols that specified the scope, content, tone, and manner of their communications?

British administration was correct in their expectation that Boston Whigs, caught off guard by this harsh and unprecedented law and confronted with overwhelming military force, would be unable to resist the closing of Boston Harbor on June 1, 1774. However, British administration underestimated the political potential of the incipient network of committees, which American Whigs had developed over the previous eighteen months. They also failed to realize that the mix of policies cooked up in Parliament in the spring of 1774—the application of firmness, constitutional reform, and force—would help turn an incipient committee network into a fully developed one. When the "electric shock" of the Port Bill strengthened and extended that network, unifying Whigs from up and down the continent in a plan to oppose British authority, it was Whitehall's turn to be shocked. It has been the habit of historians, for well over two hundred years, to give either Boston or Virginia credit for initiating intercolonial communication.[7] Instead, I will argue that we cannot understand how a network of committees of correspondence was developed, unless we grasp what Whig leaders from Massachusetts and Virginia and Pennsylvania said at the time: that credit must be distributed among the agents who bound themselves into a common network.

In a letter written in 1816, Thomas Jefferson sought to describe the effect in Virginia of the political exchanges set going by the Boston declaration of November 1772: "I felt the foundations of the government shaken under my feet by the New England townships. There was not an individual in their States whose body was not thrown with all its momentum into action" (Thomas Jefferson to Joseph C. Cabell, February 2, 1816; Jefferson 1984, 1381). With this striking language, Jefferson foregrounds two related features of the Boston committee's communication initiative. In the towns of New England, the Boston declaration "throws" the "body" of every "individual" into "action"; in this case, that action was opposition to the measures of royal government. But this political event had the added capacity to communicate itself remotely. For Jefferson insists that, because of what they had done (in New England), "I" felt the "foundations of the government shaken under *my* feet" (in Vir-

7. After the colonies became a new nation, it is perhaps inevitable that a custody battle would break out over the invention of the committees of correspondence. There is bias obvious in two early works. In Mercy Otis Warren's *History of the Rise, Progress and Termination of the American Revolution* (1805), the credit for inventing committees of correspondence goes to Boston (with Samuel Adams given the idea by Warren's husband, the Plymouth representative James Warren; M. Warren 1989, 1:62). In William Wirt's *Sketches of the Life and Character of Patrick Henry* (1817), Wirt is aware of Warren's argument, and he even quotes Warren's footnote, but Wirt's narrative gives the Virginia House of Burgesses "the merit of originating that powerful engine of resistance, correspondence committees between the legislatures of the different colonies" (Wirt 1871, 105). In some sense, historians who center their narrative on Boston—from George Bancroft to Richard D. Brown—interpret Virginia's initiative as a simple albeit important scaling up of the activity of the Boston Committee of Correspondence (Brown 1970, 140–41; see also Maier 1980, 17); by contrast, those who center their narrative in Virginia, like James Miller Leake (1917) and David Ramsay (1789), emphasize the Old Dominion's proud autonomy and its brave initiative in the cause of liberty (from the Stamp Act forward). These Virginia-centric histories see the burgesses' 1773 formation of a committee for intercolonial correspondence as the decisive innovation. I chart a course between these two positions.

ginia; emphasis mine).[8] In composing the *Votes and Proceedings*, the Boston Committee of Correspondence did not address other colonies, but, as Jefferson's words suggest, they nonetheless were heard. The colonial newspaper conducted the words of Boston's initiative to Virginia. The two Virginia gazettes reprinted, first, the Boston Town Meeting's struggle with the governor (October 26–November 2, 1772), an excerpt of the *Votes and Proceedings* (of November 20, 1772), some responses of other towns, and, finally, the debate between the governor and the Council and House. In the first months of 1773, Boston's successful development of the political potential of the committees of correspondence offered a model that Virginia Whigs borrowed and reshaped for their own political use.

It is worth tracing the steps by which the Whigs of Massachusetts and Whigs of Virginia could, across the many hundreds of miles that separated them, acquire the trust in each other that would enable them to share sensitive information, experiment with means of resistance, and learn from each other. Crucial here is the correspondence I have already described, that which flourished starting in 1773, between Richard Henry Lee and Samuel Adams (see chapter 3, "Communication, Empire, and the American Crisis"). A brief look at that correspondence will suggest the importance of this link. Richard Henry Lee, the most politically active of the five Lee brothers, was the third son of Thomas Lee, the possessor of vast landholdings of thirty thousand acres on Virginia's northern neck, and the builder, around 1730, of the stately Georgian edifice of Stratford Hall. Returning from England after nine years at the Wake field Academy, Richard Henry Lee was elected to the House of Burgesses in 1757, and by 1766 was prominent enough to run against Peyton Randolph for the position of Speaker. Richard Henry Lee's offer of a private correspondence to Samuel Adams opened a channel that could link the Whig leadership of two colonies to each other. Like so much revolutionary communication, it was triggered by a political crisis. In the winter of 1772–1773, Richard Henry Lee

8. This letter is one of a chain of letters written in the spring and summer of 1816, in which Jefferson contemplates the organization of Virginia into wards, so that "every man is a sharer in the direction of his ward-republic." Crucial to the power of those "elementary republics"—exemplified by the New England towns during the approach to the American Revolution—is the stake they gave every participating member in the action of their government. This makes their town government "the wisest invention ever devised by the wit of man for the perfect exercise of self-government, and for its preservation" (Thomas Jefferson to Samuel Kercheval, July 12, 1816; Jefferson 1984, 1399).

joined other Virginia Whigs in following two new developments: the alarming news of royal appointment of the Gaspée commission and the intensifying polemics in Massachusetts that followed the publication by the town of Boston of the *Votes and Proceedings*.[9]

After Richard Henry Lee had sent his letter to Samuel Adams, but before he had received any response, Lee worked with other Whigs from the House of Burgesses to design a systematic way to interlink the colonies. In his *Autobiography*, written in 1821, Thomas Jefferson recalls the organizational effort with these words: "We were all sensible that the most urgent of all measures was that of coming to an understanding with all the other colonies to consider the British claims as a common cause to all, & to produce an unity of action; and for this purpose that a committee of correspondence in each colony would be the best instrument for intercommunication" (Jefferson 1984, 7). To win the essential support of "our older & leading" members of the House, like Peyton Randolph, the powerful Speaker, and Robert Carter Nichols, the treasurer of the colony, Richard Henry Lee worked with the more active members to veil its more ambitious goals in a discrete rationale. So, when the motion to institute a new committee of correspondence was introduced on the floor of the House, a much more circumspect set of justifications for the formation of the committee was offered: first, "whereas, the minds of Majesty's faithful subjects in this colony" have been "disturbed" by "rumors and reports" of proceedings that threaten "their ancient, legal and constitutional rights"; second, "whereas" the "affairs of this colony are frequently connected with those of Great Britain, as well as of the neighboring colonies"; be it resolved to form "a standing committee of correspondence" of these eleven persons "to obtain the most early and authentic intelligence" of these worrisome proceedings "and to keep up and maintain a correspondence and communication with our sister colonies." In other words, anxiety and interconnection calls for communication, especially upon that "court of inquiry said to be lately held in Rhode Island," which claims the authority to move persons "accused of offences committed in America, to places beyond the seas, to be tried" (Virginia House of Burgesses 1905, 28). But why, a Tory skeptic of this initiative might ask, if there is a connection with Great Britain "as well as" our "sister colonies," is there only

9. Richard Henry Lee was chosen for special notice when, on the first day of the convening of the General Court, January 6, 1773, Thomas Cushing Jr. mailed a copy of the *Votes and Proceedings* to Richard Henry Lee; Lee acknowledged receipt of the *Votes and Proceedings* in a letter posted from Chantilly on February 13, 1773, nine days after his February 4 letter to Samuel Adams (Bancroft 1866, 6:445).

to be correspondence among the latter? When the Board of Trade read these resolves, it concluded that these "proceedings of the Virginia House of Burgesses" were pitched so directly against the authority of Great Britain that they were "of a most dangerous tendency and effect."[10]

Virginia's proposal that each colony appoint a committee of correspondence neatly complemented Boston's own networking initiative. Both promote unity, but in different ways. The Boston committee sought to increase the scope and energy of political participation, by drawing the scattered towns of Massachusetts and individual members of each town into the formulation and exchange of their opinion upon public measures. Implicit in Boston's initiative is the republican notion of the ultimate sovereignty of the people. By contrast, the House of Burgesses' initiative, by forming the Virginia Committee of Correspondence, sought to interlink the leading members of the various assemblies together, so that each colony could gather more information and, by sharing information, more effectively challenge British "proceedings," like those of the Gaspée commission. Implicit in the Virginia initiative is the authority of each colony to uphold the constitutional rights guaranteed by their charters. If the Boston initiative broadens and deepens the Whig political base, Virginia puts Whig leaders into communication with one another. While the Boston committee moved the towns of Massachusetts toward a place where they could act together (as they did in agitating against the Tea Act), the Virginia committee moved the colonies to the point where colonial assemblies could act together (in moving toward a general congress). The complementary character of these two networking initiatives is suggested by the way Virginia explicitly took Boston's example as an influence, and by the Boston committee's speedy and enthusiastic embrace of Virginia's initiative.

The deep compatibility of these two networking initiatives is readable in a broadside that the Boston committee sent to the various towns of Massachusetts on April 9, 1773 (fig. 4.1). On that day, the Boston committee held a

10. Once the House of Burgesses used the committee to initiate correspondence with other colonies, the Board of Trade expressed their alarm this way: "As these proceedings of the House of Burgesses of Virginia appear to us to be of a very extraordinary nature and we think that the inviting the other colonies to a communication and correspondence upon such matters as are stated in these proceedings is a measure of a most dangerous tendency and effect, we humbly submit to Your Majesty to take such measures thereupon as your majesty with the advice of your Privy Council shall think most proper and expedient. Entry Signatories, Dartmouth, Edward Eliot, Bamber Gascoyne" (Whitehall, Commissioners for Trade and Plantations to the King, July 1, 1773; *Documents* 1974, 6:169–70).

SIR,

THE Committee of Correspondence of this Town have received the following Intelligence, communicated to them by a Person of Character in this Place. We congratulate you upon the Acquisition of such respectable Aid as the ancient and patriotic Province of *Virginia*, the earliest Resolvers against the detestable Stamp-Act, in Opposition to the unconstitutional Measures of the present Administration. The Authenticity of this Advice you may depend upon, as it was immediately received from one of the Honorable Gentlemen appointed to communicate with the other Colonies. We are,

Your Friends and humble Servants,

Signed by Direction of the Committee for Correspondence in *Boston*,

William Cooper } Town Clerk,

To the Town-Clerk of *Westminster* , to be immediately delivered to the Committee of Correspondence for your Town, if such a Committee is chosen, otherwise to the Gentlemen the Selectmen, to be communicated to the Town.

Extract of a Letter from a Gentleman of distinction in Virginia, to his Friend in this Town, dated March 14th, 1773.

"I RECEIVED the papers * you sent me, and am much obliged to you for them, our assembly sitting a few days after, they were of use to us. You will see by the enclosed Resolutions the true sentiments of this colony, and that we are endeavouring to bring our sister colonies into the strictest union with us, that we may RESENT IN ONE BODY any steps that may be taken by administration to deprive ANY ONE OF US of the least particle of our rights & liberties ; we should have done more but we could procure nothing but news-paper accounts of the proceedings in Rhode-Island. I hope we shall not be thus kept in the dark for the future, and that we shall have from the different Committees the earliest intelligence of any motion that may be made by the TYRANTS in England to carry their INFERNAL purposes of enslaving us into execution ; I dare venture to assure you the strictest attention will be given on our parts to these grand points."

In the House of Burgesses, in Virginia March, 1773.

"WHEREAS the minds of his Majesty's faithful subjects in this colony have been much disturbed by various rumours and reports of proceedings tending to deprive them of their ancient, legal and constitutional rights.

"And whereas the affairs of this colony are frequently connected with those of Great-Britain, as well as of the neighbouring colonies, which renders a communication of sentiments necessary,

* The Votes and Proceedings of the Town of Boston, and News-Papers, containing the Governor's Speeches, and the Answers of the two Houses.

in order therefore to remove the uneasinesses and to quiet the minds of the people, as well as for the other good purposes above mentioned.

"Be it *resolved*, That a standing committee of correspondence and inquiry be appointed, to consist of eleven persons, viz. the honourable Payton Randolph, Esq; Robert Carter Nicholas, Richard Bland, Richard Henry Lee, Benjamin Harrison, Edmund Pendleton, Patrick Henry, Dudley Digges, Dabney Carr, Archibald Cary, and Thomas Jefferson, Esqrs; any six of whom to be a committee, whose business it shall be to obtain the most early and authentic intelligence of all such acts and resolutions of the British parliament or proceedings of administration, as may relate to, or affect the British colonies in America, and to keep up and maintain a correspondence and communication with our sister colonies, respecting these important considerations, and the result of such their proceedings from time to time to lay before this house.

"*Resolved*, That it be an instruction to the said committee, that they do, without delay, inform themselves particularly of the principles and authority, on which was constituted a court of inquiry, said to have been lately held in Rhode-Island, with powers to transport persons accused of offences committed in America, to places beyond the seas to be tried.

"*Resolved*, That the Speaker of this House do transmit to the Speakers of the different assemblies of the British colonies, on this continent, copies of the said resolutions, and desire they will lay them before their respective assemblies, and request them to appoint some person or persons of their respective bodies, to communicate from time to time with the said committee.

FIGURE 4.1. Boston Committee of Correspondence broadside of the resolves of the House of Burgesses instituting the Virginia Committee of Correspondence are here embedded in a letter "from a Gentleman of distinction in Virginia" (almost certainly Richard Henry Lee) "to his Friend in this Town" (Thomas Cushing Jr.), which is then embedded in a printed letter to the committees of correspondence (or the selectmen) of the various towns (here Westminster) of Massachusetts, signed by the clerk of the Boston committee, William Cooper. Photograph courtesy of the American Antiquarian Society.

special Friday meeting, attended by Speaker Thomas Cushing Jr., who, since the Massachusetts House was not in session, took the letter he had received from Richard Henry Lee,[11] which enclosed the communication of the Virginia committee, consisting of the resolutions of the burgesses instituting the committee. The letter also expressed gratitude to Cushing for sending the *Votes and Proceedings*, as well as newspapers containing the responses of the Council and the House to the governor's speeches. In such a private letter, Lee could explicitly state Virginia's goal, in terms that closely mirror Jefferson's account written forty-seven years later: "to bring our sister colonies into the strictest union with us, that we may RESENT IN ONE BODY any steps that may be taken by administration to deprive ANY ONE OF US of the least particle of our rights and liberties" (typography is that of the Boston committee broadside).

By April 9, 1774, Richard Henry Lee had written twice to Boston, once by private letter to Samuel Adams, and once in a semi-official letter to Thomas Cushing, enclosing the resolves of the Virginia Committee of Correspondence. Aware of the arrival of Lee's private letter to Adams, the Boston committee requested that its chairman, Samuel Adams, draft an official reply to Lee. I will quote from the April 10, 1774, letter at some length because it not only contains an extensive and systematic statement of the revolutionary imperative to network; it also performs the networking it describes. The letter uses six distinct threads to secure a strong bond between Adams and Lee, Massachusetts and Virginia.

Building a framework for trusted communication through expressions of esteem: "I had frequently heard of your Character and Merit, as a warm Advocate for Virtue and Liberty" (S. Adams 1904, 3:25). The Boston Committee of Correspondence, which held a "special meeting" on your resolves, "desired" me "to assure you of their veneration for your most ancient colony, and their unfeigned esteem for the gentlemen of your committee" (27). The epithet "ancient" grants Virginia its pride of place as the first successful English colony in America.

Urging the practice of general communication among the colonies: "I have often thought it a misfortune, or rather a fault in the friends of American independence and freedom, their not taking care to open every channel of communication. The colonies are all embarked in the same [ship] bottom. The

11. See Brown 1970, 140n56, on the likelihood that the letter is from Richard Henry Lee. The ardent tone of this letter makes it highly unlikely to be from Peyton Randolph, the official chair of the Virginia committee, though he would be the other possibility. For Virginia's acting with a firsthand knowledge of the *Votes and Proceedings* and the House and Council debate with Governor Hutchinson, see Bancroft 1866, 454.

liberties of all are alike invaded by the same haughty power: the conspirators against their common rights have indeed exerted their brutal force, or applied their insidious arts, differently in the several colonies, as they thought would best serve their purpose of oppression and tyranny. How necessary then is it; that *All* should be early acquainted with the particular circumstances of *Each*, in order that the wisdom & strength of the whole may be employed upon every proper occasion." Only communication that is timely, particular, and extends to "all" the colonies will enable each colony to face the "brutal force" or the "insidious arts" of Britain's "haughty power."

Noting that in facing British power separately, the record of the colonies has been uneven: Adams wishes that "the little colony" of Rhode Island "had shown more firmness" in the face of the Gaspée commission; the "compliance of New York" in providing "annual provision for a military force"; the "timidity of some colonies and the silence of other colonies is discouraging." Nonetheless, Adams insists that "the manly generosity and the steady perseverance" of Virginia and South Carolina give hope "that the fire of true patriotism will at length spread throughout the continent."

Commending to Lee's attention, for possible imitation, the system of corresponding committees that is developing so rapidly in Massachusetts: "The Friends of Liberty in this Town have lately made a successful Attempt to obtain the explicit political Sentiments of a great Number of the Towns in this Province; and the Number is daily increasing. The very Attempt was alarming to the Adversaries; and the happy Effects of it are mortifying to them. I would propose it for your Consideration, whether the Establishment of Committees of Correspondence among the several Towns in every Colony, would not tend to promote that General Union, upon which the Security of the whole depends" (26). Here Adams marks the difference between the assembly committees of correspondence that Virginia is proposing and the more numerous, local committees of correspondence that are expanding across Massachusetts. Only by winning "the explicit political sentiments" of numerous towns and counties, Adams seems to say, can we expand local political participation, thereby creating that "general union" upon which our "security" "depends."

Delivering some of that reliable information concerning the Gaspée commission that Lee had requested: Adams assures Lee that the letter of instructions to the Rhode Island governor from the American secretary, Lord Dartmouth, that "you may have seen in the News papers, may be depended upon as genuine" (27). Adams further promises to forward "an authentic copy of that commission" that he is expecting. By sharing sensitive political information, Adams returns the trust that Lee has shown him.

Ending his letter with an extravagant wish to communicate: "I have a thousand things to say to you, but am prevented by a want of time." The resemblance to first love seems more than casual. When compared with the measured tone of most of Samuel Adams's letters, the energy, candor, and high expectations for the future that are expressed in Adams's reply to Lee suggest that the exchange has incited political love. But this enthusiasm seems less a personal sentiment than one mediated by a fresh hope that Lee's letter and the Virginia resolves have excited for the cause of public liberty.

The strong and secure communication link that was forged between the Whigs of Virginia and Massachusetts over the course of 1773 did not develop from the public newspapers, from personal correspondence, or even from public bodies like the committees of correspondence alone. It required an intricate symbiosis of all three to mediate a trustworthy connection for regular intercolonial communication. Through these three distinct kinds of communications, Virginia Whigs learned from Boston's formation of a committee of correspondence and translated it into the very different constitutional and political terrain of Williamsburg. It took this complex and overlapping chain of actions to develop the communication link between Massachusetts and Virginia that would prove so important to the Revolution.

In the fourteen months between the first meeting of the Virginia Committee of Correspondence on March 13, 1773, and the arrival of the Port Bill in Boston on May 11, 1774, the Boston and Virginia networking initiatives developed more or less independently. Like the Boston committee, the Virginia committee appointed a clerk, John Tazewell, to manage its log, and it kept a careful record of the communications that it sent and received. To assure that committee correspondence was tied into the centers of power in the House of Burgesses, the Speaker of the House was made the chairman of the committee. He was joined by the treasurer of the colony, Robert Carter Nichols, and the House member from nearby York, Dudley Digges, to form a "Select Committee of Correspondence" who were authorized to write on behalf of the whole committee when, with the House not in session, most of its other members would not be in Williamsburg. The timing of the responses received by the Virginia committee suggests the greatest weakness of this network. Because Virginia's invitation to the various assemblies to appoint a committee and initiate correspondence with the other colonies arrived at a time when most assemblies were not in session, and depended upon each Speaker's interest in acting, the rate of response was widely divergent. The first colony to respond, Rhode Island, acted to appoint its committee within two months, on March 7, 1773, but the last colony to act, New Jersey, did not appoint its committee for nearly eleven months, on February 8, 1774 (Virginia House of Burgesses 1905, 41–64, 144–45). In some sense, the long period required to achieve near unanimity of action is the inevitable liability of a distributed network, where initiative is vested equally in every node on the network. It is difficult for such a network to have the agility that the Boston committee showed during the tea crisis, when it seamlessly expanded the reach of its communications from Massachusetts to include other colonies. Thus, at the meeting of December 6, the town of Boston actually adopted the tea resolves that the city of Philadelphia had adopted on October 16, and the Boston committee then disseminated those resolves to the towns. In the weeks before and after the destruction of the tea, the Boston committee sought and won support through public as well as private and informal correspondence with other colonies and towns: the Portsmouth committee of New Hampshire; committees of three towns of Rhode Island (Newport, Providence, Bristol); the Charlestown committee, South Carolina; the Hartford committee, Connecticut; New York (to and from Isaac Sears and Alexander McDougall); and Philadelphia (to and from Charles Thomson, George Clymer, Thomas Mifflin, and Joseph Reed). Because its network was organized in a star topology around itself, the Boston committee did not have to consult with anyone to initiate action. By contrast, the Virginia committee had to wait for the response of the assemblies it had addressed.[12] Nonetheless, the Virginia committee's communications took a vital new step in uniting the colonies. Because eleven out of twelve colonies responded by appointing an official standing committee of correspondence, this loose and flexible network of committees was in place and ready to respond to the general crisis precipitated by the Boston Port Bill, to disseminate the association of eighty-nine burgesses on May 28, 1774, and to send out the letter of twenty-five burgesses on May 31, 1774.

The House of Burgesses' institution of the Virginia Committee of Correspondence encouraged the development of a network with tremendous latent potential. The factors that made the network weak—that it was distributed and without an authoritative center, that initiative had to come from all its nodes, that it required near unanimity to act—are precisely what also made it a flexible and robust "learning machine," with the potential to gather the power of all thirteen colonies. Thus, when the House of Representatives of

12. The quantity of correspondence by the Virginia committee in 1773 is rather light when compared to that of the Boston committee (the Virginia committee received only fifteen communications from twelve colonies and one London correspondent; the Boston committee sent and received well over 150).

Connecticut took up the Virginia resolutions, endorsed them, and then set up its own committee, it multiplied the effect of Virginia's communication first with its own, and then with the plurality of communications it invited from others: "Resolved, that the Speaker of this house do transmit to the Speakers of the different Assemblies of the British Colonies of this Continent, Copies of these [Connecticut] Resolutions, and request that they will come into similar measures, and communicate from time to time with said committees, on all matters wherein the common welfare and safety of the colonies are concerned" (May 21, 1773; Virginia House of Burgesses 1905). The unity of the colonies could never have been achieved with a network organized as a star topology by one town (like Boston) or one colony (like Virginia). In spite of the compliments that the colonies exchanged in praise of each other, leadership or hegemony was inconsistent with the separate histories and independent claims to liberty that each colony made. Only a distributed network could support an intercolonial unity consistent with the autonomy and diversity of the thirteen colonies.

THE VARIED PURPOSES FOR A "GENERAL CONGRESS": A CRISIS MEETING AND/OR BUILDING A NETWORK HUB

If our account of the calling of a general congress is shaped by our knowledge of what the Continental Congress would later become, we can tell the following story. The "general congress" grew out of the Whig network of committees, rectified the built-in limitations of that network, and anticipated a much more ambitious federal unity. If we stay close to the uncertainty of the matrix of events out of which the congress emerged, however, a less teleological and national account becomes possible. Since the Whig networks described in this chapter had a loose structure, they also had this important virtue: networks could be reconfigured on the fly in response to events as they happened. Members at each node on the network could improvise in response to the new developments, as well as the new messages received from other nodes on the network. That is what the Virginia Whigs did in Williamsburg in late May 1774. The flexibility of networks helps to explain why the proposals for a "congress" were shaped by such different imperatives. I will examine three.

The Congress as a Bold Recourse with the Ultimately Conservative Goal of Preserving the Empire

By the summer of 1773, Benjamin Franklin's attempts to overcome tenacious differences between Massachusetts and the ministry had reached a dead end. In a long letter of July 7, 1773, Franklin suggests a "general congress" of the colonies as a canny tactical maneuver that would increase the collective weight of the colonies and might compel Great Britain to negotiate with the colonies upon the fundamental question of colonial rights. The proposal, written in an official private letter to Speaker Thomas Cushing, but later published throughout the colonies, reflects two developments: the king's definitive rejection of two petitions of the Massachusetts House and the recent successes of the committees of correspondence. Franklin reiterates his long-held view that time will steadily increase the relative wealth and power of the American colonies within the British Empire, which, combined with the high likelihood of war, would renew Britain's sense of its necessary reliance upon its American colonies. Franklin therefore recommends that the time is now right for the colonies to gather in congress: "[P]erhaps it would be best and fairest, for the Colonies in a general Congress now in Peace to be assembled, or by means of the Correspondence lately proposed after a full and solemn Assertion and Declaration of their Rights, to engage firmly with each other that they will never grant aids to the Crown in any General War till those Rights are recognized by the King and both Houses of Parliament" (July 7, 1773; Franklin 1974, 20:282). The conservative aim of Franklin's proposal—to save the unity of the empire that was threatened with division—is apparent from the way he states the goal of such a congress: "No one doubts the Advantages of a strict Union between the Mother Country and the colonies, if it may be obtained and preserved on equitable Terms." But there is an important ambiguity within this proposal: Franklin acknowledges that such a congress might "bring the dispute to a crisis," and further, that Britain might use "compulsory means" to convince us to "rescind" the resolves of such a congress. But even such a struggle would "contribute to unite and strengthen us, and in the mean time all the world will allow that our proceeding has been honorable." Franklin's goal might be to create a new basis for a "strict union" of Britain and her colonies, but his proposal also might "bring the dispute to a crisis," as indeed it did.[13] Franklin's early ideas are consistent with the conservative tenor of the rationale for a congress advanced by the Pennsylvania commit-

13. The Boston Whigs thought so well of Franklin's letter that they published part of it calling for a congress in the *Boston Gazette* of September 27, 1773. Lord Dartmouth was so disturbed by the seditious tendency of the letter that he sought help from Thomas Hutchinson in getting the original, so that it could be used in Britain in a legal action against Franklin (Franklin 1976, 20:278–79). See chapter 3.

tee, led by John Dickinson, and the Pennsylvania Assembly, led by Joseph Galloway.

A Congress Is the Logical Next Step after the Successes of the Committees of Correspondence

In his massacre oration on March 5, 1774, John Hancock proposed the convening of a congress of the colonies as a way for Whigs to build upon the success of the committees of correspondence.

> Much has been done by the Committees of Correspondence for this and other towns of this province towards uniting the inhabitants; let them still go on and prosper. Much has been done by the Committees of Correspondence for the House of Assembly in this and our Sister Colonies, for uniting the Inhabitants of the whole Continent for the security of their common interest. May success ever attend their generous endeavors. But permit me here to suggest a general Congress of Deputies from the several Houses of Assembly in this and our Sister Colonies, for uniting the Inhabitants of the whole Continent, as the most effectual method of establishing such a Union as the present posture of our affairs requires. At such a Congress, a firm foundation may be laid for the security of our Rights and Liberties; a system may be formed for our common safety, by a strict adherence to which we shall be able to frustrate any attempts to overthrow our constitution; restore peace and harmony to America, and secure honor and wealth to Great Britain. (17–18)

Hancock's massacre oration came after the destruction of the tea but before the arrival of news of the Port Bill. Although Hancock acknowledges that "much has been done" by committees of correspondence, he opens a space for a "general congress of deputies" by saying "but." What occasions this contrapuntal turn? What is the lack that a congress will repair? Hancock does not say, but his language suggests that, however coherent the network of committees, it could never become what a congress might be: fully grounded in the constitution. Hancock's language here associates the congress with the solidity ascribed to institutions built to last. At "such a congress," a "firm foundation may be *laid*" to secure our rights and liberties, and "a system may be *formed*" to reconcile parts into one whole for our "common safety." Such an institution is not represented as a constitutional innovation, but as an agency to "frustrate any attempts to overthrow our constitution." Hancock's proposal is consistent with the later proposals of the Virginia Whigs that the new congress should convene "annually."

In Order to Negotiate with Ministry on an Equal Footing,
the Congress Must Take Steps to Gather Effective Power

A congress offered a way in which a network of committees might achieve some of the institutional coherence of the ministry in Whitehall and the British Parliament. This perspective is expressed in the cover letter that Speaker Thomas Cushing Jr. wrote to Speaker Peyton Randolph in June 1773, while forwarding the first letter of the committee of correspondence of the Massachusetts House of Representatives: "That there has been a long and settled plan to subvert the political constitutions of these colonies and to introduce arbitrary power, cannot in the opinion of this house admit of doubt. Those who have aimed to enslave us, like a band of brothers, have ever been united in their councils and their conduct. To this they owe their success. Are they not in this regard worthy [of] imitation? Here it is praiseworthy to be instructed even by an enemy" (June 3, 1773; Virginia House of Burgesses 1905, 50). We are not used to hearing the ministry in Whitehall described as "a band of brothers." Nor had ministry or Parliament actually been "united in their councils and their conduct." But, by the late spring of 1774, although American Whigs were shocked and appalled at the substance of the Boston Port Bill and the other Coercive Acts, some must have envied the secrecy, coherence, and effectiveness of the British measures. If the congress that gathered in Philadelphia in early September were to achieve the robust unity of the British administration, they would need to be "instructed" by an "enemy," by imitating their tactical skill in private deliberation, secrecy, and surprise. If a congress were to open a space for free discussion, patient deliberation, and consensus building, secrecy was of the essence. Therefore, on the first full day of their meeting, September 6, 1774, the congress took steps to restrict the flow of information to the public: "*Resolved*, that the door be kept shut during the time of business, and that the members consider themselves under the strongest obligation of honor, to keep the proceedings secret, until the majority shall direct them to be made public" (Congress 1775, 23). With a few notable exceptions (like the public endorsement of the Suffolk Resolves), the congress observed a news blackout upon its proceedings, with members for the most part honoring their mutual vows of secrecy even in their private letters home.

⤛ These varied rationales for a general congress might tempt one to ask, what was the *primary* purpose of the congress: To restore the unity of the British Empire, through a statement of rights cast into the form of a petition? To build a secure constitutional foundation beneath the new network of committees? To gather the power to more boldly confront British encroachments upon American liberties? Rather than have recourse, as historians usually do, to the diverse private opinions of different members from different colonies, it is more accurate to say: all of these purposes, and others as well, served as provisional motives for a general congress. Linked to thirteen colonies, in the spring and spring of 1774, the congress was a fourteenth constituent whose role was uncertain and whose power was as yet speculative. Since the congress depended upon the constantly changing network of committees and assemblies to which it was linked, and because what it would be and could do would depend upon events that had not happened, its character was inchoate and emergent. This was one of its greatest strengths.

"A CHAIN OF FREEDOM HAS BEEN FORMED"

THE FIRST CONTINENTAL CONGRESS DEVELOPS INTO THE HUB OF AN INTERCOLONIAL NETWORK

5

. . . .

If networking helped to achieve an intercolonial convergence of Whig sentiment, unity of action would require much more. The network of committees of correspondence was by design centerless and leaderless.[1] Colonies that had grown impatient with the legal hegemony of Great Britain had little interest in accepting the leadership of even the largest and oldest colonies. While Rhode Island repeatedly showed deference to the Boston Committee of Correspondence and Maryland compliments the "great and ancient colony of Virginia," small colonies charted their own political path, and guarded their prerogative to do so. As a condition of the possibility of its loose unity, the distributive network of committees observed a strict formal equality. Thus the language that circulated among the committees had persuasive force but no administrative authority. How could scattered committees gather the diverse minds and local interests into one body, deliberate together, and determine upon one common course of action? Congress could be built out of the network of committees, but correcting the limitations of that network would be difficult. This helps explain why, in spite of their well-developed enthusiasm for the political utility of a general congress, Boston Whigs did not call for a congress when they received news of the Port Bill. Fearful of the delays that the organization of such a congress would entail, the Whigs of Boston instead called for an immediate embargo on trade with Britain. It therefore fell to other colonies like Rhode Island, New York, Maryland, and Virginia, where the effects of the Coercive Acts were not so directly felt, to call for a general congress (Ammerman 1974, 20). A congress would need to combine the broad

1. Historians sometimes speak loosely about the "leadership" of Boston or Virginia. A useful corrective to this interpretation is offered by Jack Rakove, who described the pivotal role in the deliberations of the Congress played by those who favored conciliation with Britain, like Joseph Galloway, James Duane, Edward Rutledge, and (a very latecomer) John Dickinson (Rakove 1979, 60–62; 2010, 59–64, 99–111).

reach and robust participation of a distributive network with the capacity to deliberate, decide, and act together more characteristic of a network organized according to a star topology.[2]

THE GATHERING OF THE CONGRESS

How the congress was gathered affected what it became. The Whig committees and assemblies that organized the first meeting of the congress deployed well-practiced strategies (bypassing royal authority, disruptive innovation, corporate action, popular declarations), which, in their turn, reflected Whig political values and commitments (to legal procedure, public access, virtuous initiative, and popular consent). Because all of the colonies had had long experience with trade embargos, none underestimated the difficulty of conducting this type of economic coercion. If the congress was to gather the power to endorse and organize a comprehensive trade embargo, it would need to engage the consent and participation of as many British Americans as possible. This helps explain the remarkable set of town and county meetings and provincial conventions held throughout all thirteen colonies in the months following the arrival of the news of the Coercive Acts. The thousands of actors who gathered in hundreds of meetings now entered into the communication dynamic that I have described with respect to the response of the Massachusetts towns to the Boston declaration in 1772–1773, and the responses of Philadelphia, Annapolis, and Williamsburg to the message from Boston in May 1774: they received new information concerning the imperial crisis, deliberated upon it, and translated it into resolves, which they then transmitted to other towns and committees.

To gain a panoramic view of the dispersed and concurrent actions that brought about a general congress of the colonies in Philadelphia, it is useful to

2. The name "congress" is strategically vague. On the first day of its meeting, James Duane, a delegate from New York, reports that the "question was then put, what title the Convention should assume, and it was agreed that it should be called *the Congress*" (Congress 1921, 8). The term *congress* was useful to American Whigs because it was a neutral way of describing their gathering. Literally, the noun *congress* means a "coming together," and by the eighteenth century it had been applied to the coming together of things, combatants, sexual partners, social animals, monarchs, or members of a society or organization that met periodically, like the Royal Society. The neutrally descriptive character of the term *congress* made it useful for colonists who wanted to come together, use a respectable and accurate term for designating what they were doing, but avoid the constitutional associations of possible alternatives, like *assembly*, *parliament*, or *house*, whether of *commons*, *burgesses*, or *representatives*.

TABLE 5.1. THE GATHERING OF THE FIRST CONTINENTAL CONGRESS
OUT OF THE COMMITTEES, CONVENTIONS, AND ASSEMBLIES OF TWELVE
OF THIRTEEN COLONIES

Colony with number of town and county meetings	Delegate selection convention or assembly	Total number of delegates (# on committees[a])
New Hampshire, 34 towns	July 21, 1774, Exeter: unauthorized meeting selects 2 delegates	2 (0)
Massachusetts, 267 towns	June 17, 1774, Salem: circumventing the authority of Governor Gage, the House of Representatives appoints 5	4 (1)
Rhode Island, 3 towns	June 15, 1774, Newport: General Assembly appoints 2	2 (1)
Connecticut, 12 towns	July 13, 1774, New London and Hartford: General Assembly selects 3	3 (1)
New York, 6 towns, 5 counties	July 4, 1774: committee of 51 selects 5 delegates to Congress; some counties send their own delegates	9 (3)
New Jersey, 8 towns/ counties	July 21, 1774, New Brunswick: a general meeting of county committees; 71 delegates elect 5	5 (3)
Pennsylvania, 11 towns/ counties	July 22, 1774, State House: Pennsylvania Assembly ignores the petition of the convention of the counties and appoints 7 delegates	9 (3)
Delaware, 3 counties	August 1, 1774, New Castle: representatives of the three counties select 3 delegates	3 (3)
Maryland, 2 towns, 7 counties	June 22–25, 1774, Annapolis: Maryland county committees select 5 delegates	5 (4)
Virginia, 1 town, 41 counties	August 1–6, 1774, Williamsburg: Convention selects 7 delegates	7 (6)
North Carolina, 6 towns, 30 counties	August 20, 1774, New Bern: Convention of 71 selects 3 delegates	3 (2)
South Carolina, 22 counties and parishes	July 6–8, 1774, Charleston: Convention of 104 from nearly every county and parish selects 5 delegates	5 (2)

Table 5.1 continued

Colony with number of town and county meetings	Delegate selection convention or assembly	Total number of delegates (# on committees[a])
Georgia, 1 town, 10 counties 469 meetings	August 10, 1774, Savannah: Georgia Convention 13 conventions, 56 delegates	0 1 congress

[a]Numbers of those delegates with experience as members of committees of correspondence are in parentheses.

zoom out. Table 5.1 offers a compilation of the steps by which the congress was gathered, and the complex communications feedback loop that it entailed.[3] In this chart, I have arranged the colonies top to bottom from north to south (or, as British Americans considered them, from "east to west"), starting with New Hampshire and ending with Georgia. This was the ordering used by the congress in signing all of its official documents. It reflected the colonies' reluctance to arrange themselves by order of population, physical size, economic importance, or date of founding, any one of which would have introduced a hier-

3. In developing this compilation of events, I have relied upon relevant primary documents, from the logs of the Boston and Virginia committees of correspondence, to the journals of the colonial assemblies of Massachusetts and New Hampshire, from documents reprinted in Peter Force's *American Archives*, to the substantial research gathered by a group of modern scholars, the work of which offers a distinct, but also complementary, view of this dynamic: Richard D. Brown's *Revolutionary Politics in Massachusetts: The Boston Committee of Correspondence and the Towns, 1772–1774*; David Ammerman's *In the Common Cause: American Response to the Coercive Acts of 1774*; Richard Alan Ryerson's *The Revolution Is Now Begun: The Radical Committees of Philadelphia, 1765–1776*; Jerrilyn Greene Marston's *King and Congress: The Transfer of Political Legitimacy, 1774–1776*; Bruce A. Ragsdale's *A Planters' Republic: The Search for Economic Independence in Revolutionary Virginia*. The titles of these books suggest the distinct vantage point that each offers on the political mobilization that was necessary for the convening of the Continental Congress. My study builds upon this earlier scholarship so as to provide a synthetic view and explanatory framework for the Whigs of British America's remarkable organizational achievement.

archy among the colonies. By arranging them geographically, as nature had, the congress implicitly affirmed their formal equality. This chart allows one to visualize the sequence of actions that "built" the congress. Each row, summarizing the political meetings in one colony, assumes the shape of a conceptual funnel on its side that channels the effects of decisions from left to right. In each of the thirteen colonies, local meetings were held after receipt of the news of the Boston Port Bill (column 1); they deliberated, formulated resolves, and selected delegates for thirteen provincial conventions (column 2), which, in their turn, deliberated, formulated resolves and selected delegates (column 3) for the general congress in Philadelphia.

So as to be effectively inclusive, this communication process was necessarily redundant. Like the earlier initiatives of the Boston and Virginia committees of correspondence, the calls to action in the late spring and early summer of 1774 were shaped so as to balance initiative and consultation, action by individual committees with the patience to allow as many localities as possible to participate. Robust consultation was understood to be the sine qua non of political "buy-in."[4] The effect was one of gathering in by channeling. At the end of four months of deliberation, many meetings had been channeled into one; and thousands had expressed their sentiments in many places so that fifty-six delegates could gather in one place. Since the power of the congress depended upon the number and scale of the meetings that prepared for it, communications were by design recursive and iterative, and the initiative for them was distributed.

The legitimacy that was extended to the congress even prior to its first meeting arose in part by applying the methods of public consultation and political action developed by the incipient network of the committees of correspondence. Twenty months of committee meetings, almost invariably justified by the language of political crisis, had accustomed the public to this mode of Whig association, action, and communication (see fig. 5.1). The number of delegates who had prior service in committees of correspondence appears in

4. There was a disparity in level of local activism among the colonies in the summer of 1774. In the New England colonies of Massachusetts, Rhode Island, Connecticut, and New Hampshire, where Whig committee organization had come early, delegates to the congress were selected through their regular assembly representatives, and no colonial convention needed to be organized to select delegates to a congress. But in the colonies south of New England, the delegate selection was undertaken by irregular provincial conventions that depended for their direction and legitimacy upon local meetings and committees.

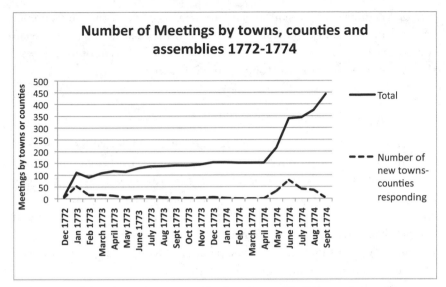

FIGURE 5.1. Meetings in response to the American crisis. This graph represents the number of meetings, as documented by scholars, held by towns and counties to respond to the political crisis between December 1772 and September 1774. Most towns and counties framed public declarations and/or developed instructions to guide delegates who were elected to attend larger provincial meetings.

table 5.1, in parentheses under delegate total in the right column. Half of the congress—twenty-nine of the fifty-six delegates—had served on committees of correspondence, whether those assembly-sponsored committees formed in response to Virginia's initiative or the committees formed (in Charleston, Philadelphia, and New York) to resist the tea.

Four leaders of the congress—Samuel Adams, Richard Henry Lee, Charles Thomson, and Christopher Gadsden—had been prime movers in founding committees in Boston, Virginia, Philadelphia, and Charleston.[5] Like the com-

5. The notable exceptions were New York, where the committee of correspondence leaders, Alexander McDougall and Isaac Sears, were excluded by the committee of fifty-one from the delegate slate, and Pennsylvania, where all of the leaders of the committee movement (except one, Thomas Mifflin) were by design excluded from the delegates by Speaker Joseph Galloway and the Pennsylvania Assembly. Marston notes that forty-seven of the fifty-six delegates had participated in colonial conventions (Marston 1987, 356).

mittee meetings before them, the larger meetings of the spring and summer of 1774 aimed at unity and consensus, but now they also adopted the slogan "deference to the congress" (Rakove 1979, 39). Local deliberations would await the corporate decisions of the congress in Philadelphia.

COLLECTING LOCAL SENTIMENT IN FAIRFAX COUNTY, VIRGINIA

We can track the relation between local meetings and the congress by considering the resolves fashioned by the meeting held at Fairfax County Court House in Alexandria, Virginia, on July 18, 1774. The resolves passed that day are both typical and distinct. Like the other forty-one Virginia meetings for which scholars have found records, they were framed so as to participate in the province-wide collection of sentiment. George Washington, who served as chairman of this meeting, was one of the twenty-five burgesses who had, on May 30, met at Peyton Randolph's house and urged the collection of the sentiments of the counties in preparation for the extralegal Virginia Convention planned for Williamsburg on August 1, 1774. The final resolve of the Fairfax County meeting was the selection of "George Washington, Esq. and George Broadwater, Gent." to attend the August meeting. The three parts of the Fairfax Resolves—a statement of rights, a list of grievances, and an address to fellow citizens proposing certain collective actions—give it the basic constituents of a popular declaration. In its articulation of Whig principles and sentiments, it is conventional, which I summarize this way: "that all English rights and privileges have crossed the Atlantic with the first settlers"; "that we can only be governed by laws to which we have given consent through legislators chosen by ourselves"; and that "therefore, the attempts of the British Parliament to exercise legislative power over them is unconstitutional and threatens us with 'despotism and tyranny.'"

There are several factors that made these resolves particularly influential when the Virginia Convention convened in Williamsburg. The resolves (by tradition attributed to Fairfax planter George Mason) offer a particularly cogent and systematic statement of American rights and grievances. Its authors also thought through the many constituents of a workable embargo, with starting dates, exemptions for certain items, and various methods for punishing those individuals, groups, or colonies that violated the embargo. Because Fairfax County was well advanced in diversifying its crops away from tobacco (toward wheat), the planters of Fairfax County were in a strong position to advocate both a general embargo upon exports to Britain and a suspension of the slave trade (Ragsdale 1996, 186–95). George Washington supported the

Fairfax Resolves with an impressive speech at the Virginia Convention, and the report that Colonel George Washington was prepared, if necessary, to outfit and lead a militia troop of one thousand men, at his own expense, added further weight to the Fairfax Resolves.

The Fairfax Resolves responded with indignation to the Coercive Acts, and repeated the formula adopted by many counties and colonies in recommending material support to Boston: "the Inhabitants of the Town of Boston are now suffering in the common Cause of all British America, and are justly entitled to its Support and Assistance." The climate of political crisis was further aggravated by an outbreak of Indian wars in the interior. George Washington gives informal and extemporaneous expression to this sense of crisis in a long letter of June 10–15, 1774, to his friend George William Fairfax:

> [I]n short the Ministry may rely on it that Americans will never be tax'd without their own consent that the cause of Boston and the despotick Measures in respect to it . . . now is and ever will be considered as the cause of America (not that we approve their conduct in destroying the tea) & that we shall not suffer ourselves to be sacrificed by piecemeal though god only knows what is to become of us, threatened as we are with so many hovering evils as hang over us at present having a cruel & blood thirsty Enemy upon our backs, the Indians, between whom & our Frontier inhabitants many skirmishes have happened, & with whom a general war is inevitable whilst those from whom we have a right to seek protection are endeavoring by every piece of art & despotism to fix the shackles of slavery upon us. (Washington 1995, 10:96–97)

Out of condemnations of British measures, calls for abstinence and boycotts, and assertions of communal virtue, a new moral superiority was fashioned. As the historian Rhys Isaac has argued, enthusiasm for the political cause can appear as "continuing revivalism": the day of fasting (on June 1) and the development of an association to enforce the boycotts became part of a moral renewal. By joining with other classes in abstaining from buying British imports, planters could curb their debt while sharing a new communitarian solidarity across religious and class lines: "Liberty, virtue and pure Protestant religion were all inextricably intertwined" (Isaac 1982, 247). This new program of moral purification is embedded in the Virginia Association that was developed and signed in August 1774 and in article 8 of the Association, adopted by the First Continental Congress in October.

The Fairfax Resolves are just one of many popular declarations written between the *Votes and Proceedings* and the Declaration of Independence. The

Fairfax County meeting, like many of the meetings throughout the colonies in the summer of 1774, observed the protocols described earlier in this study, where each protocol had a distinct effect. By observing correct legal procedure, the members of the meeting reaffirmed the constitutional foundation under its own acts; corporate action increased the effective power of local resolves; casting the resolves of each meeting as a general and systematic address to the people extended the scope of the political crisis; and these local and provincial meetings, by bravely standing up to the law and power of the British Empire, evidenced the virtuous initiative of those who pledged their support to these declarations.[6]

THE SYNERGETIC EFFECTS OF THE MEETINGS

The publicity of measures undertaken at meetings like those in Fairfax County communicated a sense that dispersed action was producing a spontaneous convergence of political effort. The most casual newspaper reader of the spring and summer of 1774 could find bountiful documentation of the intensifying political process that accompanied the appointment of delegates to provincial conventions and the general congress in Philadelphia. So, for example, one newspaper, John Dunlap's *Pennsylvania Packet* of July 4, 1774, included the text of the resolves and appointment of delegates to the congress undertaken by "a meeting of committees of several counties" in Annapolis on June 27; by the Massachusetts House of Representatives in Salem on June 17; and by the Rhode Island Assembly in Newport on June 15. In addition there was a report of the resolves and appointment of delegates to a colonial convention by a large meeting of the county of Newcastle (Delaware). Finally, there was a report of the call made on June 28, 1774, by the Philadelphia Committee of Correspondence to the towns and counties of Pennsylvania "to determine the most proper mode of collecting the sense of this province in the present critical situation of our affairs, and appointing deputies to attend the *proposed congress*." In response, there are reports of Pennsylvania meetings that had al-

6. Marston (1987, 313–19) has offered a valuable synthesis of the content of resolutions issued by 108 meetings in twelve colonies (besides Massachusetts) that she studied, which she notes is not a comprehensive survey: 68 percent pledged loyalty to King George; 92 percent specifically condemn the Boston Port Bill or the Coercive Acts in general; 44 percent raised money for Boston; 66 percent called for an intercolonial congress; and 66 percent asked for a non-importation plan.

ready taken place in Yorktown, "the Borough of Lancaster," and "the County of Northampton." This circular letter culminated in the meeting of delegates of ten counties and two towns with the Philadelphia Committee of Correspondence at Carpenters' Hall on July 15–18, 1774. By means of this public communication, one group of Whigs would learn from the actions of another. Both the meetings and the newspaper coverage of them produced a bracing spectacle of political unanimity for their Whig readers. The reader of the newspaper was implicitly invited to surmise that dispersed action was convergent and that the moral high ground that was being claimed by these many declarations had already been confirmed by concordant resolutions passed by these diverse meetings.

While the meetings of the summer of 1774 built out and scaled up the Whig network throughout the colonies and opened the prospect of a momentous meeting in Philadelphia, royal governors found that the coercive policy meant to strengthen royal power was having the opposite effect. Thus, in their official private communications with Whitehall, governors complained that they were powerless to prevent the meetings to organize a congress. Lieutenant Governor Colden of New York wrote to the American secretary, "These transactions are dangerous, my lord, and illegal but by what means shall government prevent them? An attempt by the power of the civil magistrate would only show their weakness, and it is not easy to say upon what foundation a military aid should be called in" (July 6, 1774; *Documents* 1975, 8:147). Lieutenant Governor Bull of South Carolina reported the cunning method used by the South Carolina House of Commons to circumvent his authority. The House met "privately and punctually" at 8 a.m. (instead of their usual time of ten or eleven o'clock), appointed delegates, and allocated £1,500 for their expenses. By the time that Governor Bull heard of the meeting and prorogued the House, it was too late to prevent their action: "Your lordship will see by this instance with what perseverance, secrecy and unanimity they form and conduct their designs, how obedient the body is to the heads, and how faithful in their secrets" (August 3, 1774; *Documents* 1975, 8:158). Governor Sir James Wright of Georgia, where there had been meetings "strongly incited by the Carolina Sons of Liberty," declared that "as long as these kind of summonses and meetings are suffered—a private man [to] take upon him to summons the whole province to consult upon and redress public grievances or supposed grievances—I apprehend there will be nothing but cabals and combinations and the peace of the province and the minds of the people continually heated, disturbed and distracted" (August 24, 1774; *Documents* 1975, 8:162). It was as though the turning of a vortex had become so strong that the British power to rule had disappeared into this political revolution and every effort to counteract Whig political initiatives merely contributed to them.

Of all the colonies, Georgia was the smallest by population, the most dependent upon Britain for help with the Indian wars in the interior, and the least organized in its Whig resistance to British measures (P. Thomas 1991, 128). In fact, at the end of the summer, Georgia Whigs were not organized enough to send delegates to the first congress. But even in that most southern of the colonies, Governor Wright found a fundamental breakdown of royal authority, one that led him to offer the most comprehensive critique of imperial policy offered by any of the royal governors. Wright channeled his frustration into this general assessment of the political crisis, which modulated into a call for a fundamental reassessment of the ministry's policy of coercion:

> [P]ermit me, my lord, to say how things appear to me, and I conceive that the licentious spirit in America . . . has now gone to so great a length and is such a height that neither coercive or lenient measures will settle matters and restore any tolerable degree of cordiality and harmony with the mother country; . . . America is now become or indisputably ere long will be such a vast, powerful and opulent country or dominion, that I humbly conceive in order to restore and establish real and substantial harmony, affection and confidence, and that Great Britain may receive that benefit and advantage which she has a right to expect from the colonies, it may be found advisable to settle the line with respect to taxation etc. by some new mode or constitution. (*Documents* 1975, 8:162–63)

Wright's blunt advice to ministry attempted to step back to consider what might have restored what was now clearly lost: "real and substantial harmony, affection and confidence" between Britain and its American colonies. Sounding almost like an American Whig, Wright insisted that there must be "some new mode or constitution" to fix a clear line on taxation, otherwise the flames of rebellion would break out again "with more violence." Wright's analysis grasped what was both systematic and dynamic about this political crisis. It was a situation he described with more than a little personal exasperation: "nothing but jealousies, rancor and ill blood, law and no law, government and no government, dependence and independence, if I may be allowed the expressions, and everything unhinged and running into confusion so that in short a man hardly knows what to do or how to act, and it's a most disagreeable state to one who wishes to support law, government and good order and to discharge his duty with honour and integrity" (163). Wright's chain of antitheses—"law and no law, government and no government"—expressed the vertigo felt by a supposed ruler who has glimpsed a Hobbesian state of nature beneath the remnants of royal government. But the dissolution of "law, government and good order" that Wright describes was the correlative to the emergence of new "law, government and good order" being constructed by the Whig network of committees and conventions. Royal officials lamented what Whigs celebrated: the gradual emergence of a system of government independent of the royal institutions.

By the time the delegates convened in Philadelphia, the congress had garnered a good deal of presumptive authority, but that authority was also quite circumscribed. The congress that met was by purpose, spirit, and law an extension of the committees, assemblies, and conventions that had appointed delegates to attend, and resolves to guide, the congress. Even before it convened, the congress had won a good degree of presumptive deference, especially from those who had participated in its development.[7] But the "delegates" to the congress (from the Latin *dēlēgāre*, "to assign") were not "representatives" in the usual sense: they were not authorized to undertake any action their collective knowledge and judgment might suggest (from paying for the destroyed tea to declaring independence). Both local meetings and provincial conventions had paired the appointment of delegates with the passing of resolves, so delegates understood themselves to be "assigned" to support Boston, to develop an embargo on trade with Britain, and to sustain the unity necessary to do these things. Everything that the congress ended up doing suggests the strong symbiosis between it and the network of committees and meetings from which it derived its direction and legitimacy.

CARPENTERS' HALL IN PHILADELPHIA

If the congress were to have the solitude and calm to organize itself into the hub of a new, more systematic network of American Whigs, it would need just the right place to meet. Places are invested with history and symbolic meaning. After the various colonial committees and assemblies settled upon

7. When the Connecticut delegate Silas Deane traveled to Hartford to meet the Massachusetts delegation on its way to Philadelphia, Deane told them that "the sense of Connecticut is, that the resolutions of the Congress shall be the laws of the Medes and Persians; that the Congress is the grandest and most important body ever held in America, and that the *all* of America is intrusted to it and depends upon it" (August 15, 1774; J. Adams 1961, 2:98).

Philadelphia as the place for a general congress to convene, there was a fraught political choice to be made. Speaker Joseph Galloway of the Pennsylvania Assembly had offered the imposing State House as a site for the meetings of the general congress. But instead, on the first day of deliberation, September 5, 1774, the congress unanimously confirmed an earlier decision to meet at Carpenters' Hall. In a letter to his friend and ally, the governor of New Jersey, William Franklin, Galloway interpreted this development and another made on the same day as a most troubling portent: "The congress this day met at Carpenters Hall, notwithstanding the offer of the Assembly room a much more proper place. They next proceeded to choose a Secretary, and, to my surprise, Charles Thomson (one of the most violent sons of liberty, so called, in America) was unanimously elected. The New Yorkers and myself and a few others, finding a great majority, did not think it prudent to oppose it. Both of these measures it seems, were privately settled by an interest made out of doors" (Congress 1921, 1:9). Why was Galloway so concerned by these developments, when another letter to Franklin, written only two days earlier, had expressed confidence that the congress would "behave with temper and moderation" (Congress 1921, 1:5)? Political events in Philadelphia in the months since the arrival of news of the Boston Port Bill gave the choice of Carpenters' Hall as a venue and Charles Thomson as the secretary of the congress a pointed meaning. While the committee mobilization in response to the news of the Port Bill had begun with the impromptu meeting at City Tavern on the May 20, 1774, it had culminated on July 15–18, when the Philadelphia committee convened a Pennsylvania convention of seventy-five delegates, including delegates from the ten counties of Pennsylvania as well as a large contingent of over thirty from Philadelphia. They met at Carpenters' Hall. After completing their deliberations, in the climactic act of that Pennsylvania convention, the delegates marched two blocks west to the State House, bearing a copy of their long list of carefully considered resolves as well as their suggestions for three delegates to be added to the assembly's choice of delegates to the congress: Chairman Thomas Willing, John Dickinson, and James Wilson. Entering the assembly chamber at the State House during an ongoing meeting, the convention presented a draft of their recommendations and listened quietly to the proceedings. The assembly, under the firm control of Speaker Galloway, ignored both the resolves and the convention's suggestions for delegates for the congress. Instead, meeting later behind doors firmly closed, they elected their own slate of delegates (which included only one ardent Whig, the wealthy merchant Thomas Mifflin), and bypassed the convention's detailed list of rights and grievances to offer a concise and moderately phrased single sentence of instructions to the delegates of the congress. This local provincial history gave the first acts of the congress a specific meaning. By selecting Carpenters' Hall as their meeting place, the congress shunned the elegance and convenience of the State House and asserted their independence from both royal government and the Pennsylvania Assembly. By selecting Charles Thomson as its secretary, whom Joseph Galloway dubbed "one of the most violent sons of liberty, so called, in America," the congress aligned itself with the most ardent Whig branch of the city's committee of correspondence.

There were several factors that made Carpenters' Hall a felicitous choice for a meeting that was convened to forge a new union of the colonies. The hall was a brand-new Queen Anne building just two blocks east of the State House, and set back from Chestnut Street by a spacious walk. The building was built by and for the Carpenters' Company, an association of the city's master builders, who in turn rented the second floor to the Library Company of Philadelphia. Its intimate scale encouraged easy conversation and discouraged grandeur of state; even the president of the congress, Peyton Randolph, sat neither far from, nor far above, the other members of the congress. In the eighteenth century, the first floor of Carpenters' Hall was still more intimate than it is today: it was divided into two medium-sized rooms, each about thirty by twenty feet with their own fireplaces, one room to the east, where the congress met, and the second to the west, which could accommodate a large committee. Because it belonged to the private Carpenters' Company, and because it was a quiet distance from the bustling activity of Market Street or Front Street, Carpenters' Hall protected the privacy of the deliberations of the congress. Yet Carpenters' Hall was also close enough to the new City Tavern, where delegates often ate, and to several houses of worship, such that the delegates had no difficulty dipping into the vibrant economic and social life of America's largest city.

The rigorously symmetrical classical architecture of Carpenters' Hall facilitated political unity. All four sides of Carpenters' Hall greet the viewer with an exacting but harmonious symmetry. Built on the plan of a Greek cross, exactly fifty feet across from north to south and east to west, this center-style building also featured a small cupola and entrances on both its northern and southern sides. Renaissance architects preferred the Greek to the more common Latin cross, because it was thought to unite all the worshipers and sacred objects in the church in an equal orientation upward (toward God). The center-style plan is indebted to Hadrian's magnificent Pantheon in Rome and adopted in Bramante's early plan for St. Peter's. However, Carpenters' Hall has the elegance and ease of red brick, white-painted wood, and delicate detailing so characteristic of the mid-eighteenth-century Queen Anne buildings, the favorite choice for vernacular builders throughout the American colonies, from Virginia to New England.

As long as the intercolonial network had functioned as a network, everything that was accomplished together, like planning the congress, was achieved by consensus and performed locally. Differences of religion and interest, style and dialect were submerged in the medium of a shared Whig political language. But once the delegates from the different colonies gathered at Carpenters' Hall, these differences came into clear focus: they were heard in accents, worn upon bodies, and intruded into the delegates' discourse. The congress could not conduct business as a single, large committee as if they had been appointed by a common agency. Before the delegates had fairly settled into their seats, the bottom-line issue of how properly to weight the influence of the different colonies came to the fore. So, on the opening day, the congress had little difficulty selecting Speaker Peyton Randolph of the largest and most ancient state of Virginia as its presiding officer, or "President." It settled upon a local nonmember of the congress, Charles Thomson, as secretary with some quiet grumbling. But it nearly foundered upon the question of how to vote: "whether it should be by colonies, or by the poll [of individual delegates], or by interests," which would require calculating the comparative wealth and population of each colony. The question was first posed by James Duane of New York, but it was quickly taken up by the mercurial Patrick Henry of Virginia, who insisted that a "precedent ought to be established now," and that "it would be a great injustice, if a little colony should have the same weight in the councils of America, as a great one." Major Sullivan of New Hampshire quickly rejoined "that a little colony had its all at stake as well as a great one" (J. Adams 1961, 2:123). This question was tenaciously grounded in the incommensurability of colonies, which nonetheless came together as equals to form a federal union, a union that was based upon little more than a pledge of faith or covenant. (*Federal* is derived from the Latin word *faedus*, "covenant," a cognate of "faith" [*OED*].)

The debate about voting raised the awkward question of how the congress should consider what a delegate was. Did a delegate represent the various citizens who lived in his respective colony (this would favor proportional representation), or was he part of a delegate committee appointed by the separate colonies (this would favor voting by colonies, with each colony having one vote). Did royal tyranny mean that the colonies had been dissolved "into a state of nature," as Henry claimed, or were they delegates of still legitimate colonial assemblies and conventions, which were still lodged within the English constitution (as John Jay and others maintained). Henry used the former claim to support proportional voting, while others used the latter position to justify equal voting. The question of how each colony would vote was not settled on the first day of the congress, so that it was continued to the second day. Then, after a full exploration of the issues had demonstrated the danger of this question to the very existence of a congress, four delegates led a discreet retreat from the question (Richard Henry Lee, Richard Bland, and Edmund Pendleton from Virginia and Christopher Gadsden of South Carolina). They conceded that, since there was no way to collect accurate information about the comparative wealth and population of the respective colonies, there was little choice other than to vote by colonies, with each colony having one vote. This decision reflected what the congress had emerged out of: a network with one node for each colony.

The debate about how to vote had confronted the congress with the awkward question of what it was. Most agreed that they could not be considered a proper assembly or parliament for America, for there was as yet no state possessing a council, an executive, and a judiciary, to link to such an assembly. They were surely more than a club or debating society, though when discussions seemed interminable and fruitless, some despaired that they might be little more than this. At the very least the congress provided an open-ended political opportunity. By gathering many of the most respectable Whigs from their respective colonies, they might, through effective action, develop the power and legitimacy to serve as a hub, or directing agency, for the distributed network of Whig committees, conventions, and rogue assemblies that had met throughout the previous summer. At the center of their aspiration was gathering effective power to support Boston, which "was suffering in the common cause of American liberty," to develop an effective embargo, and finally, and perhaps most crucially, to develop the unity needed to present their basic demands to Britain so it would feel obliged to yield. The debate about how to vote implicitly acknowledged that the colonies were not equal in either population or wealth, and these, all the delegates knew, were the keys to effective power—whether it was to be wielded in enforcing an embargo or in recruiting an army.

A look at the comparative population, imports, and exports of the diverse regions of British America suggests reasons why the southern states of Virginia

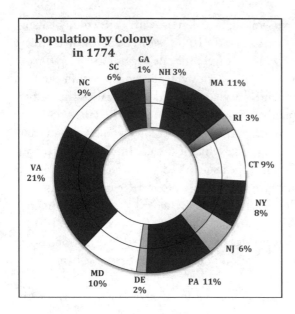

Population by Colony in 1774

GA 1%
SC 6%
NH 3%
NC 9%
MA 11%
RI 3%
VA 21%
CT 9%
NY 8%
NJ 6%
MD 10%
DE 2%
PA 11%

FIGURE 5.2.

Comparison of thirteen colonies of British America by population, with percentage of the population of all the colonies in each state. Notice that there are six colonies with populations that come in just over or under 10 percent of the whole (Massachusetts, Connecticut, New York, Pennsylvania, Maryland, North Carolina); Virginia has a full 21 percent of the free population of all thirteen colonies.

and South Carolina had opened the congress demanding proportional representation in the decisions of the congress (see fig. 5.2). The population figures in this graph do not include black slaves, which were explicitly excluded from Patrick Henry's proposal to the congress. The graph of the white population of the colonies show that the four southern states at the congress—Virginia, Maryland, and the two Carolinas—account for a full 46 percent of the total population of the thirteen colonies. While the figures on imports from Britain suggest economic influence generally equivalent to the white population throughout the colonies, the economic value of exports reveals the enormous economic power of the southern colonies. Four southern states—bolstered by the great value of tobacco, rice, and indigo—accounted for a full 81 percent of the economic value of exports to Great Britain (see fig. 5.3). When the southern states voted with New England, as they often did, for example in proposing an association modeled upon the one provided by the Virginia Convention, they spoke for colonies with 72 percent of the population, 59 percent of the imports from Britain, and 88 percent of the exports to Britain.[8] Although the

8. For population figures see Murray 2006, 20; for trade figures see Marston 1987, 109, 118. The chronic trade imbalance that these figures expose—in 1774 the American colonies imported nearly £1,000,000 more than it exported to Britain—suggests the short-term economic advantages of an embargo. It would leave British traders holding American debts.

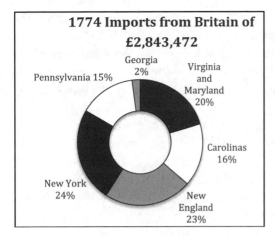

1774 Imports from Britain of £2,843,472

Georgia 2%

Virginia and Maryland 20%

Pennsylvania 15%

Carolinas 16%

New York 24%

New England 23%

FIGURE 5.3.

Comparison of thirteen colonies by imports from and exports to Britain. Notice the substantial trade imbalance in Britain's favor and the remarkable 56 percent of the North American colonies' exports coming from the two Chesapeake colonies of Virginia and Maryland.

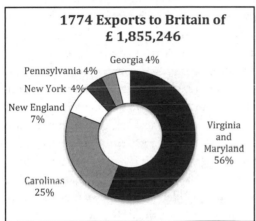

1774 Exports to Britain of £ 1,855,246

Georgia 4%

Pennsylvania 4%

New York 4%

New England 7%

Virginia and Maryland 56%

Carolinas 25%

congress finally decided to grant only one vote to each colony, Virginia's size, wealth, antiquity, and influence over the other southern delegates put her in a position to have the leading voice in the congress. By joining with the delegates from New England, this alliance could define the agenda to which the less "warm" delegates from the middle states would have to respond.

THE PROBLEM OF BOSTON

By the time Congress convened, Boston Harbor had been closed for over three months. Supported by Parliament with new laws and fresh regiments, Governor and General Thomas Gage sought to enforce the official secret instructions from Whitehall. The goal of that policy was given a most expansive and unequivocal form: "the sovereignty of the King in his Parliament over the colonies requires a full and absolute submission" (Dartmouth to Gage, April 9, 1774; *Documents* 1975, 8:88). The Whigs of Massachusetts worked tirelessly to foil Gage's mission. Throughout the six weeks of the deliberations of the First Congress, worry about Boston and periodic news from Boston kept breaking into the deliberations of Congress. The quick resolution of the dispute about how to vote may have been facilitated by the sobering news of the British cannonading of Boston, which was received by the New Jersey delegation around 2 p.m. on September 6, in the form of a broadside, printed in Norwich, Connecticut, out of a letter of General Israel Putnam. The broadside letter reported that British troops stationed in Boston had seized the gunpowder stored in a powder house near Cambridge, that six colonists had lost their lives, that the British had begun a naval bombardment of Boston, and that all the country as far away as Connecticut were now in arms and marching toward Boston (Congress 1921, 1:18; Farrand 1901). Before this rumor about the outbreak of hostilities in Boston had been refuted by the arrival of more accurate news (on September 8), Samuel Adams rose in Congress on September 6 to suggest that the Anglican minister Jacob Dupré be invited to lead Congress in prayer. Connecticut delegate Silas Deane wrote to his wife, that on September 7, "the bells toll muffled," and through Congress every face did "gather indignation and every tongue pronounces revenge" (Congress 1921, 1:18). Reverend Dupré read and developed a prayer out of Psalm 35:1–3 (King James Version): "Plead my cause, O LORD, with them that strive with me: fight against them that fight against me. Take hold of shield and buckler, and stand up for mine help. Draw out also the spear, and stop the way against them that persecute me: say unto my soul, I am thy salvation." Deane declared the extemporaneous prayer offered after the reading "worth riding one hundred miles to hear," and Rhode Island delegate Samuel Ward wrote in his diary that it was "one of the most sublime, catholic, well-adapted prayers I ever heard" (Congress 1921, 1:18–19). John Adams, incorrectly thinking that the timing of the psalm was a happy coincidence, wrote his wife, Abigail, "It seemed as if Heaven had ordained that Psalm to be read on that morning" (1:32). Congress was only three days old, but the "news" from Boston, and Congress's sympathetic response to that news, helped to couple events in Boston with the Whig political project in Philadelphia.

The ongoing crisis in Boston had occasioned the meeting of the congress, but it also threatened to render the work of Congress moot. Every member of Congress knew that a precipitous outbreak of hostilities in New England, even if it were accidental, would likely vitiate any effort to win a change in

American policy in Westminster. It would also destroy the prospect that united Congress: of restoring the colonies to a relationship of harmony with the mother country based upon their full and equal and explicitly acknowledged possession of ancient English rights. Thus, like an ellipse, the American crisis had two focal points in the autumn of 1774, one in Philadelphia and the other in Boston. Neither point was stable, and each exercised influence upon the other. Throughout the fall of 1774, towns and assemblies throughout the colonies were continuing to send assistance to Boston. The Boston Committee of Correspondence had spawned a separate Committee on Donations, which conducted a wide-ranging correspondence throughout the colonies. The congress had been called because of the Coercive Acts directed at Boston and Massachusetts by Parliament, and Congress had to find ways to "stay ahead" of the crisis in Boston if it was to shape a collective American policy to compel the Parliament to rescind its legal punishments of Massachusetts and Boston.

Throughout the First Congress, there was regular public and private communication between Boston and Philadelphia, which shaped actions undertaken in both places. News of the powder alarm was only the first of these emergency communications. On September 16, Paul Revere arrived in Philadelphia with a letter from the Boston committee enclosing a copy of the Suffolk Resolves, accompanied by an urgent request for support and advice (Congress 1775, 30–43). After an oral reading of the Resolves the next morning, Congress adopted its own resolves, urging material support for Boston, and commending the towns of Suffolk County for the "perseverance in the same firm and temperate conduct as expressed in" their Resolves. To demonstrate its solidarity, Congress then ordered the publication of the Suffolk Resolves along with the supporting resolves of Congress. Finally, on October 6, Revere arrived with another express from the Boston Committee of Correspondence, describing the British fortification of the Boston neck. The committee requested help in discouraging Gage's warlike actions, wondered whether Congress would support Massachusetts in reassuming the old Massachusetts charter of 1629, and asked Congress's opinion as to whether Boston should be evacuated. In response, a subcommittee was appointed to draft a letter to General Gage, which was sent to him under the signature of the president of Congress, Peyton Randolph, asking Gage to suspend the fortification of Boston and to desist from other menacing and oppressive measures. At the same time, Congress urged the Boston Whigs to avoid evacuating Boston, changing the constitution, or assuming an offensive posture toward the British occupiers (Marston 1987, 88–89; Frothingham 1971, 375–78).

At first glance Congress's explicit endorsement of the Suffolk Resolves may seem to be a puzzle. The Resolves' political stance was grounded in the familiar Whig orthodoxy of the *Votes and Proceedings*, and its posture was consistent with the resolves produced by the countless meetings and conventions of the previous summer. On September 12, Congress had read the Middlesex Resolves, framed in Concord, Massachusetts, on August 30, 1774, but Congress had taken no further action. The influence of the Suffolk Resolves is sometimes attributed to the stirring language of its preamble. It repeated the familiar origin story of New England settlement as grounded in the flight from religious persecution in old England, but this time with a twist. That earlier persecution, with its sacrifices in blood and treasure, with its legacy of liberty, and the debt to ancestors and obligation to children yet unborn, was now explicitly aligned with the most recent acts of Britain. "Whereas the power but not the justice, the vengeance but not the wisdom of Great-Britain, which of old persecuted, scourged, and exiled our fugitive parents from their native shores, now pursues us, their guiltless children, with unrelenting severity." By folding the memory of the past onto the present crisis, and by mobilizing stark moral polarities (justice versus power; wisdom versus vengeance), this language enabled the Suffolk County convention to represent the current struggle as an existential one.

The nineteen resolves developed a detailed recipe for resistance to British measures. Their simple declarative sentences were part of the bold, masculine style of Whig resistance. As the members of Congress listened to the resolves upon the morning of September 17, many in Congress apparently admired the careful balance they struck. They took a determined stand against British measures, but used restrained means to do so; they rejected British authority, but did so on the "defensive." We can grasp the carefully wrought dialectical form of the nineteen resolves by abridging them into one paragraph under five headings.

> *Resisting the Coercive Acts:* Although we "cheerfully acknowledge . . . George III as our sovereign" (1), "it is our indispensable duty . . . to defend and preserve [our] rights and liberties" (2). Since "the late acts of the British Parliament . . . are gross infractions of those rights" (3), "no obedience is due" to them (4) or the justices of our courts supported by those laws (5), and we will hold "harmless" any officials who refuse to support those courts (6).
>
> *Military measures* taken by Governor Gage, like the raid on the powder house and the fortification of the Boston neck, "are justly alarming" (9); therefore, we should invest militia commissions only in officers "who have

evidenced themselves the inflexible friends to the rights of the people," and the inhabitants of the towns should "use their utmost diligence to acquaint themselves with the art of war" (11). Yet "from our affection to his Majesty," "we are determined to act merely on the defensive" (12).

Communication: If our leaders are arrested, we should "seize and keep in safe custody, every servant of the present tyrannical and unconstitutional government" "until the person so apprehended be liberated" (13).

Embargo and Congress: Until our rights are restored, we should "withhold all commercial intercourse with Great-Britain, Ireland and the West Indies" (14) and appoint committees to encourage "arts and manufactures among us" (15).

Showing restraint in resistance: Although the "wicked and oppressive measures of the present administration" may encourage some "persons to commit outrage upon private property," we "would heartily recommend all persons of this community, not to engage in any routs, riots, or licentious attacks upon the properties of any person whatsoever" (18). (Congress 1775, 32–38)

For members of Congress, these resolves must have had some of the freshness and allure of news from the front. The Suffolk Resolves built upon, but also left behind, the protracted theoretical critiques of British policy that dominated so many of the earlier declarations. Instead, through the sheer scope and ingenuity of this panoply of resolves (elaborated even to the point of threatening to kidnap royal officials in retaliation for the arrest of Whig leaders), practical measures came to the fore.

The careful balance of these resolves—which were fearless yet prudent, brave but canny—also helped solve a problem that the Massachusetts delegates faced in Congress. The special challenges of the position of the Massachusetts delegates were explained by Samuel Adams in a letter to Joseph Warren of September 25, 1774: "heretofore we have been accounted by many, intemperate and rash ... there is ... a certain degree of jealousy in the minds of some, that we aim at total independency, not only of the mother-country, but of the colonies too; and that, as we are a hardy and brave people, we shall in time overrun them all." But "now," after the receipt and endorsement of the Suffolk Resolves, "we are universally applauded as cool and judicious, as well as spirited and brave." But Adams cautioned Warren that the support for Massachusetts depended upon their acting "merely on the defensive" with their continued "perseverance in a firm and temperate conduct" (S. Adams 1904, 3:158).

Boston's periodic communication with Congress brought the raw facts and feelings of the political strife unfolding in Massachusetts to the peaceful city of Philadelphia and into the secret deliberations of Congress. In response to these facts, the Boston committee asked for and received explicit support from Congress. After the explicit and unanimous endorsement of the Resolves, John Adams wrote in his diary, "This was one of the happiest Days of my life. In Congress we had generous, noble sentiments, and manly eloquence. This day convinced me that America will support the [*sic*] Massachusetts or perish with her" (September 17, 1774; J. Adams 1961, 2:134–35). But something of more lasting institutional importance was happening through this exchange between Massachusetts Whig committees and Congress. As Jack Rakove has argued, this communication feedback loop between the Boston committee and Congress expanded the effective power of Congress: "By asking Congress to judge the legality of this provincial government, the Massachusetts leaders endowed that body with authority they could never have conceded to Parliament." Implicitly, Congress was not just responding to Britain, it was showing that it could "regulate the basic political changes that would take place in every colony as the crisis deepened" (Rakove 1979, 49). By the end of the First Congress, the Boston committee had won explicit public support of Congress, but Congress had effectively restrained the Boston Whigs by praising them for their steadfastness and by warding off attempts by the Massachusetts Provincial Congress to force constitutional changes or assume the military initiative. Boston, the volatile center of the military crisis in the fall of 1774, had been properly subordinated to the deliberative political center of the crisis in Philadelphia. The wise policy of Congress had helped to increase its authority, and the ellipse had not split into two circles but become one.

CONGRESS EMERGES AS THE HUB
OF THE INTERCOLONIAL NETWORK

When Congress met at the City Tavern for a farewell dinner on October 26, 1774—the same site where the members had gathered on September 5, 1774, to walk to Carpenters' Hall to open the congress—some saw it as marking the permanent dissolution of a temporary emergency gathering. Although Congress had scheduled a precautionary date for reconvening on May 10, 1775, this would be necessary only if Britain turned a deaf ear to communications that most in Congress considered entirely reasonable. Many were optimistic that the American colonies would prevail the way they had in 1766 with the repeal of the Stamp Act. Like the Parliament, many members of Congress believed that a policy of firmness would carry the day. Richard Henry Lee even argued that the economic power of Congess's Association would mean that news of the repeal of the Coercive Acts would return from England on the same ship that carried the news of the Association. Conversely, the outbreak of hostilities might make another meeting of Congress difficult to manage and simply beside the point. On October 28, 1774, John Adams departed from "the happy, the peaceful, the elegant, the hospitable, and the polite City of Phyladelphia.—It is not very likely that I shall ever see this Part of the World again" (J. Adams 1961, 2:157).

Only retrospectively can we see this gathering of fifty-six delegates as providing the tentative beginnings for the institution that would later emerge in the Federal Union of 1789. But even in 1774, Congress began to win some powers that were distinct from the powers of the intercolonial network out of which it emerged. It did so by becoming the hub of the Whig intercolonial network. To describe the First Congress as a hub may suggest a symmetry, strength, and stability that it did not have. The word *hub* is first used to denote the central point where the spokes of a wheel are joined, so that they can sustain the stability of the wheel's rim. Much later, in describing the star topology of a hierarchical network, the hub may be the locus of command and control for all the nodes on the network. (Whitehall served this way for the British Empire in the eighteenth century.) But in the flat, distributed network of twelve colonies, members knew very well that Congress had no independent authority. Congress's leverage was positional: it came from its central position and existed only for the time interval during which the different nodes had delegated authority to it. At the hub, for a limited time, delegates gathered from various nodes of power, discussed their ideas in secret, fashioned their positions into words, and undertook actions that they hoped would articulate the purposes of the whole. Since the main power of the First Congress was hortatory and persuasive, words and actions were narrowly limited in their scope but also contentiously negotiated. If those at the hub attempted to say or do something that was out of touch with the nodes on the larger network, the hub would lose its connections to its nodes, the network would break up, and what little authority Congress had gathered would dissipate.

The pledge of mutual secrecy that opened Congress had succeeded in keeping substantive differences among the delegates out of public view. This opened, for those included within the doors of Carpenters' Hall, the space of deliberation. *To deliberate* is derived from the Latin, *delibero*: "to weigh well, consider maturely, take counsel"; which is in turn derived from the Latin, *librare*: "a balance," "a pair of scales." The metaphor embedded in this word suggests not only wise and just consideration, but also the difficulty of the decisions that the delegates had to make in confronting British measures. Deliberation is essential to an action that will be "deliberate" in the adjectival senses of the word: intentional, careful, and methodical. The public curiosity surrounding the deliberations of Congress enhanced the attention attracted to the communications that began to stream from Congress, during the last week of its meeting, in the form of broadsides and pamphlets. These were gathered for publication by William Bradford as *The Extracts from the Votes and Proceedings of the American Congress*, dated October 27, 1774. To meet demand, it was reprinted and then published by newspapers throughout the colonies (Wolf 1974, 6). Because Congress observed the privacy protocols of the petition in framing "the address to the King (George III)," that part of its work was not made public. Publication of the full *Journal of the Proceedings of the Congress* by William Bradford, as kept by Charles Thomson, the minutes of which were carefully edited for publication by a committee of several members, so key documents are interspersed with minutes of Congress, did not happen until January and February 1775 (Wolf 1974, 7). Once Congress was confident that the king had received his address, it authorized printing the "petition" independently, and the petition was added, as an appendix, to later printings of the *Journal*.

A brief anatomy of the *Journal of the Proceedings of the Congress* suggests how Congress had positioned itself at the center of an expanding network of Whig resistance to British authority (see box 5.1). Each of the six primary components of the *Journal* suggests that the acts and communications of Congress were an experimental work in progress. The journal form itself imitates the journals published annually by colonial assemblies like the Massachusetts House of Representatives and the Virginia House of Burgesses. However, the unconstitutional character of Congress becomes evident from the first part of the *Journal*. There, instead of the list of representatives elected by the various towns of Massachusetts or the burgesses elected by the various counties of Virginia, Congress placed the *resolves and instructions* (1) that were composed by the twelve colonial assemblies or conventions and carried by the delegates to Congress. The language that legitimized this extraordinary gathering, placed in the front of the *Journal* and taking up almost 15 percent of the *Journal*'s bulk, indirectly betrayed the questionable legal foundation for the meeting. The reprinting of the instructions seems to say, "Look here, this is the authority by which our congress has been convened." By inscribing the words that describe the political crisis that necessitates a congress, by listing the recommended measures (like supporting Boston and developing an embargo), Con-

BOX 5.1. THE COMMUNICATIONS INCLUDED IN THE *JOURNAL OF THE PROCEEDINGS OF THE CONGRESS* (PUBLISHED JANUARY 1775; PAGES APPEAR IN PARENTHESES)

1. Resolves and instructions from the twelve colonies that had appointed delegates (1–22).
2. Communications concerning the crisis in Boston: Suffolk Resolves and request for advice from Boston committee and letter of Congress to Governor Gage (30–43).
3. Rights and grievances (57–65): "Congress has made the following Declarations and Resolves."
4. The Association for stopping all imports and exports with signatures of all delegates (68–77).
5. Various addresses
   To the PEOPLE of Great Britain (78–92).
   To the INHABITANTS of the COLONIES (93–113).
   To the colonies of St. John . . . with the publications of the congress (114–15).
   To the agents of the colonies in London (on submitting petition to the king) (117–18).
   To the INHABITANTS of the province of QUEBEC (118–32).
   To the king, published later as a "Petition of the Continental Congress to the King" (135–44).
6. Resolve to meet on May 10, 1775, "unless the redress of grievances, which we have desired, be obtained before that time" (114).

gress gave the readers of the *Journal* the evidence to measure the *Journal*'s record of what Congress had done against its founding instructions.

Congress's carefully developed response to the crisis in Boston developed a different way to sustain a strong communications link with this most important node of the intercolonial Whig network. The *Journal* not only explicitly endorsed the Suffolk Resolves. It also incorporated them, supported them with their own resolves, and retransmitted both as part of the official public posture of Congress (2). The most conventional constituent of the *Journal* was Congress's *declaration and resolves* (3). The declaration resumed the arguments of all the other declarations from the *Votes and Proceedings* forward. By incorporating the common neo-Roman language of liberty of the previous protests against British policy, Congress made its bid to confer an authoritative statement of the meaning of this moment of the crisis. Its language sought to secure a constitutionally correct legal foundation beneath Congress, first by a statement of basic rights and liberties of British Americans and then by rejecting what they claimed were the dangerous innovations in British policy since 1763.

The most consequential, operational language of Congress is found in *the Association* (4), a comprehensive pledge to join in an agreement of non-importation, non-consumption, and non-exportation. This quasi-legal instrument, signed by all members of Congress, called upon every person in British America to join in action that would coerce Britain to rescind its policy toward the colonies. Many historians have noted that the Association was the most tangible and effective outcome of the First Congress. It helped lead to a drastic drop in both imports and exports from Britain and her possessions.[9] Congress's development of a Continental Association enabled Congress to incorporate and extend the basic architecture of the association adopted by the Virginia Convention on August 6, 1774.

The Association involved scaling up the number of committees in the American Whig network by building down to the local level of every town and county in the colonies.[10] The Association built upon the feedback loop that had operated since the first proposals for a general congress: local Whig committees and conventions supported Congress, which, in its turn, extended support to local Whig committees and conventions. The Association enhanced the power and reach of the system of committees that was so crucial to the calling of the Congress. Although each committee was to be formed by the government of "county, city, and town," it was the Association that vested local committees with a potent but limited authority to coerce people into compliance with economic warfare against Britain. The key language comes in article 11:

9. The remarkable success of the boycotts is evident from the numbers in Marston (1987, 109, 118): total imports from Great Britain dropped from £2,843,469 in 1774, to £220,355 in 1775, to £56,320 in 1776. Total exports to Great Britain dropped from £2,457,062 in 1775, to £185,816 in 1776. Of course, Great Britain itself gave added force to colonial boycotts by passing and signing the Prohibitory Act in December 1775, a law making it illegal to trade with the rebel colonies.

10. Marston (1987, 124) estimates as many as seven thousand participants in committees and conventions involved in mobilization to enforce the Association.

That a committee be chosen in every county, city, and town, by those who are qualified to vote for representatives in the legislature, whose business it shall be attentively to observe the conduct of all persons touching this association; and when it shall be made to appear, to the satisfaction of a majority of any such committee, that any person within the limits of their appointment has violated this association, that such majority do forthwith cause the truth of the case to be published in the gazette; to the end, that all such foes to the rights of British-America may be publicly known, and universally contemned as the enemies of American liberty; and thenceforth we respectively will break off all dealings with him or her.

Because an association is a group of individuals who ally themselves "to execute a common purpose" (*OED*, 2), all the meanings of *association* and *to associate* (from Latin, *associat-*, "joined," and *ad* + *socius*, "sharing, allied, friend") make it quite clear that association is voluntary. What gives article 11 of Congress's Association its sinister ring is the way *this* association is given the policing function of continuous surveillance of those in every town, village, and county of the colonies who have chosen not to associate. In fact, the Association is organized to punish and expose those who do not associate themselves with the cause of non-importation and non-exportation.

Although only fifty-six delegates from the twelve colonies voluntarily signed this association, it was now deemed to be compulsory for all Americans. Members of each community were invited to observe the rules of the Association, but if they did not, they became open to coercion. During the Townshend duties boycotts, efforts to assure compliance had been sporadic and occasional; now they were to be systematic and continuous. Enforcement was to be local, where committeemen, formally elected by those who usually vote for the colonial legislature, would be given limited coercive powers. Congress was careful not to pretend to confer full legislative or judicial authority upon the local committees of the Association—the power, for example, to tax or imprison those who violate the Association. But they urged local committees to assume a quasi-policing function—"attentively to observe the conduct of all such persons touching this association"—and to assume a quasi-judicial function—to identify violations of the Association "to the satisfaction of the majority" of the committee—and finally to use the newspaper to shame violators as "enemies of American liberty." That epithet, as the Tory experience in Massachusetts had already shown, was not very comfortable to bear.

Congress completed its work by explaining what it had done with a suite of variously inflected addresses (5). In each address Congress spoke for the whole intercolonial network, invited others to join it, and reached out to potential adversaries. The address to the inhabitants of Great Britain sought to establish solidarity with our "Friends and fellow subjects," against the policy of current administration, by appealing to a value that unites Americans and Britons, and to the rights and liberties of Englishmen. The tone of this address is urgent, and its condemnation of the policies of the present government is harsh and sometimes menacing. By contrast, the address to the inhabitants of the thirteen colonies is a report to constituents shaped to keep them close to Congress. The tone is moderate and mild to the point of sadness. Congress sought the approval and future participation of the five important non-island British American colonies that did not attend the congress: St. Johns (Newfoundland), Nova Scotia, Georgia, and East and West Florida, by sending them their publications under a brief cover letter. Special attention was extended to Quebec, which received a long address composed in both English and French, offering a primer on the English constitution and its vital rights of self-government, trial by jury, the liberty of the person from arbitrary arrest, freedom of the press—all rights that had been withheld by British ministry, but "without which a people cannot be free and happy." Congress's final "address to the King" was published as "The Petition of the Continental Congress to the King." By claiming its proper relation to their monarch, Congress could more easily refuse any constitutional subordination to Parliament, which Congress declined to address.[11] By adding the modifier "Continental" to the noun "Congress," the Pennsylvania members in charge of publication, Edward Biddle, John Dickinson, and Charles Thomson, signified the expansive ambition of Congress.

"A CHAIN OF FREEDOM HAS BEEN FORMED"

On May 10, 1775, three weeks after the commencement of hostilities at Lexington and Concord, Ethan Allen and a few hundred of the Green Mountain Boys stormed the very sparsely garrisoned Fort Ticonderoga. The fort was a great prize because of its location at the strategic juncture between Lake George and Lake Champlain, the chief inland waterway between Quebec on the St. Lawrence River and New York on the Hudson, and because of its

---

11. However, there are several factors that suggest that the petition was a perfunctory gesture. It was called an "address to the king" not a "petition" in the published minutes of Congress; it was the last document to be prepared (as a necessary afterthought); most of the work for the final revision of the address to His Majesty fell to the latecomer to Congress, John Dickinson of Pennsylvania.

abundance of cannon. The puzzled and bleary-eyed British officer in charge, "breeches in his hand," asked Allen, a famously huge man, "by what authority" he demanded surrender of the fort. Allen later reported his reply: "In the name of the Great Jehovah and the Continental Congress!" (Allen 1779, 8). How was it that less than seven months after the dissolution of the First Congress, upon the very day that Congress was scheduled to reconvene, Congress had already garnered the authority to be the political body in whose name a military commander could demand the surrender of a fort?[12]

The expanding authority of Congress was evidenced by the enthusiastic support that was garnered by its acts and resolves in the weeks after its adjournment. Just as the Boston Town Meeting gathered power only through the countersigning that the *Votes and Proceedings* received though the declarations of other Massachusetts towns, and just as the proposal by a rump meeting of Virginia burgesses for a Virginia convention succeeded only through the resolves and delegate selections of the county meetings for which it called, so too did the force and efficacy of the final acts and communications of Congress depend upon their being "countersigned" by meetings held throughout the colonies in the weeks and months after the dissolution of the First Congress. Every colony except New York and Georgia held meetings to review and endorse Congress (Burnett 1941, 61).

We can gauge the success of Congress in activating the Whig network by considering one of the local conventions, the one that was closest to "home," the convention sponsored by the Pennsylvania committees. The "Convention for the Province of Pennsylvania" was held January 23–28, 1775, at Carpenters' Hall and was attended by 106 delegates from ten counties (see fig. 5.4). The convention explicitly endorsed the Continental Association and urged measures that helped increase the production of items that the termination of trade with Britain, Ireland, and the West Indies rendered essential: sheep, woolens, dyes, flax, hemp, salt, saltpeter, gunpowder, nails and wire, steel, paper, glass, copper, grindstones, barley for malt liquors, tin plates, and printing types. In order to establish a conceptual framework for these useful resolutions, James Wilson gave a remarkable speech that was later entitled "A Vindication of the Colonies." After training at St. Andrews, Glasgow, and Edinburgh, Wilson had emigrated from Scotland in his early twenties, taught Latin at the Acad-

12. The increased authority of Congress is also evident through the petitions that began to be directed at it. For example, William Goddard petitioned Congress with his proposal for a "constitutional post" to replace the royal one; it was allowed to lie on the table (Congress 1775, 49).

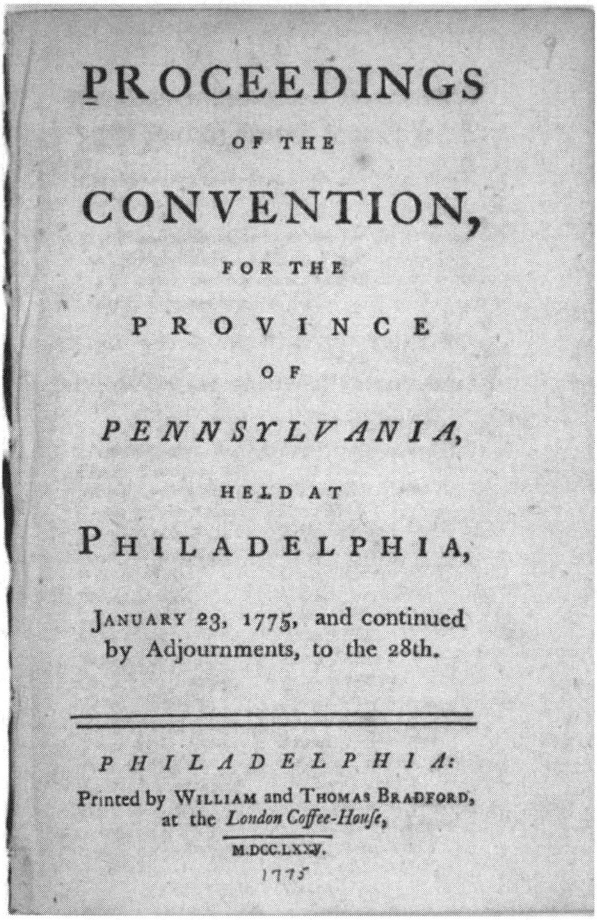

PROCEEDINGS

OF THE

CONVENTION,

FOR THE

PROVINCE

OF

PENNSYLVANIA,

HELD AT

PHILADELPHIA,

JANUARY 23, 1775, and continued
by Adjournments, to the 28th.

PHILADELPHIA:
Printed by WILLIAM and THOMAS BRADFORD,
at the London Coffee-House,

M.DCC.LXXV.

1775

FIGURE 5.4.
The pamphlet reporting the resolves of the January 1775 Pennsylvania convention in support of the Continental Congress. It is at this convention that James Wilson gave his speech in support of Congress. Photograph courtesy of the American Antiquarian Society.

emy and College of Philadelphia, read law with John Dickinson, and, by the age of thirty-two, was a successful lawyer. The previous July he had attended the first Pennsylvania convention as a member of the Cumberland County Committee of Correspondence. As noted above, the convention recognized his powers of mind and speech by recommending him to the Pennsylvania Assembly as one of a slate of three members of the convention that they hoped would be chosen for the congress.

Now, in January 1775, the speech offered a concise and eloquent justification of the collective response of the colonies to the Coercive Acts: "We were roused; we were alarmed, as we had reason to be." Wilson insists that the measures undertaken by the various colonies "have been such as the spirit of liberty and of loyalty directed; not such as a spirit of sedition or of disaffection would pursue." Wilson then offered a synoptic view of the communication innovations that have been the focus of this study. The sequence traces the steps by which a beautiful new object has come into view:

> That the sentiments of every individual concerning that important object, his liberty, might be known and regarded, meetings have been held, and deliberations carried on in every particular district. That the sentiments of all those individuals might gradually and regularly be collected into a single point, and the conduct of each inspired and directed by the result of the whole united, county committees—provincial conventions—a continental congress have been appointed, have met and resolved. By this means, a chain—more inestimable, and, while the necessity for it continues, we hope, more indissoluble than one of gold—a chain of freedom has been formed, of which every individual in these colonies, who is willing to preserve the greatest of human blessings, his liberty, has the pleasure of beholding himself a link. (Wilson 1901, 70)

Wilson's speech imbues every meeting, whether of town or county, colony or congress, with the same purpose: collecting the sentiments of "every individual" in every particular meeting of "every particular district" "to a single point." The speech celebrates the alignment of committees, conventions, and Congress, all of which "have been appointed, have met and resolved." Since the first motion of the meetings was efficient and inclusive in its ingathering of sentiments, in its second motion, after the meeting of Congress, "each" separate individual and particular meeting could be "inspired and directed" by "the result of the whole united." The past tense of the passage is important because its rhetorical charge comes from the metamorphosis these meetings had achieved. All had become part of one "chain of freedom."

The metaphor of the chain that Wilson develops here is rich with implication. First, the geography of the Atlantic coast and the history of colonization of North America by sea meant that the thirteen colonies from New Hampshire to Georgia were imagined by shipborne travelers and English mapmakers as stretched out in a curved line from north to south and east to west. But a chain, unlike the earlier device of the broken rattlesnake, never fuses into one. Because a chain is made of links of equal size that stay separate while they join, such links could represent the separateness and equality of individuals, towns, counties, and colonies that were gathered through their meetings. However, one usually associates a chain with slavery and bondage. Here, the chain condenses a paradox of American liberty: that the liberty of the colonies might only be protected if each individual will willingly linked himself or herself into one chain; that the liberty of the whole was sustained by the virtue and responsibility of each member. Because the chain is proverbially only as strong as its weakest link, each link of the chain must hold, or all might fall into bondage. In the eighteenth century, gold was considered literally "indissoluble," that which could not be dissolved (*OED*). This chain was still "*more* inestimable" in its value and "*more* indissoluble" than gold because it was not forged from physical men, meetings, or colonies; it was forged from their most precious, inward, and ideal part, their "sentiments" about the "greatest of human blessings, [their] liberty." This is why, through the alchemy of the meetings, conventions, and Congress, through the formation of a distributed network where every link was equally vital to the unity of the whole, every individual addressed and hailed by this speech could already enjoy a new kind of happiness, the "pleasure" of "beholding himself a link" of a single chain of freedom. This pleasure arrived at that moment when the citizen could say "I am free" because he or she was one link in an indissoluble "chain of freedom."[13]

13. Because of the way it separates what it joins, this figure of the chain has a resemblance to the blue field on the Betsy Ross flag, where the thirteen stars that represent thirteen states are arrayed in a circle that makes each star equally important. Intriguingly, this constellation of thirteen stars in a circle happens to bear a striking resemblance to the way a mesh network topology is usually visualized (see fig. I.4).

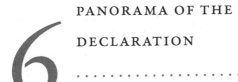

THE

PANORAMA OF THE

DECLARATION

. . . .

The Declaration of Independence [was] . . . the perfect way for an action to
appear in words. . . . And since we deal here with the written, and not the
spoken word, we are confronted with one of the rare moments in history
when the power of action is great enough to erect its own monument.
— Hannah Arendt, *On Revolution*

For American Whigs, the decade of the American crisis had produced almost unremitting anxiety about their rights and liberties. The crisis
was linked to decisions about taxation, sovereignty, and colonial rights that
were being made by those who were both powerful and remote: the king in
Parliament, the administration at Whitehall, and the Britons whom they
served. The patient development of the American Whig network, the organization of committees, the composition of declarations, and the convening
of Congress were ways to take some control over the direction of that future.
However, these Whig organizational initiatives only intensified the imperial
crisis. The sudden sense of release produced by Congress's July 4, 1776, publication of the Declaration of Independence came because it was, to use Arendt's
formulation, "the perfect way for an action to appear in words." By insulting
the king and by declaring the colonies' separation from Great Britain, the Declaration of 1776 translated an intractable crisis into an occasion to act. Now
the Declaration could be experienced as a performance to which American
Whigs could say, "Come what will, thus I willed it." Such an act of speech offered a sudden and joyful release from negotiating differences with Britain and
each other.

The potent efficacy of the Declaration, as the most influential communication of the Revolution, is suggested by its galvanizing effect upon the Whig
cause in America. In the weeks following its adoption and dissemination, the
Declaration was reprinted in newspapers and broadsides, and was proclaimed
orally in public readings in towns and villages throughout the colonies. Its
most important auditors may have been Washington's troops assembled in

brigades "on their respective parades" in Manhattan and Brooklyn, within sight of the British troops on Staten Island. After a reading of the Declaration in the State House courtyard in Philadelphia, John Adams reported in a letter to Samuel Chase that assembled "Battalions paraded on the common, and gave Us the Feu de Joy, notwithstanding the Scarcity of Powder. The Bells rung all Day, and almost all night" (July 9, 1776; J. Adams 1979, 4:372). The decisive character of the moment of the Declaration was expressed in acts of targeted destruction: royal portraits of George III were burned, the royal arms stripped from public buildings, and a fine equestrian statue of George III, which had been raised by New York Tories in 1770 on the bowling green at the southern tip of Manhattan, was overturned, later to be melted into shot.

In Boston on Thursday, July 18, the ceremonial reading of the Declaration offered the same heady mix found in many colonies: a boisterous multitude, a military parade, solemnity and celebration, violence and joy. Before the State House (i.e., the Town House), two regiments of Continental troops were assembled in King Street, arranged in thirteen divisions, while the batteries around the city were prepared to fire at the right moment. Abigail Adams describes how the moment of independence was staged:

Last Thursday after hearing a very Good Sermon I went with the Multitude into Kings Street to hear the proclamation for independence read and proclaimed. Some Field pieces with the train were brought there, the troops appeared under Arms and all the inhabitants assembled there (the small pox prevented many thousand from the Country). When Col. Crafts read from the Belcona of the State House the Proclamation, great attention was given to every word. As soon as he ended, the cry from the Belcona, was God save our American States and then 3 cheers which rended the air, the Bells rang, the privateers fired, the forts and Batteries, the cannon were discharged, the platoons followed and every face appeared joyfull. Mr. Bowdoin then gave a Sentiment, Stability and perpetuity to American independance. After dinner, the king's arms were taken down from the State House, and every vestige of him from every place in which it appeared, and burnt in King Street. Thus ends royall Authority in this State, and all the people shall say Amen. (July 21, 1776; J. Adams 1963, 2:56)

Boston's remarkable military show may be accounted for by the fact that only four months earlier General Gage had evacuated his army and naval forces from Boston (on March 17, 1776), and many still feared a military return of the British. The unanimity of sentiment in Boston that is suggested by Abigail Adams's account may be explained by the departure of approximately 1,100

Massachusetts Tories with Gage's army of 11,000. The ceremony was structured so as to climax in a moment of noisy exaltation and shared joy. After the proclamation of the Declaration by the sheriff of Suffolk County, Colonel Crofts, a reading in which, Adams tells us, "great attention was given to every word," the difference made by that proclamation was marked first by a revision of the old toast "God save our King" into "God save our American states," and then by successive waves of human and nonhuman sounds—three cheers, ringing bells, the loud report of battery cannon and militia muskets—resonating through the town and harbor. At this carefully marked moment, "every face appeared joyfull."

What is it about the Declaration that makes it possible to believe that after it had been "read and proclaimed" something fundamental had changed? How, after its reading upon the exact site of the Boston Massacre, how, after 150 years of monarchy in Massachusetts, could the reading of this document provoke the removal of every trace of the king on "King Street"? Adams gives this momentous event—"thus ends royal authority in this state"—a turn that oddly mixes her implied sentiment ("good riddance!") with a pious farewell: "and all the people shall say amen." The exaltation of the moment links this "amen" with a hopeful beginning.

Since the Declaration insulted the king and enacted a separation from Britain, why did the Whigs gathered on King Street seem to view independence less as an action fraught with peril than as a cause for joy? To explore this question, this chapter considers the means by which Congress attuned the Declaration—by its timing, method of composition, and media forms—so as to optimize its effect. It was part of the political work of the Declaration to insult the king, George III, and perform the separation of the colonies from Britain. But it was the rhetorical art of the Declaration that placed these two highly fraught actions within a calming verbal panorama, so that the Whig network that the Declaration spoke for and addressed could experience these acts as historical events: momentous, completed, and (now) part of a necessary course of human events.

TIMING THE DECLARATION

We cannot make Events. Our business is wisely to improve them.
— Samuel Adams to Samuel Cooper, April 30, 1776

Declaring independence emerged in Congress as a way to clarify the stakes of the intensifying war with Great Britain. Since May of 1775, Congress had become a war-fighting body and grappled with a succession of developments that pointed toward an ever-widening war. In the wake of the battles of Lexington and Concord and Bunker Hill, Congress had published its own "Declaration on the Necessity to bear Arms" (July 6, 1775) and authorized the invasion and conquest of Quebec. The king had proclaimed the colonies in a state of rebellion (August 23, 1775) and offered a particularly acerbic attack on the colonies in opening Parliament (October 26, 1775). News of the Prohibitory Act and the hiring of German mercenaries suggested the Crown's determination to use all available resources to prosecute the American War. Parliament's long-rumored commission to promote reconciliation with the colonies had not arrived in America. While the withdrawal of General Gage's forces from Boston to Halifax was welcome in itself (March 17, 1776), it also portended a massive invasion of New York.

In the face of a war with Great Britain, no one needed to preach the necessity of unity, but independence was precisely the issue that divided Congress. For years Tories had hurled the accusation of aiming at "independence" or "independency" so as to impugn the loyalty of American Whigs. For the many Whigs who wanted to preserve union with Britain, the charge was distressing. So as late as January 1776, Congress appointed a committee of five, which included James Wilson (PA), James Duane (NY), and John Dickinson (PA), to frame a public declaration to refute the accusation that Congress sought independence. In a draft read in Congress on February 13, 1776, the committee rejected the king's accusation "of carrying on the war 'for the purpose of establishing an independent Empire.' We disavow the Intention. We declare, that what we aim at, and what we were entrusted by you [our constituents] to pursue, *is the Defense and Re-establishment of the constitutional Rights of the Colonies*" (February 13, 1776; Congress 1906, 4:141, emphasis in the original; Rakove 2010, 95–97). While early advocates of independence in the delegations of Virginia and Massachusetts promoted it as a way to fight the war with greater resolution, for those in Congress who still cleaved to the possibility of reconciliation, independence was the point of no return that should be deferred as long as possible (Rakove 2010, 110–11).

For members of Congress opposed to independence in the spring of 1776, their strongest argument pivoted on the vexed issue of timing. All agreed that the American colonies could not hope to prevail in a war with Britain without foreign allies, most promisingly France. But this would eventually require a profound set of structural changes, only one of which was independence. In debates about independence triggered by Richard Henry Lee's resolution of June 7, 1776, Edward Rutledge (SC), John Dickinson (PA), James Wilson (PA), and Robert R. Livingston (NY) argued that it was inappropriate to declare independence from Britain before the colonies had constituted thirteen independent state governments, and, furthermore, it was absurd to attempt to bring a foreign power "into a union with us before we had united with each other" (Edward Rutledge to John Jay, June 8, 1776; Congress 1921, 1:476). This was a question that John Adams had considered carefully. In a letter written while Congress was in the midst of considering the Lee resolution for independence, Adams described the systematic steps, listed in the logically preferred order, that America should take so as to secure its future: "[1] Every Colony must be induced to institute a perfect Government. [2] The Colonies must confederate together, in some solemn Compact. [3] The Colonies must be declared free and independent states, and [4] Embassadors, must be sent abroad to foreign Courts, to solicit their Acknowledgement of Us, as Sovereign States, and to form with them, at least with some of them, commercial Treaties of Friendship and Alliance" (John Adams to William Cushing, June 9, 1776; J. Adams 1979, 4:245). Congress had made a start on John Adams's to-do list the previous month when it had passed the May 10–15 resolution requesting that each colony should "adopt such government as shall, in the opinion of the representatives of the people, best conduce to the happiness and safety of their constituents in particular, and America in general" (May 10, 1776; Congress 1906, 4:342). But ordering these four structural changes proved problematic. Forming foreign alliances (4) required a unified authority, a confederation of states (2) to conduct diplomacy; but this would be impossible to form without newly constituted states (1), a process that was proceeding quickly in some colonies (like South Carolina and Virginia) but not moving forward at all in other colonies. Declaring the states independent from Britain (3), the sine qua non of foreign alliances (4), also seemed to depend upon completing state constitutions (1) and a confederation (2), which were obviously years away. Since waiting years to declare independence might be fatal to the project of forming foreign alliances, John Adams wrote to Patrick Henry on June 3, 1776, after describing the preferred order of events: "But I fear we cannot proceed systematically, and that We Shall be obliged to declare ourselves independent States, before We confederate, and indeed before all the Colonies have established Governments" (J. Adams 1979, 4:234–35).

The compromise that Congress fashioned out of this impasse defined the context out of which the Declaration would emerge. In the wake of an explicit resolution for independence recently passed by the Virginia Convention, Richard Henry Lee, never shy about taking the initiative, introduced a triple resolution on June 7, 1776. The first part was the momentous resolution whose wording would eventually become the operative language of the Declaration.

Resolved, That these United Colonies are, and of right ought to be, free and Independent States, that they are absolved from all allegiance to the British Crown, and that all political connection between them and the State of Great Britain is, and ought to be, totally dissolved.

That it is expedient forthwith to take the most effectual measures for forming foreign Alliances.

That a plan of confederation be prepared and transmitted to the respective Colonies for their consideration and approbation. (Congress 1906, 5:425)

In discussions on June 8 and 10, Congress easily agreed to act upon the last two motions by appointing committees to frame articles for a foreign alliance (John Adams was the lead drafter for this committee) and to frame articles of confederation (where John Dickinson was the lead drafter). While members like John Adams were confident that an immediate declaration would "arouse and unite the Friends of Liberty," others countered that such a declaration would "arouse and unite Great Britain" and "put us in the Power of foreign States" (John Adams to John Winthrop, June 23, 1776; J. Adams 1979, 4:331–32). However, no consensus was developed on the resolution declaring independence. There were at least five out of thirteen states not ready to vote for independence, a measure that it was believed required unanimity to be effective. It was therefore decided "that consideration of the first resolution be postponed to this day, three weeks (July 1st)" (Congress 1906, 5:428). In the parliamentary terminology of the day, this was "laying on the table" (a resolution, petition, statute, or any other piece of business) so as to suspend its consideration until a later time.

The agreement to table the resolution was a concession to those who insisted that popular sentiment in at least five states—Pennsylvania, Maryland, South Carolina, Delaware, and New York—"were not yet matured for falling from the parent stem" (Jefferson 1984, 17). In a concession to those members favoring independence, and in order to make efficient use of the interval before July 1, Congress appointed a committee of five to draft a declaration in support of the Lee resolution. Because of the limbo into which Lee's resolution had been thrown, the first audience of the committee's draft Declaration would be those members of Congress who were still reluctant to declare independence. For the advocates of independence, including leading members of the drafting committee like Jefferson, Adams, and Franklin, independence was something that the colonies should *just do*. Then Congress might discover that unity was not the precondition of independence but rather its happy effect.

In the spring of 1776 the metaphor of the ripening fruit, by making the movement toward independence appear inevitable, became a favorite one for those favoring independence (Rakove 1979, 87). But this did not preempt efforts to hurry along the ripening. For those in favor of independence, the reluctance of certain colonies looked like a network problem that required a network solution. The May 10–15, 1776, resolution for calling conventions to organize new state government had set Whigs in motion in many colonies. Members of Congress from various colonies, like Maryland and New York, communicated with provincial congresses, urging updated advice on the question of independence, so that the instructions could be changed by the time the resolution was taken up again on July 1 (Congress 1921, 1:477, 485, 494). Samuel Chase returned to Maryland to help lead the Maryland convention toward independence, and New Jersey chose new members who were explicitly instructed to favor independence. In Pennsylvania, complex political maneuvering with the discreet covert assistance of some members of Congress led to a discrediting of the Pennsylvania Assembly and the summoning of committees of correspondence throughout the colony to meet in convention at Carpenters' Hall (June 18–25, 1775). There, the convention drafted a formal statement supporting independence.[1]

THE CULMINATING DECLARATION
OF THE AMERICAN WHIG NETWORK

What gave the Declaration its distinctive efficacy? Its galvanizing influence has led some scholars to emphasize the autonomous power of its language: the "verbal artistry" with which it justifies independence (Lucas 1989), the performative power of the climactic double assertion that "these united colonies are, and of right ought to be, free and independent states" (Derrida 2002; Honig 1991), or the way its rhetoric and pauses deliver a compelling oral performance (Fliegelman 1993). While these approaches to the Declaration are illuminating, they overemphasize the autonomous power of language. The effects of

1. For a detailed account of the complex sequence of actions that brought changes in the Pennsylvania instructions, as well as planning for the Pennsylvania constitutional convention, see Ryerson 1978, 216–46. William Hogeland's recent study, *Declaration: The Nine Tumultuous Weeks When America Became Independent, May 1–July 4, 1776*, details the way in which the radical leadership of the Pennsylvania committees benefited from the covert leadership of Samuel Adams and his old Boston collaborator, Dr. Thomas Young. Hogeland demonstrates the importance of the feedback loop between local initiatives and the resolutions of Congress (11–49).

the Declaration should not be understood as a conjuring trick of language, by which, for example, the "we" that speaks the declaration is a retroactive invention of the text of the declaration.[2] Neither does one need to enter into abstruse theoretical arguments about political representation to understand Congress's use of "we" in the Declaration to speak for "the good people of these colonies." Theoretical issues of representation and "virtual representation" had been important during the Stamp Act controversy, and they would become so again during the debates on the ratification of the US Constitution.[3]

The American Whig network that had developed between 1772 and 1776 had provided a pragmatic solution to the issue of representation. The "we" that speaks in and grounds the Declaration is literal before it is figural, tangible before it is virtual. The first referent of this pronoun is the American Whig network that had developed over the previous four years and which has been the focus of this study. The network achieved its cohesion from the inherited institutions it was built upon, its practices of association and communication, and, most notably, its innovative development of the popular declaration. There were thousands who had become participants in this network and its activities: those who had attended town and county meetings, served on committees, were delegates to conventions, ran the Association's committees of enforcement, scrupulously observed the boycott on trade with Britain over the past eighteen months, and signed up to serve in the militia or the Continental Army. These were the target audience for Congress's Declaration, and they provided a constituency that those in Congress favoring independence hoped to animate with a new clarity of purpose. This network of humans, genres, places, institutions, and protocols served as a platform so that, on July 4, 1776, a "we"—both Congress *and* the American Whig network for whom they spoke—could boldly stand forth and submit their provisional claim to speak "in the name, and by the Authority of" a still more comprehensive "we," "the good people of these colonies."

2. Putting emphasis upon the autonomous power of the language of the Declaration is itself a modern symptom of the failure of the sort of collective identification and collaborative politics that made the Revolution possible. The loss of the tangible, shared public practice of politics leads to the idea that the "we" could be a linguistic construction that is fabulous, a fable—but no less powerful for all that. For example, see Michael Warner (1990, chapter 4, especially 107–15) for an account of how the writing and printing of the Constitution allowed "the people" to constitute themselves through the "we" of the preamble of that document as both agent and object of the law.

3. For a very astute discussion of the central political issue of representation, see Downes 2002, 23–30.

1. *The Votes and Proceedings of the Town of Boston* and the
   declarations of the towns (November 1772–December 1773); the
   Boston committee functions until 1775/1776.
2. The Virginia Committee of Correspondence and the responses
   that it elicits (March 1773–May 1774).
3. The declarations of various town and country meetings and
   provincial conventions respond to the Coercive Acts and plan the
   First Continental Congress (May–September 1774).
4. The First Continental Congress: the Association; the
   "Declarations and Resolves" (stating rights and grievances;
   October 1774).
5. The declarations of various provincial and local meetings ratifying
   the acts of the First Congress, appointing new delegates, and
   implementing the Association (January–April 1775).
6. The Second Continental Congress: "Declaration of the Necessity
   of Taking Up Arms" (July 1775).
7. The declarations of various provincial and local meetings on the
   question of independence (April 12, 1776–July 6, 1776).
8. The Declaration of Independence (July 4, 1776).

The easiest way to win over to independence the members of the Whig
network was to incorporate previous declarations into this one. This helped
to finesse the legal obstacle that haunted the Declaration: there was no legal
or constitutional ground for this extra-constitutional body, Congress, to declare independence. Just as the authority of Congress depended upon thirteen extralegal colonial assemblies, the Declaration of Independence gathered
authority from the proven success and quasi-legal precedent of hundreds of
Whig popular declarations, which had been produced by committees, conventions, assemblies, and Congress over the previous three and one-half years (see
box 6.1). This declaration gathered in and incorporated the language, ideas,
and political authority of the host of preceding declarations. Like the earlier
declarations, Congress's new declaration observed the five protocols of the earlier declarations: it followed correct legal procedure, entailed corporate action,
and offered robust public access to its general and systematic address to the

people. Finally, and more explicitly than all previous declarations, *this* declaration performed its virtuous initiative by declaring independence.

While building upon these earlier declarations, Congress wrote the Declaration of Independence so that it served as a culmination that overwrote them.[4] While the earlier declarations had been explicitly British in their reiterated claims to the rights guaranteed by the ancient English constitution, the Declaration grounded its claims in universal natural rights, including the primordial right to self-defense. While canny critics of the earlier declarations—like Thomas Hutchinson and Joseph Galloway—had challenged them for harboring a dangerous spirit of independence, Congress now stepped forth to declare independence. The Declaration's distinctive and definitive message—that thirteen British colonies "are" now "free and independent states"—made the Declaration the logical end (in the sense of a telos) of all the previous American Whig declarations. The Declaration of Congress offered a new retroactive justification for the Whig network of extralegal conventions and committees and provincial congresses. No longer temporary expedients for pressing claims with Britain, they now could be understood as instituting, in the words of the Declaration, new "systems of government."

Edmund Burke was a keen observer of the breakdown of authority in Massachusetts in 1774 and the actions of the First Continental Congress. So as early as his March 22, 1775, speech to Parliament on conciliation with the American colonies, Burke warned of the way the American Whigs had gone from challenging British authority to asserting their own: "Until very lately, all authority in America seemed to be nothing but an emanation from yours. Even the popular part of the Colony Constitution derived all its activity, and its first vital movement, from the pleasure of the Crown. We thought, Sir, that the utmost which the discontented Colonists could do, was to disturb authority; we never dreamt they could of themselves supply it." Burke notes the unhappy result of a policy of parliamentary coercion and the American experiments in government that policy incited: "Some provinces have tried their experiment, as we have tried ours; and theirs has succeeded. They have formed a Government sufficient for its purposes, without the bustle of a Revolution, or the troublesome formality of an Election" (Burke 1996, 3:126). The Declaration made explicit the turn toward extra-constitutional self-government—and pointedly *adds* "the bustle of revolution."

4. In an odd fashion, the subsequent success of the Declaration of Independence—a success that was both political and literary—has had the effect of erasing the many declarations that constituted the platform upon which the Declaration was originally written.

Congress knew that *how* the Declaration was composed would affect its prospects for emerging as an expression of the corporate will of Congress. The three-and-a-half-week progress of the Declaration from resolution to broadside made Congress rather than Jefferson the author of the document. An impressive body of scholarship has reconstructed and debated this progress, usually in relation to the specter of Jefferson as author. The key stages in the development of the Declaration suggest how Congress originated and authored the Declaration. After Congress debated and then tabled the Lee resolution, it appointed (on June 11, 1776) a committee of five members, selected to represent diverse and important colonies, to draft a declaration in support of the resolution: Thomas Jefferson (VA), John Adams (MA), Benjamin Franklin (PA), Roger Sherman (CT), and Robert R. Livingston (NY). In its first meeting the committee developed the "articles," or main components, to be included in the Declaration, and Jefferson was given the task of composing the committee's first draft. The committee met several times during the next seventeen days, before delivering its draft to Congress on June 28, 1776. The Jefferson first draft, which exists only in fragments, incorporated at least forty-seven alterations before becoming the committee draft. (Some revisions were written in the hand of John Adams and Franklin.) After the formal adoption of the Lee resolution on July 2, the committee draft was read in Congress and discussed on the second and third of July, before its final adoption on July 4, 1776. During the deliberation in Congress, the committee draft received thirty-nine more alterations, many of them significant, including cuts drastic enough to reduce the length of the Declaration by one-quarter.[5]

Not only was the Declaration shaped by many hands and voices; it also incorporated arguments copied out of previous declarations as well as the whole canon of the English literature of political liberty. Generations of scholars have documented the Declaration's debt to others, whether political thinkers like John Locke or public documents like the British Bill of Rights. These debts extend down to the level of sentence or phrase. Thus, the Declaration's testament to mankind's "unalienable rights" to "life, liberty, and the pursuit of happiness" relies upon George Mason's formulation in his draft of the Virginia

5. See Jefferson 1950, 413–17, editorial note, for discussion of many changes during composition; Maier's (1997) careful reconstruction of the changes made by Congress to the committee draft are found in appendix C and involves the thirty-nine alterations mentioned by Starr 2000.

Declaration of Rights, where he affirms the right to "the enjoyment of life and liberty, with the means of acquiring and possessing property, and pursuing and obtaining happiness and safety" (Maier 1997, 134). In the prologue, the all-important pivot toward justifying revolution—"But when a long train of abuses and usurpations, pursuing the invariably the same object, evinces a design to reduce them under absolute despotism"—has been noticed by many scholars to have a more than casual resemblance to a corresponding sentence in section 225 of Locke's *Second Treatise on Government*. It is not surprising that Jefferson, in his role as lead drafter on the committee, would cut and paste from these important sources, authorities, and esteemed fellow Whigs like George Mason. In serving as the invisible drafter of the document, he most resembles a compiler and editor charged with harmonizing old arguments into a concise and compelling document that would support the bold new project of independence (Fliegelman 1993, 164). The ease with which Jefferson, the committee, and Congress incorporated previous language makes them typical practitioners of eighteenth-century authorship. Here practice is guided by neoclassical conceptions of authorship, where, as Pauline Maier (1997, 104) explains, there was a disdain for "novelty" as an end in itself and, by contrast, an admiration of "creative adaptation of preexisting models to different circumstances, and the highest praise of all went to imitations whose excellence exceeded that of the examples that inspired them."

In the last decade of his life, Jefferson had to defend himself against charges of plagiarism, and he designed his funeral monument with the epitaph "THE AUTHOR OF THE DECLARATION OF AMERICAN INDEPENDENCE." But even at the end of his life, Jefferson also remembered how restricted had been the drafting role that Congress had given him in June 1776 and how inappropriate it would have been for him to attempt to author the Declaration. Thus, in an 1825 letter to Henry Lee, Jefferson describes why the occasion of the Declaration meant he had to avoid the role of author as an original creator.[6]

> When forced, therefore, to resort to arms for redress, an appeal to the tribunal of the world was deemed proper for our justification. This was the object of the Declaration of Independence. Not to find out new principles, or new

6. Among scholars who emphasize the centrality of Jefferson's authorship, I am thinking of influential books like Garry Wills's *Inventing America: Jefferson's Declaration of Independence*, as well as other many other books that start with Jefferson's intentions and modes of writing, however much they qualify Jefferson's status as author (Lucas 1989). For a historically sensitive discussion of the institution of authorship and Jefferson, see Maier 1997, 104; and Fliegelman 1993, 164–67.

arguments, never before thought of, not merely to say things which had never been said before; but to place before mankind the common sense of the subject, in terms so plain and firm as to command their assent, and to justify ourselves in the independent stand we are compelled to take. Neither aiming at originality of principle or sentiment, nor yet copied from any particular and previous writing, it was intended to be an expression of the American mind, and to give to that expression the proper tone and spirit called for by the occasion. All its authority rests then on the harmonizing sentiments of the day, whether expressed in conversation, in letters, printed essays, or in the elementary books of public right. (May 8, 1825; Jefferson 1984, 1501)

This famous account of the imperatives that guided the composition of the Declaration helps to undo any attempt to claim authorship of it. In explaining the Declaration to Henry Lee, the son of Henry "Light-Horse" Lee III and half-brother of Robert E. Lee, Jefferson here explicitly refuses to apply to the Declaration the values of Romantic authorship that had become so influential during the forty-nine years since 1776 (Fliegelman 1993, 166). By contrast, in this letter, Jefferson argues that the Declaration did not aim at "originality" or "new principles." Jefferson's use of the passive voice and the first-person plural pronouns "we" and "our" further distances this act of writing from the Romantic conception of authorship as dependent upon the original genius of an individual. The work of the drafters required that they be self-effacing. "To justify ourselves in the independent stand we are compelled to take," they were intent upon speaking with a "tone and spirit" appropriate to purposes that were direct, public, and bold. Here the virile strength of speech would come from simplicity and clarity, rather than ingenious conceits of self-conscious authorship. Finally, to fashion writing that would provide a "justification" for a "resort to arms," the drafters had to harmonize "the sentiments of the day." The more Congress could gather to its cause, the larger its army would be. The rhetorical imperatives described by Jefferson subordinated the particularity of the drafters to the general public imperatives of the draft. Only if the drafters disappeared into the draft could the Declaration become what it aimed to be: "an expression of the American mind."

THE SHAPE-SHIFTING DECLARATION

The corporate public documents of the American Revolution were shaped to reflect and forge consensus. In order to build support for its risky collective action, dissolving "the political bands" between thirteen American colonies and Great Britain, Congress followed procedures that were similar to those followed by the Boston Town Meeting, the Virginia House of Burgesses, and the First Continental Congress. Congress appointed a drafting committee, secretly deliberated in committee and in Congress (as "a committee of the whole"), and finally published the Declaration as a corporate document. In this way the particular acts of drafting, deliberation, dispute, and revision disappeared behind the public document, thereby serving the overriding goal of presenting the Declaration to the world as the consensus of Congress. The particular drafters of the Declaration (Jefferson, the other members of the drafting committee, and those in Congress who recommended final revisions) were, by the design of this process, allowed to remain invisible to the public.

Historians have debated whether the great stir created by the publication of the Declaration should be attributed to the news that Congress had finally acted to declare the American colonies' separation from Britain, or whether it resulted from the particular qualities of the document that broadcast that news. In other words, what was more important, the declaration or the Declaration? (Maier 1997; Armitage 2000; Ferguson 1994, 476). But whether we view the document from the vantage point of eighteenth-century contemporaries, where the declaration seems primary, or from the perspective of later generations, where the Declaration looms large, it is difficult not to admire the document's canny alignment of message and media, content and form. If one charts the morphology of the Declaration—from the Lee resolution of June 7, 1776, to the Dunlap broadside of July 4–5, 1776, to the engrossed manuscript fine copy that Congress began to sign on August 2, 1776, to the printing of that document as the Goddard broadside by Congress on January 18, 1777—one can trace how Congress reshaped the form of its Declaration so as to enhance the power and authority of both Congress and the document (see box 6.2).

Over the course of its development, there were three related changes to the Declaration: its title, its addressee, and the media forms it was given as manuscript, print, and speech. The Declaration was first printed with the title "In Congress, July 4, 1776. *A* Declaration by the Representatives," positioning it as one in a series of declarations. But, after the last state to endorse independence had done so (New York), and after the Declaration of July 4, 1776, had received a rousing reception among Whigs, the title of the engrossed copy of August 2, 1776, was changed to use the definite article and the modifier "unanimous." It became "*The unanimous* Declaration," a unique event that was now explicitly rather than implicitly unanimous. Consistent with this shift was a change in who spoke in the Declaration. In an early draft of the committee, the Declaration was "of the representatives of the 13 united states," but, by the

BOX 6.2. THE MORPHOLOGY OF THE DECLARATION OF INDEPENDENCE. FROM THE INTRODUCTION OF THE RICHARD HENRY LEE RESOLUTION ON JUNE 7, 1776, TO THE FINAL PUBLICATION OF THE GODDARD EDITION WHILE CONGRESS WAS IN EXILE IN BALTIMORE, THE DECLARATION KEPT CHANGING SHAPE.

1. The Lee resolution introduced into Congress on June 7, 1776: "That these United Colonies are, and of right ought to be, free and independent States, that they are absolved from all allegiance to the British Crown, and that all political connection between them and the State of Great Britain is, and ought to be, totally dissolved." (Accepted by Congress on July 2, 1776.)
2. Thomas Jefferson is charged with writing a first draft and submitting it to committee revision (June 1776).
3. Congress receives, revises, and accepts a final version on July 4 and, immediately publishing it as the Dunlap broadside, distributes it throughout the colonies, so that it can be proclaimed at public meetings.

In Congress, July 4, 1776. A Declaration by the Representatives of the United States of American in General Congress Assembled.

4. The engrossed manuscript copy on vellum is ready to begin signing in Congress on August 2, 1776.

In Congress, July 4, 1776. The Unanimous Declaration of the thirteen United States of America.

5. Goddard broadside: "In CONGRESS January 18, 1777. ORDERED. That an authenticated Copy of the DECLARATION OF INDEPENDENCY, with the names of the MEMBERS of CONGRESS, subscribing the same, be sent to each of the UNITED STATES, and that they be desired be put on RECORD."

In CONGRESS, July 4, 1776. The Unanimous DECLARATION of the Thirteen United States of AMERICA. Baltimore, 18 January 1777.

time the committee draft was sent to Congress, it was a declaration not "of" the representatives but "by" them, and thus on behalf of the thirteen united states (Jefferson 1950, 1:423, 427). This change had the effect of emphasizing the representatives' secondary and mediating role in the act of the Declaration. The engrossed copy of August 2, 1776, went the next logical step by dropping any reference to representatives. The new title made the states themselves the "speakers" of the Declaration: "In Congress, July 4, 1776, The unanimous Declaration of the thirteen United States of America." The number of the states favoring independence, which had been discreetly dropped from the title of the Dunlap broadside because they could only number twelve, was returned with the engrossed copy.

At each stage of the Declaration's development, Congress shaped the Declaration so as to bolster the authority of Congress. In doing so, members of Congress demonstrated their expertise, acquired through a decade of practice, in using the media-communication system to develop and broadcast its message. In each of its forms, the Declaration exploited the resources of that system as well as the distinct attributes of each media form—manuscript, print, and speech—which I have expressed below in italics. During the interval opened by the three-week tabling of the Lee resolution, the Declaration was most fluid. Manuscript writing on paper had the *plasticity* essential to drafting and revision, as demonstrated by the crossings out and interlinear additions of the committee's final draft. The single unique manuscript copy, which was held by Jefferson as chief drafter of the committee, helped to guard its *secrecy* during composition. Once it had been adopted by Congress on July 4, its first publication as the Dunlap broadside allowed it to benefit from the properties of print, where it appeared as copies that were (1) *reliably identical,* (2) *portable* (allowing it to be quickly broadcast throughout the colonies), and (3) *legible,* making it appropriate for public proclamation. The copies of the Dunlap broadside that were sent to Washington and provincial assemblies were signed by the president, John Hancock, and the secretary, Charles Thomson, so their manuscript signatures *attested to the authenticity* of each copy. At the sites of reception, the *immediacy of the living voice* placed the proclaimed Declaration at the center of many *local, one-of-a-kind performances.*

While the printed Dunlap broadside had served the imperative for a *rapid multimedia broadcast,* Congress decided to give the Declaration another media form, one that was associated in eighteenth-century media ecology with documents like Magna Carta, the 1689 Bill of Rights, colonial charters, and treaties. These authoritative old documents were given *permanence* by being engrossed (literally "enlarged") with indelible ink on vellum, and they were signed by the appropriate political agents: monarchs, members of Parliament, tribal chiefs, and rivals in war. The resounding welcome that American Whigs gave the printed and proclaimed Declaration no doubt encouraged Congress to give the Declaration the authority that would be conferred by a *unique engrossed and signed parchment copy*. The personal signature upon these documents conferred force that was *evidentiary* (the signers' presence was confirmed), *performative* (the signers had acted), and *moral* (the signers had committed their word).

In the weeks after it began to sign the Declaration on August 2, 1776, Congress found ways to expand the authority of the document. Members not present on the fourth of July were allowed to sign the engrossed manuscript. *Each added signature confirmed the continued and ongoing legitimacy and force of the Declaration* and confirmed the support of the state that the delegate represented. But *each signature also renewed the "mutual pledge," or promise of loyalty to the "united states,"* that was first declared on July 4, 1776. The public importance of those manuscript signatures was reflected in Congress's final broadcast of the Declaration to the thirteen states. Driven by British troops from its de facto capital of Philadelphia, Congress, now meeting in Baltimore, voted to print a facsimile of the now authoritative engrossed manuscript copy of Declaration. "In CONGRESS January 18, 1777. ORDERED. That an authenticated Copy of the DECLARATION of INDEPENDENCY, with the names of the MEMBERS of CONGRESS, subscribing the same, be sent to each of the UNITED STATES, and that they be desired be put on RECORD." Here the document finally received its familiar title as "the Declaration of Independenc[e]." More importantly, in this final form, attested copies of the printed Declaration, with signatures very readable, were destined for a *permanent archive*, the place for depositing the first traces at the origin, which helped to authorize the new systems of government being developed by each state.

AN ACT OF FREE SPEECH

Let those flatter, who fear: it is not an American art.
— Thomas Jefferson, "A Summary View"

In this chapter, I have argued that the success of the Declaration depended upon the laboriously negotiated timing of its appearance, the mobilization of the network of American Whigs in support of independence, a practice of corporate authorship, and, finally, the shape shifting that assured that the Declaration reached a large audience in the most effective possible ways. But the success of the Declaration also depended upon the "software" of its language: the logical structure of its argument, the affective power of its rhetoric,

Title: In CONGRESS, July 4, 1776. A DECLARATION.

1. **Introduction.** "WHEN in the course of human events, it becomes necessary . . . that they should declare the causes which impel them to the separation."
2. **Prologue Statement of Rights.** "We hold these truths to be self-evident, that all men are created equal . . . to alter their former systems of government."
3. **List of Grievances.** "The history of the present King of Great-Britain is a history of repeated injuries and usurpations. . . . A prince, whose character is thus marked by every act which may define a tyrant, is unfit to be the ruler of a free people."
4. **Reproach to our "British Brethren."** "Nor have we been wanting in attentions to our British Brethren . . . and hold them, as we hold the rest of mankind, enemies in war, in peace, friends."
5. **Separation Performed.** "We, therefore, . . . do . . . solemnly publish and declare, that these united colonies are, and of right ought to be, FREE AND INDEPENDENT STATES . . . we mutually pledge to each other our lives, our fortunes, and our sacred honor."

Signed by ORDER, and in BEHALF of the CONGRESS,
John Hancock, President; ATTESTED Charles Thomson, Secretary

and the scope of its grand style. In the rest of this chapter, I will look closely at the language of the Declaration to show how it advanced American separation from Great Britain. First, the Declaration *used boldly* free speech to insult George III. Second, it not only argued the necessity of American independence, the Declaration showed American Whigs what it felt like to already be so. Finally, the Declaration created a verbal panorama that allowed those who heard and read it to experience American independence as a singular event within "the course of human events."

At the center of the Declaration was an act of free speech: an insult to the monarch of Great Britain, George III (see box 6.3). By "free" I mean speech that was bold, disrespectful, and not softened by politeness, balance, or any attempt at fairness. We can recover the rude asperity of this speech by reading the Declaration through the eyes of one of its first readers, Ambrose Serle. Serle was a devout Church of England Tory, with evangelical leanings, who had been appointed undersecretary of state in 1774 by the secretary of the American Department, Lord Dartmouth. Serle had traveled to the American colonies in that year. By 1776, at the age of thirty-two, Serle was serving as personal secretary to Lord Howe, commander in chief and admiral of the British fleet, which invaded New York in 1776 with the largest seaborne invasion since ancient times: 427 warships and transports, 1,200 cannons, 32,000 troops, and thousands of seamen.[7] On July 12, 1776, Serle disembarked on Staten Island and reported in his diary that they had heard "that Congress had now announced the Colonies to be INDEPENDENT STATES, with several other articles of intelligence, that proclaim the villainy & madness of these deluded people." If the bare news of the Declaration of Independence suggested that the American Whig rebels were a "deluded people," Serle's reading of the text of the Declaration, reported in his next day's diary entry, suggests something much worse.

> The Congress have at length thought it convenient to throw off the Mask. Their Declaration of the 4th of July, while it avows their Right to Independence, is founded upon such Reasons only, as prove *that* Independence to have been their Object from the Beginning. A more impudent, false and atrocious Proclamation was never fabricated by the Hands of Man. Hitherto, they have thrown all the Blame and Insult upon the Parliament and ministry: Now, they have the Audacity to calumniate the King and People of Great Britain. 'Tis impossible to read this Paper, without Horror at the daring Hypocrisy of these Men, who call GOD to witness the uprightness of their Proceedings, nor without Indignation at the low scurrilous Pretences by w[hi]ch they attempt to justify themselves. Surely, Providence will honor its own Truth and justice upon this Occasion, and, as they have made an appeal to it for Success, reward them after their own Deservings. (July 13, 1776; Serle 1940, 30–31)

There are several layers to Serle's indignation with Congress. First, Serle notes the change of the target of their political complaints, from Parliament

---

7. These figures come from Raphael 2009, 263. Later in the war, Serle helped to manage the royalist newspaper operation in New York (*Dictionary of National Biography*).

and ministry to the king and people of Great Britain. For years Whigs had defended their resistance to the policy of ministry and Parliament by affirming their loyalty to king and constitution. But Congress had "now" shown the "audacity" to "calumniate," that is "to make false and defamatory statements" about, "the King and People of Great Britain." While this speech is free in one sense—bold and loose to the point of libel—it is also openly seditious: the prologue's statement of rights is structured so that it culminates in an argument for the overthrow of the king's government. In other words, while Whig writing on both sides of the Atlantic had for years deflected the government's prosecution for seditious libel, here was a document whose writers explicitly crossed that line. What Tories had always darkly suspected, they could now find openly proclaimed.

Of course, Serle could hardly be surprised that rebels would engage in sedition. He even welcomes the fact that they have finally put aside "the mask," and have shown that they had been scheming for independence "from the beginning." The intensely personal animus with which he responds to the Declaration had another source. For Serle, this document's extremity of evil—"A more impudent, false and atrocious proclamation was never fabricated by the hands of man"—came from its appeal, in the final paragraph of the Declaration, to "the Supreme Judge of the World" and "the Protection of Divine Providence." Serle responds first by registering his own moral shock at the "daring hypocrisy of these men, who call GOD to witness the uprightness of their proceedings." Then, with dry understatement, Serle expresses his confidence that "Providence will honor its own truth and justice" and "reward them after their own deservings."

Serle's Tory moral righteousness justified harsh military reprisals against American "rebels." Thus, Serle's account of the Declaration was immediately preceded in his July 13 diary entry with news received from the northern theater of battle. Burgoyne had "overtaken the rebels, who had penetrated into Canada, driven them into a swamp, and put above 500 of them to the sword. The troops hold them very cheap, and long for an opportunity of revenging the cause of their countrymen, who fell at Bunker's Hill" (Serle 1940, 30). Serle obviously held Congress as "cheap" as Burgoyne's troops held the "rebels." Rather than reading the act of Congress with any analytic detachment, for example as a strategic move in a game of Atlantic politics, Serle assessed the Declaration to be "impudent, false and atrocious." This intensely personal response, and the indignation and rage it brought, was concomitant to a sentimental posture of Serle's loyalty to king and country. Serle's response also suggests how the Declaration served as a war-fighting document. By clarifying the stakes of the war for Whigs, it did the same for Tories, making conciliation short of a full-scale war most unlikely.

Whig auditors and readers of the Declaration enjoyed the very insults to the king that had so offended Serle. For Whigs, aggregating the various acts that had been committed by governors, Parliament, and ministry over ten years and then laying all twenty-seven grievances at the foot of the king helped to effect an emotional separation of king and subject. However unfair this apportionment of blame might be, the sentimental calculus of the Declaration made it *feel* right. In her study of the history of the sensibility in British America in the 1770s, Sarah Knott (2009, 64) shows that "sentimental reading presumed, valued and sought to effect a particular mode of selfhood: sensible, responsive, and receptive." For the past decade, the American petitioners to the king had hoped to find such a sympathetic reader of colonial grievances in their own monarch, but had failed to do so. Now the king, who had shown so little receptivity to and sympathy for his subjects, would receive none from them.

No list of grievances, no matter how long or deeply felt, would bring independence. Independence would require an act by American Whigs that explicitly rejected the comfortable old analogy between king and people, father and sons, parents and children. The cascade of insults to the king that make up the central section of the Declaration were not the result of transient anger or a lapse of good manners. Scholars of the Revolution have described the various ways in which the Declaration helped the colonists "get over" their attachment to the system of monarchy, by which the union of subjects was secured by the person of the monarch. The listed grievances became "counts" in a figurative court where the king was the "defendant" and the colonists were the "righteous accusers" (Ferguson 1994, 474–75). The staccato repetition of the third-person pronoun—"*he* has . . . *he* has . . . *he* is"—helps to objectify the king as a relentless persecuting agent, so that the "we" who speaks in the Declaration became his corporate victims. When the king becomes the bad father, the son must demonstrate "filial freedom" by spurning him in favor of a higher father, God (Fliegelman 1982, chapter 6). The young son's bitter renunciation of one who was once honored as a father gave the Declaration the personal antagonism of a family fight. The free speech of the Declaration worked to solve a practical imperative of the war with Britain, as described by the historian Timothy Breen (2010, 243): "persuading ordinary people of the legitimacy of using violence against a constitutional government that no longer protected their rights." By vilifying George III, Whigs could feel justified in attacking the troops and ships that fought under the king's arms.

> *The allegiance of thirteen states . . . by a solemn declaration . . . was a consideration of*
> *solemnity, a bold resolution, an experiment of hazard: especially when the infancy of*
> *the colonies as a nation, without wealth, resources, or allies, was contrasted with the*
> *strength, riches, and power of Great Britain.*
> — Mercy Otis Warren, *History of the Rise, Progress and Termination of the*
>   *American Revolution*

In the nearly 250 years since Congress issued its Declaration, citizens and scholars have most commonly treated it as a beginning.[8] But in order to begin, it also had to end decades of colonial rule, and the Declaration did this by performing an act of separation. By terminating the colonial relation with Great Britain, the Declaration served as the zenith of nearly four years of American Whig networking. Considered in this way, the Declaration's essential character was improvisational, pragmatic, and, in Mercy Otis Warren's suggestive formulation, an "experiment at hazard." Like the many other declarations that preceded it, it was an experiment that sought to enhance the power, unity, and authority of the American Whig network. By declaring separation from Britain, Congress also hoped to begin the transformation of that network, with Congress at its operational hub, into the constituents of an independent political agency strong enough to prevail in a war with Britain. As an instrument in fighting a war, the Declaration began its work by delivering a kind of anti-petition by insulting George III. This insult implied but also prepared for the decisive act of declaring independence.

8. Many studies of the American political system make the Declaration the starting point in early American constitutional history that continues through the Articles of Confederation (1781) to the US Constitution (1787) and the Bill of Rights (1789) (Wood 1969; Rakove 1979). Although many historians emphasize that American identity is an anachronism projected upon those whose primary affective affiliation remained with their colony or state (Wills 1979), some cultural historians and literary critics have noted that the Declaration was one of the first places where Americans proclaimed a distinctly American, as opposed to a British, national identity (Fliegelman 1993, quoted in *New York Times*, July 4, 2001, Art Section, by Robert D. McFadden). More recently, Elisa Tamarkin (2007) and Leonard Tennenhouse (2007) have described the various ways in which the Americans of the early Republic strived to be American by being more English than the English. Finally, social and intellectual histories have described the Declaration's role in the commemorative celebrations of the founding of the nation, where it figures as the nation's charter of rights, its most beloved textual monument, its "national treasure," its "American scripture" (Maier 1997; De Bolla 2008).

The boldness and bravado of the document were ways to deflect the anxiety and uncertainty that resulted from the weakness of Congress's position in the late spring and early summer of 1776. This weakness had several sources. First, Congress acutely felt its military weakness. The late spring brought news of the defeat of the northern American army in Quebec. For months Congress had heard rumors of the British forces converging on New York from Halifax, from Ireland, from England, and from various German states. With a huge armada landing in New York and another British army moving south from Canada, would these armies join forces and cut New England off from the other colonies? Would Britain use its overwhelming naval superiority to lay waste to every port and coastal town as they had Falmouth, Massachusetts? Would the British army succeed in rallying the thousands of Tory supporters throughout the colonies into formidable royal brigades? Would a parliamentary commission, through a canny policy of negotiation and selective pardon, peel away the colonies that were less "warm" in the struggle for liberty? Since trade with other nations had not yet replaced the suspended trade with Britain, the weakness of the colonies was also economic and material. It left them chronically short of supplies for the war effort: muskets with bayonets, cannon, and gunpowder. Finally, on the brink of its declaration of independence, Congress was also embarrassed by fundamental political weaknesses. Congress pretended to speak for the united *states* of America, but many colonies were still very far from replacing their colonial charters with new state constitutions, and the "united states" were only beginning the deliberation upon the terms for a viable confederation. These many real and perceived debilities helped motivate Franklin's celebrated advice, during the deliberation on independence: "We must, indeed, all hang together, or assuredly we shall all hang separately."[9] Weakness, uncertainty, and anxiety were constituents of the brave but hazardous document approved on the fourth of July, and they are registered in many features of its rhetoric, to which I will now turn.

In the fifth paragraph of the Declaration, which contains the operational language that separates the thirteen American colonies from Great Britain, the tortuous complexity of the language is a symptom of the weakness and uncertainty that haunted Congress's declaration of independence. If Congress felt fully authorized to declare independence, it might have done so simply and directly, with words like this: "We declare that these united colonies are Free and Independent States and that all political connection between them and

9. Quoted as an anecdote in *The Works of Benjamin Franklin* by Jared Sparks (1856). However, it was a commonplace found in earlier sources.

the State of Great Britain is dissolved." Instead, Congress fashioned a serpentine sentence that begins with the subject ("We"), adds two modifying phrases ("the Representatives of the UNITED STATES OF AMERICA"; "in general congress Assembled") and one long modifying clause ("appealing to the Supreme Judge of the world for the rectitude of our intentions"), a compound verb ("publish and declare"), modified by a clause ("in the Name, and by Authority of the good People of these Colonies") and an adverb ("solemnly"), and two clauses in the objective case: the first, the Lee resolution approved by Congress on July 2, 1776, and the second, an enumerated list of the powers that these states enjoy because of this declaration (see table 6.1). Each modifying word and clause seeks to fortify the subject, verb, and objects of this declarative sentence. Taken together, these modifying additions weave an armature of legitimacy. For example, the "we" is specified as "the representatives of the UNITED STATES OF AMERICA," which gets further amplification through a capital font. By also specifying the "we" as "in general congress assembled," Congress assures the reader or auditor that they are properly convened. Finally, "we" act not in a casual or thoughtless manner, but "solemnly," and we act by the "authority of the *good* [rather than the bad Tory] people of these colonies."

Nothing more clearly indexes Congress's efforts to fortify its own uncertain authority than the often-remarked equivocation that lies at the center of the Lee resolution. There it is declared that "these united colonies *are, and of right ought to be*, FREE AND INDEPENDENT STATES" and that all "political connection between them and the state of Great Britain *is, and ought to be, totally dissolved*" (emphasis mine). What is the meaning of this apparent equivocation? The committee had submitted a draft to Congress that supported the sense of the Lee resolution but avoided its equivocal language in favor of a clear, direct, and decisive performance of independence: "We . . . reject & renounce all allegiance . . . to the kings of Great Britain . . . we utterly dissolve all political connection . . . and finally we do assert and declare these colonies to be free and independent states" (Jefferson Rough Draft, in Boyd 1999, 4).

Shouldn't the final paragraph of the Declaration be the climactic, self-confident moment where Congress *makes* history? Isn't it with these words that political independence happens? Although the committee draft had attempted this sort of decisive speech act, if we look at the operational language of the document that was approved by Congress on July 4, 1776, we find the equivocal language of the Lee resolution. One can imagine this commonsense query: "wait, *are* these states free and independent, or *ought* they to become independent at some future time?" They decline the sort of heady power Thomas Paine wanted the Whigs of America to claim, in his pamphlet *Common Sense*:

Subject	"**We,** therefore,
First modifying phrase	the Representatives of the UNITED STATES OF AMERICA,
Second modifying phrase	in General Congress, Assembled,
First modifying clause	appealing to the Supreme Judge of the world for the rectitude of our intentions,
First verb (secondary)	**do,**
First clause modifying verb	in the Name, and by Authority of the good People of these Colonies,
Second and third verbs (primary) modified by adverb	solemnly **publish and declare,**
Object 1: The three clauses of the Richard Henry Lee resolution that were introduced on June 7, discussed and then tabled on June 10, and ratified by Congress on July 2, 1776	**That these United Colonies** *are,* *and of Right ought to be,* **FREE AND INDEPENDENT STATES,** that they are absolved from all Allegiance to the British Crown, **and that all political connection between them and the State of Great Britain,** *is and ought to be* **totally dissolved;**
Object 2: The future implications of the Lee resolution, once realized, are clarified by Congress's enumerating the powers claimed for these "independent states"	and that as FREE AND INDEPENDENT STATES, they have full Power to levy War, conclude Peace, contract Alliances, establish Commerce, and to do all other Acts and Things which INDEPENDENT STATES may of right do.
Second sentence: The supplementary promise of the signatories binding them to support the words with which Congress had declared independence	And for the support of this declaration, with a firm reliance on the protection of divine providence, we mutually pledge to each other our lives, our fortunes, and our sacred honor."

Note: The only indispensable elements of the sentence are printed in boldface.

"We have it in our power to begin the world over again" (2004, 92). Congress refused the allure of the performative moment of revolution, when, within a propitious moment of crisis and opportunity, fluid events and decisive acts, a corporate actor could *just do* revolution.[10] By inserting the exact text of the Lee resolution in the Declaration, Congress gave the Declaration a more narrowly subsidiary relation to the Lee resolution.[11]

The political crisis of June and July 1776 made the restoration of the Lee resolution to the text of the Declaration utterly appropriate. The equivocal language of the Lee resolution neatly reflected the countercurrents that shaped the debate about whether to declare independence. After the Virginia Convention came out in support of independence, Lee submitted his multipart resolution to Congress. In the three clauses of the Lee resolution, the "are/ought to be" (free and independent states) and the (connection) "is/ought to be" (totally dissolved) compounds don't express the precise wording of the Virginia Convention, which simply "propose" to Congress "TO DECLARE THE UNITED COLONIES FREE AND INDEPENDENT STATES" (Virginia Convention resolutions in *Boston Gazette*, June 24, 1776; capitals in the original). However, the equivocal formulation of the Lee resolution did reflect the divided opinion in both Congress and the colonies in the spring of 1776, and this provided the most immediate context for the drafting of the Declaration. Influential and important skeptics, like John Dickinson, James Duane, John Jay, and Edward Rutledge, doubted that Congress had the legal authority or effective power to declare independence. So at the level of the political calculus of July 1776, the first sense of the "are/is" statements is that American colonies are already "de facto" independent: because we are at war with Britain, because of the burning of coastal towns, because, as John Adams claimed, the Prohibitory Act, by removing American shipping from the king's "protection," meant that Parliament had already declared the thirteen colonies independent. All

10. Derrida's philosophical reading of this passage, using the concepts of the trace, the supplement, and the signature as they are developed elsewhere in his philosophy, is particularly useful for its critique of the wishful self-present moment of self-constitution, as though all action flowed from that moment. Derrida's analysis of this language points to the latent complexities and odd deferrals that enable a text to seem to found a new institution or a new nation, even though the agency to make such a declaration is not yet in place (see Derrida 2002; Honig 1991).

11. Julian Boyd speculates that returning to the Lee resolution stayed closer to the "parliamentary practice" and "political principle" of Congress's original assignment to the committee; it also allowed Congress to avoid the explicit reference to Parliament in the committee draft (Boyd 1999, 35–36).

these arguments, made in the course of debates inside and outside of Congress, could make the declaration appear to be a belated recognition of the status quo.

The thesis that the American colonies "are" already independent was supported by arguments that we "ought to be" this way. Important here were old arguments about long-term population trends (developed by Benjamin Franklin), the momentum of economic development (as laid out by Sir Thomas Pownall in *The Administration of the Colonies*, by Edmund Burke in his speeches to Parliament, and by Franklin), as well as newer, more piquant arguments like Thomas Paine's in *Common Sense*, that "there is something very absurd, in supposing a continent to be perpetually governed by an island" (2004, 69). Here the "ought to be" is persuasive, instructive, and hortatory. It exhorts the vacillating that independence is a sensible goal.

However, separation from Britain was more than a practical recourse in the tactics of war. It entailed a radical change in the constitution of government. Here, the "are/is" "and of right ought to be" takes on a new set of meanings. With the verbs "are/is," the bond between Great Britain is declared to be broken. The words, by denoting a change in the very being of the states and empire, take on the character of "an event," a big one. Here words have the potential effect of a performative, a speech act like the "I do" in a wedding ceremony or an "I declare war" that initiates hostilities. But considered as a performative, this "are/is" is defective. The success of the "I do" in a wedding depends upon marriage certificates and the authority of civil or religious agents to marry others; even the "I declare war" depends, by the international laws of war, on possessing the status of a recognized state (pirates, rebels, and terrorists cannot declare war). So this primary ontological sense of "are/is"—which aspires to bring the condition of independence into existence in the very moment of enunciation—must lean up against and solicit the supplement of "and of right ought to be FREE AND INDEPENDENT STATES."

It is appropriate to put the last words in capitals, as they appear in both the Dunlap broadside and the engrossed copy of the Declaration, because at the heart of the ideological labor of the document is the articulation of the traditionally shared political value, freedom, with the risky new political arrangement, independence. For Tories, of course, independence from Britain was an anathema, for it would cut them off from the liberty of its ancient English constitution, and expose them to rule by Whig committees and/or the mob. But for American Whigs, independence from Britain was to secure freedom, so that it is what "of right ought to be." Perhaps as a way to strengthen their claim to the virtue necessary for this new political arrangement, Congress added the modifying clause to the subject of this sentence, "We": "appealing to the Supreme Judge of the world for the rectitude of our intentions." An appeal to heaven shored up potentially dubious political intentions by inviting divine scrutiny of them.

The doubleness of "are" and "ought to be" also suggests something crucial about the temporal structure of the Declaration. It works to strengthen the fragile and uncertain present of its own action by speculating upon the future that might be brought by its action. In this way the Declaration offers an instance of a *prolepsis*: "representing something in the future as already done or existing." This temporal framework enables the Declaration to overwrite the palpable gaps in the "now" that would begin the new epoch of independence. In other words, because its performative statements can declare but not secure independence, the Declaration obscures this uncomfortable fact by speaking in the future perfect, so the readers and auditors of the text can imagine what it will feel like when we "will have been independent." Thus, the Declaration's equivocation between the present and the future is only apparent. In fact, through its rhetorical art, the Declaration acts in the present *and* figures the future. The Declaration inhabits both temporalities and binds them together with its "and." Not choosing between a "real" present and a speculative future, to succeed, the Declaration requires *both* the present *and* the future it solicits. It performs independence in the present, but it also invokes a future that will bring that present to fruition.

What are the practical implications and palpable effects of declaring independence? The sentence that declares independence answers this implicit worry by going beyond the words of the Lee resolution. The second object of the verbs "publish and declare" specifies the powers that these "free and independent states" now claim: "to levy war, conclude peace, contract alliances, establish commerce." This enumeration does double duty. On one hand, it explicitly denotes the practical advantages of independence by projecting a future where, because the former colonists will have contracted foreign alliances and established commerce free of British constraints, it will be easier to "wage war" and (eventually) "conclude peace." On the other hand, this list of state powers allows those who hear the Declaration with sympathy to envision what it will be like to live as part of this fabulous new entity, "the united states of America."

If the Declaration had ended with its sinuous, complex penultimate sentence, worried Whigs might well have reason to join skeptical Tories by asking, "What supports this extraordinary declaration?" To preempt this question, Congress ends its Declaration with this sentence: "And for the support of this declaration, with a firm reliance on the protection of divine providence, we mutually pledge to each other our lives, our fortunes, and our sacred honor."

What supports this Declaration is a promise. The members of Congress made a "mutual pledge" to support the Declaration, and the pledge was secured by their most valued possessions: "our" lives, "our" fortunes, and "our" sacred honor. It is apt that "our sacred honor" is placed as the climactic final phrase of the Declaration. Every gentleman of honor makes his word his bond, so only this honor can assure that a man will do in the future what he has promised in the past and therefore have the right to make promises.[12] Since the Declaration had severed old ties with the king and our "British brethren," it feels emotionally correct to end with words that bind American Whigs, through a "mutual pledge," to each other. Breaking old political bands enables the formation of these new ones. To give this mutual pledge still more authority, Congress augmented the committee draft by adding a modifying clause that bolsters the confidence of the "we" who makes "our" pledge: "with a firm reliance on the protection of divine providence." Unsure of the outcome of its audacious experiment in independence, Congress seems to have been intent upon securing divine as well as human covenants.

Building upon the committees and assemblies of the American Whig network, the Declaration offered the citizens of the "thirteen united states" a new platform upon which to build their future. But nothing assured the successful adoption of this newly independent political system. That is what makes this "mutual pledge" of the members of Congress to each other so important and why Congress protracted its deliberations so that its declaration could be unanimous. Because Congress had made this crucial culminating mutual pledge in so public a fashion, scholars have noted that the last sentence of the Declaration implies the presence of subscribing signatures. These are absent in the Dunlap broadside, but they are added to the engrossed manuscript copy of the Declaration. Not until January 18, 1777, did the Goddard broadside make a full list of the signers and their "signatures" publicly available in printed form. The new system of government would only slowly emerge, where it would be guaranteed by the thin swirls of ink of the signers' signatures upon parchment.

12. A network that could act together requires a well-developed capability for its members to make promises today for what they will do tomorrow. In *The Genealogy of Morals*, Nietzsche (1968, 495) sees "the right to make promises" as a form of self-mastery, of sovereignty over the self, that only emerges at the end of a long and violent history. Hannah Arendt (1963, 170–75; 1998, 243–47) argues that promising is one of the indispensable resources for collective political action, one that is especially crucial in a republic. For a comparative discussion of promising in Nietzsche, Arendt, and Derrida, see Honig 1991, 102–5.

While the piety directed at this political "scripture" appeared inappropriate to some, it has turned out to be powerfully sustaining.[13]

THE DECLARATION AS A VERBAL PANORAMA

While the Declaration contains dangerous political provocations, its tone is calm, its mood equable, and its posture collected. In choosing Jefferson as drafter of the Declaration, Congress chose the most skilled and gifted Whig writer on the western side of the Atlantic. If any Whig was equipped to give "an expression of the American mind" the "tone and spirit called for by the occasion," Jefferson was. Scholars have given exacting attention to the literary art of the Declaration. They have admired the symmetrical architecture of its five interrelated parts, the purity and perspicuity of its language, its avoidance of metaphor and rhetorical ornament, the calm cadences of its monosyllabic language, and the artful "pauses" that prepare it for oral proclamation. Many have concluded that it is a masterpiece of "political literature."[14] In spite of the contributions of this kind of analysis, it has the problematic tendency to turn the Declaration into an end in itself, as though a central goal of Congress was to produce a literary masterpiece. In fact, at its inception, the Declaration lacked the formal means by which art is set apart from the world: the pedestal, the frame, or the book cover. The Declaration was published as a broadside and proclaimed so that it could promiscuously mix with the audiences it addressed. Rather than doing art for art's sake, Congress and its members deployed the powers of rhetoric to support their collective political goals. The nuanced rhetorical art of the Declaration places two fraught political acts—

13. It is the unique engrossed parchment copy of the Declaration, now faded into illegibility, that receives the pious attention of millions of annual visitors. For Arendt, the new centrality of text and scripture, and the piety directed toward this writing, is not an error that we must seek consciously to avoid, as Pauline Maier (1997, xvi) argues with much zest, so that we can come to terms with the "grubby world of eighteenth-century American politics" that produced it. Instead, Arendt insists that it is the very absence of any religious support for early American politics that leads to revering these early documents as "*religare*, Latin, for a binding themselves back to a beginning" (Arendt 1963, 198).

14. For the best general analysis of the style of the Declaration, see Lucas 1989; for an analysis of the way the art of Jefferson's pauses fits the document to be spoken and heard, see Fliegelman 1993, 20–28; for an impassioned appreciation of the "literature of public documents," see Ferguson 1994, 495. For a more wide-ranging appreciation of Jefferson's language, see Wills 1979.

insulting King George III and separating from Great Britain—into a textual framework that would calm the anxieties that these two portentous acts were likely to arouse. It does so by embedding them within a verbal panorama.

Bruno Latour has suggested that panoramas are one of the main ways that local spectators can see their relation to a global horizon and extend credibility to shared narratives. In July 1776, the panorama offered members of the far-flung American Whig network a way to experience the moment of the declaration of independence together. While Latour cautions us to be skeptical of the truth claims of panoramas, his description of their political and social utility resonates with the verbal form and political occasion of the Declaration:

> Far from being the place where everything happens, as in their director's dreams, [panoramas] are local sites to be added as so many new places dotting the flattened landscape we try to map. But even after such a downsizing, their role may become central since they allow spectators, listeners, and readers to be *equipped with a desire for wholeness and centrality*. It is from those powerful stories that we get our metaphors for what "binds us together," the passions we are supposed to share, the general outline of society's architecture, the master narratives with which we are disciplined. (Latour 2005, 189)

Understanding the Declaration as a verbal panorama allows us to grasp its limits as well as its powers. Mere mortals in the small chambers of Philadelphia promulgated it, and it transmitted the limited purposes mobilized in those places and upon that particular occasion. However, it succeeded in animating the network of American Whigs by, to use Latour's formulation, fortifying their "desire for wholeness and centrality." The Declaration also left the sorts of valuable traces brought by other panoramas: metaphors for what binds America together, shared passions, an outline of a society, and a master narrative. All these are condensed in the Declaration's final "mutual promise."

Before reading the Declaration as a verbal panorama, it will be useful to describe the first panoramas, those introduced in London and other major European cities starting around a decade and a half after the Declaration. The word *panorama* (from the Greek *pan*, "all," + *orama*, "that which is seen") was coined by the Irish painter Robert Barker to describe his painting of a view of London, which he mounted upon a cylindrical canvas and displayed in a special-purpose building in Leicester Square. Audiences viewed the 360-degree panorama from a raised platform, under a skylight that diffused light evenly to the whole panorama (Oettermann 1997). There are several noteworthy features of the panorama that resonate with the art of the Declaration. First, the panorama was understood as providing a view at one glance of a "complete and comprehensive survey or presentation of a subject"; second, it provides a continuous and "unbroken view of the whole region surrounding an observer" (*OED*); and, finally, and more implicitly, it does so by harmonizing a very diverse range of materials.[15] Barker's panorama was granted a patent in 1787, which suggests that it was understood to be a distinctive new technology. To achieve its effects, the panorama must remove the viewer from the given world, for example, the ordinary street-level vistas of London, and place him or her in a contrived place, where the inchoate "all" that has been left behind can be viewed as a reduced reproduction within the panorama. This artful mediation of the view of city or battlefield enabled the panorama to achieve its paradoxical effects: it miniaturizes in order to enlarge, it brings many elements close so that they can be seen together, as if they were far away. In this way, they can be seen together in one panoramic sweep. Through techniques that are enclosing and immersive, the panorama sets viewers at a contemplative distance.

In order to offer its reader or auditor a comprehensive view of Congress's momentous response to the political crisis, the Declaration had to offer a highly condensed redaction of eleven years of political strife. Arguments, ideas, and facts had to be selectively incorporated into one synthetic view. This required language that was precise in reference, general in scope, and elegant in its economy. In order that the whole performance would have the seamless sweep of a panorama's continuous view, each part of the Declaration had to seem to prepare for what came next and follow from what came before. By offering a brief reading of the Declaration, I will argue that its panoramic effects are indispensable to its political work. Set within the grand sweep of a verbal panorama, the act of separation from Great Britain changes character, so a momentous action appears as an event.

"When in the Course of Human Events"

The beginning words of the Declaration open up an interval in time that is to be filled with an account of the action of Congress. In this brief introduc-

---

15. The appeal of holding all together in "one glance" is made explicit in the early advertisement for Barker's spectacle: a 1791 panorama is advertised this way: "The public are most respectfully informed, that the subject ... is a view, at one glance, of the cities of London and Westminster" (*OED*). That such a spectacle involves tricking the eye is evident from a diary entry from 1793, "We all walked to Leicester Fields, and there saw the Panorama, a fine deception in painting of the British & Russian Fleets at Spithead (J. Woodforde *Diary* 26 June [1929] IV. 37)" (*OED*).

tory sentence, Congress offers a quick view of the three factors that occasion this speech act: first, an action that is said to be "necessary" ("for one people to dissolve the political bands which have connected them to another"); next, its grounding legal justification ("the laws of nature and of nature's God"), and, finally, the social value that motivates this declaration ("a decent respect to the opinions of mankind"). But who speaks this sentence? Although it refers to the "one people" whose "decent respect" leads them to "declare the causes which impel them to the separation," the language is structured to assume the impersonal vantage point of history. When compared with previous declarations, like the *Votes and Proceedings*, the Declaration pulls off a remarkable shift in scale: it zooms out from the particular to the general, from the chambers of Congress to "the world," from the specific differences between the American colonies and Britain to a sublimely elevated view of "the course of human events."

"We Hold These Truths to Be Self-Evident"

The active agent of declaration—the first-person plural "we"—now enters to speak in its own name. Building upon the enormous physical and temporal remove of the introduction, the prologue's five carefully linked, magisterially paced sentences continue to avoid particularity of reference. Instead, the prologue moves the reader and auditor into the prehistorical state of nature, where the primary radicals of politics are said to take form: equality; the rights to "life, liberty and the pursuit of happiness"; "that to secure these rights, governments are instituted among men"; that when "government becomes destructive of these ends," the people have the right "to throw off such government" and "to institute new government." By casting politics in such general terms, Congress strips away the British and English political contexts to which these ideas are clearly indebted. The reference points of the earlier declarations—like the ancient English constitution, the Bill of Rights of 1689, and the rights that it guaranteed—have now faded from view. Congress eschews the issues of colonial rights and parliamentary sovereignty so central to the earlier pamphlets, petitions, and declarations, because separation makes them irrelevant. In its place is a credo about unalienable rights that constitute "our creator's" endowment to us. The distinctive tone of this language—firm, elevated, and confident—is an effect of distance. Its steady cadence aspires to express the mandate of history. Noisy polemics have been sublimated into crystalline logic, and they persist within this Olympian perspective only as an afterimage.

*"The History of the Present King of Great-Britain
Is a History of Repeated Injuries and Usurpations"*

The long list of the "injuries and usurpations" of the king offers a comprehensive view of actions, policies, laws, and war measures of the previous dozen years. Many scholars have noted the way this part of the Declaration personalizes the conflict by opposing the "we" of the prologue with the "he" and "him" of the catalog of grievances. But, in fact, there are several ways that this list of grievances also keeps the reader and auditor at a significant remove from its target, the king. The grievances are not narrated in chronological order or placed in relation to specific events, like the destruction of the tea, which occasioned them. By reducing a complex history to a list, events are extracted from the particular context of their emergence so they can be reduced to "facts" that illustrate "a prince whose character is thus marked by every act which may define a tyrant." However, we are still kept at a distinct remove from this man. To say anything too specific about his history, lineage, age, appearance, personal character, or even his place in the structure of government might introduce mitigating factors. In order that each grievance can serve as a count in a mock indictment, each must be familiar and straightforward enough so that merely naming it will draw a nod of immediate assent from American Whigs. Jefferson's wordy and tortuous attempt to blame the king for the continued slave trade in America survived committee review but was expunged by Congress. No doubt this excision reflected, as Jefferson claimed, the interest of the slaveholders of Georgia and the Carolinas and of slave traders in certain northern colonies. But it also reflected the need for these grievances to have the same self-evident truthfulness as the political axioms of the prologue. Every grievance must stand out with the vivid singularity of a fact "submitted to a candid world," which declaring independence will immediately redress. Then George III, as the king for the American colonists, would be "history," one more tyrant who had lost his job.

"Nor Have We Been Wanting in Attentions to Our British Brethren"

If, in order to be accommodated within the Declaration's calming panorama, rights must appear as timeless "truths" and grievances as simplified "facts," how was the Declaration to present the vexed feelings of American Whigs toward "our British brethren"? Separation entails loss, and losing these "ties of our common kindred" seems to have been acutely felt by many of the signers. Some of the members of Congress had attended school or university or read law in England. All American Whigs were grateful for vigorous support of leading British Whig allies like John Wilkes, Richard Price, Joseph

Priestley, Catharine Macaulay, and many others. In addition, separation from Britain meant turning away from the stalwart defenders of America in Parliament, like Lord Chatham, the earl of Shelburne, Edmund Burke, Thomas Pownall, and many others. The document's rhetorical strategy for effecting this break is to merge supporters and opponents into the single category, "British brethren," and then to move their own feelings into the past: "we *have* warned them . . . we *have* reminded them . . . we *have* appealed to their native justice . . . we *have* conjured them." But since they "have been deaf to the voice of justice and of consanguinity," the Declaration shifts into a new, post-separation reality, expressed in the present tense: we must "acquiesce in the necessity" to "hold them, as we hold the rest of mankind, enemies in war, in peace friends."

"We, Therefore, . . . Solemnly Publish and Declare"

The word *therefore* tethers the final paragraph to the first four sections of the Declaration, making performing independence the logical and rhetorical culmination of what has gone before. The distinct rhetorical powers of the panorama—comprehensiveness, continuity, and a distant view—are an effect of the argument of the previous three paragraphs of the Declaration: the abstract rendering of man's universal natural rights, the plethora of grievances hurled at the king, and the definitive farewell to "our British brethren." This foreshortening of the American crisis, by fixing the reader and auditor of the Declaration within the Whig political perspective, prepares for the decisive action contained in the language of the Lee resolution ("These united colonies are and by right ought to be . . ."). Set within the grand sweep of a verbal panorama, however, the act of separation from Great Britain changes character: a momentous action now appears as an event, one that is presented so it appears as natural and necessary as any other outcome within "the course of human events."

For the thousands of Whigs who heard or read the Declaration in the weeks following July 4, 1776, this shift from proposed action to completed event assumed a public form. The celebrants who shouted "hazzah" three times in Philadelphia, Boston, New York, Charleston, and many other towns experienced independence as an accomplished fact. They could celebrate with their cheers and antics and dinners because they had, in their own minds, resolved the equivocation in the Lee resolution. Accepting the hortatory proposition that the united colonies "by right ought to be" independent states, Whigs who read or heard the Declaration evidently accepted its performative: "that these united colonies are . . . free and independent states." Appearing before them as a fact, separation was "countersigned" by crowds of Whigs with their cheers;

or, conversely, we might say that, by countersigning it with their cheers, they turned the action proposed by Congress (independence) into an accomplished event. Even before the members of Congress had officially signed the Declaration, thousands of happy Whig celebrants had joined their own lives, property, and sacred honor to the "mutual pledge" of the document's last sentence.

THE NECESSARY BIAS OF THE PANORAMA

As Congress's most ambitious broadcasting initiative, the Declaration was fashioned as a panorama so that all American Whigs, reading and listening in dispersed locations, could "see" and experience the political moment of independence in the same way together. But to make independence commonly shared required a host of elisions and omissions. Thus, none who read or heard the Declaration in 1776 were likely to apply its expansive concept of natural rights to Native Americans, who were described within one of the list of grievances as "merciless Indian savages, whose known rule of warfare, is an undistinguished destruction of all ages, sexes and conditions." Chattel slavery was a topic that had to be set aside if slaveholders who reviewed the document on July 2–4, 1776, were to endorse the Declaration's ringing endorsement of equality. Therefore Jefferson's effort to align the Declaration with the House of Burgesses' effort to end Virginia's role in the Atlantic slave trade was excised from the document. Governor Dunmore's opportunistic offer of freedom for Virginia's slaves and indentured servants in return for loyal service to the king was reduced to this grievance against the king: "He has excited domestic insurrections amongst us."

No clause of the Declaration has been more quoted and more contested than the simple five-word statement, "All men are created equal." Nearly four months before Abigail Adams joined many others in celebrating a reading of the Declaration before the Town House in Boston on July 18, 1776, Abigail wrote her husband, John, urging him to use the moment of revolution to include women, in an explicit fashion, in the new rights and laws that it would proclaim. "I long to hear that you have declared an independancy—and, by the way in the new Code of Laws which I suppose it will be necessary for you to make, I desire you would Remember the Ladies and be more generous and favourable to them than your ancestors." Although Abigail's suggestion was "by the way," that is ancillary to declaring independence, it was nonetheless integral to her understanding of what political emancipation should mean. Thus, Abigail Adams easily extended the neo-Roman theory of liberty as well as the Whig right to revolution to women's determination to win equal rights under the law. She continues: "Remember all Men would be tyrants if they could. If perticular care and attention is not paid to the Laidies we are determined to foment a Rebelion, and will not hold ourselves bound by any Laws in which we have no voice, or Representation" (March 31, 1776; J. Adams 1963, 1:370). Although this letter begins an exchange with John that is by turns serious and playful, Abigail Adams had made a crucial point about the debilities of the sort of general proclamation that the Declaration would eventually use: "all men are created equal." If "particular attention" is not "paid to the ladies" in the language of the text, it could simply prolong or even strengthen the long history of men's subjection of women. So Abigail insists to John that "your sex are naturally tyrannical," urges him "to be happy willingly to give up the harsh title of master for the more tender and endearing one of friend," and join "men of sense in all ages [in] abhor[ring] those customs which treat us only as vassals of your sex."

By way of response, John Adams took Abigail's "code of laws" as a form of special pleading that was dangerous to the Whig cause. Abigail's letter, he suggested, offers evidence that, along with children, apprentices, Indians, and negroes, "another tribe more numerous and powerful than all the rest were grown discontented" (April 14, 1776; J. Adams 1963, 382). John Adams's response was by turns patriarchal ("we know better than to repeal our masculine systems"), arch ("you know they are little more than theory"), and coy ("in practice you know we are the subject," "we have only the names of masters"). By aligning Abigail's complaint with other particular complaints to and about Congress, John Adams suggests that particular claims would disable the collective declaration that Congress is framing. Perhaps without intentional simplification and active forgetting, there could be no shared experience of British tyranny and no acting together in a common Declaration. By the way it subsumed the particular into the general and invited every American to experience freedom through independence, the Declaration created a plausible (if illusory and provisional) experience of unity. The absence of any reference to the rights of women in the Declaration, like countless other elisions and omissions, became constitutive rather than accidental.

A general statement of rights may have been useful for getting the majority of American Whigs—including Whigs like Abigail Adams—to accept the Declaration's affirmations. But subsuming the particular into the general (e.g., women into men) is an effect of the distant view and deceptive art of the panorama. Within its scale and sweep, differences may appear indifferent. However, there is nothing in the concept of universal human rights that justifies excluding women from equality as it is affirmed in the prologue to the Declaration. Thus, in the Seneca Falls Declaration of Sentiments (1848), the group committing itself to the political struggle to win the suffrage for women can pick upon the promissory note embedded in the panoramic general language of the Declaration of Independence, by proclaiming a revisionary repetition of its first self-evident truth: "that all men and women are created equal."[16]

PUBLIC HAPPINESS IN THE EVENT

Abigail Adams's enthusiasm for the Declaration appears no less sincere for the failure of Congress to take up the "code of laws" that would align the liberation of women with the liberation of America. Adams's account of the public reading of the Declaration on King Street with which we started this chapter neatly characterizes the public happiness of the event. Of the conclusion of the reading and the moment of the ceremonial firing of the cannons and muskets, Adams declared, "Every face appeared joyful." What are the sources of this happiness, a joy that is described in so many accounts of the ceremonies developed around the public reading of the Declaration throughout the colonies and which Americans have tried to echo in many later celebrations of the fourth of July? (Hazelton 1906, chapter 11).

This moment of happiness recalls others discussed in this study. Each was experienced by Whigs at a moment when there was a success in checking the encroachment of British tyranny: the day after the Boston Massacre, when the town meeting ended the day expressing their "high satisfaction" for compelling the governor to remove all British regulars from Boston; the day after the destruction of the tea, which John Adams describes as "so bold, so daring, so firm" that it must become "an epoch in history"; the day that the First Continental Congress voted to endorse the Suffolk Resolves, which John Adams described as "one of the happiest days in my life"; and finally, the speech at the

16. A full consideration of the vexed and important question of how groups bypassed by the rights claims of the founders have later submitted their claims through appeal to the words of the Declaration lies beyond the scope of this study. However, the most powerful statement of the exclusions and built-in limitations of the Declaration's panoramic view was formulated in Frederick Douglass's 1852 speech "What for a Slave Is the Fourth of July?" Robert Ferguson (1994, 496) has argued that Enlightenment republicanism in America is "both the source of ideas and the boundary placed upon them in revolutionary America, both the expression of broad aspirations and the enforcement of narrow instrumental controls." For a canny analysis of the broad implications of the exchange between Abigail Adams and John Adams, see Ferguson 1994, 497–99.

Pennsylvania Convention, when James Wilson characterized the succession of meetings that culminate in the First Continental Congress as forming "a chain of freedom" where each "has the pleasure of beholding himself a link."

What do these moments of public happiness have in common? First, these events in the political crisis had taken a direction that was happy, because, drawing upon the meaning of the root of the word *happy* ("hap"), the events appeared more lucky or fortunate than Whigs had dared to hope. For some the events marked the beginning of a new epoch, for others an objective sign of providential favor. Second, each of these episodes was a collective victory for an expanding revolutionary movement. Finally, at each of these moments, an individual or a group paused to take stock of what had been achieved and experienced joy in reflecting upon the collective strength of those American Whigs who had, in acting together, experienced their freedom, as if to say, "Since it is *we* who have done this, it is *we* who are free."

The Declaration was drafted and distributed by Congress in hopes that the whole network of American Whigs would celebrate the collective decision for independence and confirm the bond formed by their mutual pledge of life, property, and honor. In the weeks following July 4, 1776, those who read the Declaration and heard it proclaimed could repeat, in a boldly public and collective manner, the insults to the king and the dissolution of all political connection with Great Britain. In doing so, an evanescent moment of joy was savored in a ceremony, and agents could experience their freedom by acting together, in view of shared principles. But that moment was also haunted by a sense of loss. For even the first time it was proclaimed, the Declaration commemorated what had happened and what the "we" of this Declaration had already done.

CONCLUSION

THE AMERICAN REVOLUTION AS A GIFT

. . . .

*T*he American Revolution has never concluded. By this proposition I refer not to the annual July Fourth celebrations or the constitutional system that was put into practice in 1789. Instead, I'm pointing to the intermittent redeployment of the methods that were first used to challenge British sovereignty in America as I have described them: the political agency of the standing committees of correspondence, the genre of the popular declaration, and finally, the observation of a set of protocols of legal procedure, corporate action, open access, systematic address, and virtuous independence, which enabled a dispersed group to develop a network and act together. In the years since the American Revolution, these methods, all grounded in the premise that sovereignty is vested in the people, have served as a political tool kit for those who set out to challenge instituted authority. In this way, the American Revolution has served as a kind of trust fund, legacy, or gift.

Are these Whig political innovations most useful for founding a new political order, or for "unfounding" an old one? The account offered in this book contributes to an account of nation building. Such a narrative would emphasize the evolution from the Whig network of committees to the gathering of the First Congress and the development into a loose confederation of states under the Articles of Confederation, and, finally, the constitutional system framed in 1787. By this account *The Votes and Proceedings of the Town of Boston* becomes a precursor of the Declaration of Independence; a congress convened in 1774 evolves into *the* Congress, and a president, as "one who presides," into *the* President. Such a narrative, by subordinating the revolutionary movement to the founding of a new nation, values revolutionaries as the founders and framers, as those who build. But this teleological, results-driven history obscures another potential of the communication innovations described in this study. As instruments improvised in the heat of crisis, these Whig innovations were as much about challenging as instituting political authority, as much about "unfounding" the British Empire in North America as founding their own system of government. In this sense Tories were correct in grasping the anarchic and destructive potential of these Whig political methods.

Although Whig communication innovations gathered power by the way they emerged from specific American conditions, they also had a general formal character that has allowed others outside the thirteen colonies to adopt them for their own purposes. My account of the expansion of the Whig networks in America shows how they emerge from and build upon local institutions (like town and county government), legal frameworks (like the royal charters), and traditional practices (like a New England town's instructions to their representatives). But once the American Revolution had demonstrated the efficacy of the committee, the declaration, and the protocols in unsettling the authority of an existing political order, Whigs in Britain adapted them to their own purposes. Although parliamentary reform was one theme of the Wilkes agitation as early as the 1770s, it was only after the organizational successes of American Whigs that British Whigs developed the association movement of 1780–1781, where county committees were gathered, framed declarations, and formed an association linking different towns (Black 1963, 28–103). Parliamentary reform was pursued through the 1780s and 1790s by a loosely associated group of societies and committees in both the metropolis and the provinces. For example, members of the London Revolution Society and the Society for Constitutional Information welcomed the French Revolution in 1789 and exchanged correspondence with the National Assembly (Goodwin 1979, 107–35). For these reformers, the success of the American Revolution, and now the French Revolution, heralded a victory for parliamentary reform in England.[1]

Witnessing revolutions in America, France, and Haiti, as well as those many revolutions that resulted from Napoleonic conquest and the eclipse of Spanish power in South America, a wide range of contemporary commentators— from the dissenting English radical Richard Price to the German philosopher G. W. F. Hegel to the American historian George Bancroft—argued

1. By the account of one of the founders of the London Corresponding Society, it was the example of the American Revolution and their rereading of the pamphlets that had been published by British Whigs in its defense that served as a model for their organizational efforts in 1792 (Thomas Hardy in Thale 1983, 5–6). The leaders of the French Revolution, in order to gather the power to act upon their more radical reforms, made a still more pervasive and effective use of the committee, the popular declaration, and the convention.

that a single powerful idea, "the spirit of liberty," was spreading throughout the world. Sometimes this notion of liberty's inexorable advance was bolstered by the affiliated notion of the *translatio studii*, by which knowledge and culture was being successively translated westward, from Greece through Rome to western Europe to America. But this study suggests what is deeply flawed about this familiar grand narrative, one that continues to have surprising currency in our own day. In these narratives, the victories of liberty through revolution are construed as spontaneous, isomorphic, and irresistible, which, by reflecting an idea "whose time has come," evidence a vector-like irreversibility. By contrast, my account of one revolution is grounded in tangible practices of communication, which were initiated by a relatively small group, emerged from a specific contingent political emergency, and produced results that were fragile and open to revision.

Ideal and universalistic accounts of revolution obscure the nuanced communications at the heart of a revolution's success. So, while American Whig networking allowed dispersed actors to share ideas, gather power, and act together, this networking effected a unity that was provisional and partial. Thus, as noted above, the efficacy of the American Whig networking depended upon sustaining the autonomy of each node even during coordinated political action. The communications of such a network are narrow in scope and produce weak, limited ties. Links hold apart and filter as well as connect, censor as well as share. Thus, for example, the momentous issue of chattel slavery was kept discreetly out of the spirited Whig communications that linked New England with Virginia. When Jefferson made it one of the complaints against the king in his draft of the Declaration, his colleagues in Congress excised it, much to his chagrin.

No amount of communication and shared action allows a distributed network to coalesce into a single common identity. John Durham Peters (2001, 1), a historian of Western ideas of communication, has described the persistence, evident from Plato to the latest electronic device, of the dream of communication as "the mutual communion of souls." This idea of communication "invites us into a world of unions without politics, understandings without language, and souls without bodies" (30–31). Peters describes why acts of communication never elide the difference between two humans. Those who communicate must make do with unreliable mediators: codes, language, symbols, gestures, but also the noise and misunderstandings that haunt their circulation. Every act of communication carries the potential to obscure the message that it seeks to communicate. Because communication is shadowed by miscommunication, the otherness of two minds is never overcome. The enabling revolutionary communications among the dispersed American Whigs of thirteen states were fashioned so that they could be effective despite the inevitability of some miscommunication. The Articles of Confederation formed a union just good enough to prevail in the Revolutionary War. Though the Constitution of 1787 was framed "in Order to form a more perfect Union," it was never meant to *be* perfect. It safeguarded the sovereignty of the individual states, which would plunge into civil war around the very issue (chattel slavery) the discreet avoidance of which had been the condition of the possibility of revolutionary unity.

When former revolutionaries framed a new constitution, suspicion of state power was embedded as a structural feature of the Constitution. During the ratification debates, some of those who had led the Revolution, like Richard Henry Lee, Patrick Henry, Samuel Adams, and John Hancock, expressed concern about the extensive new powers given the federal government. Many in the ratifying conventions worried that the proposed constitution's absence of a bill of rights meant that it would leave individuals and groups without the legal instruments necessary to protect themselves from the power of the new federal government. For this reason, the ratifying conventions of Massachusetts, Virginia, and New York recommended that the first federal Congress enact, as part of its first business, a series of amendments that would explicitly safeguard the rights of the citizens of the new republic.[2] Of course, the new Bill of Rights was not explicitly designed to encourage revolution. But by protecting individual and collective rights, the first federal Congress reaffirmed the principle of the ultimate sovereignty of the people and set up protections for precisely the sort of decentralized communication acts that had been essential to the Revolution's challenge to British rule. In short, Congress supported an information policy that would make possible future challenges to government. The legal underpinnings of that policy were laid down by the First Amendment (1789), the first Copyright Act (1790), and the first Postal Bill (1792).

With the First Amendment, the founders developed a powerful formula

2. It is evident from the debates recorded in the Congressional Register of August 1789 that Congress felt that, in the wake of the ratification debates, their first duty was to take up amendments securing basic rights (Veit 1991, 104–213). For an account of the amendments proposed by ratifying conventions and the crucial question of whether they would be required as a condition of ratification or be proposed after ratification, see, for Massachusetts, Beeman 2010, 388–90, and Maier 2010, 197; for Virginia, Beeman, 399–400, and Maier, 294–309; and for New York, Beeman, 402–3, and Maier, 388–98.

for protecting freedom of speech and press as constitutive elements of the politics of the new republic. I quote, preserving the three-part division observed in legal studies:

1. Congress shall make *no* law respecting an establishment of religion, or prohibiting the free exercise thereof;
2. or *abridging* the freedom of speech, or of the press;
3. or the right of the people peaceably to assemble, and to petition the Government for a redress of grievances. (emphasis mine)

Here five expressive rights and freedoms are protected together: to worship, to speak, to print, to assemble, and to petition the government. These range from the most personal and private (religious worship) to the most public (to assemble and petition government for redress). Because the critique of British policy published in the newspaper and other printed documents was indispensable for mobilizing prerevolutionary opposition, here freedom of the press is linked to explicitly oppositional forms of public expression: peaceful assembly and the petition for redress of grievances. These freedoms are protected from legislative control with a verbal formula that gets its power from a double negative: "Congress shall make *no* law . . . *abridging* freedom of speech or the press" (emphasis mine). This double negative is a law against law. It hollows out a theoretical space for freedom of speech and the press prior to, and immune from, the lawmaking powers of Congress.[3]

The framers also took steps to grant authors and inventors a tangible but limited reward for their labors. The Constitution granted Congress the power "to promote the Progress of Science and useful Arts, by securing for limited Times to Authors and Inventors the exclusive Right to their respective Writings and Discoveries" (article 1, section 8). To implement this clause of the Constitution, the first American copyright bill, passed in 1790, adopted the

---

3. Here the contrast with the contemporary Declaration of the Rights of Man and the Citizens, also adopted in 1789, is instructive. Article 11 states, "The free communication of ideas and opinions is one of the most precious of the rights of man. Every citizen may, accordingly, speak, write, and print with freedom, but shall be responsible for such abuses of this freedom as shall be defined by law." Note that while the French declaration, like the First Amendment, defines freedom of expression as a "right" of "every citizen," its qualification of that right "as shall be defined by law" opens a much easier pathway to legislative definition of what speech is free and what is proscribed. This was an act of distinction that the French revolutionary assemblies quickly exercised, leading to a harsh foreshortening of freedom of speech. By contrast, the First Amendment explicitly precludes allowing the state to become the speaker of last resort.

limited copyright and patent law that then prevailed in Britain (a fourteen-year term, renewable once). By adopting British copyright, as it had been restricted in the recent ruling of the House of Lords in *Donaldson v. Becket* (1774), the founders ensured that writing and inventions would pass quickly into the public domain and become free to users. The Postal Bill of 1792 encouraged development and circulation of American newspapers as a means to link far-flung states into one print media sphere: first, by setting postal rates so that personal and commercial letters provided a substantial subsidy to newspapers, heavily traveled eastern routes supported new western routes, and the American postal system was conceived as a subsidized public service rather than a for-profit business (John 1995, chapter 2). In short, the successful Whig activism in the years before the American Revolution helped to explain why certain terms—"open," "public," and "free" (of government control)—articulate both the content and the form, both the informing values and the information protocols, of the communication system of the early republic.

The committee, the declaration, and the network proved invaluable to those political movements that sought redress for the "rights blindness" of the political order that they confronted. It is here that the political tool kit of the American Whigs of the Revolution proved indispensable, and their methods of revolutionary communication lived on in the many popular movements in the first half century of the federal republic. The movement for the abolition of slavery and the movement to win the suffrage for women used the same basic organizational innovations (the committee, the declaration, and the distributed network) that revolutionaries had developed in the 1770s. The Seneca Falls Declaration of Sentiments (1848), by parodying the form and language of the Declaration of Independence, builds upon but critiques that revolutionary inheritance. In his celebrated speech, "What for a Slave Is the Fourth of July?" (1852), Frederick Douglass used the same double articulation, of affirming the value of founders' freedom but exposing its hypocritical application. Revolutionary communications also become a model for political initiatives of a less liberal cast. When a South Carolina committee developed the Articles of Nullification (1832) and the first Declaration of Succession (1852), they based their right to do so in the primary role of sovereign states in making and realizing the freedom claims of the Revolution. Each of these political movements challenged a fundamental feature of the existing system—slavery, women's exclusion from full citizenship, the federal government's presumption that the union was indissoluble—in the name of a still more fundamental human right. The Americans who undertook these actions have often seen themselves as realizing the highest purposes of the Revolution. "It is through *these* acts," they seem to say, "that we are living up to the freedom that the founders practiced in winning independence from Great Britain." The basic political stance of a return to the origin of America in the Revolution, which aims to reclaim the "better angels of our nature," can be heard in the progressive movement, in the civil rights movement of the 1950s and 1960s, in the revival of the conservative movement with Goldwater and Reagan, with the Obama campaign of 2008, and, most recently, in the Tea Party and "Occupy" movements. In each of these popular political movements, however different their goals or tendentious their claims, the "lost treasure" now recovered is the practice of freedom through action invented by American Whigs in the years before the Revolution.[4]

4. The notion that the American Revolution is a "lost treasure" comes from Hannah Arendt (1963, 215–81). The centrality of action to revolution may help explain divergent popular attitudes toward the US founding documents. Many observers have noted that the Declaration of Independence is much more widely admired and enjoyed than the Constitution. This may be the effect of what each is. While the Declaration is action in the form of words, the Constitution is a framework of government built out of words. Thus, while Americans celebrate, memorize, and declare the first, we interpret, dispute, and litigate the second.

REFERENCES

PRIMARY SOURCES

Adams, John. 1818. John Adams to Hezekiah Niles, February 18. In *The Annals of America,* vol. 4, *1797–1820,* 465–69. Chicago: Encyclopedia Britannica, 1968.

———. 1961. *Diary and Autobiography of John Adams.* Edited by L. H. Butterfield. 2 vols. Cambridge, MA: Belknap Press of Harvard University Press.

———. 1963. *Adams Family Correspondence.* Edited by L. H. Butterfield. 2 vols. Cambridge, MA: Belknap Press of Harvard University Press.

———. 1979, 1989. *Papers of John Adams.* Edited by Gregg L. Lint. 15 vols. Cambridge, MA: Belknap Press of Harvard University Press.

———. 2000. *The Revolutionary Writings of John Adams.* Edited by C. Bradley Thompson. Indianapolis: Liberty Fund.

Adams, Samuel. 1865. *The Life and Public Services of Samuel Adams: Being a Narrative of His Acts and Opinions, and of His Agency in Producing and Forwarding the American Revolution.* Edited by William V. Wells. 3 vols. Boston: Little, Brown and Co.

———. 1904. *The Writings of Samuel Adams.* Edited by Harry Alonzo Cushing. 4 vols. New York: G. P. Putnam's Sons.

Allen, Ethan. 1779. *The Narrative of Colonel Ethan Allen.* Bedford, MA: Applewood Books.

Blackstone, Richard. 1769. *Commentary on the Laws of England.* 4 vols. Oxford: Clarendon Press.

Boston, Town of. 1772. *The Votes and Proceedings of the Town of Boston.* Boston: Edes and Gill.

———. 1772–1775. *Minute Books of the Boston Committee of Correspondence.* 5 reels. Bancroft Collection, New York Public Library.

———. 1773. Copy of Certain Letters sent to Great-Britain by His Excellency Thomas Hutchinson, the Hon. Andrew Oliver, and several other persons, born and educated among us. Which original letters have been returned to America, and laid before the Honorable House of Representatives of this province. Boston: Edes and Gill.

———. 1883. "Minutes of the Tea-Meetings." Massachusetts Historical Society Collections, 20:10–17. Boston: Massachusetts Historical Society.

———. 1889. *Rededication of the Old State House, Boston.* Fifth edition. Boston: printed by order of the City Council.

Boston Gazette. 1770–1776. Edited by Edes and Gill. In *Early American Newspapers,* series 1, 1690–1877. Readex.

The Briefs of the American Revolution. 1981. Edited by John Phillip Reid. New York: New York University Press.

Burke, Edmund. 1981–1996. *The Writings and Speeches of Edmund Burke.* Edited by Paul Langford. 9 vols. Oxford: Clarendon Press.

Congress. 1775. *Journal of the Proceedings of the Congress Held at Philadelphia September 5, 1774.* Philadelphia: William and Thomas Bradford.

———. 1777. Extract from the Minutes. Charles Thomson, Secry. Philadelphia: John Dunlap. Early American Imprint no. 15669.

———. 1779. *Observations on the American Revolution.* Philadelphia: Styner and Cist. Evans no. 21861.

———. 1906. *Journals of the Continental Congress.* 34 vols. Washington, DC: Government Printing Office.

———. 1921. *Letters of Members of the Continental Congress.* Edited by Edmund C. Burnett. 2 vols. Washington, DC: Carnegie Institution of Washington.

Documents of the American Revolution, 1770–1783. 1972–1976. Edited by K. G. Davies. 21 vols. Dublin: Irish University Press.

Fairfax County Resolves. July 18, 1774. Available at http://www.constitution.org /bcp/fairfax_res.htm.

Finlay, Hugh. 1774. *Journal Kept by Hugh Finlay, Surveyor of the Post Roads on the Continent of North America, September 19, 1773–May 24, 1774.* Reprint. Edited by D. F. Drinkwater. Washington, DC: United Press Association, 1867.

Force, Peter. 1837–1853. *American Archives.* Series 4, vol. 1. Washington, DC: Congress.

Franklin, Benjamin. 1964. *The Autobiography of Benjamin Franklin.* Edited by Leonard W. Labaree. New Haven: Yale University Press.

———. 1974–2012. *The Papers of Benjamin Franklin.* Edited by William B. Willcox. 40 vols. New Haven: Yale University Press.

———. 1987. *Writings of Benjamin Franklin.* New York: Library of America.

Gage, Thomas. 1933. *The Correspondence of General Thomas Gage, 1763–1775.* Vol. 2. Edited by Clarence Edwin Carter. New Haven: Yale University Press.

Goddard, William. 1774. "The Plan for Establishing a New American Post-Office." Boston: Edes and Gill. Early American Imprint no. 42609.

Gordon, William. 1789. *The History of Rise, Progress, and Establishment, of the Independence of the United States of America.* 4 vols. Freeport, NY: Books for Libraries Press, 1969.

Hancock, John. 1774. *An Oration; Delivered March 5, 1774.* Boston: Edes and Gill. Early American Imprint no. 13314.

Hutchinson, Thomas. 1936. *The History of the Colony and Province of Massachusetts-Bay.* Edited by Lawrence Shaw Mayo. 3 vols. Cambridge, MA: Harvard University Press.

———. 1971. *The Diary and Letters of His Excellency Thomas Hutchinson, Esq.* Edited by Peter Orlando Hutchinson. 2 vols. New York: Burt Franklin.

Jefferson, Thomas. 1950. *The Papers of Thomas Jefferson.* Edited by Julian P. Boyd. 35 vols. Princeton: Princeton University Press.

———. 1984. *The Writings of Thomas Jefferson.* New York: Library of America.

Lee, Richard Henry. 1829. *The Life of Author Lee.* 2 vols. Boston: Wells and Lilly.

———. 1911. *The Letters of Richard Henry Lee.* Edited by James Curtis Ballagh. 2 vols. New York: Macmillan Co.

Leonard, Daniel. 1972. *Massachusettensis; or, A Series of Letters.* Introduction by George Athan Billias. Boston: Gregg Press.

Massacusetts. 1980. *Journals of the House of Representatives of Massachusetts, 1772–1773.* Vol. 49. Boston: Massachusetts Historical Society.

Massachusetts Council. 1770. "PROCEEDINGS of his Majesty's Council of the Province of Massachusetts-Bay, Relative to the Deposition of Andrew Oliver, Esq; Secretary of the said Province, Concerning what passed in Council in Consequence of the unhappy Affair of the 5th of March 1770." Early American Imprint no. 11737.

Milton, John. 1951. *Areopagitica and Of Education.* Edited by George Sabine. Wheeling, IL: Harlan Davidson.

Oliver, Peter. 1961. *Peter Oliver's Origin & Progress of the American Rebellion: A Tory View.* Edited by Douglass Adair and John A. Shutz. Stanford, CA: Stanford University Press.

Paine, Thomas. 2004. *Common Sense.* Edited by Ed Larkin. Peterborough, Ontario: Broadview.

Pownall, Thomas. 1949. *Topographical Description of the Dominions of the United States of America.* Edited by Lois Mulkearn. Pittsburgh, PA: University of Pittsburgh.

———. 1993. *The Administration of the Colonies.* Facsimile reproduction, with introduction by Daniel A. Baugh and Alision Gilbert Olson. Delmar, NY: Scholars' Facsimiles and Reprints.

Price, Richard. 1776. *Observations on the Nature of Civil Liberty, the Principles of Government, and the Justice and Policy of the War with America.* London: T. Cadell.

Proceedings and Debates of the British Parliaments Respecting North America, 1754–1783. 1982–1987. 6 vols. Edited by R. C. Simmons and P. D. G. Thomas. Millwood, NY: Kraus International Publications.

Ramsay, David. 1789. *The History of the American Revolution.* 2 vols. Philadelphia: R. Aitken and Son.

Serle, Ambrose. 1940. *The American Journal of Ambrose Serle, Secretary to Lord Howe, 1776–1778.* Edited by Edward H. Tatum Jr. San Marino, CA: Huntington Library.

Thale, Mary. 1983. *Selections from the Papers of the London Corresponding Society, 1792–1799*. Cambridge: Cambridge University Press.

Thomson, Charles. 1879. *In Collections of the New-York Historical Society for the Year 1878*. New York: New-York Historical Society.

Trenchard, John, and Thomas Gordon. 1995. *Cato's Letters; or, Essays on Liberty, Civil and Religious, and Other Important Subjects*. Edited by Ronald Hamowy. 2 vols. Indianapolis: Liberty Fund.

Veit, Helen E. 1991. *Creating the Bill of Rights: The Documentary Record from the First Federal Congress*. With Kenneth R. Bowling and Charlene Bangs Bickford. Baltimore: Johns Hopkins University Press.

Virginia House of Burgesses. 1905. *Journals of the House of Burgesses of Virginia, 1773–1776, Including the Records of the Committee of Correspondence*. Edited by John Pendleton Kennedy. Richmond: Library Board of the Virginia State Library.

Warren, James. 1917. *Warren-Adams Letters*. Boston: Massachusetts Historical Society.

Warren, Mercy Otis. 1989. *History of the Rise, Progress and Termination of the American Revolution*. Edited by Lester H. Cohen. 2 vols. Indianapolis: Liberty Fund.

Washington, George. 1995. *The Papers of George Washington: Colonial Series, March 1774–June 1775*. 10 vols. Charlottesville: University Press of Virginia.

Wilson, James. 1901. "A Vindication of the American Colonies." In *American Eloquence: A Collection of Speeches and Address*, edited by Frank Moore, 1:68–74. New York: D. Appleton.

SECONDARY SOURCES

Ammerman, David. 1971. "Annapolis and the First Continental Congress: A Note on the Committee System in Revolutionary America." *Maryland Historical Magazine* 66, no. 2: 169–80.

———. 1974. *In the Common Cause: American Response to the Coercive Acts of 1774*. Charlottesville: University Press of Virginia.

Arendt, Hannah. 1963. *On Revolution*. London: Penguin Books.

———. 1998. *The Human Condition*. Chicago: University of Chicago Press.

———. 2000. *The Portable Hannah Arendt*. Edited by Peter Baehr. London: Penguin Books.

Armitage, David. 2000. *The Ideological Origins of the British Empire*. Cambridge: Cambridge University Press.

Atlantic Monthly. 1863. "The Hancock House and Its Founder." 11:692–707.

Bailyn, Bernard. 1965. *Pamphlets of the American Revolution*. Vol. 1, *1750–1765*. Cambridge, MA: Belknap Press of Harvard University Press.

———. 1967. *The Ideological Origins of the American Revolution*. Cambridge, MA: Belknap Press of Harvard University Press.

—————. 1974. *The Ordeal of Thomas Hutchinson.* Cambridge, MA: Harvard University Press.

Baker, Keith Michael. 1990. *Inventing the French Revolution: Essays on French Political Culture in the Eighteenth Century.* Cambridge: Cambridge University Press.

Bancroft, George. 1866. *The History of the United States from the Discovery of the American Continent.* 10 vols. Boston: Little, Brown and Co.

Barker, Hannah. 1998. *Newspapers, Politics, and Public Opinion in Late Eighteenth-Century England.* Oxford: Clarendon Press.

Beeman, Richard. 2010. *Plain, Honest Men: The Making of the American Constitution.* New York: Random House.

Bercovitch, Sacvan. 1978. *The American Jeremiad.* Madison: University of Wisconsin.

Black, Eugene Charlton. 1963. *The Association: British Extraparliamentary Political Organization, 1769–1793.* Cambridge, MA: Harvard University Press.

Botein, Stephen. 1975. "'Meer Mechanics' and an Open Press: The Business and Political Strategies of Colonial American Printers." *Perspectives in American History* 11:127–225.

—————. 1980. "Printers in the American Revolution." In *The Press & the American Revolution,* edited by Bernard Bailyn and John Hench, 11–57. Worcester, MA: American Antiquarian Society.

Boyd, Julian P. 1999. *The Declaration of Independence: The Evolution of the Text.* Edited by Gerard W. Gawalt. Hanover, NH: University Press of New England.

Breen, T. H. 2010. *American Insurgents, American Patriots: The Revolution of the People.* New York: Hill and Wang.

Brewer, John. 1989. *Sinews of Power: War, Money and the English State, 1688–1783.* New York: A. A. Knopf.

Brown, Richard D. 1970. *Revolutionary Politics in Massachusetts: The Boston Committee of Correspondence and the Towns, 1772–1774.* Cambridge, MA: Harvard University Press.

—————. 2000a. "Early American Origins of the Information Age." In *A Nation Transformed by Information: How Information Has Shaped the United States from Colonial Times to the* Present, edited by Alfred D. Chandler Jr. and James W. Cortada, 39–53. Oxford: Oxford University Press.

—————. 2000b. "Periodicals and Politics: Part 2: The Shifting Freedoms of the Press in the Eighteenth Century." In *The History of the Book in America,* edited by Hugh Amory and David D. Hall, 366–76. Cambridge: Cambridge University Press.

Burnett, Edmund Cody. 1941. *The Continental Congress.* New York: Macmillan Co.

Bushman, Richard L. 1985. *King and People in Provincial Massachusetts.* Chapel Hill: University of North Carolina Press.

Butler, Ruth L. 1928. *Doctor Franklin, Postmaster General.* Garden City, NY: Doubleday.

Cappon, Lester J. 1976. *Atlas of Early American History*. Princeton, NJ: Princeton University Press.

Carp, Benjamin. 2010. *Defiance of the Patriots: The Boston Tea Party and the Making of America*. New Haven: Yale University Press.

Castells, Manuel. 1996. *Rise of the Network Society Information Age*. Vol. 1. New York: Wiley.

Chandler, Alfred D. Jr., and James W. Cortada. 2000. *A Nation Transformed by Information: How Information Has Shaped the United States from Colonial Times to the Present*. Oxford: Oxford University Press.

Clark, Charles E. 1994. *The Public Prints: The Newspaper in Anglo-American Culture, 1665–1740*. New York: Oxford University Press.

——. 2000. "Periodicals and Politics: Part 1, Early American Journalism: News and Opinion in the Popular Press." In *The History of the Book in America*, edited by Hugh Amory and David D. Hall, 347–65. Cambridge: Cambridge University Press.

Cohen, Matt. 2010. *The Networked Wilderness: Communicating in Early New England*. Minneapolis: University of Minnesota Press.

Culligan, Gerald. 1968. *The Post Office Department*. New York: Frederick A. Praeger.

De Bolla, Peter. 2008. *The Fourth of July and the Founding of America*. Woodstock, NY: Overlook Press.

Derrida, Jacques. 2002. "Declarations of Independence." In *Negotiations: Interventions and Interviews, 1971–2001*, edited and translated by Elizabeth Rottenberg, 46–54. Stanford, CA: Stanford University Press.

Dierks, Konstantin. 2009. *In My Power: Letter Writing and Communications in Early America*. Philadelphia: University of Pennsylvania Press.

Dillon, Elizabeth. 2004. *The Gender of Freedom: Fictions of Liberalism and the Literary Public Sphere*. Stanford, CA: Stanford University Press.

Doerflinger, Thomas M. 1986. *A Vigorous Spirit of Enterprise: Merchants and Economic Development in Revolutionary Philadelphia*. Chapel Hill: University of North Carolina Press.

Douglass, Frederick. 1852. "What for a Slave Is the Fourth of July?" Available at http://teachingamericanhistory.org/library/index.asp?document=162.

Downes, Paul. 2002. *Democracy, Revolution, and Monarchism in Early American Literature*. Cambridge: Cambridge University Press.

Elliott, Emery. 1994. "New England Puritan Literature." In *The Cambridge History of American Literature*, vol. 1, *1590–1820*, edited by Sacvan Bercovitch, 171–306. Cambridge: Cambridge University Press.

Ellison, Julie. 1999. *Cato's Tears and the Making of Anglo-American Emotion*. Chicago: University of Chicago Press.

Enders, Jody. 2009. *Murder By Accident*. Chicago: University of Chicago Press.

Farrand, Livingston. 1901. *Israel Putnam: Pioneer, Ranger, and Major-General, 1718–1790.* Ithaca, NY: Cornell University Library.

Ferguson, Robert A. 1994. "The American Enlightenment, 1750–1820." In *The Cambridge History of American Literature,* vol. 1, *1590–1820,* edited by Sacvan Bercovitch, 345–537. Cambridge: Cambridge University Press.

Fischer, David Hackett. 2005. *Liberty and Freedom.* New York: Oxford University Press.

Flavell, Julie M. 2001. "Intercepted Letters and Colonial Opinion." *William and Mary Quarterly* 58, no. 2: 403–30.

Fliegelman, Jay. 1982. *Prodigals and Pilgrims: The American Revolution against Patriarchal Authority, 1750–1800.* Cambridge: Cambridge University Press.

———. 1993. *Declaring Independence: Jefferson, Natural Language, and the Culture of Performance.* Stanford, CA: Stanford University Press.

Forbes, Esther. 1942. *Paul Revere & the World He Lived In.* Boston: Houghton Mifflin Co.

Fox, Adam. 2000. *Oral and Literate Culture in England, 1500–1700.* Oxford: Oxford University Press.

Frothingham, Richard. 1971. *The Life and Times of Joseph Warren.* Boston: Little, Brown and Co.

Galloway, Alex. 2004. *Protocol: How Control Exists after Decentralization.* Cambridge, MA: MIT Press.

Goodwin, Albert. 1979. *The Friends of Liberty: The English Democratic Movement in the Age of the French Revolution.* Cambridge, MA: Harvard University Press.

Gould, Eliga H., and Peter S. Onuf. 2005. *Empire and Nation: The American Revolution in the Atlantic World.* Baltimore: Johns Hopkins University Press.

Green, James N. 2000. "English Books and Printing in the Age of Franklin." In *The History of the Book in America,* edited by Hugh Amory and David D. Hall, 248–97. Cambridge: Cambridge University Press.

Gross, Robert. 2002. "Print and the Public Sphere in Early America." In *The State of American History,* edited by Melvyn Stokes, 245–64. Oxford: Oxford University Press.

Gustafson, Sandra. 2000. *Eloquence Is Power: Oratory & Performance in Early America.* Chapel Hill: University of North Carolina Press.

Habermas, Jurgen. 1991. *The Structural Transformation of the Public Sphere: An Inquiry into a Category of Bourgeois Society.* Cambridge, MA: MIT Press.

Hancock, David. 1995. *Citizens of the World: London Merchants and the Integration of the British Atlantic Community, 1735–1785.* Cambridge: Cambridge University Press.

Harlow, Ralph Volney. 1975. *Samuel Adams: Promoter of the American Revolution.* New York: Octagon Books.

Hazelton, John H. 1906. *The Declaration of Independence: Its History*. New York: Dodd, Mead and Co.

Henkin, David M. 2006. *The Postal Age: The Emergence of Modern Communications in the Nineteenth Century*. Chicago: University of Chicago Press.

Hogeland, William. 2010. *Declaration: The Nine Tumultuous Weeks When America Became Independent, May 1–July 4, 1776*. New York: Simon and Schuster.

Honig, B. 1991. "Declarations of Independence: Arendt and Derrida on the Problem of Founding a Republic." *American Political Science Review* 85:97–113.

Hosmer, James K. 1885. *Samuel Adams*. Boston: Houghton Mifflin Co.

Irvin, Benjamin H. 2002. *Samuel Adams: Son of Liberty, Father of Revolution*. Oxford: Oxford University Press.

Isaac, Rhys. 1982. *The Transformation of Virginia, 1740–1790*. Chapel Hill: University of North Carolina Press.

John, Richard R. 1995. *Spreading the News: The American Postal System from Franklin to Morse*. Cambridge, MA: Harvard University Press.

Kaestle, Carl F. 1968. "The Public Reaction to John Dickinson's 'Farmer's Letters.'" *Proceedings of the American Antiquarian Society* 78, no. 2: 323–59.

Kelly, Kevin. 1994. *Out of Control: The New Biology of Machines, Social Systems and the Economic World*. New York: Addison Wesley.

Knott, Sarah. 2009. *Sensibility and the American Revolution*. Chapel Hill: University of North Carolina Press.

Labaree, Benjamin Woods. 1979a. *The Boston Tea Party*. Chicago: Northwestern University Press.

———. 1979b. *Colonial Massachusetts: A History*. Millwood, NY: KTO Press.

Lakoff, George. 2002. *Moral Politics: How Liberals and Conservatives Think*. Chicago: University of Chicago Press

———. 2004. *Don't Think of an Elephant! Know Your Values and Frame the Debate*. White River, VT: Chelsea Green.

Latour, Bruno. 2005. *Reassembling the Social: An Introduction to Actor-Network Theory*. New York: Oxford University Press.

Leake, James Miller. 1917. *The Virginia Committee System and the American Revolution*. Baltimore: Johns Hopkins University Press.

Lewins, William. 1864. *Her Majesty's Mails: An Historical and Descriptive Account of the British Post-Office*. London: Sampson Low, Son, and Marston.

Looby, Christopher. 1996. *Voicing America: Language, Literary Form, and the Origins of the United States*. Chicago: University of Chicago Press.

Loughran, Trish. 2007. *The Republic in Print: Print Culture in the Age of US Nation Building, 1770–1870*. New York: Columbia University Press.

Lucas, Stephen E. 1989. "Justifying America: The Declaration of Independence as a

Rhetorical Document." In *American Rhetoric: Context and Criticism*, edited by Thomas W. Benson, 67–130. Carbondale: Southern Illinois University Press.

Maier, Pauline. 1972. *From Resistance to Revolution: Colonial Radicals and the Development of American Opposition to Britain*. New York: A. A. Knopf.

———. 1976. "Coming to Terms with Samuel Adams." *American Historical Review* 81, no. 1: 12–37.

———. 1980. *The Old Revolutionaries: Political Lives in the Age of Samuel Adams*. New York: A. A. Knopf.

———. 1997. *American Scripture: Making the Declaration of Independence*. New York: Vintage.

———. 2010. *Ratification: The People Debate the Constitution, 1787–1788*. New York: Simon and Schuster.

Marston, Jerrilyn Greene. 1987. *King and Congress: The Transfer of Political Legitimacy, 1774–1776*. Princeton, NJ: Princeton University Press.

Massachusetts Historical Society Collections. 1858. Fourth series. Boston: Little, Brown.

McLuhan, Marshall. 1967. *The Medium Is the Massage*. Designed by Quentin Fiore. New York: Bantam Books.

Meinig, D. W. 1986. *The Shaping of America: A Geographical Perspective on 500 Years of History*. Vol. 1, *Atlantic America, 1492–1800*. New Haven: Yale University Press.

Miller, James C. 1936. *Samuel Adams: Pioneer in Propaganda*. Boston: Little, Brown and Co.

Murray, Stuart A. P. 2006. *The American Revolution*. Irvington, NY: Collins.

Nietzsche, Friedrich. 1968. *The Basic Writings of Nietzsche*. Edited by Walter Kaufmann. New York: Random House.

Oettermann, Stephan. 1997. *The Panorama: History of Mass Media*. New York: Zone.

Oxford Dictionary of English Etymology. 1966. Edited by C. T. Onions. Oxford: Clarendon Press.

Paulson, Ronald. 2010. *The Art of the Riot in England and America*. Baltimore: Owlworks.

Peters, John Durham. 2001. *Speaking into the Air: A History of the Idea of Communication*. Chicago: University of Chicago Press.

Ragsdale, Bruce A. 1996. *A Planter's Republic: The Search for Economic Independence in Revolutionary Virginia*. Madison, WI: Madison House.

Rakove, Jack N. 1979. *The Beginnings of National Politics: An Interpretive History of the Continental Congress*. New York: A. A. Knopf.

———. 2010. *Revolutionaries: A New History of the Invention of America*. Boston: Houghton Mifflin Harcourt.

Raphael, Roy. 2001. *A People's History of the Revolution: How Common People Shaped the Fight for Independence*. New York: Perennial.

———. 2002. *The First American Revolution before Lexington and Concord*. New York: New Press.

———. 2009. *Founders: The People Who Brought You a Nation*. New York: New Press.

Ryerson, Richard Alan. 1978. *The Revolution Is Now Begun: The Radical Committees of Philadelphia, 1765–1776*. Philadelphia: University of Pennsylvania Press.

Said, Edward. 1994. *Culture and Imperialism*. New York: Viking Press.

Schlesinger, Arthur M. 1952. "Liberty Tree: A Genealogy." *New England Quarterly* 24, no. 4: 435–58.

———. 1958. *Prelude to Independence: The Newspaper War on Britain, 1764–1776*. New York: A. A. Knopf.

Siegert, Bernard. 1999. *Relays: Literature as an Epoch of the Postal System*. Stanford, CA: Stanford University Press.

Siskin, Clifford. 2010. "Mediated Enlightenment: The System of the World." In *This Is Enlightenment*, by Clifford Siskin and William B. Warner, 164–72. Chicago: University of Chicago Press.

Siskin, Clifford, and William B. Warner. 2010. *This Is Enlightenment*. Chicago: University of Chicago Press.

Skinner, Quentin. 1998. *Liberty before Liberalism*. Cambridge: Cambridge University Press.

Sly, John Fairfield. 1967. *Town Government in Massachusetts, 1620–1930*. Hamden, CT: Archon Books.

Snow, Caleb H. 1825. *A History of Boston, the Metropolis of Massachusetts*. Boston: Abel Bowen.

Sparks, Jerad. 1856. *The Works of Benjamin Franklin*. Boston: Whittemore, Niles, and Hall.

Starr, Thomas. 2000. "Separated at Birth: Text and Context of the Declaration of Independence." *Proceedings of the American Antiquarian Society* 110, no. 1: 153–99.

Stern, Jeremy A. 2010. *The Overflowings of Liberty in Massachusetts, the Townshend Crisis and the Reconception of Freedom, 1766–1770*. UMI 3401587. Ann Arbor, MI: ProQuest.

Tamarkin, Elisa. 2007. *Anglophilia: Deference, Devotion, and Antebellum America*. Chicago: University of Chicago Press.

Tennenhouse, Leonard. 2007. *The Importance of Feeling English: American Literature and the British Diaspora, 1750–1850*. Princeton, NJ: Princeton University Press.

Thomas, Peter D. G. 1987. *The Townshend Duties Crisis: The Second Phase of the American Revolution, 1767–1773*. Oxford: Clarendon Press.

———. 1991. *Tea Party to Independence: The Third Phase of the American Revolution, 1773–1776*. Oxford: Clarendon Press.

Tocqueville, Alexis de. 2000. *Democracy in America*. Chicago: University of Chicago Press.

Warner, Michael. 1990. *The Letters of the Republic: Publication and the Public Sphere in Eighteenth-Century America*. Cambridge, MA: Harvard University Press.

Warner, William B. 2007. "Networking and Broadcasting in Crisis; or, How Do We Own Computable Culture?" In *Media Ownership: Research and Regulation*, edited by Ronald E. Rice, 77–102. New York: Hampton Press.

Wills, Garry. 1979. *Inventing America: Jefferson's Declaration of Independence*. New York: Vintage.

Windsor, Justin. 1881. *The Memorial History of Boston*. 4 vols. Boston: James R. Osgood and Co.

Wirt, William. 1871. *Sketches of the Life and Character of Patrick Henry*. Philadelphia: Claxton, Remsen and Haffelfinger.

Wolf, Edwin. 1974. Introduction to *Journal of the Proceedings of the Congress Held at Philadelphia, September 5, 1774*. Philadelphia: Library Co. of Philadelphia.

Wood, Gordon S. 1969. *The Creation of the American Republic, 1776–1787*. Chapel Hill: University of North Carolina Press.

———. 1993. *The Radicalism of the American Revolution*. New York: Vintage.

———. 2002. *The American Revolution: A History*. New York: Modern Library.

Yirush, Craig. 2011. *Settlers, Liberty, and Empire: The Roots of Early American Political Theory, 1675–1775*. Cambridge: Cambridge University Press.

Zaret, David. 2000. *Origins of Democratic Culture: Printing, Petitions, and the Public Sphere in Early-Modern England*. Princeton, NJ: Princeton University Press.

Zobel, Hiller B. 1970. *The Boston Massacre*. New York: W. W. Norton.

INDEX

Page numbers in italics refer to illustrations.

American crisis: March 6, 1770, as expression of, 3–10; "succession of crises" narrative, 8–9; traced through articles in *Gentleman's Magazine* from 1763–1785, *149*

American Revolution: familiar accounts of, 20–24; founder narratives, 21–22, 22n4; grounded in communication practices, 1, 268 (*see also* American Whig communication networks; communication networks, colonial); intellectual histories of, 22, 22n4; methods of as tools for challenging authority in future, 266; people's histories, 22, 22n4; problem with view of liberty as origin and end of, 22–24, 29

American Weekly Mercury, 143

American Whig communication networks, 148–51, 267; communication dynamic, 170–71; Declaration of Independence as culminating declaration of, 233–36; deferral of defining specific goals of struggle, 161; distributed networking as response to events, 161, 164–65; evolution of network into confederation and federal republic, 29; formation of intercolonial network of committees, 179–89; innovative development of popular declaration, 24, 25, 27–28, 74, 234; meetings by towns, counties, and assemblies, 1772–1774, 198, *199*; movement from challenging to asserting authority, 236; organization in star topology, 188; pragmatic solution to issue of representation, 234; and problem of unity, 162–65, 268; and proposals for a general congress, 189–93; reconfiguration of royal post as Continental post, 151–54; timing

as weakness of, 187–88; trustworthy private correspondence system, 150–51. *See also* Boston Whigs, communication innovations of

Ammerman, David, 25, 177n6

Anderson, Benedict, 140n15

Annapolis Committee of Correspondence, Virginia: formation of, 177; letter to Virginia House in response to Port Bill, *167,* 170, 171, *172–73,* 176–77, 178; organizational challenges, 176; as relay point on network from north to south, 177

Arendt, Hannah, 91, 255n12; notion of American Revolution as "lost treasure," 272n4; *On Revolution,* 9–10, 227; "What Is Freedom?," 10, 91, 91n6

Articles of Confederation, 232, 248n8, 269

Articles of Nullification, 271

Associated Press (AP), 129

Association, the (boycotts of British imports and exports), 34n3, 220–21, 220n10; compulsory for all Americans, 221; success of, 220n9

Atlantic trading and communication system, 24, 28, 148

Bacon, Edward, 86

Bailyn, Bernard: *The Ideological Origins of the American Revolution,* 60, 61

Baker, Keith, 3

ballad, 26n8

Bancroft, George, 22n4, 23n6, 24, 180n7, 267

Bancroft Collection, 32

Barker, Hannah, 130n7

Barker, Robert, panorama of London, 257–58, 258n15

Barnstable, MA, 86

of meetings of elected assemblies, 98; and Tea Act, 12, 113–19; underestimation of political power of Whig committees, 179; weakening of, 1–2, 96–97. *See also* General Court; George III; Hutchinson, Thomas; Privy Council

British Bill of Rights, 237, 242

British "country party" ideology, 60

British Empire: topology of administrative network, 20, *21*; Whig ideal of as empire founded in free circulation of goods and information, 147–48. *See also* communication networks, and British Empire

British Whigs, adoption of American Whig methods for reform, 267

broadcasting *vs.* networking, 145n17

broadsides: Dunlap broadside, 240, *241*, 242, 253, 255; Goddard broadside, 240, *241*, 255; postal system as distribution system for, 29, 122, 124; used by Boston Committee of Correspondence, 92, 94–95, 94–96, 183–85; used by First Continental Congress, 218

Brookline, MA, 116

Brown, Richard D., 25, 77–78, 158n24, 180n7

Bull, William, 1–2, 203

Bunker Hill, Battle of, 230, 246

Burke, Edmund, 13, 236, 253, 261

Bushman, Richard L., 55n11

Cambridge, MA: declaration, 81, 83; resistance to tea, 116

Camden, Lord, 13

Campbell, John, 128

Carpenter's Hall, Philadelphia, 205–8

Carroll, Charles, 173

Carter, John, 128

Castle William, 35, 36, 114

Cato's Letters (Trenchard and Gordon), 147, 155

Censor, 158n24

"chain of freedom," metaphor of, 225–26, 226n13

Charles I, 59

Charles II, 71

Charlestown, MA, declaration, 83

Charlestown Committee of Correspondence, South Carolina, 188

Chase, Samuel, 173, 177, 233

Chatham, Lord (William Pitt), 13, 261

Church, Benjamin, 37n6, 48n8

Clark, Charles E.: "Early American Journalism: News and Opinion in the Popular Press," 148n19; *The Public Prints: The Newspaper in Anglo-American Culture, 1665–1740*, 126

Clymer, George, 188

Coercive Acts of 1774, 1, 29, 149, 165, 192, 213

Colden, Lieutenant Governor of New York, 203

colonial meetings: Fairfax, VA, meeting, 200–201; meetings by towns, counties, and assemblies, 1772–1774, 198, *199*; synergetic effects of, 202–5. *See also specific towns and colonies*

colonies, American: comparison of thirteen colonies by imports from and exports to Britain, *211*; comparison of thirteen colonies by population, *210*; economic power of southern colonies, 210; majority of exports to Britain from Virginia and Maryland, *211*; military and economic weaknesses in 1776, 249; reforms and resistance in, *12–13*

as act of free speech, 243–47; as act of separation, 248–56; "All men are created equal" statement, 262–63; "are/is" *vs.* "ought to be," 250, 252, 253–54; bolstering of congressional authority with each change of title, 240, 242; claims grounded in universal natural rights, 236; as culminating declaration of American Whig network, 233–36; diagram of sentence of separation, *251*; drafting of, 237–39; Dunlap broadside, 240, *241*, 242, 253, 255; effect on Whig cause in America, 227; engrossed manuscript copy, *241*, 243, 253, 255, 256n13; enumeration of effects of declaring independence, 254; facsimile of engrossed manuscript copy for each state, 243; five parts of, *244*; Goddard broadside, 240, *241*, 255; insults to the king, 229, *244*–45, 247, 248, 257, 260; morphology of, 240–42, *241*; necessary bias of, 262–64, 264n16; neoclassical concepts of authorship, 237–38; overwrote earlier declarations of American Whigs, 236; as panorama, 244, 256–62; as prolepsis, 254; prologue statement of rights, *244*, 246; public enthusiasm for, 264–65; public reverence for original engrossed copy, 256n13, 272n4; reading of in Boston, 228–29; reproach to British, *244*, 260–61; separation statement, *244*, 249–52, 257, 261–62; shaped to reflect and forge consensus, 239–43; successive waves of declarations preceding, *235*; support for declaration, 254–55; timing of, 229–33; use of five protocols of earlier declarations, 235–36; "We Hold These Truths to Be Self-Evident," 259; "When in the Course of Human Events," 258–59

Declaration of Rights of 1689, 57

Declaration of Succession, 271

Declaration of the Rights of Man and the Citizens, 270n3

declarations of towns, protocols of, 83–92; corporate action protocol, 84, 85–86; first embedded in *Votes and Proceedings,* 84; legal procedure protocol, 84–85; protocol of systematic and general address to people, 88–89; public access protocol, 84, 86–87; virtuous initiative protocol, 89–92

Declaratory Act, 12

Delacroix, Eugène: *Liberty Leading the People,* 23

Derrida, Jacques, 252n10

Dickinson, John, 36, 150n20, 175, 191, 194n1, 222, 224, 230; doubted authority of Congress to declare independence, 252; lead drafter of Articles of Confederation, 232, *Letters from a Pennsylvania Farmer,* 50, 150

Dierks, Konstantin, 123n3, 152n22

Digges, Dudley, 187

Diggs, Thomas, 33

Dillon, Elizabeth, 73n19

distributed networks, 226; Boston Committee of Correspondence, 92–96, 161, 163–65; committees of correspondence, 78–79; Continental Congress as hub for, 209, 217; evolution into confederation and then republic, 29; imperfections of, 268–69; use of in later social movements, 271; Virginia Committee of Correspondence, 179–89

Donaldson v. Becket, 271

Dorchester, MA, 116

ation with Britain, 194n1; support for throughout the colonies, 223; three imperatives for, 189–93

Fischer, David Hackett: *Liberty and Freedom*, 72–73, 128n5

Florida, East and West, congressional address to, 222

Fort Ticonderoga, 222–23

founder narratives, 21–22, 22n4, 33n2

Fox, Adam, 26n8

Foxcroft, John, 139n13, 152

franking privileges, of colonial newspapers, 28, 129, 131

Franklin, Benjamin, 24, 42, 106, 107, 151–54; advice about "hanging" together, 249–52; *The Autobiography of Benjamin Franklin*, 140n15, 142–43; commitment to politics of unity, 133–34; composition of first draft of Articles of Confederation, 133; and drafting of committee of Declaration of Independence, 237; "Edicts of the King of Prussia," 132n11; and Hutchinson letters affair, 108–13, 110n14; "Join or Die" snake in *Pennsylvania Gazette*, 132; "A Letter from London," 152–53; preface to *The Votes and Proceedings of the Town of Boston*, 31, 51, 52n10; proposal for general congress to save empire, 190; support for thesis that American colonies were already independent, 253

Franklin, Benjamin, as communications engineer, 132–44; accounting system for deputy postmasters, 136–40, *138*; "Additional Instructions to Deputy Postmasters," 142–44; "Apology for Printers," 134, 141–42; appointment as postmaster general of Continental Post Office, 125, 152; belief in need

for supplement of italics and capitalization in written discourse, 132n11; extended post as distribution system for all newspapers, 142–44; fired by British as postmaster general for America, 28, 152; "Further Instructions to Deputy Postmasters," 134; "Instructions to Deputy Postmasters," 135–40; linking of expanded public communication to unity, 132–33; and need for supplement of italics and capitalization in written discourse, 132n11; official communication with London, 108, 133; personal investment in postal system, 140n16; reform of postal system, 123, 124–25, 134

Franklin, William, 132n11, 133, 206

freedom: and attachment to and responsibility for community, 72–73; as collective, principled, public action, 10; modern liberal and neoliberal concepts of, 72

freedom of assembly, 270

freedom of religion, 270

freedom of speech, 270

freedom of the press, 155–59, 270

freedom to redress grievances, 270

French Revolution, 3, 267; use of committee, 267n1

Furet, François, 3

Gadsden, Christopher, 199

Gage, Thomas, 11, 95, 171, 211–12, 213, 214; evacuation of military forces from Boston, 228–29, 230

Galloway, Alex: *Protocol: How Control Exists after Decentralization*, 18–19, 18n3

Galloway, Joseph, 133, 191, 194n1, 199n5, 206, 236

determination to enforce Tea Act in Massachusetts, 114; development of government-sponsored newspaper, 158n24; exile in England, 107n12; initial offer to town meeting, 5–6, 7, 8; lack of power to disperse of meeting of "the body of the people," 117–19; optimism about royal government in 1771, 37; refusal to discuss administrative changes or convene General Court, 43–44; response to *Votes and Proceedings,* 76, 98, 103, 104, 107; on "rise of the committee," 112–13; scholarly history of Massachusetts Bay, 102; speeches to the General Court, 97, 98–108; suspicion that Franklin hatched the plan to establish the Boston Committee of Correspondence, 34n4; view that committees of correspondence spread sedition, 77

Hutchinson letters affair, 108–13, 152; circulation of copies of letters, *109*

imperial historians, 60
Internet, 92n8, 122
invention, earliest meaning of, 33n2
Ipswich, MA, 83, 85
Isaac, Rhys, 201

Jay, John, 209, 252
Jefferson, Thomas, 167, 168; attempt to blame king for continued slave trade in Declaration draft, 260, 262, 268; *Autobiography,* 182; description of effect of Boston's communication initiatives on Virginia, 180–81, 181n8; explanation for avoiding role of original creator of Declaration, 238–39; funeral monument, 238; as invisible drafter of Declaration of Independence, 237–39, 240, *241*, 242, 256; letters about political organization of Virginia, 181n8; *A Summary View of the Rights of British America,* 51, 243

Johnson, Thomas, Jr., 173, 177
Journal of the Proceedings of the Congress (William Bradford), 218–20; the Association, 220; communications included in, *219*; declarations and resolves, 219–20; neo-Roman language of liberty, 220; resolves and instructions, 218

Junius letters, 155

Kames, Lord, 67n14
Knott, Sarah, 247

Latour, Bruno, 257
Leake, James Miller, 180n7
Lee, Arthur, 36, 37n6, 39, 102n11, 151
Lee, Henry, 238, 239
Lee, Henry "Light-Horse," III, 239
Lee, Randolph, 169
Lee, Richard Henry, 24, 39, 91, 127, 167, 240, *241*; account of Boston Port Bill crisis, 165–66; correspondence with Samuel Adams, 151, 181–82; delegate to first congress, 169; efforts to systematically link the colonies, 182; expected repeal of Coercive Acts, 216–17; founding of Virginia Committee of Correspondence, 199; and pragmatic unity, 133, 184; receipt of copy of *Votes and Proceedings* from Cushing, 182n9; suggestion that each colony have one vote, 209; triple resolution for independence, 231–32. *See also* Lee resolution of June 7, 1776
Lee, Robert E., 239

Onuf, Peter, 11
oral media, as vehicles of resistance, 25–26
Osborne, Francis, 59
Otis, James, Jr., 26, 33n2, 36, 48, 86, 96, 102, 160

Paca, William, 173, 177
Paine, Thomas: *Common Sense,* 51, 250, 252, 253
panoramas, 257–58
Peace of Paris of 1763, 1, 11
Pembroke, MA, declaration, 81–82
Pendleton, Edmund, 209
Penn Ledger, 146
Pennsylvania Assembly, ignored Convention's resolves and suggestions for delegates, 206–7
Pennsylvania Chronicle, 150n20
Pennsylvania convention, resolves and suggestions for delegates to Continental Congress, 206
Pennsylvania Evening Post, 146
Pennsylvania Gazette, 126, 129, 132; open plan, 133
Pennsylvania Packet: coverage of Boston Port Bill and following events, 150; documentation of appointment of delegates to general congress, 202–3
Peters, John Durham, 268
Petersham, MA, declaration, 82, 93
petition of right for redress of grievances: built upon hierarchies of eighteenth-century monarchy, 55; forms and protocols, 56; fundament of English liberty, 55; gradual decay of practice, 27, 54; as justification for formation of Boston Committee of Correspondence, 45; mutually acknowledged asymmetry of power,

55; routine use of prior to Boston Committee of Correspondence, 55; special mode of protected political speech, 54–5
"Petition of the Continental Congress to the King, The" 222
Philadelphia Committee of Correspondence, response to Port Bill, *172–73,* 178
Phillips, William, 162
political jeremiad, 64
political pamphlets, 25, 26n8, 50–51, 218
popular declaration, 2, 54, 266; innovation of Boston Whigs, 24, 25, 27–28, 74, 234; revolutionary potential, 27–28; spread to all thirteen colonies, 28–29; *The Votes and Proceedings of the Town of Boston* as first, 35, 53, 66
Portsmouth Committee of Correspondence, New Hampshire, 188
Postal Bill (American) of 1792, 269, 271
Postal Bill (British) of 1765, 124
postal system, British-American, 24, 28; Allen improvements, 124; basic communication traits of, 121–22; British invasion of mails coming from and going to colonies, 152–53; colonial post offices in 1774, 130; development of address protocol, 123; as distributed topology, 20; distribution system for newspapers and broadsides, 29, 122, 124; evolution of from monopoly patent to service for the public, 122, *124–25;* and extension of power of writing, 122; form and development of in eighteenth century, 121–25; Franklin improvements, 124–25; as mediator of American crisis, 120; op-

erational integration with newspapers, 129–32, 131n10; Postal Bill of 1765, 124; Queen Anne Postal Law, 123, 124, 134; reconfiguration as Continental post, 28, 125, 151–54; required new public infrastructure, 121, 123, 129; and standardization of street names and numbering, 121, 123; used to subvert British authority in colonies, 28

post roads, 123, 124

Pownall, John: secretary of Board of Trade, 9, 76, 99, 103; wrote one of first documents of "succession of crises" narrative, 8–9

Pownall, Thomas, Jr., 13, 14, 109–10, 253, 261

Price, Richard, 23, 260, 267

Priestley, Joseph, 260–61

Privy Council: approval of Pownall recommendations, 9; determination to reform colonial governance, 11, 13; firing of Benjamin Franklin as head of North American post, 111; review of governance and changes to Massachusetts charter, 8–9, 35

Proclamation Line of 1763, 12

Prohibitory Act, 220n9, 230, 252

promising, and collective political action, 255n12

proportional voting, 209, 210

protocols: and computerized networks, 18; corporate action protocol, 84, 85–86, 235, 266; developed by the Boston Committee of Correspondence, 18–19, 34; in diplomatic practice, 18; earliest use of word, 17–18; as enabling constraints, 17; legal procedure protocol, 84–85, 235, 266; public access protocol, 84, 86–87, 235, 266; social use of, 18; systematic and general ad-

dress to people, 88–89, 235–36, 266; virtuous initiative protocol, 89–92

Providence Committee of Correspondence, Rhode Island, 188

Providence Gazette, 128

Province of Massachusetts Bay, 85

public access protocol, 84, 86–87, 235, 266

Public Advertiser, 132n11, 146

public virtue, 91

Puritans, settlement of New England, 17

Putnam, Israel, 212

Quebec, 222

Queen Anne Postal Law, 123, 124, 134

Quincy, Josiah, 37n6

Ragsdale, Bruce A., 25

Rakove, Jack N., 194n1, 216

Ramsay, David, 180n7

Randolph, Peyton, 182, 200; call for suspension of fortification of Boston, 213; chairman of Virginia Committee of Correspondence, 169; convening of rump House of Burgesses, *167*; moderator of Virginia Association, 168; president of First Continental Congress, 207, 208

Reed, Joseph, 175, 175n4, 188

Reid, John Phillip: *The Briefs of the American Revolution,* 52n10

religious jeremiad, 64

Representatives' Hall, *100*

Reuters, 129

Revere, Paul, 15, 150, 213; *The Bloody Massacre,* 4n1; and resistance to tea, 117

Rhode Island Committee of Correspondence, 187

Rind, William, 129